The Kingdom, Power

by

CHUCK & NANCY
MISSLER

The King's High Way Ministries, Inc.

The Kingdom, Power & Glory

New and Revised Edition, 3rd Printing August 2010

Published by *The King's High Way* Ministries, Inc.
P.O. Box 3111
Coeur d'Alene, ID 83816
www.kingshighway.org

ISBN 978-0-9795136-4-0

All Scripture quotations are from the King James Version of the Holy Bible.

Cover design by Koechel Peterson & Associates, Minneapolis, Minnesota.

PRINTED IN THE UNITED STATES OF AMERICA

Dedication

Lord, You are the *Source* of it all;
We dedicate this book back to You.

"For Thine is, the Kingdom, the Power and the Glory forever . . ."

—Matthew 6:13

"He that *overcometh* shall inherit all things, and I will be his God, and he shall be My son."

—Revelation 21:7

Table of Contents

Section 3: The Power (Colossians 1:10-15)

Appendices:

Chart Index

Foreword

John must have been puzzled. Exiled to the lonely island of Patmos, he has just begun to receive what will become known as the most elevated vision of things to come given to any person in the history of planet earth. The vision begins with a resurrected, immortal Jesus of Nazareth dictating seven letters for delivery to the pastors of seven churches that existed during the latter half of the first century. With eyes of flames like fire and feet like bronze that glows in a furnace, the God-man—who once was dead and now is alive forevermore—is ill.

Call the dictated letter eschatological symbolism if you will. Label it literary allegory. Or classify it as apocalyptic literature influenced by Jewish visions of the end of the world from the time between the Old and New Testaments. You can even think of the story as mere literary license.

It really doesn't matter what name we use to describe the event, because the reality of the letter to the church of Laodicea is that Jesus is sick of lukewarm Christianity. He is about to vomit, writes the Apostle John in Revelation 3:14–17:

> 14"To the messenger of the church in Laodicea, write: 'The Amen, the witness who is faithful and true, the originator of God's creation, says this:
>
> 15'I know your actions, that you are neither cold nor hot. I wish you were cold or hot. 16Since you are lukewarm and neither hot nor cold, I am going to spit you out of my mouth. 17You say, "I am rich. I have become wealthy. I don't need anything." Yet you don't realize that you are miserable, pitiful, poor, blind, and naked." (ISV v2.0)

Bluntly speaking, Jesus of Nazareth is sick of useless Christian lifestyles. But he doesn't leave the Laodicean pastor without a solution to the problem:

> 18"Therefore, I advise you to buy from me gold purified in fire so you may be rich, white clothes to wear so your shameful nakedness won't show, and ointment to put on your eyes so you may see. 19I correct and discipline those whom I love, so be serious and repent! 20Look! I am standing at the door and knocking. If anyone listens to my voice and opens the door, I will come in to him and eat with him, and he will eat with me. 21To the one who conquers [overcomes] I will give a place to sit with me on my throne, just as I have conquered [overcome] and have sat down with my Father on his throne.

[22]'Let everyone listen to what the Spirit says to the churches.'" (ISV)

As I write the words of this *Foreword* on a rainy, blustery wintery day in early 2009 here in southern California, the United States of America and the world in which it exists is entering the most terrifying time in history. The economies of virtually every nation on earth are collapsing. Unwise American politicians are creating dollars out of thin air, voting into existence more than a trillion dollars merely by agreeing to loan them to businesses that would otherwise have been reorganized through the discipline of the bankruptcy courts and free enterprise business realities.

Meanwhile, the whole Western world that only six months ago was saying, "I am rich. I have become wealthy. I don't need anything," is now about to find out from personal experience what it will mean to hear the third horseman of the Apocalypse cry out, "A quart of wheat for a denarius, or three quarts of barley for a denarius" (Revelation 6:6, ISV v2.0).

All of this trouble has been allowed by a God who loves us and who corrects and disciplines those whom He loves. And that's why Chuck and Nancy Missler's *The Kingdom, Power and Glory* message is going to be your road map through the times of trouble that are about to refine God's children and judge all of God's enemies. God's people need to read this book, from cover to cover. And then read it again. And tell all of their friends, family, and acquaintances about what is contained herein, for the time is at hand.

The counsel contained in this remarkable volume will explain what the life of faith is intended by its Author to lead to, which is divinely ordered *preparation* for rulership in the coming Kingdom. For those who are in the midst of that certain and inevitable God-ordained discomfort called *adversity*, *The Kingdom, Power and Glory* is just what you'll need to make sense out of a world turned upside down.

With respect to Christ's call to embrace our God-ordained adversity as a means to be trained on how to rule for eternity, may all of the readers of *The Kingdom, Power and Glory* learn to be firmly entrenched "overcomers" who have no need of exhortation. May we not be the cowardly ones who bury their talents in the ground, wrongly convinced that the God whom we serve reaps where He doesn't sow.

Meanwhile, the ancient words of a centuries-old poem haunt me. They're carved in a gothic, medieval alphabet on a towering, ornate cathedral door right in the heart of a small town in Germany. From the looks of that door, the words carved therein date back to the days of Martin Luther. For all I know, Dr. Luther read them one day, and maybe the message contained in that poem started him on his spiritual journey that eventually led him to reform first his own life, and then the Church of 16th-century Germany. Translated into modern English, the words take the form of a frightening poem. No. Surely I misspoke. It's a *terrifying* poem. Here is what the poem says:

You call me eternal, then do not seek me.
You call me fair, then do not love me.
You call me gracious, then do not trust me.
You call me just, then do not fear me.
You call me life, then do not choose me.
You call me light, then do not see me.
You call me Lord, then do not respect me.
You call me Master, then do not obey me.
You call me merciful, then do not thank me.
You call me mighty, then do not honor me.
You call me noble, then do not serve me.
You call me rich, then do not ask me.
You call me Savior, then do not praise me.
You call me shepherd, then do not follow me.
You call me Way, then do not walk with me.
You call me wise, then do not heed me.
You call me Son of God, then do not worship me.
When I [sentence] you, then do not blame me.

May all of the readers of Chuck and Nancy Missler's *The Kingdom, Power and Glory* heed the warnings of this poem, embracing that necessary virtue we call spiritual bankruptcy, which is that certain, mandatory, and abject condition of total poverty of spirit and soul that marks the beginning of true Christian maturity and fitness for service in eternity.

May we all allow God to carry us on to maturity and fitness for ruling as kings and queens in the coming Kingdom as we rightly respond to the circumstances and adversities of this present life. "For I reckon that the sufferings of this present time are not worthy to be compared with the glory which shall be revealed in us" (Romans 8:18).

William Welty

Executive Director
The ISV Foundation
Paramount, California
Translators of the Holy Bible: International Standard Version

Preface

We suspect that many Christians who get to heaven will be seriously disappointed. If that shocks you, then this book is for you.

We have been serious students of the Bible for over five decades of our marriage, and God has also blessed us with numerous mentoring relationships with many of the great people of faith of our time. However, we have also come to the sobering assessment that the "Body of Christ" ostensibly isn't really producing the results we should expect. Consider the following:

- The divorce rate among Christians is no better than that of the secular world.
- Too many high profile leaders appear to stumble with disturbing regularity.
- There are too few examples of those who really "walk the talk."
- People are weary of hearing extraordinary claims from ordinary lives.
- Contemporary Christianity, thy name is compromise.

Despite the fact that we have always maintained a "high view" of inspiration, and have generally followed a very literal hermeneutic, we have been shocked to discover how many ways we have failed to appreciate the practical, day-to-day need to become "overcomers" and to pursue requisite diligence regarding our inheritance. Our behavior matters! The emphasis on what Dietrich Bonhoeffer dubbed "cheap grace"—as it is widely taught today—has disseminated a casualness toward our commitments to our Savior. We enjoy the security of our "get-out-of-hell-free card" without a real awareness of the coming events, and how they will involve us, *after* the *Harpazo,* and with little concern over the possibility of intense *disappointments* when we *do* "get to heaven"!

(We have discovered that one of the apparent distinctives of the church in China is their focus on maintaining a "Kingdom perspective": exploiting the current "Kingdom of Preparation" in order to prepare themselves for the "Kingdom of Inheritance"—as they refer to the forthcoming Millennium.)

We hope this study will prompt a serious re-examination of the explicit promises and imperatives of our Savior, and that it might facilitate a revival *among us Christians* that we all so desperately desire.

During our intense research underlying these studies, we encountered a number of surprising textual discoveries, which have subsequently been confirmed by exegetical experts, and which puncture several widespread erroneous presuppositions that interfere with truly comprehending the real import of the Biblical text.

Over the 50 plus years that we have been Christians, as we have grown and matured we have had to alter our views many times. But as we review those occasions, we notice that it was always in the direction of taking the text ever more seriously—literally—than before. Every "jot and tittle" demands recognition.

For over four decades, our trademark verse has been Acts 17:11, speaking of the Bereans: "These were more noble than those in Thessalonica, in that they received the Word with all readiness (openness) of mind, and searched the scriptures daily, to prove whether those things were so."

We have usually emphasized the second part, "searching the Scriptures" to confirm the various aspects of the text. In more recent years, however, we have come to regard the first part as the larger challenge: to receive the Word with an open mind—blindfolding our prejudices and presuppositions and letting the text speak for itself, unbridled by our traditional presumptions.

There are many good scholars who have differing views on the many aspects of the Biblical text. We have expressed, as best we can, why we hold the views we do. But our goal, and that of the Koinonia Institute we're committed to, is for you to resolve the critical issues through your own study. It is our prayer that you will be guided by the Holy Spirit in discovering for yourself the many treasures which awaits the diligent inquirer.

Good hunting!

In His Name,

Chuck and Nan Missler
Coeur d'Alene Idaho
(On our 52nd Wedding Anniversary)

Section One

Introduction

"Cease not to give thanks for you, making mention of you in my prayers; that the God of our Lord Jesus Christ, the Father of glory, may give unto you the spirit of wisdom and revelation in the knowledge of Him: [that] the eyes of your understanding being enlightened; *that ye may know what is the hope of His calling*, and *what the riches of the glory of His inheritance* in the saints, and *what is the exceeding greatness of His power (dunamis)* to us-ward who believe, according to the working of his mighty power."

—Ephesians 1:16–19

Chapter One

Prologue

Why This Book?

Welcome, to what we consider one of the most important books we have ever written.

After being Christians for more than fifty years, what we have learned during the past couple of years in our research for *The Kingdom, Power and Glory* has totally revolutionized our personal walks with the Lord. *We consider the truths that you are about to read to be some of the most life-changing principles we've encountered since our new births.*

We are passionate about this material because it has made the whole Bible come alive for us. Passages of Scripture that we have known for years are now taking on a new depth of understanding; passages that have stumped us are being enlightened; and passages we never saw before as millennial are now jumping off the page.

We pray that we'll be able to adequately communicate all that God has taught us and that then you can take what you hear back to the Word of God and see if the Lord confirms the same thing to your hearts. We are going to cover some controversial issues—issues that probably will go against some of your traditional views—so we first of all encourage you to be open and teachable, but then to check out everything with God's Word. Acts 17:11: "*They received the Word with all readiness of mind*, [but] then they searched the Scriptures to see if these things be so."

If intense warfare is any indication of the importance of a spiritual message, then this has to be one of the most important messages we have ever given! The warfare in preparing for this book, and the DVD series that accompanies it, has been greater than anything we've faced in preparing other studies or materials.

Get ready for a real roller-coaster ride!

How We Live Our Lives Has Eternal Consequences

One of God's purposes for calling us is "to be conformed to His image" (Romans 8:29). We used to believe that to be the extent of our calling. What we didn't grasp is that God's calling is far more extensive than that.

The real reason for our salvation is to be able to rule and reign with Him in the Millennial Kingdom and after that for eternity. Everything moves toward this goal.

Being conformed into His image is critically important. Being a living example of Christ is what will bring others to the Lord, but the real purpose for our calling is to have positions of authority alongside of Christ in the coming Millennial Kingdom and forever in heaven. *Our life here on earth is simply the training ground, the proving ground, and the testing ground for that next life!*

D. L. Moody said in his book *The Overcoming Life*, "I have an idea that we are down here in training, that God is just *polishing* us for some higher service." (Remember the word *polishing* as it will become important later.)

The Millennial Kingdom that we will be focusing on is *not* heaven; it's that literal, physical kingdom on earth where Jesus Christ will reign *in person* for a thousand years. It's a place where we will recognize each other, a time when we will have intimacy with the King of kings, and a realm in which we will rule and reign alongside of Christ.

When we say "rule and reign" with Christ (which we will mention quite often in this book) we simply mean we will hold positions of authority (or levels of responsibility) that Christ will entrust to us. It might be authority over a country, over a state, a city, a town, or simply a housing complex. It all depends upon our faithfulness here in this life. Christ is the One who knows the truth and He will decide.

Most Christians acknowledge this Millennial Kingdom to some degree or another, but many have absolutely *no* idea as to *what criteria is required* (if any) to enjoy a significant role there. We certainly didn't.

We asked one young believer recently, "Does what you do here on earth as a believer influence your position in the coming kingdom?" He immediately responded, "Oh yeah, we get rewards or something like that!" That was the extent of his understanding. To be honest, that was the extent of our own understanding until a few years ago.

Many of us have not been taught about the Millennium. We don't understand that not only our rewards, but also our place of responsibility in this future kingdom will either be won or lost according to our "fruitfulness" in this life. Consequently, there is an urgent need in the Christian body for a renewed recognition of our own personal accountability. It's imperative that we see our lives here on earth in the context of eternity. We need that Fear of God back! We must understand that once we are saved, we are still responsible for what we do with the rest of our lives here and now. It isn't "cheap grace"! *Living faith is more than just belief.* It's more than just knowing the Scriptures! And it's more than just going to church on Sundays. *Living faith is learning how to be a partaker of Christ's Life*—which means not only *receiving* His Life at our new birth (being born again), but also *living* His Life every day![1]

The Bible calls these kinds of Christians "overcomers."

What Is an Overcomer?

The Greek word *to overcome* is *nikao,* which means "victory over hostile powers," to subdue something or to prevail over something. Suffice it to say, an overcomer is a conqueror or a winner. This victory has as its foundation the victory already won by Jesus Christ. In other words, Christ is the real conqueror and winner. He is the true overcomer! The only way we can become overcomers, is to yield ourselves to Him and allow Him to conquer, subdue, and prevail through us.

Overcomers are those faithful and obedient Christians who not only *talk* about doing the will of God, but who also *do* it. "Not every one that saith unto Me, 'Lord, Lord,' shall enter into the kingdom of heaven; but he that *doeth* the will of My Father which is in heaven" (Matthew 7:21). By doing God's will, we are able to overcome the world, the flesh, and the devil.

As we begin to talk about overcomers, we want to make something absolutely clear. We are *not* talking about someone who is perfect or religious or good. *We're talking about someone who simply recognizes their choices, confesses them, and then chooses to turn around and go God's way!*

Remember David in the Old Testament? He was an overcomer and yet remember all the ways he blew it? The New Testament even calls him "a man after God's own heart" (Acts 13:22). In other words, *David knew how to confess his sin, how to repent of it, and how to go God's way.* This is the kind of overcomer that we are talking about in this book.

This is something that we didn't stress enough in our first edition of this book and some people jumped to the conclusion that overcomers are somehow "perfect," i.e., believers who have it all together. They are *not*! An overcomer is just a regular *person*—he or she is someone who has simply learned to choose God's way. He could be that janitor in the school building down the street, or that laundry woman in the back room of that large downtown hotel or that widow in the country who faithfully gives her one dollar every week to the Salvation Army. In our opinion, these believers are often more faithful overcomers than the most popular Christian television personalities. In no way is being an overcomer dependent on our socio-economic status. God is the only One who knows our hearts. So, He's the only One who knows the truth and the only One who can judge us.

Why Is Being an Overcomer So Important?

Okay, so why is learning about being a faithful overcomer so important? Why make such a big deal about it?

It's important because the Bible teaches us that overcomers are the only ones who will inherit the Millennial Kingdom and possibly rule and reign with Christ. Revelation 21:7: *"He that overcometh shall inherit* all *things and I will be his God and he shall be My son."* Overcomers are the ones who will have various levels of responsibility in the coming kingdom.

What we are saying is that *all* Christians will *enter* the Millennial Kingdom, be "with Christ" and have eternal life (John 14:3; John 3:16). But only the "faithful overcomers"—the ones who have fulfilled the conditions set down by God in His Word—will *inherit* and possibly rule in that kingdom.[2]

Some of those conditions are found in Romans 8:17 and 2 Timothy 2:12, which say, *if we don't suffer with Him*, we will jeopardize our being able to reign with Him. Matthew 24:45–47 says that *if we are not faithful*, we could endanger our being made "rulers" over His household. And finally, James 2:5 warns that *if we don't love (agapao) Him*, we could forfeit our being heirs of His kingdom. (Note: There are two different kinds of inheritances, see page 55.) In addition to these scriptures, Ephesians 5:1-5 gives us a list of other things that if we do, we will not inherit.

So, Scripturally there's a huge difference between simply *entering* the Millennial Kingdom and being a "subject" there (which all believers will do) and actually *inheriting* that kingdom and being a "sovereign" there (which only the faithful overcomers will do).[3] All born-again believers will enter, but only the triumphant overcoming Christians will rule and reign. *The deciding factor is how we live our lives here and now.*

This is why learning how to become an overcomer is so very important! What we do in this present life *does* affect our role in the future kingdom because there's a distinction between *entering* a realm and *inheriting* that realm. We will explore this more in chapter three.

The Kingdom Perspective

At the beginning of the "church age," this *kingdom perspective* (that we are being trained *here* to rule and reign with Christ *there*) was the central message and the prevailing thought taught throughout Christendom.[4] Now, however, at the end of the age, this message has been essentially forgotten.

Except by a few great men.

Charles Stanley (Baptist pastor, radio preacher, and author of forty-five books) in his book *Eternal Security* wrote: "Does our behavior matter once we are assured of our salvation? You bet it does. *Are there any eternal consequences when a believer sins? Absolutely*. Will eternity be the same for those who follow Christ faithfully and those who live for themselves? Not a chance. Our God is a God of justice as well as grace. His offer of grace is continually extended to even the most vile sinner. But His justice moves Him to keep a careful record of those who remain faithful and those who do not. His grace moved Him to sacrifice His only Son to provide a way for our salvation. But His justice causes Him to take special note of those believers who are willing to sacrifice for His Son."[5]

DONALD GREY BARNHOUSE (Presbyterian pastor, pioneer of radio preaching, and author of many theological books) in his commentary on Romans said: "We can be sure that at the Judgment Seat of Christ there will be a marked difference between the Christian who has lived his life before the Lord, clearly discerning what was for the glory of God . . . and a nominal Christian . . . All will be in heaven, but *the difference between them will be eternal*. We may be sure that the consequences of our character will survive the grave and that we shall face those consequences at the Judgment Seat of Christ."[6]

ERWIN LUTZER (Pastor of Moody Church in Chicago, radio personality, and author of thirty books, including *One Minute After You Die*) in his book *Your Eternal Reward* wrote: "The assumption that "rewards" are nothing more than the crowns themselves is false in my opinion. Rewards have more to do with *levels of responsibility* that will be given to us. When we become like Him, we will be qualified to share with Him in the inheritance, and to work with Him in important positions of high responsibility over the whole universe."[7]

TIM LAHAYE (Pastor and author of the Left Behind Series and fifty other books) in his book *The Popular Bible Prophecy Workbook* said: "Apparently Christians will be assigned to specific areas of service in the kingdom directly proportionate to the amount of "good works" performed while alive on earth."[8]

DR. SPIROS ZODHIATES in his wonderful commentary *The Complete Word Study New Testament (with Parallel Greek)* made the comment: "Entrance into heaven is gained by accepting Christ's sacrifice for justification, but a person's rewards in heaven will be determined by what he did for Christ here on earth."[9]

GRANT JEFFREY said in his book called *Heaven*: "One of the reasons for the lack of holiness in Christianity today, is because *we have lost sight of our inheritance in heaven.*"[10]

JOHN WALVOORD, in his book *The Millennial Kingdom,* KENNETH WUEST in his *Expanded Translation of the Greek New Testament*, and THAYER in his *Greek/English Lexicon* all talk about this kingdom perspective.[11]

An article in the LAYMAN'S PERSPECTIVE said: "The church today is basking in the illusion that 'being born again' is the ultimate goal of preaching the Gospel. But a thorough investigation of the ministry of Jesus and the apostles, clearly shows that regeneration (new birth) is simply the *prelude* to the intimate relationship God desires to have with each one of us. But, it's a relationship that we each must seek . . . because *there are consequences to a careless Christian life—*"[12]

Our Message

The message we would like you to consider is this: *All* Christians will be "with Christ" (John 14:3) in the Millennium, but only the *overcomers*—only those faithful and obedient ones who recognize their choices and allow Christ to live His Life out through them—will inherit that kingdom and have positions of authority there.[13] This includes not only the throne (Revelation 3:21), but also the crown (2 Timothy 4:8). Therefore, it is imperative that we learn *what* makes us overcomers, *how* we become overcomers, and *what* the future holds for overcomers.

It's grievous that the church today seems to be relying upon the illusion that being born again and bringing others to Christ is the ultimate goal of preaching the gospel. It's not! This is just the beginning. *Working alongside Christ in the coming kingdom is the final and ultimate goal! Philippians 3:14 tells us that it's the prize of the "high calling" of God.*

Fear and Condemnation

Before we go any further, we want you to be aware of something very important. And, again, this is something we didn't stress enough in the first edition of this book. The enemy hates this message of "overcoming." He hates it more than any other subject because it reveals his total inability to defeat Christ. Therefore, he is going to try everything he can to put *fear* and *condemnation* upon you, in order to keep you from reading and learning this material. His goal is the destruction of all doctrine surrounding the future Kingdom of Heaven. If this fear occurs, we want you to recognize *where* it is coming from and realize it is *not* from God. Scripture tells us that "Love casts out all fear" (1 John 4:18). Therefore, *knowing that God loves us needs to be the foundation upon which any new biblical truth is built* (Jeremiah 31:3).

As far as God is concerned, it doesn't matter how badly we've blown it in the past; it doesn't matter what horrible things we've done; and it doesn't matter how many times we've failed. That's what 1 John 1:9 is all about: "*If we confess our sins, He is faithful and just to forgive us our sins and to cleanse us from all unrighteousness*." This is the basis of *how we are able to overcome* and the means by which we *can* become faithful. Don't let the enemy get to you and feed you lies. This material is too important!

Remember, there's a big difference between *conviction*, which is from the Lord's Love (John 16:8) and will ultimately draw us closer to Him, and *condemnation* (guilt, reproach, accusations), which comes from the enemy and pushes us further away from the Lord. Romans 8:1 assures us that "there is therefore, *no* condemnation to them which are in Christ Jesus."

The Challenge of This Study

This study is in no way meant to be frightening, condemning, or intimidating. In fact, we pray it will prove to be just the opposite. We pray the material will challenge each of us to become faithful overcomers in our personal lives, our professional lives, and our spiritual lives. And we pray that *if we are* not *overcomers now, these principles will challenge us to turn around and become so; if we are* not *obedient now, they will show us how to be obedient in the future; and if we are* not *faithful now, they will convince us that it's* not *too late to learn steadfastness.*

Proof: We received a letter from a friend who has been in prison for many, many years. He shared in his letter that any of us can learn to become overcomers, no matter where we are in life. No matter what we've done, who we've hurt, or how far we have fallen, there's still time to turn around.

Listen to what he wrote:

> I feel like an overcomer when I choose the difficult over the easy. It might be loving someone unlovely (and there are many here that qualify) or it might be accomplishing the goals I've penned in my daily planner. My accomplishments here have been miniscule. I've written no books, have no substantial savings, etc. But somehow *I think God sees me as an overcomer. And how He perceives me is all that truly matters anyway* . . . I'm very thankful for prison and for my hardships, because *they have clothed me with humility.*

We believe this man is one of God's special "saints." Like that washerwoman in the hotel and the janitor in the school, he's going to have a special place in the future kingdom, because he *is* a faithful overcomer right where he is now. After hearing his testimony, *none of us can say, "I can't do this!" "It's too difficult!"* If a guy in prison (without much temporal hope) can become an overcomer, then any of us can!

From now on, when we talk about overcomers throughout this study, think of this prisoner as an example. Again, he's not perfect, he's just someone who recognizes his choices.

Are We All Overcomers?

Many Christians believe and teach that *all* of us become overcomers the moment we are born again and they use 1 John 5:4–5 as a proof text: "Whatsoever is born of God overcometh the world; and this is the victory that overcometh the world, even our faith. Who is he that overcometh the world, but he that believeth that Jesus is the Son of God."

Consequently, *the idea that a Christian can somehow fail to be an overcomer and lose his inheritance is a totally foreign notion to many.* This fallacy (that we are all *automatically* overcomers) has robbed the church of the truth, clouded its perspective of grace, and played right into the enemy's hands. Now, it's true that "positionally" we are overcomers when we are first born again because Christ lives in us. (He is the true overcomer!) But "experientially," how many of us really are overcoming the world, the flesh, and the devil, even after being Christians for years? Not very many of us!

There is no teaching quite as conducive to godless living on the part of Christians than the teaching that *all Christians, no matter how they live their lives here and now, will someday rule and reign with Christ.* This philosophy frees Christians from any responsibility toward God in regards to daily living. This is the type of theology that has caused our kids to say, "Hey, I'm saved; that's all I care about, it doesn't really matter how I live my life now."

Well, it *does* matter! It matters tremendously how we live our lives in the present, because our part, our place, and our position (our level of responsibility) in the Millennium reign of Christ depends upon it. Paul even called our inheritance in Christ *the "prize" of the high calling of God.* And he told us we are to seek that prize with everything we have (Philippians 3:14).

A Greatly Neglected Area

Unfortunately, this teaching about overcoming in order to inherit is one of the most neglected areas of eschatology—the study of the end times. It has been obscured because of the strong emphasis on grace during the past several decades. *Grace* wonderfully brings us to God, but it doesn't relieve us of our responsibility to live our lives as God desires. We must remember God is a God of justice as well as a God of mercy.

Being born again by asking the Holy Spirit into our lives will get us *into* the Millennial Kingdom, but *faithfulness, obedience,* and *perseverance* in this life are what will render us the "prize" and allow us to inherit positions of responsibility in that kingdom. And there's a huge difference between these two. Failure to distinguish between "eternal Life" (which is assured if we are born again) and "participation in the coming kingdom" (which is assured if we have been faithful) has resulted in tremendous confusion in the body of Christ. James had it right all along: "hearers of the Word" are given eternal life where "doers of the Word" will gain an inheritance in His kingdom (James 1:21–22; 2:5).

Thus, it's absolutely imperative that we recognize the need for our own personal accountability, the need to be faithful, and the need to overcome—*because we're going to decide today what kind of a Millennial Kingdom we're going to enjoy tomorrow.*

The Purpose of This Study

The purpose of this study is to explore three things: *Why are we here?* (Why were we called?) *Where are we going?* (What's the future hold?) And, *what do we have to do to get there*? (How do we become those overcomers—those faithful ones—who inherit the kingdom?)

Our motive for writing is to help believers understand the real reason for our salvation, which is "our inheritance in Christ." Ephesians 1:17–18 explains: "May the God of our Lord Jesus Christ, the Father of Glory, give you the spirit of wisdom and revelation in the knowledge of Him. The eyes of your understanding being enlightened; that you may know *what is the hope of His calling* and [that you may know] *what the riches of the glory of His inheritance in the saints*."

How many of us really know what the "hope of our calling" is and what the "riches of the glory of our inheritance" are?[14] (Ephesians 1:16-19)

Both of us have been Christians for more than fifty years and we are only just now learning these things and seeing the ramification of what all this really means. We want to help believers realize why God has called them and why He has laid hold of them. Philippians 3:12 validates the importance of this: "that I may apprehend that for which I am apprehended." In other words, to be given divine understanding of "things to come."

Hope Realized

If we had only two words to describe what this study has meant to us, they would be "Hope Realized." Through learning and applying these principles, our hope in Christ has been realized, apprehended, understood, and embraced. We now know *why* we have been called, *where* we are going, and *what* we have to do to get there.

Proverbs 13:12 tells us that when our "hope is realized," it will become a "tree of life." In other words, when we realize (apprehend or understand) the real reason why we have been called, it puts everything together for us—the whole Bible comes alive. The symbolism of the tree of Life in the Bible represents "equipping believers with divine wisdom and understanding" in order to have levels of responsibility in the coming kingdom (Proverbs 3:13–18). It also stands for the possibility of ruling and reigning with the King of kings over all the earth.

Interestingly, Proverbs 13:12 also tells us, "*hope deferred makes the heart sick*." This describes what so many believers are experiencing today and why the enemy is making such inroads in our lives—hopelessness.

In the Bible the words *salvation, hope,* and *inheritance* are all interconnected. Only when we are *saved*, can we possess *hope*. But we can only have that hope when we really understand our future *inheritance in Christ*. (See Romans 8:24.) That's our "hope realized"! It's what Ephesians 1:18 promises: "understanding the riches of our inheritance." This hope is the anchor of our soul (Hebrews 6:19; 1 John 3:3).

Thus, the purpose of this study is to help believers understand the real reason for their salvation—our inheritance in Christ in the coming kingdom (Titus 2:13). And to help them implement these principles in their lives in a practical way.

It's important to understand this future hope does *not* replace our temporal hopes (our hopes for marriage, careers, family, ministry, etc.); it simply enhances (magnifies, amplifies, and strengthens) them. In other words, when our temporal hopes fade (and they will because they are temporal), our eternal hope will always be there to carry us through. Our *temporal hopes are fleeting* (brief, they pass away quickly), *but, the "hope realized" that we are talking about here—our inheritance in Christ—is eternal* (Romans 15:13).

It's like God's *Agape* Love. When the human loves fade away and die, which they often do because they are human, God's Love (*Agape*) will always be there to carry us through. It's the same thing with the "hope of our salvation"—it will always be there to carry us through life's ups and downs. This is the answer to the hopelessness that so many Christians are experiencing today.

Encouragement and Hope for the Future

Our aim with this book will be to integrate "the sanctification process" (actually learning *how* to live Christ's Life) *here* on earth with "the reward of inheritance" (co-reigning with Christ) *there* in the kingdom.

We will explore each of the passages that seem to hint of a Millennial disinheritance, along with the Greek and Hebrew words in each Scripture. We will also share some of the verses that absolutely revolutionized our theology when we first began to understand the full ramifications of what they really meant. We want to put all this information at your fingertips and then let you decide what you believe and how it will affect your own personal walk with the Lord. We want you to be like the Bereans and study these verses and see what the Holy Spirit shows you.[15]

Our purpose is to provoke one another "unto love and to good works" (Hebrews 10:24).

As older Christians, who have at times blown it just like everyone else, we have learned through the grace of God how to turn around (1 John 1:9), how to give things to God (Romans 12:1–2), and how to overcome.

> Nay, in all these things we are *more than conquerors* [overcomers] through Him that loved us. For I am persuaded that neither death, nor life, nor angels nor principalities, nor powers, nor things present, nor things to come, nor height, nor depth, nor any other creation, shall be able to separate us from the Love of God that is in Christ Jesus, our Lord.
>
> —Romans 8:37–39

Our intention is to give encouragement and hope for the future, to shed more light on God's specific plan of redemption, and to answer those three important questions: *Why are we here? Where are we going? What do we have to do to get there*? Once we understand God's answers to these questions, it should give us the incentive to live here and now, as God desires, *because this life truly is the training ground for the next.*

> He that *overcomes shall inherit all things* and I will be his God and he shall be My Son.
>
> —Revelation 21:7

The bottom line is: The way we live our lives here and now will have eternal and unchangeable consequences in the next life. In other words, what we do after we have been born-again dramatically affects our role, our position, our place, our status, and our authority in the coming Millennial Kingdom.

Chapter Two

Eternal Security

Why Are We Here?

The first part of this chapter might seem a little technical, but bear with us as this information is absolutely necessary in order to build a solid foundation.

As we said, our purpose with this book is to integrate the sanctification process here on earth with the reward of inheritance in the kingdom. In order to do this, there are three important questions we want to answer: *Why are we here? Where are we going? What do we have to do to get there?*

The first question we want to explore is: *Why are we here?* In other words, what is God's purpose in calling us?

Genesis tells us that man was originally called into existence *to reign over the whole earth with the King of kings.*

> And God said, Let us make man in our image, after our likeness: and *let them have dominion* over the fish of the sea, and over the fowl of the air, and over the cattle, and over all the earth, and over every creeping thing that creepeth upon the earth . . . And God blessed them, and God said unto them, be fruitful and multiply and replenish the earth and subdue it; and *have dominion over* the fish of the sea and over the fowl of the air and *over every living thing that moveth upon the earth.*
>
> —Genesis 1:26–28

Man was created in the image of God so that one day he could become a "servant-king" and rule the world alongside the true king, the King of kings.[1] There was just one problem—Lucifer. Ezekiel 28 explains:

> Thou hast been in Eden the garden of God; every precious stone was thy covering . . . thou art the anointed cherub that covereth; and I have set thee so: thou wast upon the holy mountain of God; thou hast walked up and down in the midst

of the stones of fire. Thou wast perfect in thy ways from the day that thou wast created, *till iniquity was found in thee.*

—Ezekiel 28:13–15[2]

Lucifer was determined to thwart God's plan in any way he could. He came up with a scheme to deceive Adam and Eve, the first Mr. and Mrs. Man. At his prompting, Adam and Eve disobeyed God's rule (they ate of the Tree of the Knowledge of Good and Evil) and as a result of their sin, three things happened: 1) *they died spiritually (i.e., they became separated from God)*; 2) *they forfeited their right to rule and reign*; and 3) *Lucifer* (Satan) *became their mortal enemy* (Genesis 3:23–24).

Because of their sin, *all* mankind has inherited those same three consequences: 1) We are all born naturally separated from God; 2) God's future plans for us to rule and reign alongside of Him have been forfeited; and 3) We have the same mortal enemy as Adam—Satan.[3]

These consequences have been passed down through every generation. The Epistle of Romans tells us that every person since Adam is born with a sin nature, not a spiritual nature, and thus has automatically "fallen short of the glory of God" (Romans 3:23). In other words, without Christ's intervention, *all* of us are born guilty of sin, the penalty of which is death (eternal separation from God). Consequently, not only was man's fellowship with God broken because of Adam's sin, we also have forfeited our future rulership in the coming kingdom.

(For a more thorough explanation of *The Origin of Evil*, be sure to see our DVD advertised in the back of this book.)

God Inaugurated a New Program

God, however, loved man so much that He inaugurated a new program to bring his sin-marred creation back into the *blessings of a future glorious reign* (Psalm 8:5–6). He chose a way of deliverance from man's inevitable destiny (death) and set about to reclaim the kingdom for us.

He sent His only Son, Jesus Christ, to bridge the gap and make it possible for us to once again have fellowship with Him and participate in the future kingdom.[4] Christ's mission is to deliver us out of the authority of darkness into the kingdom of the Son's Love (Colossians 1:13). Jesus (who knew no sin), became sin on our behalf and voluntarily gave His Life as a ransom so that we could: 1) *be reconciled back to the Father;* 2) *be trained as companions of Christ to rule and reign* with Him in the future; and 3) *be given the authority and power to overcome the enemy* in the present.[5]

John 3:17 says, "For God sent His Son into the world *not* to condemn the world; but *that the world through Him might be saved.*"

This is what salvation is all about.

What Is Salvation?

The word *salvation* means "to liberate, to set free or to loose." It literally means to deliver from bonds (chains or shackles) by a payment or a ransom. (A "ransom" is something that is given in exchange for a life.) Matthew 20:28 tells us that Christ paid that ransom for us.[6] He exchanged His Life for ours by shedding His blood on the Cross.[7] He freed us from our sins by His blood and "loosed us from the pangs of death."

Salvation then is a free gift that Christ wants everyone in the world to have. [8] All that's needed is for us to believe in what Christ did on the Cross (for the redemption of all mankind) and to choose to be obedient to His commandments. By believing in Him, He promises that we will not perish, but have everlasting life.[9] Romans 10:9 says: "If you confess with your mouth the Lord Jesus, and shall believe in your heart that God hath raised Him from the dead, you will be saved." This *simple act of belief* is what makes one "declared not guilty" (or justified) before God (Romans 3:26; 4:5–6).

By accepting what Christ has done for us on the Cross, five things occur: 1) we are set free from our bonds of sin and reconciled to Him, 2) we are delivered from the penalty of death, 3) we are guaranteed an entrance to the Millennial Kingdom (and to heaven), 4) we are given the gift of a brand-new spirit (which is like a "down payment," a pledge or a seal that assures us His promises are true) (Ephesians 1:13–14), and finally, 5) we are given His eternal Life (His Love, wisdom and power) in our hearts (Colossians 1:27; Romans 5:5).

(If you have never made a commitment like this to Christ, and you want to do so now, there is a prayer at the end of this book that might help. Please see page 285.)

Christ's death on the Cross signified the end of the Old Covenant (old covenant with Israel) and the beginning of a new one, which provides regeneration and the forgiveness of sin through faith in Christ.[10] Consequently, our salvation does *not* depend upon us, but rather upon Christ and His faithfulness. The Father and the Son and the Holy Spirit, in fact, actually guarantee our salvation (Ephesians 1:4–6, 11–12).

Justification

When we first come to Christ and are born again, we are declared righteous and holy just like Romans 10:9 tells us. This is called *justification*, which is a judicial term meaning "to be declared *not* guilty before God." The word *justification* (Strong's #1344, *dikaioo*) means "to be acquitted, to render just, innocent or righteous" (2 Corinthians 5:21). Christ has already paid the penalty for us and there is nothing more we can do to add to it (Romans 3:24). *It's a free gift!* (Titus 3:5). The price has already been paid. God uses the instrument of grace to accomplish this justification.[11]

Being justified also means that we are guaranteed an entrance to the Kingdom of Heaven on the basis of what Christ has already done. He is the righteous and holy One, and He has imputed that righteousness and that holiness to us. The down payment, or the pledge or seal of this future redemption is the gift of His Spirit indwelling our own spirit (Ephesians 1:13). In other words, at our new birth, our spirit is saved (Ephesians 1:13–14; 2:8).

Even though at our new birth, we are positionally (an approved fact) reconciled to God, justified and declared not guilty before God, experientially (in our life actions), our character, our disposition, and our temperament really haven't changed a bit! We are still the same mentally, emotionally, and spiritually. Christ has simply imputed (*accredited*) His righteousness to us by means of a new spirit. It's at this point that *we* must begin the long road toward *true life* transformation and this process is called "sanctification." Therefore, being justified before God is really just the *first step* toward our total salvation. The completed work of justification is what introduces the complimentary work of sanctification, and eventually, glorification. It works something like this:

> Our spirit (which is the energy source or power source of our lives) is *saved* at our new birth (Ephesians 2:8–9). This is called "justification."[12] This means freedom from the *penalty of sin.*
>
> Our soul (which is made up of our own natural thoughts, emotions, and desires) is in the *process of being saved* through the "sanctification process" that we are all in now (James 1:21; 1 Peter 1:8–9).[13] This means freedom from the *power of sin.*
>
> Our bodies *will be saved* in the future at the resurrection, which is called "glorification."[14] This means freedom from the *presence of sin.*

In other words, *"salvation" in the broad sense—spirit, soul and body—is really a lifelong process* (1 Thessalonians 5:23).

See *Chart 1: A Lifelong Process*

I Peter 1:9 says that we receive the salvation of our souls *at the* end *of our faith, not* the beginning. "Receiving the end of your faith, even the salvation of your souls." Hebrews 10:39 says the very same thing. Therefore complete salvation doesn't consist of one simple choice at the beginning of our faith (to accept Christ), but thousands upon thousands of choices to stay faithful, obedient, and persevering until the very end. The actual saving of our soul is dependent upon our constant choice to "put off" our sin and self and "put on" Christ. James 1:21 validates this: "Wherefore, put away all filthiness and naughtiness and receive with meekness the engrafted Word, which is able to save your souls." (See also Philippians 2:12.)

So, even though we have a redeemed spirit as a result of justification, we still have an unredeemed soul and body.

This is what justification, the first step, might look like:

See *Chart 2: Justification*

A Lifelong Process

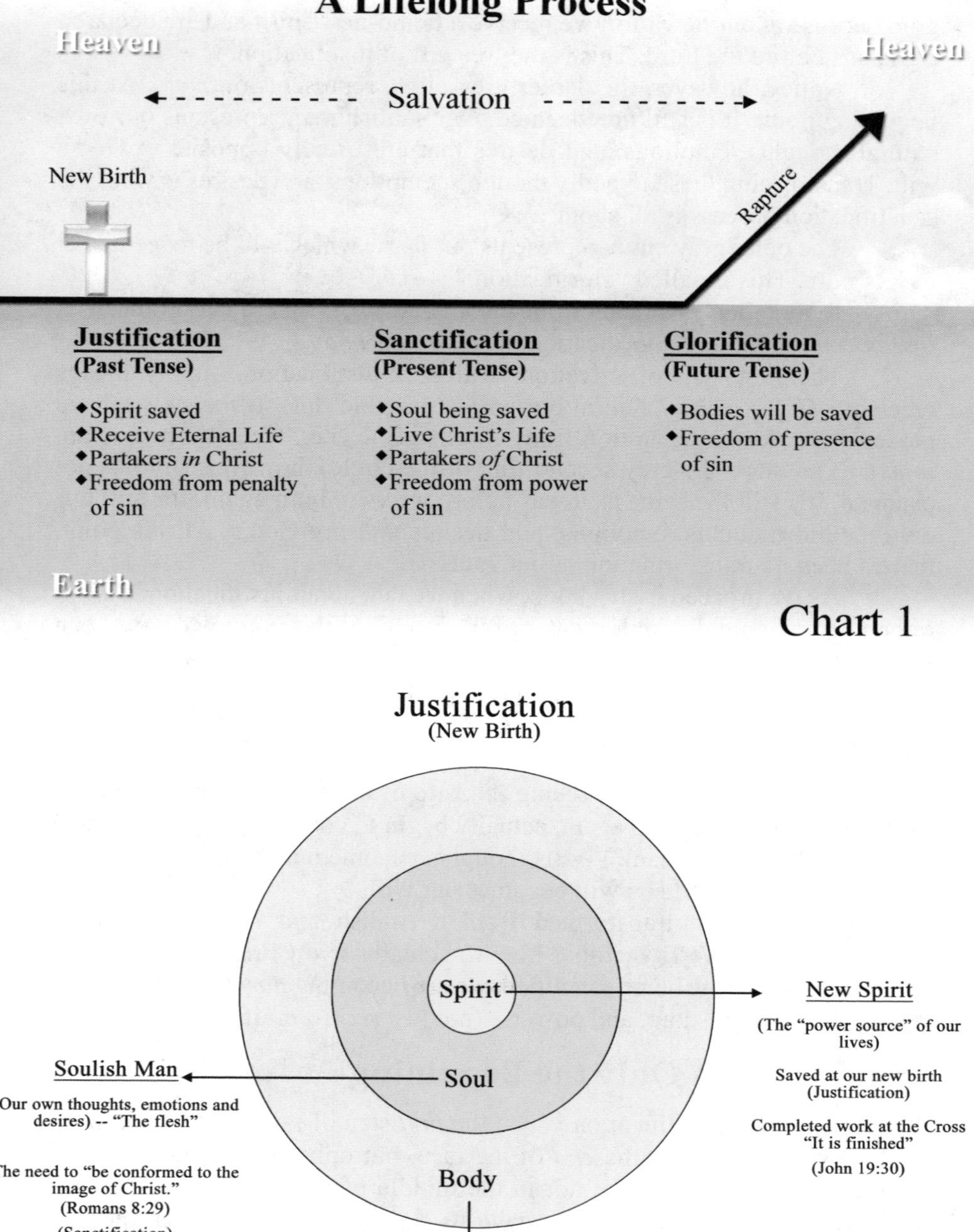

The gold dot in the middle of the circles represents our *spirit*. It is gold because at our new birth we receive a brand-new spirit and are declared righteous before the Lord. This is the free gift of justification.

Notice, however, the darker grey circle represents our *soul*. At this beginning point, it is still unredeemed. Our soulish man represents our own natural thoughts, emotions, and desires that are usually opposite to God's will. Transforming these to godly thoughts, emotions, and desires is what the sanctification process is all about.

The outer grey circle represents our *body*, which will be redeemed at the Rapture. This is called "glorification."

Remember, justification means a *new spirit*; sanctification means a *transformed soul*; and, glorification means a *new body*.

The first step of salvation, which is justification, simply means receiving *God's eternal Life* in our spirit (the gold dot). It means we have passed from death (separation from God) to Life (i.e., God is, once again, *in us*).[15] Our soul (the grey second ring of the circle), however, still has not changed. It's still the same as it was before we were born again. It's still our own natural thoughts, emotions, and desires and *not* God's. At this point, there's been no transformation of our soul.

As we proceed in this book, when we talk about justification, always remember the gold dot in the center of the circle. At this point, we have been saved, we'll go to heaven, but no sanctification has yet taken place.

This is what sanctification might look like:

See *Chart 3: Sanctification Process*

Sanctification means seeing the Life of God that was placed in our hearts when we were born again, actually begin to come forth and transform our souls (that "gold beam")—His thoughts become our thoughts, His Love becomes our love, and His will becomes our will.[16]

We're being transformed from a soulish and fleshly man to a "spiritual man." We're learning how to actually live Christ's Life. At this point, because we are being sanctified, we are becoming *partakers* of *Christ's Life*—His Love, wisdom, and power—(not just *receivers* of His Life).

Justification Is Only the Beginning

Therefore, justification is just the *first* step of salvation, speaking in the broad sense. It's *not* the *end* of the race, but only the *beginning* of our walk with the Lord. (It's the dot in the middle of the circle, not the beam of light!) God wants to literally make us righteous, holy, and set apart in character and action so that "beam of light" (God's Life) *can* come forth. Unfortunately this transformation doesn't happen automatically. It's going to be our constant and continuing choice.

Receiving the Holy Spirit in our spirit is like the down payment—the pledge or the seal—of a much greater commitment that is yet forthcoming

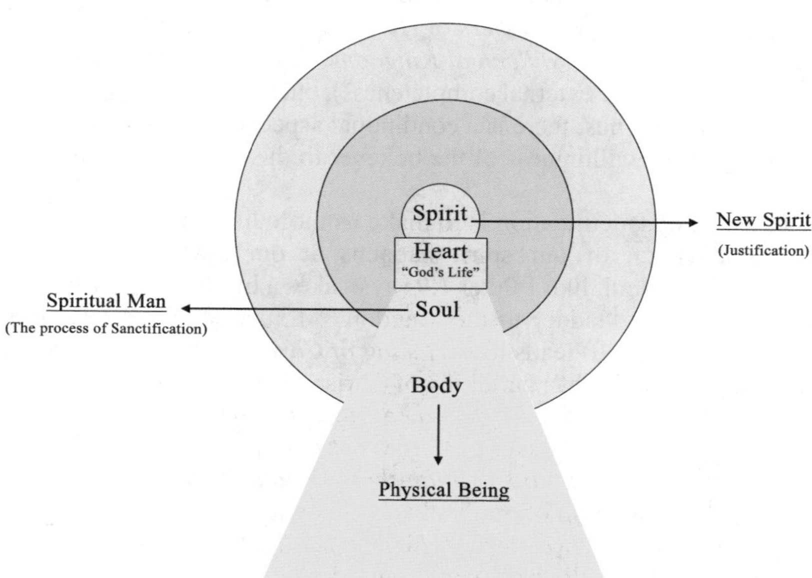

Partakers of Christ's Life

Chart 3

(Ephesians 1:13). The union of our spirits (justification) is simply a symbol of our "betrothal." Our wedding is still forthcoming! Justification is what gets us into the Millennial Kingdom and heaven. It is what opens the door for us, but sanctification (learning to actually live and partake of Christ's Life) is what will make us those faithful and obedient overcomers who will rule and reign there with Christ.

Christ is the One who will accomplish this transformation in our lives by the power of His Holy Spirit. But *we* are the ones who must choose to let Him do so moment-by-moment.

Justification is a free gift that we simply receive and embrace, whereas, *sanctification* is the process that will outwardly reveal that we have, indeed, been saved (John 13:35). The whole point is that salvation in the broad sense—body, soul, and spirit—truly is a lifelong process. It begins with justification and the gift of a new Spirit, but the *real work* comes with the sanctification process because that's what qualifies us to co-reign with Christ. Therefore, sanctification is what the majority of this book is going to be about.

What Is Sanctification?

The word *sanctification* (Strong's #38, *hagiasmos*) simply means "separated unto God." It means to become clean, holy, and righteous in all we think, say, and do. "Positional" sanctification happens when we first accept Christ (Hebrews 10:10); whereas "experiential" sanctification happens when we choose, moment by moment, to be cleansed by the Holy Spirit (1 Thessalonians

4:3). Sanctification is simply the process by which God conforms us back into His image, which was lost when Adam and Eve sinned (Romans 8:29). *It's the means God uses to make us partakers* of *His Life so that we* can *become those overcomers who inherit the Millennial Kingdom.* Yes, the "ransom work" has already been finished (the external completeness), but the inward completeness must still be secured. Thus, there is a conditional aspect of sanctification. This will depend upon the willingness of the believer to die to self and to be alive unto God.

The goal of sanctification is to make us more like Christ.[17]

The salvation of our spirit happens at our new birth, but the sanctification of our soul, like 1 Peter 1:9 says, takes a lifetime. Sanctification is the first step in the "ladder to the kingdom": Experiential *sanctification* (being open and cleansed) leads to *partaking of Christ's Life* (actually living His Life—that beam of light); partaking of Christ's Life leads to *overcoming;* and, overcoming leads to *inheriting and co-reigning with Christ.* We'll refer to these steps over and over again.

God has chosen us "to *salvation through sanctification*" (2 Thessalonians 2:13). Sanctification of our soul is God's will for every believer, but again it's going to be *our own moment-by- moment choice* whether we allow Him to accomplish His will or not (Ephesians 5:26).

Our fulfillment, our meaning, and our significance in this life and the next all rest upon this important *first step* of *sanctification.* If we are not sanctified, we won't be able to partake of Christ's Life, which prevents us from overcoming, which in turn, forfeits our "inheritance" (which will be explained in depth in chapter three). If we are not sanctified, nothing else will happen. It stops the whole cycle. Therefore the measure of our usefulness to the Lord in the future kingdom will be found in the measure of our sanctification here and now.

(For more information on "What Is Sanctification?" see the Supplement Study Note Section of the Appendix.)

The Purpose of Our Salvation

God's whole purpose in saving us (and *the reason He has called us*) is to place us back in the position for which we were originally created—to be "joint-heirs" with Christ ruling and reigning with Him over the earth (Genesis 1:26).[18] Since this was *not* fulfilled at the beginning of time because of Adam and Eve's sin, God has determined to accomplish this purpose in the Millennium where *man will finally occupy a regal position* over a restored earth (Acts 3:21).

Ruling and reigning with Christ *is the mark or the goal of the high calling of Christ.* In Philippians 3:10–14 Paul said,

> That I may know Him, and the power of His resurrection, and the fellowship of His sufferings, being made conformable

> unto His death. If by any means I might attain unto the resurrection of the dead. Not as though I had already attained, either were already perfect, but I follow after, if that I may apprehend that for which also I am apprehended of Christ Jesus. Brethren, I count not myself to have apprehended, but this one thing I do, forgetting those things which are behind and reaching forth unto those things which are before, *I press toward the mark for the prize of the high calling of God in Christ Jesus.*

Incredible as it may seem, God seeks our fellowship, our communion, and our love. He actually wants to dwell among us. We were created for His pleasure. "Thou art worthy, O Lord, to receive glory and honor and power: for Thou hast created *all* things, *and for Thy pleasure they are and were created*" (Revelation 4:11).

See *Chart 4: The Purpose of Our Salvation*

The purpose of our salvation, therefore, is not only an earthly mission (to be conformed into the "image of Christ" for a witness to others), but also to regain the blessings of a future glorious kingdom. *Now* is just the testing ground! *Faithful, obedient, and sanctified believers* (the overcomers) who depend upon the Holy Spirit for everything will be qualified *to inherit that kingdom* (Hebrews 10:23). *Unfaithful, disobedient, and carnal believers* (the overtaken) will *enter* that kingdom, but forfeit the privilege of having levels of responsibility there.

Romans 8:30 is an interesting verse in this context. It tells us that God has decreed from the very beginning "our complete salvation." It says, "Moreover, whom He did *predestinate*, them He also *called*; and whom He called, them He also *justified*; and whom He justified, them He also *glorified*."[19] Notice a couple of very important points: 1) Sanctification is not even mentioned in this verse. In other words, sanctification is God's will, but it requires our own moment-by-moment choice (2 Thessalonians 2:13). 2) Also, notice that those Christ predestined, He also called; those He called, He also justified; and those He justified, He also glorified. So according to this verse, our redemption is guaranteed if we are justified (regardless of our sanctification). We have that eternal security.

The Role of the Holy Spirit

The role of the Holy Spirit is to help believers reach the goal of inheriting the kingdom. First of all, the Holy Spirit is sent to seal us, then to sanctify us, and finally, to transform us into Christ's image for our future inheritance. *The Holy Spirit will provide the power that will enable us to become partakers, overcomers, and inheritors.* He is the Source of it all. Christ's ministry, as our High Priest and Advocate, is to *not* lose anyone that the Father has given Him. John 10:28–29 tells us, “I give unto them eternal Life; and they shall never perish, neither shall any man pluck them out of My hand. My Father, which gave them Me, is greater than all; and no man is able to pluck them out of My Father’s hand.” Thus, every circumstance in our lives is designed to make us more like Him, so we *can* learn to be partakers of His Life; overcome the world, the flesh, and the devil; bear “fruit”; and inherit His kingdom.

The Holy Spirit is the power source that will enable us to produce this kind of fruit. In the Bible “fruit” is spoken of as *actions, deeds, or “good works” that are accomplished by the Holy Spirit through us*. Ephesians 2:10 tells us “fruit” was God’s plan all along. It says we were “*created in Christ Jesus unto good works [to bear fruit]*, which God has ordained that we should walk in them.”[20] God’s will, then, is that we not only *receive* His Life in our *spirit* at our new birth, but that we also learn how to *live* His Life out in our *soul* so we might bear fruit.

Fruit—deeds done by the Holy Spirit through us—should be a natural outgrowth of receiving His eternal Life (James 2:14–18). He wants us to be delivered from sin and self, be reconciled to Him, and then pass along

Purpose of Our Salvation

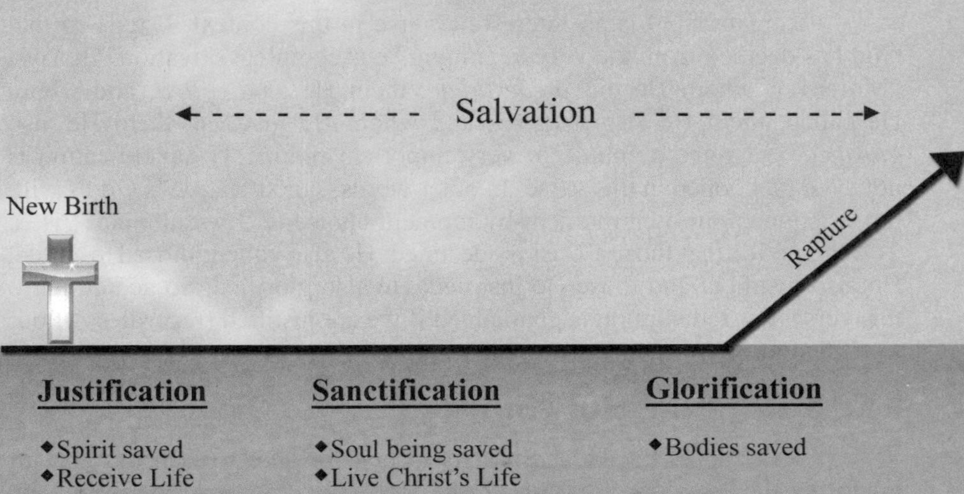

His Life—the fruit of the Spirit—to others. Christians are saved with a view toward bringing forth fruit, because fruit—or good works done by the Holy Spirit in us—as you will see in the coming chapters, becomes the benchmark by which we inherit the kingdom or not.

How Secure Is Our Salvation?

The question then becomes: What about those believers who come to Christ in genuine faith and are "justified" before God, but over time they quench God's Spirit by sin, "lose their first love," and end up producing *no* fruit at all (Romans 8:5)? They don't walk by faith, they don't seek God's will, and eventually they return to the lifestyle they had before they knew Christ. They're *not* sanctified; they're *not* partakers of His Life; and thus, they're *not* overcomers.

What about these believers? Where do they fit in? Are they saved or not? And where will they be in the coming Millennial Kingdom?

There has been a centuries-long debate about just such Christians and their salvation. On the one hand, some would say that their lives of sin show that they were *never* saved to begin with. In other words, because they

Chart 4

blew it here, it shows they never had the Spirit of God in their hearts at all. They weren't saved. Consequently, they won't participate in the Millennium. Theologically, this is part of what is called *Calvinism*.

There are also those believers who insist that these backsliding Christians were indeed saved at one time, but they have lost that salvation because they denied Christ by their actions. In other words, because they blew it here, they will lose their salvation and, again, be unable to participate in the Millennial reign. Theologically, this is part of what is called *Arminianism*.

In this study we want to present a third and what we think is a very provocative way of looking at these things. And, one that we think really resolves the problem on both sides of the argument. This might be called the "Overcomer's Viewpoint."

Once we understand that salvation in the broad sense not only includes the *justification of our spirits,* but also the *sanctification of our souls,* and eventually, the *glorification of our bodies*, we can begin to understand that the above mentioned unfaithful and backsliding believers were fully justified, but simply were *not* making any headway in the process of sanctification. Their free will allowed them to choose a life of sin, which ended up "shipwrecking" their faith.[21]

The Overcomer's Viewpoint says that if we are genuinely justified at some point in our lives, but eventually blow it, God will chasten us and discipline us because He loves us (Revelation. 3:19). But in the end He will save us and out of His Love retrain us again in His way of holiness. That's His character! That's His way! That's His Love!

We believe that the saving of our spirits (no matter how we live our lives here) is eternal, irrevocable, and indestructible. It cannot be altered under any circumstance. All of a Christian's sins—past, present, and future—are under the Blood of Christ.[22] But, we must not stop there. What about our mind, will, and emotions? Philippians 2:12 tells us we must go on and "work out our salvation [the sanctification of our souls] with fear and trembling."

Are Carnal Believers in the Millennium?

The question then becomes: What happens to these "carnal, backsliding, nominal" believers in the Millennium? Are there consequences to their unfaithful lifestyle here?

You bet there are!

If we don't learn sanctification here on earth, we will run the risk of jeopardizing our place and our position in the coming kingdom. We *will* still be a part of the Rapture; we *will* still be a part of the Millennium; and we *will* still go to heaven (John 3:15–16). *But, if we* don't *learn holiness here, we will forfeit the possibility of future positions of honor*.[23]

There is so much at stake!

We understand that Calvinists and Arminianists will be challenged by some of the things we will be sharing. But instead of arguing about predestination versus free will, we need to be exhorting each other to follow hard after the Lord Jesus Christ and the experiential sanctification that He desires in each of our lives. "If any man, therefore, purge himself from these [sinful things], he shall be a vessel unto honor, sanctified, and *fit for the master's use* and *prepared* unto every good work" (2 Timothy 2:21). We need to encourage one another to press on to the end and not argue about doctrine that fails in the end to produce any righteousness.

All we ask is that you stay open and teachable as you read, then compare it in the light of the Word to see what it says (Acts 17:11).

(For a more thorough look at this age-old debate (Calvinism vs. Arminianism), we strongly suggest Dr. Joseph Dillow's book *The Reign of the Servant Kings*. You will find all the information in the bibliography. Be sure to also read "Predestination versus Free Will" in the Supplemental Study Note Section of this book.)

God's Love and Justice

The question at hand is: *Where will* we *spend our Millennial Kingdom days*?

Will we be rejoicing and fellowshipping with each other in the presence of the King of kings, or will we be in some other separate region or "separate place" experiencing profound regret and remorse as we look back on a life full of lost opportunities? John Greenleaf Whittier wrote, "Of all the words of tongue and pen, The saddest are these, 'It might have been.' "[24]

In other words, are there consequences to our carnal and self-centered actions here and now?

Charles Stanley answered this earlier: "God's *grace* is extended to the worst sinner, but His *justice* moves Him to keep a record not only of those who are faithful, but also of those who are not . . . God's Love is such that He accepts us just the way we are, but loves us too much to leave us that way."[25]

Speaking of God's grace and justice, Psalm 89:14 tells us that *justice and judgment* are the habitation of God's Throne but *mercy and truth* always go before Him (Romans 11:22). Just because we are "eternally secure" and we are going to heaven, does *not* mean we have a license to sin. "Behold, therefore, the goodness and the severity of God: on them which fell severity; but toward thee, goodness *if* thou continue in His goodness: otherwise thou also shalt be *cut off*" (Romans 11:22).

Therefore, justification is *not* all that matters, because heaven, after the Rapture, is just a stopover. We are all coming back to earth for one thousand years one way or another. And everything we will be assigned to do in the future kingdom will have everything to do with what we have done here! We have a choice *now* of what it will be like for us *there*. It will *not* be the same for every believer. Someone is watching and someone is taking detailed notes. Malachi tells us there is a "Book of Remembrance" that records everything we say and do (Malachi 3:16).

God's motive in all that He allows in our lives is Love; but His Love is always based upon His holiness and His justice. Love without justice is partiality, and justice without Love is despotism. So yes, everything God does in regards to us is based upon His Love, but incorporated into that Love is His justice. Revelation 3:19 confirms this: "As many as I love, I rebuke and chasten." Chastening is different from punishing. Please hear this loud and clear! *God does* not *punish His own, He simply disciplines us*. And there's a huge difference between these two. "To punish" means "*to inflict harm*"; whereas "to chasten" means *"something that is done for our profit and for our benefit."*

No discipline from God will involve our destruction. Yes, the Lord *scourges* (Strong's #3164—lays open or examines) every son whom He receives as Hebrews 12:6 tells us He must. His absolute justice demands a review of all of our lives. This is what the Bema Seat of Christ is all about. We are sinners saved by grace who need to be made holy. God's holiness compels Him to disassociate Himself from us as sinners, but His Love prompts Him to restore and establish us. Sin results in separation, but God promises that He will *never* take away His Love. (See Psalm 89:30–33; Romans 8:38-39.) There will be no godly wrath toward those who have been justified through faith. Yes, we can expect chastening and discipline, but God's motive in this will always be Love. As we'll see, *discipline begins in this lifetime and probably will continue on into the next!*

Chastisement seems to be God's highway to perfection. Psalms 94:15 validates this: "Judgment [from God] shall return unto righteousness." That's His plan from the very beginning.

Complete Salvation

In review: Once we have made a commitment to believe in Jesus Christ (affirming what He did for us on the Cross, and have asked the Holy Spirit to come into our lives), we are *eternally* saved—eternally justified (John 3:15–16). At that point, we receive a new Spirit and Christ's eternal Life in our hearts. "Eternal Life" simply means the very life of God Himself—*His* Love, *His* wisdom, and *His* power residing in us. As 1 John 5:13 says, "These things have I written unto you that believe on the name of the Son of God, that ye may *know that ye have eternal life*, and that ye may believe on the name of the Son of God." As a result, all believers will receive an entrance to the Millennial Kingdom (John 5:24).

If, however, we are not experientially sanctified here on earth, we will run the risk of jeopardizing our place and our position in the coming kingdom. As said before, we will still be translated, judged at the Bema Seat, and return with Christ for the Millenium. *But, if we* don't *learn holiness here, we will forfeit the possibility of ruling and reigning with Him there* (Galatians 5:19–21).

"Complete salvation," therefore, means not only *receiving God's Life* in our spirits (justification), but also *renewing every part of our souls and bodies* as well (sanctification) (1 Peter 1:9). Many Christians take only the first step of salvation (justification) and stop there. Like the Israelites, they put Christ's blood on the doorposts of their homes (Exodus 12:22), but they forget to purge the leaven from their lives. They trust God for the salvation of their spirits, but they fail to declare war on their flesh. Consequently, they prevent the power of God from doing the work of sanctification in their lives, which would entitle them to positions of authority in the coming kingdom.

This can all be changed, because when we begin to understand the *real reason* why we have been called—to co-reign with Christ—it will become a "tree of life" (Proverbs 13:12).

See *Chart 5: Salvation of a Believer*

"Complete salvation," again in the broad sense, then is not only *believing in the Lord,* it's also *walking with the Lord,*[26] which entails *partaking of His Life; overcoming* the world, the flesh, and the devil; *producing fruit;* and being faithful to the end.[27] Thus, you can see how confusing the term "salvation" can be.[28]

So, from now on, when we speak of the salvation of our spirits (our born-again experience) we will call it *justification*—which means "declared righteous before God." We have been saved from the "penalty of sin."[29] When we speak of the salvation of our souls, we will call it *sanctification*—which means making one righteous in all their deeds. This person is saved from the "power of sin."[30] And finally, when we speak of the salvation of our bodies, we will call it *glorification*—which means separation from the presence of sin by receiving a new heavenly body.[31]

Therefore, after our initial conversion (justification), God deals with us on an entirely different plane. He now deals with us as "servants" with a view toward the Millennium. In this season, God looks at *our faithfulness, our obedience, and our perseverance.*

In Conclusion

Maybe now you can see why having a kingdom perspective at the present time is so very important. It will not only affect how we live our lives here and now (making us *stop* before we react, *think* before we respond, and *pray* before we move), it will also affect our kingdom positions there.

A woman wrote us after she had read the first edition of the book and said, *"I will absolutely never be the same again!"* Another couple called and said, "After being Christians for thirty-one years, this material is stirring up the depths of our souls to seek the Lord as we never have before." Another woman wrote last week, "The Bible makes total sense to me now for the first time since becoming a Christian in 1974." And it's true! Passages of Scripture that you have known and studied for years will come into a whole new light. They will literally jump off the page with new meaning.

The "hope of our salvation" is our inheritance in Christ, and that includes positions of authority in the coming Millennial Kingdom. When that hope is embraced, apprehended, and made real in our lives, it will become a tree of Life!

Salvation of the Believer

(1 Thessalonians 5:23)

← - Salvation - - - - - - - - - -

Justification	**Sanctification**
(Romans 3:26)	(1 Peter 1:15-16)
Believing *in* the Lord	**Walking *with* the Lord**
◆Declared Righteous (Rom.3:26)	◆Making us Righteous (1 Thes.4:3)
◆"Free Gift" (Eph.2:8)	◆Earned by Merit (Heb.3:14)
◆No "works" Necessary (Eph.2:8-9)	◆"Fruit" Necessary (Eph.2:10)
◆Sealed with the Holy Spirit (Eph.1:13)	◆Empowered by the Holy Spirit (1 Pet.1:5)
◆Receive Everlasting Life (John 3:36)	◆Experience Abundant Life (John 10:10)
◆A Follower of Christ	◆A True Disciple of Christ (Lk.14:33)
◆Partaker in Christ (1 Cor.10:17)	◆Partaker of Christ (Heb.12:10)
◆Betrothed (Hosea 2:19)	◆Preparing for the Wedding (Rev.19:7-8)
◆Believers and Receivers (John 3:16)	◆Overcomers (Rev.21:7)
◆Enter the Kingdom (Gal.4:7)	◆Inherit the Kingdom (Col.3:24)
Spirit Saved (1 Cor. 6:17) *from "Penalty of sin"*	**Soul Saved** (1 Pet. 1:9) *from "Power of sin"*

Judgment Seat of Christ

Glorification
(1 Thes. 4:16-17)

"Judgment of Works"
(1 Corinthians 3:13-15)

Rapture
"Be with Him" (John 14:3)
New Body (1 Cor.15:51-53)

Body Saved (Phil.3:20-21)
from "Presence of sin"

Chart 5

Chapter Three

Inheritance

Review

So far we have learned that the way we live our lives here and now will have eternal and unchangeable consequences in the coming kingdom. In other words, what we do *after* we have been born again dramatically affects our roles, our positions, and our places in the future reign of Christ. This coming kingdom is *not* heaven, but a literal kingdom that will exist back on earth for a thousand years where Jesus Christ will rule and reign. (Be careful not to confuse what happens in the Millennium with what occurs in heaven at the end of the thousand years, because they are two different realms.)

All believers will be with Christ in the coming Millennium, but only the overcomers—the ones who constantly recognize their choices and choose to turn around and follow Christ—will inherit levels of responsibility in that kingdom. So not only our rewards, but also our places of responsibility in the future kingdom will be won or lost according to our faithfulness, perseverance, and obedience in this life. Our life here is simply the training ground for the next life there.

Consequently, there is an urgent need in the body of Christ for a renewed recognition of our own accountability and a refreshed understanding of the reason for our salvation, which is not only to be conformed to the image of Christ, but also our inheritance in Him. Philippians 3:12 tells us we need to apprehend (or understand) that for which we have been apprehended by Christ.

Two Kinds of Inheritance

The subject of our future inheritance in the Millennial Kingdom is one of the major themes of the Bible. There are 1,518 verses in the Old Testament and hundreds in the New Testament that speak about this coming kingdom and the importance of our being able to inherit it. What makes the subject of inheritance rather confusing, however, is that the Bible uses the word *inherit* or *inheritance* in two different ways.

1. First of all, the Bible speaks of an "*inheritance by birth*" or a "*sonship inheritance*" (Strong's 2816, *kleronomeo*). This is an inheritance that belongs to us simply because we are sons of God and we are heirs. It means that because we are "born again" ("justified"—and have the Spirit of

God in our hearts) we have God Himself as our inheritance. Galatians 4:6–7 confirms this: "And because ye are sons, God hath sent forth the Spirit of His Son into your hearts, crying, Abba, Father. Wherefore, thou art no more a servant, but a son; and if a son, then an heir of God through Christ."[1]

This *sonship* inheritance is unconditional and automatic, such as something you might receive in a will.[2] Once you are a son, you will always remain a son.[3]

Therefore, inheritance by birth is a free gift (no works are needed). It guarantees us eternal Life and is open to absolutely everyone who will accept it (Ephesians 1:11, 14). It's an unconditional inheritance.

2. The second type of inheritance that the Bible speaks about is called an *inheritance from the Lord* (Strong's #2817, *kleronomia*). This is an inheritance *given by the Lord* because of faithfulness, obedience, and perseverance.[4] It's an earned inheritance and it entitles one to positions, rewards, authority, and blessings in the Millennial Kingdom. Colossians 3:24 calls this "a reward of inheritance." So this type of inheritance is conditional.

Here are some Old Testament Scriptures that deal with the requirements for an inheritance from the Lord. (Keep in mind that inheriting the land in the Old Testament is symbolic of inheriting the kingdom in the New Testament.) Deuteronomy 6:18 tells us that, "*If* they [the Israelites] do what is good and right," *then* they will not only go into the land, but also possess it. And Deuteronomy 19:9–10 confirms this: "*If* they shall keep the commandment, *then* they will inherit the cities and the land." And finally, Deuteronomy 11:22–23, "*If* ye shall diligently keep all these commandments which I command you, to do them, to love the Lord your God, to walk in all His ways, and to cleave unto Him, *then* will the Lord drive out all these nations from before you, and ye shall possess greater nations and mightier than yourselves."

Here are a few New Testament Scriptures that speak of some of the requirements for this second type of inheritance: Matthew 24:43 and 47 say, "*If* we are faithful, [then] He will make us ruler over all his goods"; 2 Timothy 2:12 says, "*If* we suffer, [then] we shall reign with Him"; and James 2:5 says, "*If* we love Him, we will be heirs of His kingdom." (See also Hebrews 10:35.)

"Inheritance from the Lord," both in the Old Testament and in the New, is always conditioned upon behavior.

All Christians are sons of God and therefore possess the free gift of an *inheritance by birth* that they can never lose. But *not* all Christians will receive an *inheritance from the Lord* because this position is earned by faithfulness, obedience, and perseverance.[5]

Just like a slave cannot pass straight from the slave market right into the royal palace and the throne, so a one-time pardon of a sinner doesn't entitle him to become a king or a sovereign. Much is required to prepare and fit such a person for that blessing and that total change of life.

Christ pardons and purchases us in a moment of time—He imputes His righteousness to us at our justification—but then He spends the rest of our lives cleansing, renewing, and sanctifying us for positions in the coming kingdom.

A Personal Example

Here's a personal example that might help explain the difference between these two types of inheritance—*a sonship inheritance* and *an inheritance from the Lord.*

Nan and her mom, Rusty, had a wonderful relationship. Nan was one of those fortunate people to have had an ideal mom (much like the *Brady Bunch* family). They were best friends for more than sixty years, with never a harsh word between them. Even though they didn't live in the same city, they talked at least once every day.

In November 2001, we found out that Rusty had pancreatic cancer and had only a few weeks to live. Nan immediately flew down to Northern California to be with her. By December, Rusty was so sick that Nan and her brother, Marty, had to place her in one of the hospice facilities for the terminally ill. Rusty died January 4, 2002.

The inheritances that Nan and her brother received as a result of Rusty's passing, remind us of these two different biblical types of inheritance that we have been talking about. In Rusty's will, Marty and Nan received a *sonship inheritance* that they split evenly—Rusty's house, her car, her investments, etc.

But the following day, Marty and Nan were told by Rusty's lawyer to go down to her safe deposit box at the bank where she had left them something very special. What they found there were two individual "love letters" from Rusty to both of them. Rusty had written pages on what they each had meant to her and how she loved them and would always be with them. But the added blessing in Nan's envelope was the gift of a beautiful gold and diamond ring that Nan's dad had given Rusty on their fiftieth anniversary. It had a diamond cross in it. In her note to Nan, Rusty said the ring was a "thank you" for the incredible love relationship that they had shared all those years.

This ring—which is probably the most beautiful earthly love gift anyone could ever imagine—reminds Nan and me in a small way of what *our inheritance from the Lord* (that second type of inheritance) might be like. "Eye hath not seen, nor ear heard, neither have entered into the heart of man, the things which God hath prepared for them that love [*agapao*] Him" (1 Corinthians 2:9). (We will talk about *agapao* love in chapter eight.)

This second type of inheritance is something that is *in addition to* sonship inheritance and it's obtained by obedience, faithfulness, and perseverance. It includes not only entering the kingdom, but also inheriting different levels of responsibility and authority there. It means to take possession of something that is already assigned to us.

The Thayer Greek Lexicon of the New Testament says that "*to inherit means to be a partaker* (*of* Christ's Life)."[6] This second type of inheritance is promised to those who are sanctified by faith and to those who overcome.[7] It means that we will, in some way, have *ownership* of the kingdom in the Millennium, rather than just being a resident there (Matthew 6:20).[8]

Again, this is the hope of our salvation in Christ!

Tony Evans, in his book *What a Way to Live*, wrote: "There are Christians who have been set free from spiritual bondage, but who will never enjoy the full rights and privileges they could have inherited in the coming kingdom. That's because these benefits accrue to believers based on their faithfulness to Christ here on earth."[9]

Inheritance from the Lord (co-reigning with Him) is earned; whereas, sonship is not.

Huge Difference Between Entering and Inheriting the Kingdom

Another way of saying all of this is that all Christians are *heirs of God* (they are assured of eternal life and a place in heaven); but not all Christians will inherit the kingdom *from Him* (and receive positions of authority in that kingdom).

Being an heir is unconditional, but being a co-ruler with Christ is conditional upon our spiritual obedience and faithfulness. We cannot lose our eternal life, but we *can* lose a position of authority in His kingdom. This is the basic difference between a Christian who will only *dwell in* the Kingdom of Heaven and one who will *inherit* or *rule over* it.[10] The latter will actually participate in the coming glory of Christ.

So, there's a huge difference between simply *entering* the kingdom and *inheriting* it. They're *not* the same thing at all! We *enter* (Strong's #1525, *to come into*) the kingdom because of our new birth and because we have received God's Spirit. But we *inherit* that kingdom (Strong's #2816, *obtain, receive or possess it*) as a reward for an obedient and faithful lifestyle here on earth. It's the prize for being an overcomer and for making choices to live Christ's Life. Again, we won't do it perfectly, but at least we will recognize our choices and continue to choose to follow Christ as best we can.

He who receives God's Spirit (through Jesus Christ) *enters* the kingdom; but he who partakes *of* Christ's Life and overcomes the world, the flesh, and the devil will *inherit* that kingdom.[11] Thus, the Millennial Kingdom will be inhabited by born-again Christians, but positions of honor will be held by faithful and obedient overcoming Christians.

Not All Christians Will Inherit

What we are saying is that we *cannot* lose our eternal life, but we *can* lose our rewards and our positions of authority in God's future Millennial Kingdom by our lifestyle here and now (Mark 9:41). We are warned about this: "Look to yourselves, that we lose not those things which we have wrought, but that we receive a full reward" (2 John 8). This hints of a variation in rewards and that they are *not* all the same, as many of us have supposed.

Tim La Haye commented about this passage in his book, *The Popular Bible Prophecy Book.* He said, "2nd John warns us that it is *possible* to lose those things we have worked for. Although we will *not* lose our salvation (our justification), *it is possible to forfeit our rewards* by indulging in temptation."[12]

Consequently, inheriting the kingdom is conditional upon our spiritual walk here and now, *not* just our beliefs. To believe something is very easy. It means "to mentally ascribe to something or assent to something" (Strong's #5219, *hupakoue*). Whereas, to be obedient, faithful, and persevering means *seeing that belief acted out* in our lives. It's not only *hearing* His will, it's actually *doing* His will. It's putting feet to our belief, which is the crucial test of our faith.

The more we understand this message, the more we will appreciate James, who said all along: "Be ye *doers of the Word* and *not hearers only*, deceiving your own selves" (James 1:22).

To be obedient, then, not only means hearing God's will, but also choosing to do His will. Luke 6:46 tells us, "Why call Me Lord, if you don't *do* the things I tell you?" We must actually make the choice to be sanctified (1 Thessalonians 4:3), to be partakers of Christ's Life (Hebrews 3:14), and to be faithful overcomers (Revelation 21:7) in order to inherit the kingdom. It's not automatic! It's God's will; but only our continual choice implements it.

(We won't do this perfectly. Remember, an overcomer is not perfect! He is simply one who recognizes his choices, recognizes when he blows it, and chooses to turn around and follow Christ. He is *not* perfect, good, or religious. An example, remember, was David in the Old Testament. He blew it big time, but he recognized it, he repented of it, and then he chose to follow God. In the New Testament, David is called "a man after God's own heart" (Acts 13:22). David was a faithful and obedient overcomer.)

The second type of inheritance—*inheritance from God*—is a very precious commodity because Scripture tells us *it can be lost* (Revelation 3:11; Matthew 10:42).

Examples of Forfeiture of Inheritance

The Old Testament gives us some graphic examples of believers who inherited the land and those who did not. It very clearly shows us the distinction between simply *being in the land* and inheriting or *owning the land*. Owning the land was a reward for faithfulness and obedience. Owning the land is often compared to the "rest of God" (or the Millennial Kingdom) as we will see in chapter fourteen.

Abraham, for example, was *guaranteed* the land by an oath (Genesis 15:18), but he only *obtained* (possessed) that land by spiritual obedience (Genesis 17:1–2). The appropriation of that blessing was conditional upon his obedience. Joshua and Caleb were given the land because they obediently followed God and had finished the work that had been given them.[13] We, too, must be diligent to finish the work God gives us to do here on earth so we can *enter into His rest* (possess the kingdom).[14]

The Old Testament also gives us many examples of those who forfeited their inheritance. Esau, for example, forfeited his birthright and his blessings because of disobedience (but, *not his sonship*). Genesis 27:35–40 tells us the whole story. Isaac told Esau, "Your brother [Jacob] came subtly and took away your blessing." The only blessing Isaac had left for Esau was recorded in verse 39: "Thy dwelling shall be the fatness of the earth, and of the dew of heaven from above." He went on to predict that Esau would live by his sword, which, of course, he does. His descendants are the Edomites. He is an example of one who forfeited his birthright and his blessing, but not his sonship (Hebrews 12:16–17).

Then there's Reuben in 1 Chronicles 5:1 who defiled his father's bed, and thus his birthright was taken away from him and given to the sons of Joseph. Nevertheless, again, he still retained his sonship.

And of course, there's Moses in Deuteronomy 4:21–22 where God expressed His anger at him for striking the rock and misrepresenting His character. As recompense, the Lord disqualified Moses from entering into the land of Canaan and from obtaining his inheritance, but we do see Moses again on the Mount of Transfiguration in Matthew 17:3.

Finally, there were the *two million Israelite* believers who were supposed to inherit the blessings of the promised land, but they failed to do so because of their disobedience and lack of faith. *They were saved* (they had put the blood on the doorposts of their homes), but they were unable to receive their inheritance and go into the promised land (a foreshadow of the Millennial Kingdom) because of doubt, disobedience, and unfaithfulness. Only Caleb and Joshua of that generation inherited the land and the blessings from God.

Forfeiting Our Inheritance

These scriptural examples infer that we, too, can forfeit our inheritance from God and be disqualified. First Corinthians 3:13–15 (speaking about the Judgment Seat of Christ) tells us, "Every man's work shall be made manifest: for the day shall declare it, because it shall be revealed by fire; and the fire shall try every man's work of what sort it is. *If any man's work abide which he hath built thereupon, he shall receive a reward. But if any man's "work" shall be burned, he shall suffer loss; but he himself shall be saved; yet so as by fire.*"

This refers to believers who made it to heaven—they had eternal security—but they lost their reward of inheritance (Colossians 3:24).

Paul took this even further and in 1 Corinthians 9:24 he wrote: "Know ye not that *all* run in a race, but [only] *one* receiveth the prize?" And then he exhorts us: "So run, that ye may obtain [that prize]." Remember Philippians 3:14, which tells us that *the prize is "the mark of the high calling of God.*" It's co-reigning with Christ. It's inheriting the kingdom! It's the "reward of inheritance." It's enjoying the blessings, the intimacy, and the rest that God has planned for us all along. Again, it's our hope realized.

The New Testament tells us that a *gift* and a *prize* are two different things. A *gift* is "something that is bestowed freely upon someone," like our justification before the Lord.[15] Whereas a *prize* is "something that is *gained through some performance*," like our sanctification.[16]

This prize then must be sought after with *all* our effort, or we too will miss it.[17]

The warnings in the book of Hebrews are all about the possibility of believers losing *not* their sonship, but their reward of inheritance from God. (See Hebrews 3:7–14; 4:1, 11; 10:26–39; 12:25–29.)

"Sons of the Kingdom" (Matthew 8:11–12)

Speaking of losing our inheritance, there are several more Biblical passages (about forfeiting the kingdom rule) that have absolutely turned our theology upside down. The first one is the narrative in Matthew 8:11–12: "And I say unto you, that many shall come from the east and west, and shall sit down with Abraham, and Isaac, and Jacob, in the *kingdom of heaven [the Millennial Kingdom].* But [some of] *the children [sons] of the kingdom* shall be cast out into outer darkness: there shall be weeping and gnashing of teeth."

First, a little background on this verse: Jesus is the One talking here and He's talking to His own followers—Jewish and Gentile believers. While in Capernaum, He came across a believing centurion (a Gentile) who displayed tremendous faith. Jesus commented on this man's faith by saying, "I have not found so great a faith, no, not in Israel" (verse 10).

Verse 11 tells us that Jesus was talking about an event that will happen in the future—in the "kingdom of heaven"—where Abraham, Isaac, and Jacob will be present. This is very important because, as you will see later, this Kingdom of Heaven refers to the Millennial Kingdom where resurrected saints like Abraham, Isaac, and Jacob will be present. Verse 12 then says that the people who will be "cast out" from this event are the "children [or sons] of the kingdom."

Who are these "children [sons] of the kingdom"? The common interpretation of the *children* in this narrative is that they are Israelites, nonbelieving Jews. But, in fact, they are Messianic believers! Matthew 13:38 makes it very clear that the "children [sons] of the kingdom" are "the good seed," i.e., the believers. They are not the tares (or the unbelievers). Thus, it is *not* to the unregenerate that this fate occurs, but to the children [sons] of the kingdom . . . to whom the calling naturally belongs.[18]

This Scripture then is speaking about *truly saved Jewish believers* who of all people should have demonstrated great faith like the centurion. But like so many of us, they showed only marginal, nominal, and carnal faith. These are the ones who are found to be disqualified to inherit the kingdom, so they are *cast into the darkness outside* where there will be weeping and gnashing of teeth.

What is the Meaning of "Outer Darkness"?

Throughout this book we will be expanding upon many of these unsettling scriptural phrases. Please don't jump to conclusions ahead of us.

Dr. Spiros Zodhiates, in his wonderful commentary, *The Complete Word Study New Testament (with Parallel Greek)* commented on "the outer darkness" and the "weeping and gnashing of teeth." He said: "These terms may be applied to *believers* who have failed the Lord in their service . . . In this instance, the 'outer darkness' may be a reference to a place or a position of far less rewards for the servants who proved themselves less diligent than those who used and exercised their talents to the fullest." Kenneth Wuest in his *Greek New Testament* said, "This darkness is simply the darkness that is outside the King's banqueting house. It is *not* hell." Also, Charles Stanley in his book *Eternal Security* wrote, "The outer darkness here simply refers to being thrown outside a building into the dark. It is not a description of hell."[19]

This term "darkness," which so many of us have always associated with "hell," is used extensively throughout Scripture, *not* as a reference to hell, but as a reference to being *outside of the Lord's presence*. For instance, 1 John 2:9–11 says: "He that saith he is in the light, and hateth his brother, is in *darkness* even until now. He that loveth his brother abideth in the light and there is no occasion of stumbling in him. But he that hateth his brother is in *darkness*, and walketh in *darkness*, and knoweth not where he goeth, because *darkness* hath blinded his eyes."

This is a believer that John was talking about because he referred to him as "a brethren." God is still in this believer's heart, but because he has quenched the Spirit by poor choices, he is seen as "walking in darkness." The darkness in this Scripture is the same Greek word used in the above Matthew narrative.

Isaiah 50:10 in the Old Testament says, "Who is among you that feareth the Lord, that obeyeth the voice of his servant, that walketh in *darkness,* and hath no light? Let him trust in the name of the Lord, and stay upon his God."

Again, this is obviously a believer who is being referenced here.

So the word *darkness* gets its meaning from the context of the Scripture. Therefore, when you hear the term "outer darkness," don't jump to the conclusion it's talking about hell. It is not! There are much deeper meanings here that will be covered in detail later in this book.

It's very plain that God is trying to communicate something very important here to us, because these are believers that He is talking about. And something very drastic happens to them. They are "cast out into the darkness outside" where there is weeping and gnashing of teeth.

Amazingly, this is *not* the only passage like this in the Bible. There are several other parables that talk about the very same thing. Next chapter, we will expand on these words "outer darkness," "cast out," and "weeping and gnashing of teeth."

We know that many of you have very strong preconceived ideas about these terms, especially "the outer darkness" and "weeping and gnashing of teeth." We did too. All we ask is that you stay open and teachable, don't pre-judge until you've heard all the facts. Then, take it all back to the Word of God and see what the Lord says to you (Acts 17:11). The only certain barrier to truth is the presumption that you already have it.

"Outer Darkness" is *not* Purgatory

We want you to know right up front that the concept of "outer darkness" is *not* at all like the Catholic doctrine of "purgatory." Outer darkness is *not* a place of punishment. It's *not* a place of purging!

God does not punish us. He loves us back to health, wholeness, and renewal. Don't let the enemy put fear and condemnation on you at this point because of a Catholic background. God is *not* a harsh judge who is interested only in our perfect behavior. He is a loving Father who accepts sinners as His children and then in His compassion and love renews them back to wholeness. His judgments are not punitive. Hebrews 12:5–6 validates this: "My son, despise not thou the chastening of the Lord, nor faint when thou are rebuked of Him; For whom the Lord loveth He chasteneth" (see 1 Corinthians 11:31–32; Psalm 94:15). It's simply child discipline, beginning in this life and possibly extending into the next.

In the coming chapters we will discuss not only what the outer darkness is and what exactly happens there, but we will also find out who are the ones God puts there and why there will be weeping and gnashing of teeth.

We will be looking at several passages in Matthew that speak about "the Kingdom of Heaven," "being cast out," "the outer darkness," and "weeping and gnashing of teeth" (Matthew 8:12; 22:13; 24:51; 25:30). *These parables of Jesus in Matthew are the only places that use the terms "the kingdom of heaven," "being cast out into the outer darkness," and "weeping and gnashing of teeth" all in the same verse.* In fact, the term "outer darkness" is used nowhere else in Scripture but in these particular Matthew parables having to do with believers.

The reason Matthew seems to focus on the Kingdom of Heaven is because his is the only Gospel that records Christ's announcement to turn His attention from the Jews to the Gentiles and build "His church." Matthew 21:43 says, "The kingdom of God shall be taken from you [meaning the Jews] and given to a nation [meaning the 'body' of Christ] bringing forth the fruits thereof." In other words, Matthew's Gospel highlights *the change* to whom His message is being proclaimed (from the Jews to "the body of Christ").

Thus, there is something very important that God is trying to convey to us in these parables.

(Be sure to see Chapter 5 "Thy Kingdom Come" (the difference between the Kingdom of God and Kingdom of Heaven) and in the Supplemental Study Note Section of this book "The Epistomology Cycle.")

See *Parable Chart 1: Matthew 8:12*

In order to help us understand what exactly God is saying in this Scripture, we have laid out in one chart all the Matthew parables we're going to be studying so we can compare them. With each parable, we want to know: *To whom was Jesus speaking? About whom was He talking? What had they done wrong? What was their loss? Which kingdom was He speaking about? And, what is the lesson for us to learn?*

Take a look at Matthew 8:12 on the chart. To whom was Jesus speaking? *The Gentile centurion.* About whom was He talking? *The sons of the kingdom (Jewish believers).* What did they do wrong? *They lacked faith and didn't embrace the kingdom message.* What was their loss? *They were cast into the darkness outside where they experienced weeping and gnashing of teeth.* What is the lesson for us? *We need to have faith like that of the centurion.*

Jesus Christ Himself told all of the parables that we will be studying and *directed them to the entire body of believers*—Jewish believers, Gentile believers, His own servants, the church, and any believer waiting for His return. These are the ones Jesus was warning about being "cast out into the outer darkness" where there will be weeping and gnashing of teeth. *Consequently, these parables are not addressed to nonbelievers, but to the whole body of Christ.* This is why it's so crucial for us to take note of exactly what is going on here.

See *Chart 6: Who Will Inherit?*

Looking at this chart you can see that as a result of the Judgment Seat of Christ, there will be two kinds of inheritance. One is an inheritance that belongs to us simply because we are sons (a sonship inheritance). This is a free gift that all true Christians enjoy and one that will allow us to freely *enter* the kingdom. The second type of inheritance refers to a meritorious

PARABLE CHART 1 (MATT. 8:12)

STORY OR PARABLE	TO WHOM IS JESUS SPEAKING	ABOUT WHOM IS HE TALKING	WHAT HAD THEY DONE WRONG	WHAT WAS THEIR LOSS	WHAT EVENT IS BEING PREDICTED	WHAT IS THE LESSON FOR US
Matt. 8:12 Sons of the Kingdom "Story"	Gentile Centurion	"Sons of the Kingdom" - Jewish believers	Lack of Faith	Cast into outer darkness-weeping and gnashing of teeth	Preparation for the Kingdom	Need to have faith
Matt. 24: 45-51 Faithful & Wise Servants "Story"	Disciples ("What are the signs of Your coming?")	Any believer waiting for his Lord's return	Thought the Lord would not come-Mistreated his fellow servants	Cut him asunder & appointed him a place with "hypo-crites"-weeping and gnashing of teeth	The Rapture	Need to always be looking for His soon return
Matt. 25:14-30 10 Talents "Parable"	Disciples ("What are the signs of Your coming?")	His own servants	Wicked servant didn't do anything with his talent	Take talent away Cast into outer darkness-weeping and gnashing of teeth	The Bema Seat	Need to be faithful with the abilities God gives us
Matt. 25:1-13 10 Virgins "Parable"	Disciples ("What are the signs of Your coming?")	The "Church"	They had no intimacy with the Lord. He did not "know" them	Locked out of wedding - The door was shut & they were left out	The Wedding Ceremony	Need to know the Lord intimately
Matt. 22: 1-13 Man without a Wedding Garment "Parable"	Pharisees	Gentile believers at wedding (original ones called were not "worthy")	No wedding garment (no "fruit")	Bind him - cast into outer darkness-weeping and gnashing of teeth	The Marriage Supper	Need to wear the appropriate wedding garment

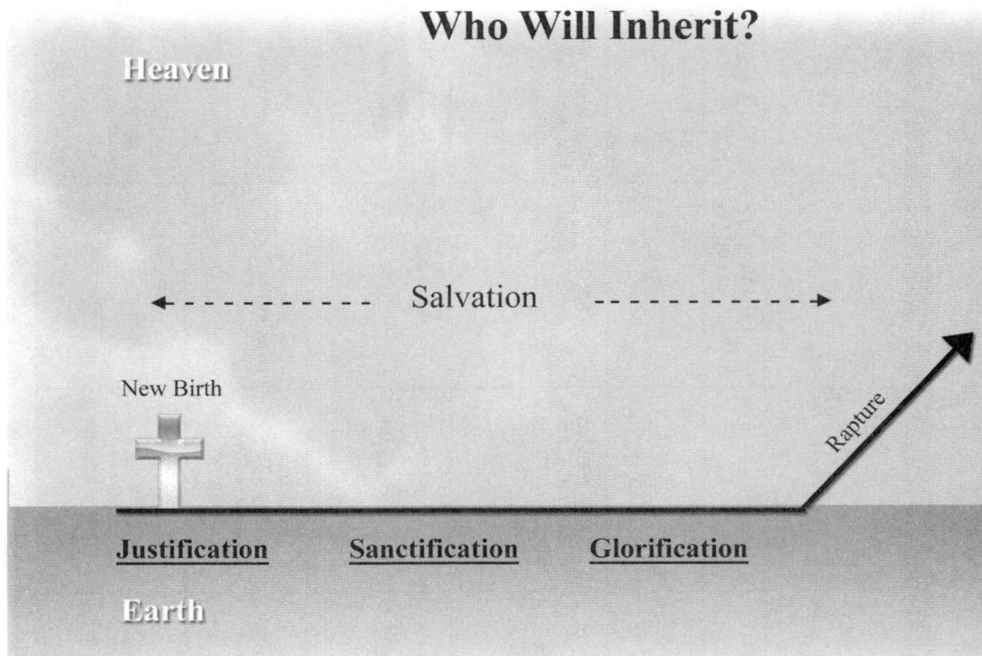

reward that only overcoming Christians will receive for their obedience, faithfulness, and endurance. This reward will allow us to *inherit* the kingdom (an inheritance from the Lord). This inheritance allows us to attend the Marriage of the Lamb in heaven, the Marriage Supper on earth and share in Christ's Millennial reign. These are the ones who not only will be *subjects* in the coming kingdom, they will be also *sovereigns* (and co-rulers with Him).

Revelation 21:7 says, "He that overcometh shall inherit all things, and I will be his God, and he shall be My son."

From now on, when we refer to Christians who will *"inherit, possess, or rule over the kingdom,"* we will be referring to those believers who are not only experientially sanctified but who also are partakers of Christ's Life and thus, overcomers. When we refer to those who only *"enter the kingdom*," however, we will be referring to those who have *not* been obedient or faithful in their walk with the Lord. They are justified, but *not* sanctified. They have not relied upon the Power of God to endure to the end. They are nominal Christians, lukewarm Christians, backsliding Christians (believers who once had fruit in their lives) but who have decided *not* to make the choices needed to stay in God's will. The world, the flesh, and the devil have overtaken them because they have quenched God's Spirit in their hearts.

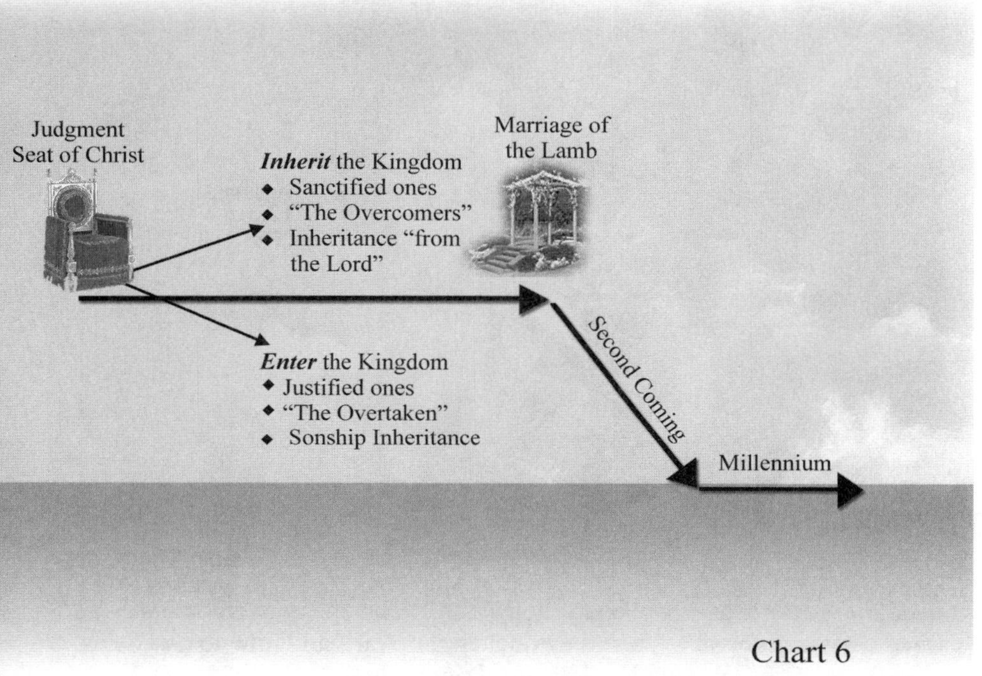

Chart 6

See *Chart 7: "Quenching the Spirit"*

This believer still has a new spirit and a new heart filled with God's eternal Life, *(the gold dot)* but because he has made *emotional choices* to follow his own desires rather than God's, God's Life in his heart has been quenched and blocked, and thus, "self life" (his own thoughts, emotions, and desires) is showing (1 Thessalonians 5:19). *So rather than a beam of light coming forth (God's Life), notice the black shadow (of self) that blocks that light.*

If this believer continues *not* to recognize that he has quenched God's Spirit and he never chooses to turn around (and repent), he will ultimately be deemed unfit, unprepared, and unqualified to inherit the kingdom.

See Chart 8: "Filled with the Spirit"

Take a look at Chart 8 and see what happens when we make faith choices to turn around and follow God. These are the believers who have denied themselves (the flesh) and have chosen to let Christ's Life come forth (that beam of light). These are the experientially sanctified ones, the partakers of Christ's Life, and the overcomers.

We want to emphasize that these overcomers are *not* perfect. *The light does* not *always stay on and the beam of light does* not *always flow*. It

Quenching the Spirit

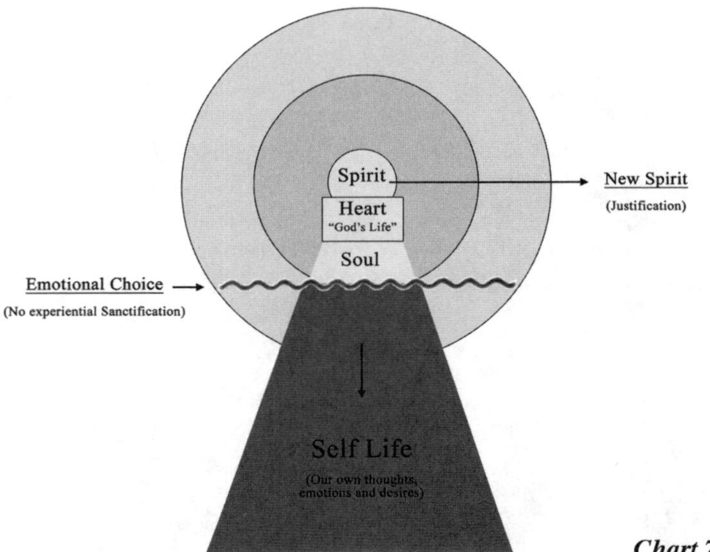

Chart 7

comes and goes, depending upon their choice. But these overcomers have learned how to recognize when they quench the Spirit and how to *let Christ, who is the perfect One, live His Life out through them.*

These are the ones who will inherit, possess, and rule in the coming kingdom with the King of Glory.

What Are the Requirements for Inheriting?

One of the most common questions we get asked is, what do I have to do in order to be *worthy* of inheriting from the Lord? For example, what does Matthew 10:38 really mean? "He who taketh not his cross and followeth after Me, is *not worthy* of Me." What does the word *worthy* in this Scripture mean?

There are two Greek words for the term *worthy* (and they are important for us to understand because we will be referring back to them often):

1. The first one is the Greek word *kataxioo* (Strong's #2661), which means "to be counted worthy; to be deemed entirely deserving." We are "counted worthy" only because of what *Christ* has already done for us on the Cross. He has redeemed us; *He* has imputed His righteousness to us and has given us His holiness. In other words, *He* is the One who is really worthy. We are only counted worthy because of what *He* has already done. Luke 21:36 validates this: "Watch ye, therefore, and pray always, that ye may be *accounted worthy [kataxioo]* to escape all these things that shall come to pass, and to stand before the Son of man."[20]

Filled with the Spirit

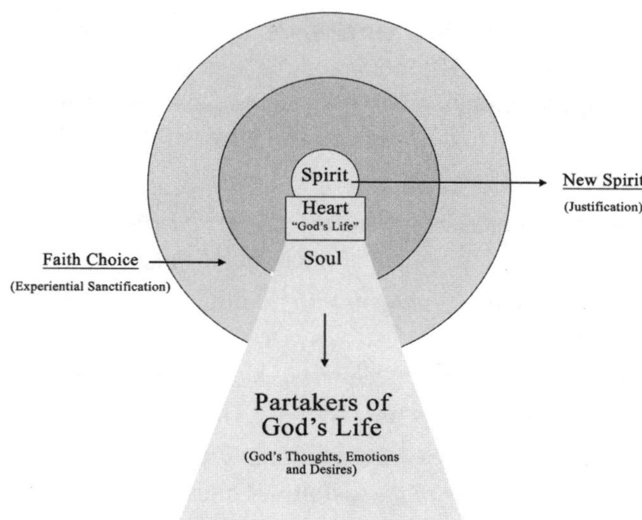

Chart 8

According to this, *all* true believers in Jesus Christ (faithful or not) are *accounted worthy* to escape the things to come and to stand before the Lord—to be a part of the coming kingdom. (Luke 15:21-24.)

2. The second definition of the word *worthy* (and the one we are really interested in) is the Greek word *axios* (Strong's #514), which means to be "worthy of" on the grounds of being fit, meet, or prepared. In Revelation 3:4 where Christ was talking about the church of Sardis, He said: "I have a few names even in Sardis which have *not* defiled their garments; and they shall walk with Me in white; *for they are worthy.*"

This is the kind of "worthy" that we have been talking about in relation to *inheriting the kingdom.* It means being fit, prepared, and qualified to rule and reign with Christ and hold levels of responsibility.[21]

See *Chart 9: Requirements for Inheriting*

What are some of the qualifications that will make us worthy of inheriting the kingdom?

Here's a list of some of the specific things the Bible says we need to attend to in order to be worthy of (fit, prepared, and qualified) to inherit the kingdom.[22] We will be covering most things on this list in detail in the Power Section of this book. So, again, don't get ahead of us.

Some of the things we will be learning in the coming chapters are:

- *How to be experientially sanctified* or conformed into Christ's image (Romans 8:29). How to give Christ the complete rights to our lives on a daily basis. How to submit to His absolute Lordship.

How to be set apart for Him (1 Thessalonians 4:3). How to be clean and open vessels (Ephesians 5:1–5).

- *How to be a partaker, a participant, and a sharer* of *Christ's Life* (Hebrews 3:14; 12:10), not just a receiver of His Life, but actually living and experiencing His Life. How to love others with His Love (2 Peter 1:3–4). How to produce the "fruit of the Spirit" (Galatians 5:22–23).
- *How to overcome the world, the flesh, and the devil* (Revelation 21:7). What is the practical application of this?
- *How to be obedient and faithful* (Matthew 7:21). How to do the will of God.
- *How to abide in Christ's fellowship* by daily presenting yourself to Him as a cleansed vessel (Romans 12:1–2).
- And when we do sin or when self raises its ugly head, *how to go to the Cross and deal with those things*. Unless the Cross is a constant part of our life, we will not experience Christ's overcoming Life. John 12:24–25 tells us, "Life only comes from death" (death of our

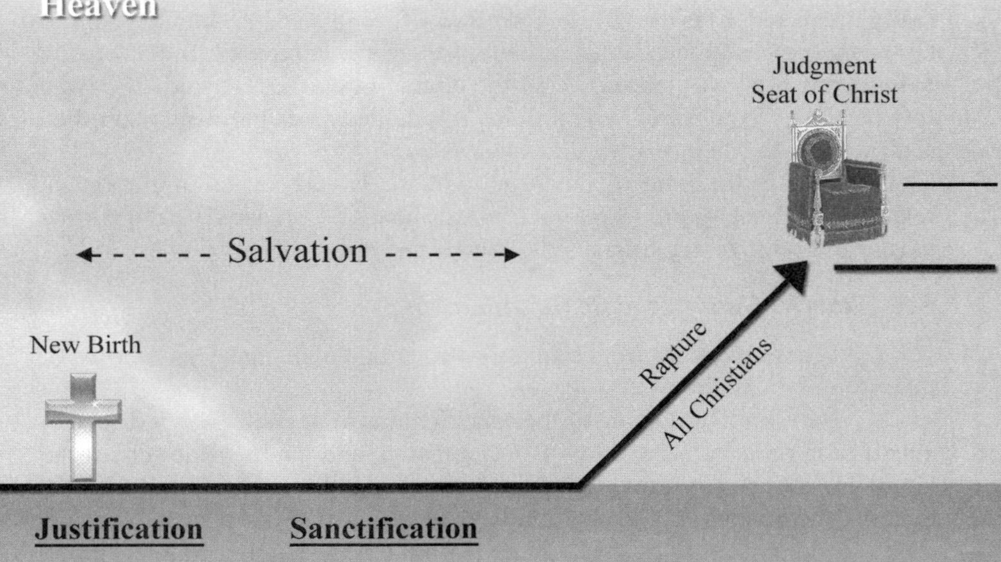

"self-life"). Chapters eight through twelve of this book deal with this subject in detail.

- *How to be diligent in prayer, dwell in His Word, be obedient to His commands, and follow the leading of the Holy Spirit* (2 Timothy 2:15).
- *How to persevere to the end, no matter what the trial*, and continually watch for His soon return.[23] (See also "*What More Can We Do?*" in the Supplemental Notes Section of the Appendix for more suggestions and Scriptures.)

In Conclusion

If you look at this list and say, "*There's no way in the entire world that I can do all those things. It's totally impossible!" then* we want you to again remember our prisoner friend whom we spoke of in chapter one. If he can learn to be sanctified, a partaker of Christ's Life, and an overcomer in his situation, then any of us can. The first place to start is simply recognizing your choices. Recognize when you blow it and quench God's Spirit. Then learn how to make faith choices to turn around and go God's way. Christ will do the rest. *He's* the One who will sanctify us; *He's* the One who will make

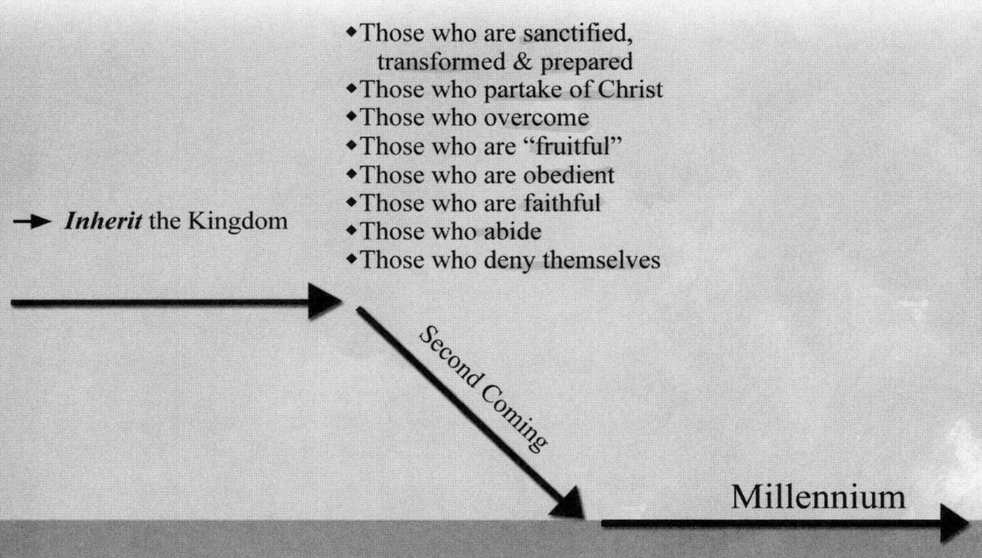

Chart 9

us partakers of His Life; and *He's* the One who will help us persevere unto the end. In other words, *He's the Overcomer*, not us. All He wants from us is our willingness to let Him do these things through us. *That's His will; but it's going to be our own choice whether or not we allow Him to do it.*

Learning how to do the above things *in a practical way* is what this book is all about.

The sobering part of all of this is that our eternal destiny depends upon these daily, moment-by-moment choices. The Life we are living now is just the testing ground or proving ground. The Kingdom Reign is the prize.[24] *Entering* the Kingdom of God simply means being born again and having faith in Christ's completed work; whereas merit and obedience are required in order to *inherit* that prize (John 3:3–8).

This kingdom perspective will not only have a profound effect on our daily lives here and now, it will also be the basis for encouragement in the difficult times that lie ahead. Remember Proverbs 13:12, "*Hope deferred makes the heart sick," but when that hope (our inheritance in Christ) is realized (apprehended, taken hold of), it will become a tree of Life.*

It certainly has in our lives and we pray it will in yours also. Our eternal destiny depends upon it.

Chapter Four

Who Are the Overcomers?

The Message of Overcoming

So far we've learned that *all* Christians are *called* to be overcomers, but *not* all Christians *choose* to be. The question is why not?

It's not so much that the body of Christ doesn't want to be overcomers. They do! It's just that they have not been taught how to become overcomers. The first part of the nineteenth century, the theology that we all must become an overcomer in order to reign in the Millennial Kingdom was taught, treasured, and applied. Now a hundred years later, this message has been so watered down that it has been replaced with a more liberal approach—that if we are believers, we *all* will rule and reign with Christ. As a result, much leaven has crept into the church and many have purposely chosen to neglect the topics of "overcoming," "inheriting," and the "Kingdom of Heaven." They avoid these subjects because 1) they are controversial; 2) they are divisive; and 3) they don't fill the pews like messages of grace do. As a result, these truths have become a foreign subject to many, causing us to miss out on one of the most central messages of the entire gospel.

Scripture exhorts every believer to become an overcomer so we might have positions of authority in the coming kingdom. For example, in Revelation 3:21, Jesus said, "To him that overcometh will I grant to set with Me in My throne, even as I also overcame, and am set down with My Father in His throne."

The Bema Seat Judgment at the end of this dispensation, where Christians will be judged for their fitness and their qualifications to inherit the Millennial Kingdom, will reveal man's response to this call. It will reveal which Christians have overcome the world, the flesh, and the devil and have produced wonderful "fruits" of righteousness by the Holy Spirit. It will also reveal the Christians who were overcome by the world, the flesh, and the devil and, consequently produced no fruit.

This book was written primarily to fill in some of the gaps about overcoming the world, the flesh, and the devil and inheriting the kingdom that perhaps were not adequately covered in our typical Christian upbringing.

"To Overcome" Means

The word *overcome* (Strong's # 3528, *nikao*) means "*to conquer or to gain victory over something*." The inherent thought in the word *overcome,* is to be a conqueror or victorious in a contest or conflict. Overcomers are those conquerors and those winners who have successfully run the race of faith and conquered the numerous obstacles encountered along the way. They are those fruitful believers for whom special rewards are offered. (Again, they are not perfect, religious, or good; they are just ordinary believers who have made continuing choices to follow Christ, regardless of how they feel.)

We can only be overcomers *because Christ lives in us. He is the true overcomer* (Romans 8:37). And He can only overcome through us when we choose to surrender our flesh (go to the Cross) and then let His Life come forth. Unfortunately, there is no middle road. We will either let Him *overcome* the world, the flesh, and the devil through us (by being "filled with the Spirit"—that "beam of light"), or we will *be overcome* (because we have "quenched the Spirit"—"that dark shadow"). There's no such thing as being half-filled!

In chapter twelve, we will explore exactly *what* an overcomer is and *how* we become one. In this chapter, however, we simply want to understand *who* the overcomers are and what is promised to them.

Promises to the Overcomers

Chapters 2 and 3 of Revelation speak extensively about *overcomers.* The blessings of the future kingdom are assured to these overcomers.[1] Listen to some of the incredible promises God makes to these overcomers:

- They will be clothed in white. (Revelation 3:5a)
- They will be "pillars" in the Lord's temple. (Revelation 3:12a)
- They will be granted power over the nations. (Revelation 2:26)
- They will enjoy the tree of Life. (Revelation 2:7)
- They will not be subject to spiritual death. (Revelation 2:11)
- Their names will be acknowledged by Christ. (Revelation 3:5b)
- They will be fed out of the hidden manna. (Revelation 2:17a)
- They will have a white stone with their name on it. (Revelation 2:17b)
- Christ will write His own Name upon them. (Revelation 3:12b)
- They will sit with Christ on His Throne. (Revelation 3:21)

All of the above promises are Millennial in scope. These blessings clearly reveal that overcomers not only will enter the kingdom, but also will have positions of significance.

Overcomers are those Christians who, by being partakers of Christ's eternal Life, are able to conquer, prevail, and subdue the temptations of the world, the desires of the flesh, and the wiles of the devil. They have learned to love with God's Love, make faith choices according to His wisdom, and depend upon His power to accomplish their deeds.

Overcomers in the Churches of Revelation

If you haven't already, take a moment to reread Revelation 2:1 through Revelation 3:22, which talks about the "seven letters to the seven churches." This passage of Scripture was given to John by Jesus not only about *seven existing churches at that time*, but also about *all churches* in general and about *each of us individually*. These letters were written to all churches of all ages and all individuals in every age. The rewards of inheritance that are promised to each of these churches, and to the individuals in them who overcome, apply to all of us. We need to listen carefully to what Jesus was saying because each of the rewards He gives corresponds to the exact measure of faithfulness the believer manifested in his life.

It's important to also note that seven times in these letters to the seven churches, Jesus said (through John), *"I know your works."* Jesus was emphasizing works in these letters. In fact, in Revelation 2:26 He said, "He that overcometh and keepeth *My works* to the very end, I will give power [authority] over the nations." Jesus was talking about the Millennial Kingdom and He was stressing a special kind of work that a believer must do. "My works," Jesus said. He was talking about the things that are done *by the Holy Spirit* through us. He was *not* referring to the works of the flesh, but to the works of the Spirit.

The Seven Churches of Revelation

Let's take a moment to look at *who* the overcomers are in each of these seven churches, and let's pay close attention to *what God promises* them in return for their faithfulness, obedience, and endurance. Remember, these letters are addressed not only to churches in general, but also to each of us individually!

1. Ephesus (Revelation 2:1–7) —Ephesus represents the *apostolic church,* which endured great hardships, but God said He knew their "good works," their labor, and their patience. These saints were strong on doctrine, but they had forgotten and forsaken the most important thing—their first love, that special intimacy with the Father. He exhorted them to repent.

God's promise to the faithful and obedient overcomer in the church of Ephesus was that he would eat of the tree of Life (the tree of Life means being equipped with a "special wisdom and knowledge" for the future kingdom).[2]

This tree of Life first appears in Genesis where it says *man was created to rule and reign* with the King of kings over all the earth (Genesis 1:26–28 and 2:9). Then it disappears on the earth for six thousand years because man was *not* in a position to rule and reign with Christ. But here in Revelation, it shows up again as man will, once again, be in a position to co-reign. So the tree of Life has something to do with our future inheritance in the Millennial Kingdom. It has to do with special wisdom and knowledge in order to co-reign with Christ (Proverbs 3:13–18).

2. Smyrna (Revelation 2:8–11)—Smyrna represents *the persecuted church* or the suffering church, whose elders said they were Jews, but really were not. Some were Jews in name only. God told this church that He knew their poverty and their suffering, but He promised them if they were faithful and obedient unto death, He would give them the "crown of life" (James 1:12).

Interestingly enough, this was the only church (besides Philadelphia) that had *nothing bad said about it.*

God's promise to the faithful and obedient overcomers in the church of Smyrna was that they would not be hurt in the "second death." (The second death—where death and hell are cast into the lake of fire—comes at the end of the Millennium and involves unbelievers at the White Throne Judgment.)[3] Because of their perseverance, even unto death, God promised the overcomers a victorious crown.

(Someone recently asked us a very good question: "If the overcomers in the church of Smyrna will *not* be hurt in the second death, *what about the non-overcomers in this church?* What happens to them? Will they be hurt in the second death? Do they lose their salvation?" We wrestled with this question for a while. But we know that God's Word always has an answer for everything, if we just wait. We did. Finally, it came. *Smyrna, remember, is the only church that had nothing bad said about it, so in essence, there were* no *non-overcomers!* This letter was just assuring them that they *all* will be a part of the first resurrection and not be hurt in the second death.)

3. Pergamus (Revelation 2:12–17)—Pergamus represents *the church that was married to the world* (Constantine's era). As God puts it, these are the ones who "dwell where Satan's throne is." This church had allowed the evil *doctrine of Balaam* (which means monetary gain by compromise) and the *doctrine of the Nicolaitans* (which means corruption of delegated authority) to come in.[4] God exhorted them to repent.

God's promise to the faithful and obedient overcomer in the church of Pergamus was that he would eat of the "hidden manna" (divine physical provision for the future) and receive a "white stone," which is a victory stone for Christians whose works endure the fire. This stone will have a new name written on it that no one knows, except the one who receives it (Revelation 2:17).

4. THYATIRA (Revelation 2:18–29)—Thyatira represents *the orthodox church* where the evil spirit of Jezebel was allowed to reign. (You might want to read about Jezebel, the patron of Baal worship, in 1 Kings 16:30–34 and 21:25 because in the end times this spirit is said to return.) The goal of the spirit of Jezebel was (and will be) to seduce God's faithful servants into disobedience and fornication. As John phrased it, Thyatira hit the "depths of Satan." Revelation 2:22 says that God is going to cast Jezebel and her followers into the great Tribulation unless they repent. Therefore, God exhorted the faithful to "hold fast" till He comes. He said they will also receive the "morning star," which means they will have a special relationship with Jesus Himself (Revelation 22:16). They will shine like the Lord, reflecting His brightness and glory.

God's promise to the faithful and obedient overcomers in the church of Thyatira is that they will reign with Christ while He rules the nations with a rod of iron (speaking of the Millennial Kingdom).

5. SARDIS (Revelation 3:1–6)—Sardis represents those in *the denominational church* who say they are alive, but who really are dead. The Spirit told Sardis that if they didn't wake up, He was going to come "like a thief in the night" and they wouldn't even know it. Their name said they were alive, but in reality they were dead. God exhorted them to be watchful and repent and strengthen the things that remain.

There is nothing good said about Sardis.

God's promise to the *overcomers* in this church was, "Thou hast a few names even in Sardis that have *not* defiled their garments, and they shall walk with Me in white, for they are worthy" (verse 4).

The word *worthy* here is the same Greek word, *axios,* that we talked about last chapter, which means "worthy of" on grounds of being fit, prepared, and ready.

The "white" raiment has to do with the "wedding garment" that Revelation 19:7 says all of us are now supposed to be preparing for ourselves. (We'll talk more about this wedding garment in chapter six.)

The word *defiled* in this Scripture is the Greek word *moluno* (Strong's 3435) and means to blacken oneself, to pollute oneself or dirty one's clothing (Jeremiah 23:11). The basic meaning here is to color something by staining it. Defilement means that it needs cleaning. It's the declaration that we have morally or spiritually transgressed. A simple meaning is that we have defiled the purity of Christ and have become *unfaithful*.

It's interesting that the root of the word *defiled* in this Scripture is the word *black*. In other words, to defile yourself means to *"blacken yourself."* As you look back over our Spirit-Quenched Chart from last chapter, you can see that's exactly what happens when we make choices that block God's Spirit and cause us to walk in darkness.

Note that this Scripture is telling us that it *is* possible to defile our garments even after we become Christians.

God then continues His promise to the overcomer in Sardis (Revelation 3:5) by saying He will *not* blot his name out of the "book of life" (which will be opened at the Judgment Seat of Christ),[5] but He will confess it before the Father and His angels.[6]

6. PHILADELPHIA (Revelation 3:7–13)—Philadelphia represents *the raptured church* (the caught-up-to-heaven church) and the church, of course, we all want to be associated with (1 Thessalonians 4:17). Verse 7 says that Philadelphia is the church that has the "key of David," which Scripture says, "he that openeth, and no man shutteth; and shutteth, and no man openeth." This sounds very similar to the "keys to the kingdom" found in Matthew 16:19 and 18:18, which we will explore in depth in chapter twelve.

The Spirit told this church that He knew they had little strength of their own, but He also knew that they had *not* denied His Name (to deny His Name would disqualify them for the prize). In other words, they had faithfully and obediently rested on God's resurrection power even through the hard times (2 Corinthians 13:4). They had suffered because of His Name. And, because of their faithfulness to keep the "word of His patience," He would keep them from the very hour of temptation that is to come upon the earth. He would also make those who say they are Jews, but are not, bow at their feet. God exhorted them to "hold fast to that which you have, so no one will take your crown." (Does this mean we can lose our crown?)

God's promise to the faithful and obedient overcomers in the church of Philadelphia is that He will make them a pillar in His temple. A pillar is symbolic of a steadfast figure of strength and durability.[7] Thus, these faithful saints will remain secure and firm in their positions of strength at the Lord's side and enjoy tremendous intimacy with Him. And because of this intimacy, they will not go out of the sanctuary any more. (Interestingly enough, this verse ties the Millennial Temple to being a major part of the coming kingdom.) The Lord also said He would write upon them the Name of God, the name of the city of God (Jerusalem), and also His own name.

7. LAODICEA (Revelation 3:14–22)—(This is the church we are all a part of now, so we need to pay special attention here.) Laodicea represents *the last days church*, which is neither "hot nor cold." This includes the "seeker friendly" churches that we see springing up everywhere. The music and worship programs create excitement, but the message is so watered down that it does not stimulate a renewed personal commitment of obedience and faithfulness to the Lord. As this Scripture notes, it is "neither hot nor cold." It is lukewarm! Today's deadness in churches comes from following the truth only with our minds, *not* with our hearts or our lives. These saints said they were rich and in need of nothing, but in truth and from God's perspective, they were *wretched, miserable, poor, blind,* and *naked.* (Note the word *naked* here because we'll talk a lot about this in chapter fourteen.) He is speaking about nominal and unfaithful Christians who are found to be "naked" because they do not have

on the appropriate clean and white wedding garments. Revelation 16:15 tells us, "Behold, I come as a thief. Blessed is he that watcheth and keepeth his garments, lest he walk *naked* and they see his shame." (See page 269 for an explanation of the two different kinds of garments).

Unfortunately, *there was nothing good said about this church.*

God then exhorted the saints in Laodicea (verse 18) to "buy of Him gold tried in the fire" (in other words, begin to produce "works of gold" that will withstand the fire of God's coming judgment). He said *if they do*, they will be clothed in that white raiment (that wedding garment we will talk about in chapter six) and "the shame of their nakedness will not appear."

Then He makes an interesting statement in verse 19: "As many as I love, I rebuke and chasten." (Remember in chapter two, we spoke about how God *never* punishes His own, but He does discipline and chasten us "for our profit." That discipline begins in this lifetime and may extend to the next.)

Notice something else interesting here. The Scripture we always hear quoted referring to unbelievers is verse 20 which says: "Behold I stand at the door and knock; if any man hear My voice, and open the door, I will come in to him, and will sup with him, and he with Me." The question is: Who is God really speaking to here? These are supposedly believers, right? They are *not* unbelievers! Yet, Christ is on the "outside" knocking on these believers' hearts (those who are "naked") asking them to let Him in! He is pleading with them to repent, turn around, and be clothed—i.e., let Him live His Life out through them. In other words, be partakers of His Life, which will allow them to become real overcomers.

The Church of Laodicea corresponds to the epistle of Jude where it says "a form of godliness" remained in the church, but they had "denied the power thereof" (2 Timothy 3:5). Materialism had so permeated this church that they were spiritually destitute (Jude 17–19). *Christ stood on the outside, not within.* At the end of this present dispensation, apostasy is again predicted to prevail. This is referred to in the parables of Matthew 13, these seven churches in Revelation, and the books of 2 Peter and Jude (1 Timothy 4:1).

God's promise to the faithful and obedient overcomers in the Laodicean church is that Christ will let them sit with Him on His Throne. In other words, the overcomers in this church will have a "joint participation" in the throne room of the King (Revelation 3:21).

It seems to us that the "rewards of inheritance" escalate from *wonderful* blessings for the overcomers in the church of Ephesus to *incredible* blessings for the overcomers in the church of Laodicea. These phenomenal promises should be an incentive for all of us to strive (press on, struggle, contend, fight, labor) diligently to become faithful overcomers.

Justification is a free gift, with no works needed. Experiential sanctification, however, is different. It entails a fight and a battle to continue to stay sanctified, obedient, and faithful so we can earn "an inheritance from the Lord."

Characteristics of the Overcomers

Some of the characteristics of these Revelation 2 and 3 overcomers are worth mentioning again:

- They did *not* deny Christ. (Revelation 3:8, 10b)
- They did *not* defile their garments. (Revelation 3:4)
- They kept the word of His patience. (Revelation 3:10a)
- They remained loyal to God. (Revelation 2:1–3)
- They overcame tribulation and remained faithful. (Revelation 2:8–10) They were spiritually zealous. (Revelation 2:19)

The greatest incentives that God has placed in His Word for us to live godly lives are found in these promises to the overcomers. Such glorious promises should stir the hearts of all believers and cause us to diligently strive to personally apprehend them.

The bottom line is: *we will either overcome or be overcome.*[8]

Paul's Paranoia

Let's leave the overcomers and their promises for just a moment and take a good look at how Paul, the great apostle, viewed entering and inheriting this future Millennial Kingdom.

Paul wrote fourteen books of the Bible (Romans, 1st and 2nd Corinthians, Galatians, Ephesians, Philippians, Colossians, 1st and 2nd Thessalonians, 1st and 2nd Timothy, Titus, Philemon, and probably Hebrews), yet he told us in 1 Corinthians 9:24–27 that *he was fearful of not winning the prize (the prize of the reward of inheritance) and, somehow, becoming a "castaway"*:

> Know ye not that they who run in a race run all, but one receiveth the prize? So run, that ye may obtain. And every man that striveth for the mastery is temperate in all things. Now they do it to obtain a corruptible crown, but we, an incorruptible. I, therefore, so run, not as uncertainly; so fight I, not as one that beateth the air; But I keep under my body, and bring it into subjection, *lest by any means, when I have preached to others, I myself should be a castaway.*

The word *lest* (Strong's #3381, *mepos*) means "God forbid that I should."

The word *castaway* (Strong's #96, *adokimos*) in this Scripture means someone who is unapproved, rejected, and worthless. It means someone who is tested for proof, but who fails the test (is not able to withstand it) and is then rejected. *Castaway* means one who is *not worthy* (*axios*) of inheriting because he is not fit, prepared, or ready.

Kenneth Wuest said in his book, *Word Studies in the Greek New Testament*, "Castaway means disapproval after having failed to meet the requirements." He said that if a Greek runner broke training, he would be forbidden to race. *Castaway* simply means "disqualified."[9]

Titus 1:16 further demonstrates Paul's concern about being a castaway when he talked about *our works* portraying the truth about our lives: "They profess that they know God [Strong's #1492, *eido*—"to know intimately"], but *in works* they deny Him, being abominable, and disobedient."

What is it that the apostle Paul was so intent about keeping, while at the same time, acknowledging that it *could* be lost? He never doubted his justification for a moment, as he preached in Romans 8:38–39 that "nothing would separate us from the Love of God." But he *was* concerned about losing the *prize of the reward of inheritance*.

Paul knew that it was possible to be saved and yet still not participate in the coming kingdom (to be justified and yet *not* have a part or a role in the Millennium), i.e., to be a castaway (1 Corinthians 9:27). And this made him apprehensive. I'm sure he probably remembered Moses, who was *not* permitted to enter the promised land because of disobedience at the end of his life (Deuteronomy 3:25–26). Paul was worried that his own life's work could be burned in the end and he could suffer loss. That's why he wrote 1 Corinthians 3:15: "If any man's work abide which he hath built upon it, he shall receive a reward. [But] if any man's work shall be burned, *he shall suffer loss*; but he himself shall be *saved, yet as by fire*."

"Saved, yet as by fire" means "barely saved," or saved with difficulty. *Loss* in this Scripture means to forfeit one's inheritance or something that could have been in one's possession.

Who was Paul talking about here? Nonbelievers? No way. He was talking about believers *because according to the above 1 Corinthians 3 Scripture these people* are *saved in the end*. He was talking about "believers who suffer loss." They became castaways not worthy of inheriting.

Paul was warning us that ruling and reigning in the coming kingdom is *not* a given; it's *not* automatic; and, we all won't win the prize! It's very possible to defile our garments like those in Sardis did, fail the test, and become "a castaway."

Martyn Lloyd Jones quoted 1 Corinthians 3:15 in his book *Life in the Spirit* and commented: "This is a great mystery . . . but the teaching seems to be clear. It does not mean that a man can fall from grace; but it does mean that a man who is saved can know the terror of the Lord."[10]

In Philippians 3:13–14 Paul exhorted us: "Brethren, I count not myself to have apprehended; but this one thing I do, forgetting those things which are behind, and reaching forth unto those things which are before,

I press toward the mark for the prize of the high calling of God in Christ Jesus."

See *Chart 10: Running the Race*

Just as Paul *agonized* and *strained* every muscle of his being as he sought to win the prize of the high calling, so he was exhorting every one of us to "lay aside every weight and *run the race*" (Hebrews 12:1). He wanted us to win! (1 Timothy 6:12; 2 Corinthians 11:25–28). He didn't want us to be overtaken by the world, the flesh, and the devil, but to be overcomers. He wanted our works to withstand the test of fire, so that we would be welcomed into the kingdom and win the prize.

The end of the race for us will be either victory or defeat. We either will overcome or be overtaken. The goal of the race is that we might become "partakers of His holiness [conformed into His image]" and win the prize (Hebrews 12:10). This is the reason why Satan is on such a rampage to destroy the message of overcoming and inheriting the kingdom. He can't let us win! He must keep us failing the test, becoming castaways, and losing the prize. (Yes, the prize can be lost!)

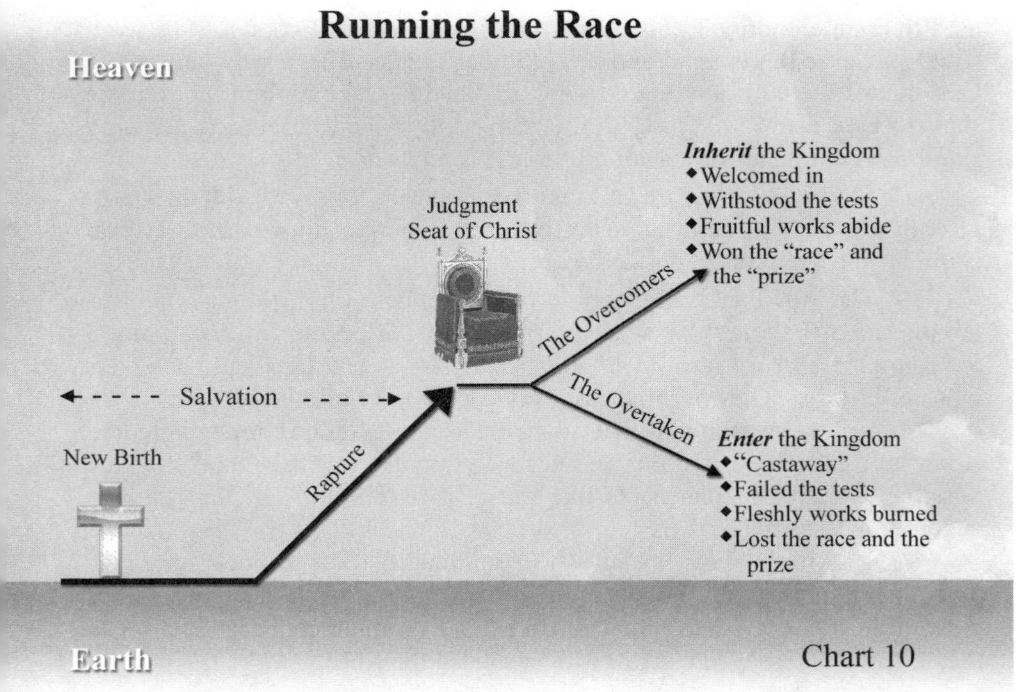

Life Is Like a Contest

Paul said that the Christian Life is like a contest or a race. Every one of us, whether we like it or not (if we are believers), is enrolled in that race. Therefore, if we want to win, we must lay aside every weight and run the race with all our might.[11] Our conversion experience simply *enters* us into the race. But, then, like Paul, we must press on toward the goal of "the prize of the high calling"—a share in the Millennial reign of Christ. As in all races, prizes will be given out at the very end (1 Corinthians 9:24). Hebrews 11:6 confirms this: "Without faith it is impossible to please Him; for he that cometh to God must believe that He is, and that He is a *rewarder* of them that diligently seek Him." The Kingdom of Heaven is set before us as an object to be sought and a prize to be won.[12]

Justification is a gift that is bestowed upon us without a price and earns us a place in the kingdom;[13] *whereas, sanctification is part of a prize gained through performance.*[14] *All of us can run the race, but only the overcomers will win the prize.*

Our life here and now just happens to be the testing ground or the proving ground to see how we do in that race. *It's the score card!* Every choice we make and every action we take is being registered and weighed for approval in the next life. There are five books in heaven, which we will talk about in chapter six, that record everything we do here and that will be opened and read at the Judgment Seat of Christ. As we said, being born again simply *enters* us into the race. But then, like Paul, we must each press on toward the goal, or the prize of the high calling, in order to finish the race (Philippians 3:14; Hebrews 12:1).

God has given each of us different talents, abilities, and giftings to advance the Kingdom of God here on earth. The question is: What have we done with these talents? Have we used them wisely, squandered them, or buried them?

The Parable of the Ten Talents (Matthew 25:14–30)

(See picture.)

This brings us to the parable of the Ten Talents in Matthew 25:14–30. This is the second of the Matthew passages that speak about "the kingdom of heaven," "being cast out of fellowship," the "outer darkness" (or *the darkness outside*), and "weeping and gnashing of teeth."

Before we begin to examine this parable, let's again remember Acts 17:11: "They received the Word *with all readiness of mind*, [but then] they searched the Scriptures daily whether those things were so." This is just exhorting us to always be open to new thoughts, new ideas, and new ways of looking at Scripture, but then prayerfully take these things back to the Word and see if it validates them.

The Ten Talents

Jesus told the parable like this:

[14]For the kingdom of heaven is as a man traveling into a far country, who called his own servants, and delivered unto them his goods. [15]And unto one he gave five talents, to another two, and to another one; to every man according to his several ability; and straightway took his journey. [16]Then he that had received the five talents went and traded with the same, and made *them* other five talents. [17]And likewise he that had received two, he also gained other two. [18]But he that had received one went and digged in the earth, and hid his lord's money. [19]After a long time the lord of those servants cometh, and reckoneth with them.

[20]And so he that had received five talents came and brought other five talents, saying, Lord, thou deliveredst unto me

> five talents: behold, I have gained beside them five talents more. [21]His lord said unto him, Well done, thou good and faithful servant: thou hast been faithful over a few things, I will make thee ruler over many things: enter thou into the joy of thy lord. [22]He also that had received two talents came and said, Lord, thou deliveredst unto me two talents: behold, I have gained two other talents beside them. [23]His lord said unto him, Well done, good and faithful servant; thou hast been faithful over a few things, I will make thee ruler over many things: enter thou into the joy of thy lord.
>
> [24]Then he which had received the one talent came and said, Lord, I knew thee that thou art an hard man, reaping where thou hast not sown, and gathering where thou hast not strawed: [25]And I was afraid, and went and hid thy talent in the earth: lo, there thou hast that is thine.
>
> [26]His lord answered and said unto him, Thou wicked and slothful servant, thou knewest that I reap where I sowed not, and gather where I have not strawed: [27]Thou oughtest therefore to have put my money to the exchangers, and *then* at my coming I should have received mine own with usury. [28]Take therefore the talent from him, and give *it* unto him which hath ten talents.
>
> [29]For unto every one that hath shall be given, and he shall have abundance: but from him that hath not shall be taken away even that which he hath. [30]*And cast ye the unprofitable servant into outer darkness: there shall be weeping and gnashing of teeth.*

The master was very upset at this servant and in verses 26–29 he said: "You *wicked* (Strong's #4190, meaning hurtful in influence, *but not in character*) and slothful [unprofitable] servant, you knew I reaped where I sowed not and gathered where I did not winnow, therefore you ought to have put my money with the exchangers [bankers]. Then I could have at least gotten some interest from it. Therefore, I am going to take the one talent I gave you and give it to my servant who has ten talents. For everyone that has shall be given more; but to him who has not, even that which he has will be taken away." As a consequence, in verse 30 he said, *"Cast the unprofitable servant into the outer darkness [the darkness outside] where there shall be weeping and gnashing of teeth [profound regret]"* (author's paraphrase).

An Explanation and a Little History

Dwight Pentecost wrote in his book *Things to Come*: "The purpose of the writing of the Gospel of Matthew was to record the presentation of Jesus

Christ as Messiah; to trace the opposition to Him and His offered kingdom by the nation and to record the official and final rejection of that King and kingdom by Israel."

The Kingdom of Heaven was offered to Israel by not only John in Matthew 3:2, but also by Jesus for three and a half years.[15] Israel, however, rejected not only the coming kingdom, but also its King (Matthew 11:2–16:12). And thus, Christ announced to the Jewish leaders of that day that He was going to turn His attention to another (holy) nation—"a nation bringing forth fruits thereof," i.e, "the church" (Matthew 21:43). Even though the church did not exist yet, Christ had previously spoken of it in Matthew 16:18-19. The church is that "holy nation" of 1 Peter 2:9 whose main purpose is to bring forth "fruit" with a view toward occupying positions of responsibility in the coming Millennium. This new nation is described as a "chosen generation" and "a royal priesthood."

Consequently, the Messianic Kingdom was postponed, but will be reoffered to the Jews during the Tribulation. (See Hosea 5:15; Romans 11:13–21; Galatians 3:6–14.) Christ pointed out that since Israel failed as stewards of the mysteries of the Kingdom of Heaven, many will be destroyed and their city leveled. A "new nation" will then be appointed to take their place, but on the condition of bearing fruit.

Comments About the Parable of the Ten Talents

Before we dissect this parable, we need to understand that a parable is simply a truth told in story form in order to help explain a previously taught truth. *Para* actually means *"to come alongside."* The previous truths in Matthew 24 and 25 are all about the Rapture, how we are to watch for Christ's return at any moment, and the coming Kingdom of Heaven (Matthew 24:32—25:30). The reason Jesus spoke in parables is so that His disciples and followers could understand, but His detractors could not (Matthew 13:10–11).

Parables are prophetic in nature. The particular parables we will be studying, Matthew 8:11–12; 22:1–13; 24:45–51; 25:1–13, and 25:14–30, are prophetic of all the events between the rejection of the Kingdom of Heaven by Israel and the fulfilling of the destiny of the Church—including the Rapture, the Bema Seat, the Wedding, and the Marriage Feast.

It's important we notice Jesus' change of focus here in this particular parable—from the Jewish nation to His own disciples, the first members of His church. Right after Matthew 24 He stopped speaking to the Jewish people and began to talk to His body of believers (notice especially verses 36–44). The doctrine that Jesus then taught to His disciples became the foundation upon which the church would be built (Matthew 28:19–20). Consequently, what Jesus spoke to His disciples, He was also speaking to His church: "Go ye therefore, and teach all nations, baptizing them in the Name of the Father, and of the Son, and of the Holy Ghost: *teaching them to observe* all *things whatsoever I have commanded you."*

Therefore, it's scriptural for us to apply to our own lives what Jesus spoke to His disciples through these parables.

The servants that Jesus was talking about here are *His own servants—those who belong to Him*. In other words, they're believers. (You can't say that only two of the servants were saved and the third one was not. They were *all* "servants" and they were *all* "saved"—because they were *all* waiting for His return.) In fact, the word *servant* (Strong's #1401, *doulos*) in this Scripture is used to describe all three of these individuals. We cannot arbitrarily dismiss the third servant as being unsaved, simply because we don't understand the terms "cast out," "outer darkness," and "weeping and gnashing of teeth" in regards to a Christian.

The talents (or the money) in this parable was not a gift, but represented a *special privilege or stewardship* that was given to each of these servants in accordance with their own capacity for business. It was a loan, so they could decide for themselves what they wanted to do with it, just as God gives us the free choice to decide our own course of action.

The number ten suggests "a measure of human responsibility."

The first servant doubled his master's investment, proving that he was merciful and honest in exercising trust for another's benefit. He was also faithful to his master's interests.[16] The second servant did the same, only not to the same degree. The last servant, however, thought there would be no consequences to what was done with his master's talent. Thus, he made no effort to improve what was given to him. He never exercised the grace that his master gave him.

This parable, then, is really concerned with the *actions* of the servants of God. It was *not* the possession of the talents that determined their reward or punishment; it was the servants' use of them. It was their faithfulness—what they *did* with the blessings the Lord gave them. The first two faithful servants wisely used the privilege that was afforded them. And the Lord was pleased and said, *"Well done, good and faithful servant, you have been faithful over a few things, I will make you ruler over many things. Enter into the joy of the Lord"* (Matthew 25:21).[17] These servants were then ushered into God's presence and His fellowship.[18]

Cast into the Outer Darkness

But the third "unprofitable servant" wasted the talents the Lord gave him, so he was then cast into the outer darkness where there is "weeping and gnashing of teeth."

Now the word *unprofitable* (Strong's #888) simply means "not worthy of" (in the sense of not being fit or prepared. It's again the Greek word *axios*—the second definition of the word *worthy* that we talked about last chapter.) This man was *not* worthy of entering the joy of the Lord's presence, because he had not been faithful, obedient, or persevering. Thus he wasn't qualified to enter the joy of the Lord.

The word *cast out* has two definitions: *Ekballo* (Strong's #1544) means he was cast forth from his original position *grudgingly, a position he was once a part of* but was now ejected, sent forth, and sent away. This Greek word is always used in connection with the outer darkness or the darkness outside.

Whereas *ballo (*Strong's #906) is always used for casting away, throwing out *violently*, not caring where it falls. This Greek word is always used in connection with being cast into hell or fire.

And the word *outer darkness* (Strong's #1857, *exoteros,* and Strong's #4655, *skotos*), which we talked about last chapter, means the "darkness outside" and is so rendered in the ISV Bible. It's simply *the darkness outside the light of God's presence*. It's another region or another area outside of where the joy of the Lord was being experienced by the first two faithful and obedient servants. It's a place *outside* the room where the obedient servants are enjoying God's presence, but evidently contiguous to it. The unprofitable servant can see what is going on in the other region, but he cannot enter in. He is a castaway—he was cast out of fellowship. Now we might be able to understand a little more clearly why Paul was so apprehensive about this.

In this darkness outside, the unfaithful servant will experience *weeping and gnashing of teeth,* which simply means "profound regret." Keep in mind that God does not wipe away our tears until the *end* of the Millennium. Revelation 21:4 says, "I will wipe away all tears from their eyes," speaking of heaven, *not* the Millennium. (Revelation 7:17 refers to the Tribulation saints.)

Before you are unnerved by the terms "outer darkness" and "weeping and gnashing of teeth," which many of us have always associated with *hell* or the *lake of fire*, it's important to remember that there are many other places in the Bible that speak of Christians "walking in darkness." We talked about a couple of them in the last chapter. Remember 1 John 2:10–11, "He that loveth his brother abideth in the light, and there is none occasion of stumbling in him, but *he that hateth his brother is in darkness and walketh in darkness and knoweth not whither he goeth, because that darkness hath blinded his eyes*." John was talking about a believer because he referred to him as a brother. God was still in this believer's heart, but because he had quenched God's Spirit by emotional choices, the Scripture says he was *walking in darkness*. The word *darkness* here in 1 John is the same Greek word that is used in the Matthew parable, and it has *nothing* at all to do with hell or the lake of fire.

Many of us have been so influenced by our preconceived ideas about certain terms in the Bible that it's often very difficult for us to be open to new ideas and new interpretations. That's why Acts 17:11 is so important.

Let's hear what some well-known theologians have to say about this parable and about these particular terms.

Comments by Theologians

Charles Stanley talked about this "outer darkness" in his book *Eternal Security*: "The final verse of this parable is so severe that many commentators assume it is a description of hell. *It is not!* Keep in mind that this is a parable. A parable makes one central point. The point of this parable is that in God's future kingdom, *those who were faithful in this life will be rewarded, and those who were not, will lose any potential reward.* Some will be given more privileges and responsibility while others will have none. The outer darkness refers to 'being thrown outside a building into the dark' and in that place there shall be weeping and gnashing of teeth" (emphasis added).[19]

Kenneth Wuest in his *Expanded Translation of the Greek New Testament* said, "The outer darkness is the darkness that is outside of the King's banqueting house."[20] In other words, it is not hell!

Erwin Lutzer, in his book *Your Eternal Reward*, wrote, "These warnings are addressed to believers . . . God does not let His children get by with disobedience even though their place in heaven is secured and their transgressions legally forgiven."[21]

Thayer's Greek / English Lexicon says that the outer darkness is "the darkness outside the limits of the lighted palace."[22] It's evidentially a space in the kingdom, but outside the circle of men and women whose faithfulness earned them a special rank. *Among the privileges of the overcomers is nearness to Christ.* The opposite of this is the darkness outside of His presence. The unprofitable servant is simply being excluded from the light and the joy of the feast with the Lord. One either *enters into* the joy of the Lord and is included; or one is *cast out* from that joy and is excluded from the fellowship.[23]

Dr. Spiros Zodhiates, in his wonderful commentary, *The Complete Word Study New Testament (with Parallel Greek)* commented on "the outer darkness" and the "weeping and gnashing of teeth." He said: "These terms may be applied to *believers* who have failed the Lord in their service . . . In this instance, the "outer darkness" may be a reference to a place or a position of far less rewards for the servants who proved themselves less diligent than those who used and exercised their talents to the fullest. The expression would then refer to the degrees of the enjoyment of heaven rather than referring to hell . . . *Entrance into heaven is gained by accepting Christ's sacrifice for justification, but a person's rewards in heaven will be determined by what he did for Christ here on earth* (Matthew 5:3–12; 7:21–23; Luke 6:20-26; Acts 10:4, 31; Romans 2:1–16; 1 Corinthians 3:13; 4:5; 2 Corinthians 5:10; 1 John 4:17). The Christian's faithfulness to his tasks and responsibilities in the world is considered of such paramount importance that the same metaphor, the *"outer darkness,"* that was used by the Lord to indicate the punishment of the unbeliever for his rejection of God's salvation, *is also used of the believer who does* not *live in obedience to the light he has received.* In the case of the nonbeliever, it will be a punishment of fire and burning (Matthew 13:30; John 15:6). In the case of the believer, it will be weeping or expressing sorrow over not having used the opportunities God provided. The phrase "gnashing of teeth" indicates anger at oneself for ignoring the marvelous opportunities that he had on earth" (emphasis added).[24]

Warren Wiersbe in his *Bible Exposition Commentary* (speaking of "weeping and gnashing of teeth") said, "We need not see this treatment as punishment in hell, but rather the *deep remorse of a man* who was an unfaithful servant. He grieves deeply in the darkness outside of the King's palace, but he is still a servant and thus, will be welcomed back into the King's estate. The man was dealt with by the Lord, lost his opportunity for service and gained no praise or reward. To me, this is outer darkness!"[25]

And finally, Tony Evans in *The Prophecy Study Bible* quoted Zane Hodges as saying: "Every Christian will be rewarded based on his words, deeds and faithfulness. Those Christians who are unfaithful (Matthew 25:28–30) will have their rewards taken from them and given to those who were faithful and they will be cast out into outer darkness, the place where there shall be weeping and gnashing of teeth. *The outer darkness described in this passage is likely a lesser state in God's kingdom.*"[26]

Sounds a Little Like "Purgatory"

When we first began to write this book and were sharing a little about these principles with others, especially the part about the "outer darkness" and the "weeping and gnashing of teeth," many who had Catholic backgrounds quickly said: "This place sounds a little like purgatory!"

Since neither of us have a Catholic background, we were surprised by this response. So we want to make a clear distinction between "purgatory" and the "outer darkness." *The Catholic Encyclopedia* says: "Purgatory is a place or condition of temporal punishment for those who, departing this life in God's grace, have not fully paid the satisfaction due to their transgressions." In other words, it is a place where men and women go to be temporarily purged by fire for their sin. This Catholic doctrine comes from 2 Maccabees 12:41-46.

Contrary to this, Romans 5:8 clearly states that Jesus paid the penalty for *all* of our sins. The idea that we have to suffer for our sins after death is contrary to everything the Bible says about salvation. Neither Jesus, nor Paul, nor any modern Protestant churches teach the existence of a place of purgatory. Paul, throughout his epistles, made it very clear that *God's judgment of believers is* not *punitive!*[27] (We've tried to make this point over and over again.) Revelation 3:19 tells us that those God loves, He *rebukes* and *chastens, but He does not punish.* And Hebrews 12:10 says the only reason He chastens us is so that we might be "*partakers of His holiness*" and thus, be able to inherit the kingdom.

The sins of a believer have already been paid for at the Cross. It's a finished work. He does not have to go through a period of purging before he goes to heaven (Titus 2:14; Hebrews 1:3). The outer darkness is *not* a place of punishment!

The basic difference between the Catholic doctrine of purgatory and what we are sharing here is that, first of all, there *is* going to be a literal Messianic Kingdom here on earth for a thousand years. All believers will be raptured and all believers will enter that kingdom. However, *only the true overcomers (those who recognize their choices and choose to follow Christ) will be able to inherit regal positions*. Christians who are overcome (or overtaken) by the world, the flesh, and the devil will have their works burned, but they themselves will be saved. First Corinthians 3:13 and 15 confirms this: "*Every man's work* shall be made manifest; for the day shall declare it, because it shall be revealed by fire; and the fire shall test *every man's work* of what sort it is . . . If *any man's work* shall be burned, he shall suffer loss; but he himself shall be saved." Thus, it's <u>not</u> *the person* who is burned but simply *his fleshly works*—works motivated by the believer himself and then performed in his own strength and for his own self-glorification. These are things he did in his own power and through his own love. The burning of these fleshly works is done at the Judgment Seat of Christ, *not* in the outer darkness.

The issue at stake in this parable is *not* the unfaithful servant himself (since he is a believer, his sins have already been judged and forgiven at the Cross). The issue is his works and his deeds here on earth. The issue is that he didn't use the talents that God gave him to produce fruit.

This outer darkness then is *not* a place of dark suffering like hell, but a place where God in His Love will "retrain" these unfaithful believers back to His way of holiness. It's a place of renewal, new beginnings, fresh starts. As Psalm 94:15 says, "God's judgment shall return unto righteousness." Just as the Lord cleanses, refines, purifies, and separates the vine for the purpose of making more fruit, He does the very same thing with us. And, apparently, He will do this in the Millennial Kingdom also.

No Fear in God's Love

As you hear terms like the "darkness outside" and the "profound remorse" experienced there, don't let the enemy put fear and condemnation upon you. Recognize the difference between conviction (from God) and condemnation (from the enemy). Remember how much God loves you. Remember, *God does* not *punish His children*. He chastens us and He does so because He loves us and knows it's for our benefit.

Hebrews 12:8 tells us, "if we are not chastised, we are really not sons—"

Here's a modern day example of what this outer darkness may be like: Picture in your mind a young family going on a summer vacation in their SUV. They have three small children, two of whom have behaved wonderfully the whole trip, but the third child has been incorrigible. The parents don't throw that child out of the car into the dark night, never to see him again. They love him. And because they love him, they make him sit in the very backseat of the car until he acknowledges his mistakes. When he does so, again because they love him, *they take the time to retrain him in the right way to behave.* This might be exactly what God is going to do with His disobedient children in the coming kingdom.

Just like the parents of that disobedient child—first, they disciplined him, but then they took the time to restore, instruct, and retrain him in the right way to act. God might do the very same thing with us. It's called "tough Love." But it's still Love! That's God's way. That's His character. And, that's His methodology.

(Note: God's Love (*Agape*) has two sides to it. It's not only a longsuffering and merciful Love, it's also a tough and discipline Love. Both are God's Love. The darkness outside may be a part of God's tough Love, but it is still *Agape*. "Behold the goodness and the severity of God" (Romans 11:22).

See *Parable Chart 2: Matthew 25:14–30*

This brings us to our Parable Chart again.

Remember, at this point the "Kingdom of Heaven" had been rejected by the Jews and thus, Christ had just offered it to "a nation bringing forth fruits" (i.e., the church) (Matthew 21:43).

To whom was the Lord speaking? He was talking to His own disciples. *About whom was He speaking?* He was speaking about His own servants—the coming church. *What had they done wrong?* They hadn't invested the talents that He had given them wisely. They had squandered them. *What was their loss?* They lost what they did have and were cast into the darkness outside, where they experienced weeping and gnashing of teeth. *What occasion does this remind us of?* Possibly, the Judgment Seat of Christ. *What is the lesson for all of us?* We need to be faithful with the talents and abilities that God has given each of us here and now.

See *Chart 11: Overcomers vs. the Overtaken*

The bottom line is that at the Judgment Seat of Christ (which we will speak more about in chapter six), the *overcomers* (the faithful believers) will be informed of their welcome into the region of Light, where they will experience the joy of the Lord.

The *overtaken* (those nominal, lukewarm Christians), however, will be informed that they will be cast into a sphere of darkness *outside the light and joy of the Lord,* where they will experience tremendous remorse and regret.

PARABLE CHART 2 (MATT. 25: 14-30)

STORY OR PARABLE	TO WHOM IS JESUS SPEAKING	ABOUT WHOM IS HE TALKING	WHAT HAD THEY DONE	WHAT WAS THEIR LOSS	WHAT EVENT IS BEING PREDICTED	WHAT IS THE LESSON FOR US
Matt. 8:12 Sons of the Kingdom “Story”	Gentile Centurion	“Sons of the Kingdom” - Jewish believers	Lack of Faith	Cast into outer darkness-weeping and gnashing of teeth	Preparation for the Kingdom	Need to have faith
Matt. 24: 45-51 Faithful & Wise Servants “Story”	Disciples (”What are the signs of Your coming?”)	Any believer waiting for his Lord’s return	Thought the Lord would not come-Mistreated his fellow servants	Cut him asunder & appointed him a place with “hypo-crites”-weeping and gnashing of teeth	The Rapture	Need to always be looking for His soon return
Matt. 25:14-30 10 Talents “Parable”	Disciples (“What are the signs of Your coming?”)	His own servants	Wicked servant didn’t do anything with his talent	Take talent away Cast into outer darkness-weeping and gnashing of teeth	The Bema Seat	Need to be faithful with the abilities God gives us
Matt. 25:1-13 10 Virgins “Parable”	Disciples (“What are the signs of Your coming?”)	The “Church”	They had no intimacy with the Lord. He did not “know” them	Locked out of wedding - The door was shut & they were left out	The Wedding Ceremony	Need to know the Lord intimately
Matt. 22: 1-13 Man without a Wedding Garment “Parable”	Pharisees	Gentile believers at wedding (original ones called were not “worthy”)	No wedding garment (no “fruit”)	Bind him - cast into outer darkness-weeping and gnashing of teeth	The Marriage Supper	Need to wear the appropriate wedding garment

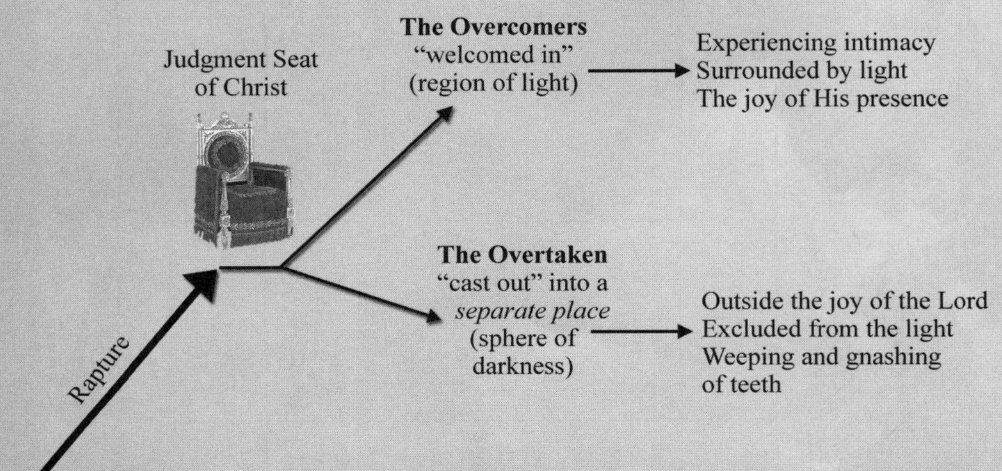

Studying this subject of inheriting the kingdom and co-reigning with Christ in the Millennium has been such an incredible eye-opener for both of us. It's absolutely set the Bible on fire for us and illuminated every single page. We've both been Christians for more than fifty years and yet are only now getting the full impact of what all of this really means. It's too horrible to even contemplate the possibility of forfeiting our inheritance from God (our eternal rewards) and learning at the Judgment Seat of Christ that our lives have been wasted.

It's Not Too Late!

But thankfully, it's *not* too late! If you are reading this now, then *it's not too late for a renewed commitment*! It doesn't matter how badly you've blown it in the past; or what horrible things you've done or how many times you have failed. That's what 1 John 1:9 is all about: "If we confess our sins, He is faithful and just to forgive us our sins and cleanse us from all unrighteousness." *In other words, one choice and we can be back on the road (God's High Way) again toward becoming an overcomer!*

Overcomers are *not* perfect. They fail just like the rest of us, but they keep on getting up, keep on repenting, and keep on being willing to surrender themselves to Christ and letting Him, who is the only perfect One, work and produce "fruit" through them.

God promises us that *if we are faithful over a few things here*, then He will give us authority over many things *there* (Matthew 25:21).

That's His promise! That's our hope! And that's the tree of Life!

Section Two

The Kingdom

"That I may know Him, and the power of His resurrection, and the fellowship of His sufferings, being made conformable unto His death; if by any means I might attain unto the resurrection of the dead. Not as though I had already attained, either were already perfect: but I follow after, if that I may apprehend that for which also I am apprehended of Christ Jesus. Brethren, I count not myself to have apprehended: but this one thing I do, forgetting those things which are behind, and reaching forth unto those things which are before, *I press toward the mark for the prize of the high calling of God in Christ Jesus."*

—Philippians 3:10–14

Chapter Five

Thy Kingdom Come

In the model prayer that the Lord taught His disciples—commonly called "the Lord's Prayer"—one of the key petitions is "Thy Kingdom come."[1] Most Christians today, however, have no real idea what this means. Yet there are more promises and prophecies about this "kingdom" than any other period in the entire Bible!

The lack of any realistic perspective on the kingdom may be the root source of the widespread apostasy that characterizes our contemporary churches today. Leonard Ravenhill, the famous minister and preacher from England, said:

> Is there then a forgotten truth from the holy and imperishable Word of the living God that could shake this Laodicean Church from its creeping paralysis? I believe there is. If there is no word from the Lord in this hour, there certainly is no word for the Church from anyone else. One day I grasped two handfuls of books of sermons and found that not one of them had a message on the [Millennial Kingdom] or *the Judgment Seat of Christ. This, I am persuaded after much thought, is the most neglected part of eschatology.* Sermons there are and books without number on the Second Coming of Christ, but books dealing as a sole subject [of the Millennial Kingdom] and the Judgment Seat of Christ can be counted on one hand. Why is this? Does meditation on such a penetrating truth terrify the minister? Well it might.[2]

It is tragic that most of the major denominations—Roman Catholic and Protestant—embrace an eschatology ("study of last things") that is *amillennial:* a view that does not envision a literal rule of Christ on the Throne of David on Planet Earth.

While there are many different, yet defendable, views regarding many aspects of end-time prophecies, this basic divergence—denying a literal Millennium—is particularly hazardous since it would appear to be an attack on the very character of God! It does violence to His numerous and explicit promises and commitments that pervade both the Old and New Testaments.

The Old Testament is replete with commitments for a literal Messiah ultimately ruling the world through Israel from His throne in Jerusalem. There are at least 1,845 references in the Old Testament and 17 books that give prominence to the event. The ancient rabbinical aspirations were dominated by it. In fact, this obsession obscured Israel's recognizing the Messiah when He made His initial appearance.

There are at least 318 references in 216 chapters of the New Testament and 23 of its 27 books give prominence to the event. The early church looked longingly for His promised return as their "Blessed Hope" to rid a desperate world of its evil rulers.

(For a summary of the origin of these traditions see *Historical Basis of Amillennialism* in the Supplemental Study Notes. For a perspective of how hermeneutics (theory of interpretation of Scripture), eschatology (the study of last things), and ecclesiology (the study of the church), impact each other, see *the Epistemological Cycle* in the Supplemental Study Notes.)

The Davidic Covenant

One of the hazards of the amillennial view is the failure to take the covenants of God seriously. There are a number of major covenants—commitments—of God throughout the Old Testament. Four of them are *unconditional* (that is, unilateral commitments on God's part):

1. The Abrahamic Covenant[3]
2. The Land Covenant[4]
3. The Davidic Covenant[5]
4. The Everlasting Covenant[6]

Throughout the world today anti-Semitism continually challenges the Abrahamic Covenant. Most New Testament Christians have an inadequate understanding of the Old Testament roots of our faith and the ultimate destiny of Israel in God's program for mankind.

The Land Covenant, and Israel's right to the land, is the primary challenge of the militant agenda of Islam today.

The postmodern church, in its Replacement Theology that ignores the passages outlining the ultimate destiny of Israel, dismisses the Davidic Covenant. Paul's definitive statement of Christian theology we call the book of Romans hammers away in three chapters—9, 10, and 11—that God is not finished with Israel and emphasizes its future restoration. The fulfillment of the Davidic Covenant—and its implications for Christians in our day—is the subject of this book.

The Throne of David is central to many of the Messianic prophecies, for example:

> For unto us a child is born, unto us a son is given: and the government shall be upon his shoulder: and his name shall be called Wonderful, Counsellor, The mighty God, The

> everlasting Father, The Prince of Peace. Of the increase of his government and peace there shall be no end, upon the *Throne of David,* and upon his kingdom, to order it, and to establish it with judgment and with justice from henceforth even forever. The zeal of the LORD of hosts will perform this.
>
> —Isaiah 9:6–7

In the New Testament, the angel Gabriel confirmed this very Throne in his annunciation of the birth of the Messiah:

> And, behold, thou shalt conceive in thy womb, and bring forth a son, and shalt call his name JESUS. He shall be great, and shall be called the Son of the Highest: and the Lord God shall give unto him the Throne of his father David: And he shall reign over the house of Jacob for ever; and of his Kingdom there shall be no end.
>
> —Luke 1:31–33

The Throne of David, however, did not exist during the Messiah's earthly ministry. So the Thorn-crowned One has yet to assume that very Throne and to fulfill this destiny!

One of the pivotal episodes in the book of Acts was the Council of Jerusalem, when James explained:

> And after they had held their peace, James answered, saying, Men and brethren, hearken unto me: Simon hath declared how God at the first did visit the Gentiles, to take out of them a people for his name. And to this agree the words of the prophets; as it is written, *After this I will return, and will build again the Tabernacle of David,* which is fallen down; and I will build again the ruins thereof, and I will set it up: That the residue of men might seek after the Lord, and all the Gentiles, upon whom my name is called, saith the Lord, who doeth all these things. Known unto God are all his works from the beginning of the world.
>
> —Acts 15:13–18

James was quoting from the Old Testament prophet Amos:

> In that day will I raise up the *Tabernacle of David* that is fallen, and close up the breaches thereof; and I will raise up his ruins, and I will build it as in the days of old.
>
> —Amos 9:11

Revelation 20 details the fulfillment of these kingdom commitments in which a specific period of one thousand years is designated and thus yields the common label the "Millennium." (Although most of what we know about this period accrues from other related passages.[7]) The Millennial Kingdom is a one-thousand-year literal and visible reign of Christ upon the earth during which Satan is bound, Israel as a people is restored, the Jewish Temple rebuilt. Jesus will be the King of kings ruling over a literal kingdom, in the literal land of Israel, located in the literal city of Jerusalem.

The Kingdom of Heaven

Matthew used a specific phrase, "the Kingdom of Heaven" in his Gospel. He was the only one to use this phrase. Mark, Luke, and John, in similar passages, always used the phrase "the Kingdom of God." Many assume that these are simply synonyms. Careful exegetical study suggests that they are not precisely equivalent: Kingdom of God is all-inclusive; Matthew's use of Kingdom of Heaven is more specific and a denotative subset within the all-inclusive term.

The Kingdom of God

The Kingdom of Heaven

Matthew used "Kingdom of Heaven" thirty-three times and "Kingdom of God" only five times.[8] It is astonishing to discover what his specificity reveals denoting the fulfillment of the Davidic Covenant.

The all-inclusive Kingdom of God is always portrayed in sevens: seven churches, seven spirits before His throne, etc. The Kingdom of Heaven, however, is always portrayed in twelves: twelve tribes, twelve apostles to reign over the twelve tribes,[9] twelve Kingdom Parables, twelve Kingdom Mysteries, twelve thousand sealed from each of twelve tribes.[10] And it climaxes in the New Jerusalem with twelve gates, twelve foundation stones, and measuring twelve thousand furlongs in each of (at least) three dimensions.[11]

The illuminating discovery is that the Millennium is the fulfillment of the Davidic Covenant. It is also important to realize that it is a physical kingdom on the Planet Earth.

See *Chart 12: Defining the Kingdom*

The Kingdom of Heaven is sequenced as the fifth in the list of kingdoms in Daniel's interpretation of Nebuchadnezzar's dream:

> And in the days of these kings shall the God of heaven set up a kingdom, which shall never be destroyed: and the kingdom shall not be left to other people, but it shall break in pieces and consume all these kingdoms, and it shall stand for ever.
>
> Forasmuch as thou sawest that the stone was cut out of the mountain without hands, and that it brake in pieces the iron, the brass, the clay, the silver, and the gold; the great God hath made known to the king what shall come to pass hereafter: and the dream is certain, and the interpretation thereof sure.

—Daniel 2:44, 45

It seems we are too often victims of our own presuppositions. It is useful to recognize that in Hebrew (and in German), the words *of* and *from* are the same word. In German, when we say "von Hapsburg," we really mean "of Hapsburg" in the sense of being "from (the place called) Hapsburg." In Hebrew, to speak of "the Kingdom *of* Heaven" actually means "the Kingdom *from* Heaven." Grammatically, it is a genitive of source, rather than a genitive of apposition as is often assumed. It is too easy to confuse an entity with the location of its source. Matthew's references are to a physical kingdom on the earth that will be established *from* heaven for some very specific purposes.

It is also interesting to carefully consider the offer of the "kingdom, power, and glory" by Satan to Christ:

> And the devil, taking him up into an high mountain, showed unto him all the kingdoms of the world in a moment of time. And the devil said unto him, All this power will I give thee, and the glory of them: for that is delivered unto me; and to whomsoever I will I give it. If thou therefore wilt worship me, all shall be thine. And Jesus answered and said unto him, Get thee behind me, Satan: for it is written, Thou shalt worship the Lord thy God, and him only shalt thou serve.

—Luke 4:5–8

One of the most provocative aspects of this encounter is that the "kingdoms, power, and glory" were Satan's to give—*or it wouldn't have been a temptation!* Jesus didn't challenge Satan's possession of them. It is the ultimate victory over the usurper—*and the Kingdom, Power, and Glory*—that the Bible is all about.

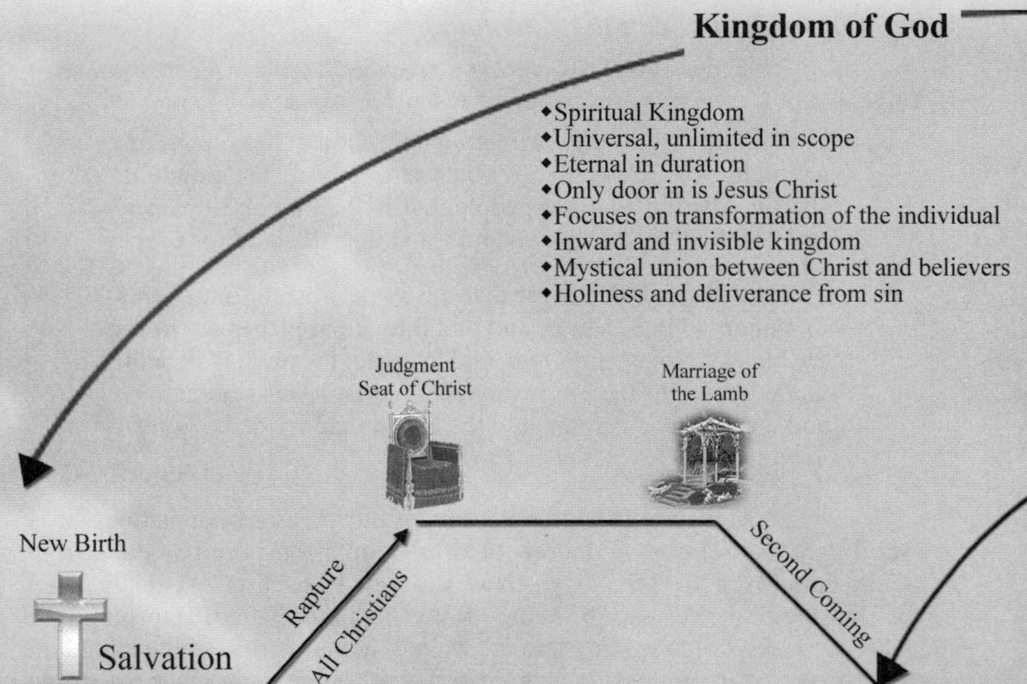

The Purpose of All History

Jesus summarized the purpose, tragedy, and triumph of all history:

> O Jerusalem, Jerusalem, thou that killest the prophets, and stonest them which are sent unto thee, how often would I have gathered thy children together, even as a hen gathereth her chickens under her wing.
>
> —Matthew 23:37

The Tragedy of All History

> But ye would not! Behold, your house is left unto you desolate.
>
> —Matthew 23:38

When Jesus came, they rejected Him, attributed His miracles to Satan, and began plotting His death.[12] From that day on, He preached publicly only in parables. His explanations were reserved in private sessions with His

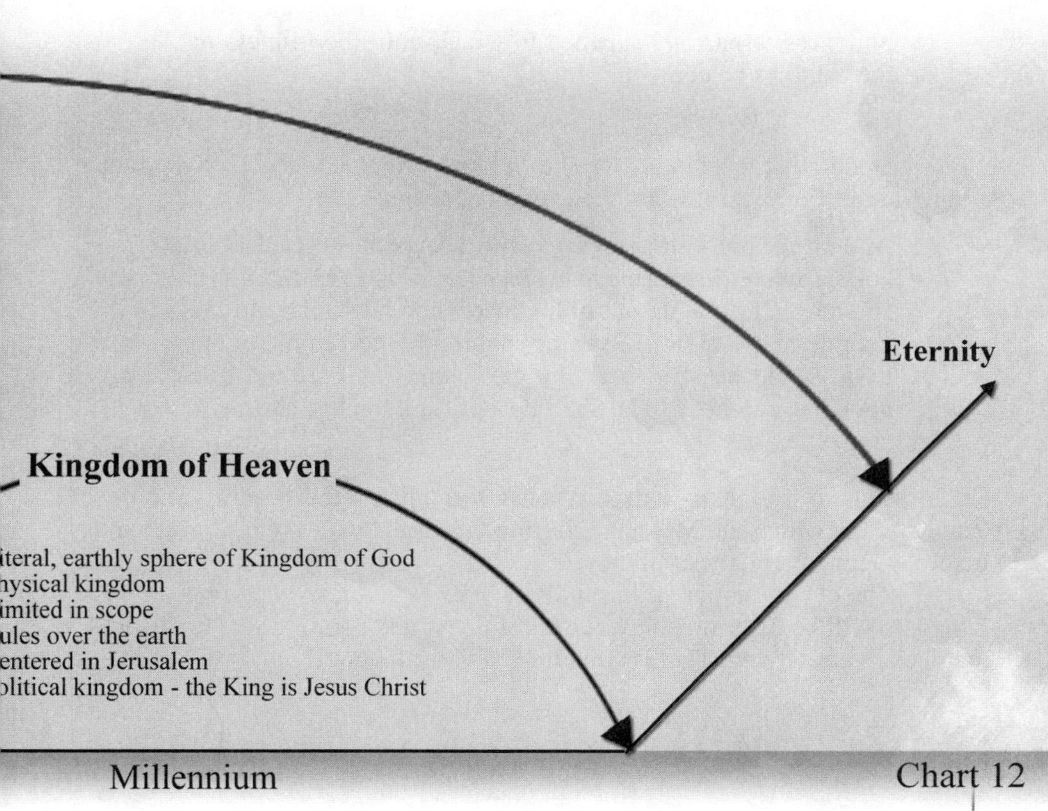

disciples.[13] It will require the Great Tribulation to ultimately drive them to repentance:

> I will go and return to my place, till they acknowledge their offence, and seek my face: in their affliction they will seek me earnestly.
>
> —Hosea 5:15

The Triumph of All History

> For I say unto you, Ye shall not see me henceforth, till ye shall say, Blessed is he that cometh in the name of the Lord.
>
> —Matthew 23:39

Because of their rejection, national blindness was decreed upon Israel as Jesus rode that donkey into Jerusalem, presenting Himself as the Messiah on the very day that Gabriel had established with Daniel.[14] But that blindness would not last forever:

> For I would not, brethren, that ye should be ignorant of this mystery, lest ye should be wise in your own conceits; that blindness in part is happened to Israel, until the fullness of the Gentiles be come in.[15]
>
> —Romans 11:25

Upon His return in power, the Messiah will establish His Kingdom, and build the Temple, fulfilling the Davidic Covenant.

> And speak unto him, saying, Thus speaketh the LORD of hosts, saying, Behold the man whose name is The BRANCH; and he shall grow up out of his place, and he shall build the Temple of the LORD: Even he shall build the Temple of the LORD; and he shall bear the glory, and shall sit and rule upon his Throne; and he shall be a priest upon his Throne."
>
> —Zechariah 6:12–13

This is the Kingdom predicted throughout the Psalms and the Prophets,[16] in which the Messiah will rule the earth "with a rod of iron" and before whom "every knee will bow."[17]

The determination of our individual roles and responsibilities in this Kingdom will be determined by our faithfulness and commitment in this life that we are now living. That is what this book is all about.

Chapter Six

Kingdom Events

Where are we going and what does the future hold? Let's examine some of the events that will occur at the close of this age, just before the Kingdom from Heaven begins.

See *Chart 13: What Happens After the Rapture*

First, there will be the Rapture—which is the surprise catching up of *all* the saints by Christ to be with Him always. 1 Thessalonians 4:16–18 contains an incredible promise: "For the Lord Himself shall descend from heaven with a shout, with the voice of the archangel, and with the trump of God; and the dead in Christ shall rise first; Then we who are alive and remain shall be caught up together with them in the clouds [the whole body of Christ] to meet the Lord in the air; and *so shall we ever be with the Lord.* Wherefore, comfort one another with these words." Note Christ's instructions that we are to comfort one another with these words: *"so shall we ever be with the Lord."*

This takes care of any thought of "partial Rapture." We are *all* going to be caught up together in the air and we are *all* going to be with Him forever! (For a more in-depth look at the *harpazo*, be sure to see "The Rapture" in the Supplemental Study Notes Section of this book.)

This is the time we will receive our glorified bodies and, finally, be freed from the presence of sin. Remember, in chapter two we said that at our "justification" we are freed from the *penalty of sin* by Christ's Blood; through "sanctification" we will be freed from the *power of sin*; and at our "glorification" we will be freed from the *presence of sin*, i.e., the sin factor is removed altogether.

After the Rapture, the Tribulation will begin on the earth. This will be a time of trouble that the world has never before seen[1] (Daniel 12:1). It will be a period of the worst famines, earthquakes, persecution, hatred, and lawlessness that the world has ever experienced.

While the Tribulation is occurring on the earth, the believers who have been raptured and taken up to heaven will encounter two big events. 1) First, they will *all* be judged at the Judgment Seat of Christ for their fitness, their worthiness, and their qualifications to inherit the Millennial Kingdom.[2]

2) Next, depending upon the outcome of their Bema Seat Judgment, they will be escorted into the "Marriage of the Lamb," which also occurs in heaven (Revelation 19:7).

Let's explore these two events in a little more detail.

The Judgment Seat of Christ

The Judgment Seat of Christ or the "Bema Seat Judgment," as it is often called, is the place where Christ will judge believers. It is called the Bema Seat because that was the name given to the place where officials sat, judged, and sentenced people.[3] For example, Pilate sat on a Bema Seat, as did Festus, Gallio, Agrippa, and Felix.[4]

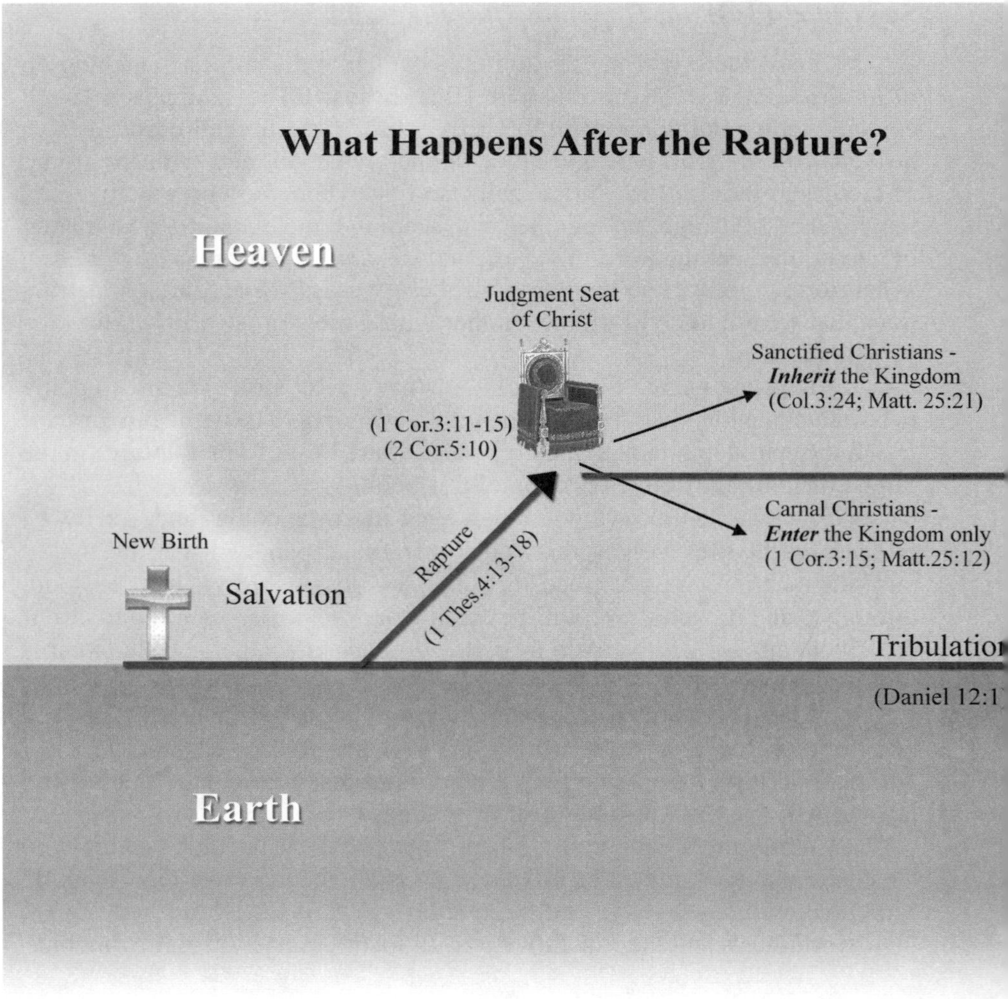

It is here that every Christian's position in the coming thousand-year reign will be determined. Christ will be the judge and He will evaluate us by our fruits, our faithfulness, and our obedience. At this judgment every Christian will either qualify for kingdom rule or not (2 Timothy 2:12). Christ's Throne of Grace is replaced here with His Throne of Judgment. Many think that the Bema Seat is only a place of rewards and *not* judgment. Nothing could be further from the truth. The Bema Seat actually means a "judicial evaluation" by a judge, not only of positive results and the giving out of rewards, but also of negative results.[5] 2 Corinthians 5:10 tells us "For we [Christians] must *all* appear before the Judgment seat of Christ; that every one may receive the things done in his body, according to that he hath done, whether it be *good or bad.*" The outcome of this judgment will determine our place, our role, our status, our position, and our authority within the coming kingdom.

This Bema Seat Judgment is *God's gateway to the Millennial reign* (2 Timothy 4:1). "Judgment must begin at the house of God" (1 Peter 4:17). In other words, *all* Christians must appear at this Bema Seat and give an account of ourselves (Romans 14:10; 1 Corinthians 4:3-5; James 2:12-13).

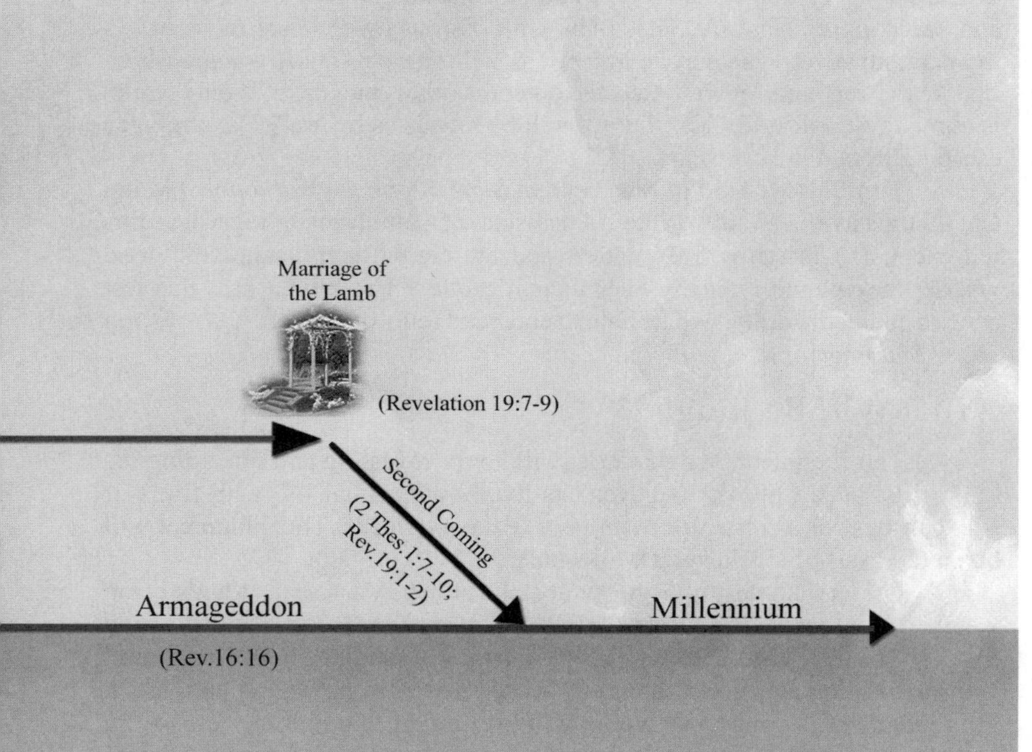

Many Christians do not like to hear that there is going to be an accounting and a judging of ourselves (not only for the good things we have done, but also for the bad). Those who are deemed "worthy" (again, that second definition, *axios,* which means "those who are prepared and fit"), will inherit blessings and privileges (Colossians 3:24). Those who are found *not* worthy will suffer loss. 1 Corinthians 3:13–15 tells us, "Every man's work shall be made manifest: for the day shall declare it, because it shall be revealed by fire; and the fire shall try every man's work of what sort it is. If any man's work abide which he hath built thereupon, he shall receive a reward. If any man's work shall be burned, *he shall suffer loss;* but he himself shall be saved; yet so as by fire."

The "loss" here simply means loss of rewards, positions of responsibilities, and privileges. *Loss* in 1 Corinthians 3 means "to forfeit something that is already in one's possession." Some may have had righteous works in their lives at one time, but because of a lack of perseverance, they will lose any reward. God wants us *all* to possess the kingdom by being sanctified and partaking of His Life. That's His will. It's our own choice moment-by-moment, however, whether we accept His will or not.[6] And if we don't hold fast "to the very end," it will affect the outcome of this judgment. If our "work" is burned, we will suffer loss, but we will be saved "as by fire" (like a refugee escaping from a fire).

Tim LaHaye said in his *Popular Bible Prophecy Workbook*, "Many Christians have been lulled into a false state of complacency regarding this judgment. If Christians truly understood the eternal significance of 'good works,' they would radically alter their lifestyle." Those who pass this test and are counted worthy, will be able to enter and fellowship at the *Celebration of the Marriage of the Lamb*.

What Will Be Judged?

The Judgment Seat of Christ will be for revealing and rewarding the kind of Christian life the believer has lived—a spiritual life with fruits of righteousness or a carnal life with very few good deeds. This judgment will be on the basis of a believer's works only.[7]

Our eternal destiny is never at stake at the Bema Seat. What's being weighed is our worthiness, our qualifications, our fitness, our readiness, and our preparation for positions or levels of responsibility in the future kingdom.[8] Our justification is never in jeopardy. We are eternally secure in that respect. This judgment is where our works will go through the refining test of fire and the Lord will search our hearts and minds and expose the truth.[9] This is also the time that each of us will give an account of our faithfulness, our obedience, and our perseverance (Romans 14:12). We will be evaluated on the basis of what we did with the time, the talents, and the treasures that we were given here on earth (1 Timothy 5:24–25).

Remember the parable of the ten talents? The Judgment Seat of Christ is where the reward ("enter into the joy of the Lord") or the loss ("cast into the darkness outside") is pronounced; but the actual carrying out of the sentence doesn't happen until much later. Michael Huber from Dallas Theological Seminary said: "There is no special judgment for the believer *after* the Millennium begins, but simply the execution of the judgment already given by Christ at the Bema Seat."[10]

The Bema Seat judgment will be for those who didn't take advantage of the forgiveness of sins that Christ provided at their new birth. Therefore, unconfessed sin will be judged because it quenched God's Spirit and prevented any "works of righteousness" from being produced. Because these carnal believers didn't apply 1 John 1:9 in order to cleanse their lives, they quenched God's Spirit in their hearts and, consequently, no "fruit" could be produced.

The only exception to the outcome of this judgment will be for those who have already confessed and repented of their sin and given it to God. These are the believers who have daily relied upon 1 John 1:9: "If we confess our sins, He is faithful and just to forgive us our sins, and to cleanse us from all unrighteousness." God has already forgiven them, already cleansed them from *all* unrighteousness, and already produced "fruit" in their lives.

God is not only a *loving* God, He is also a *just* God. His Love brings us to Him as a gift, but His justice demands a review of our lives—every thought, word, and deed, whether good or bad.[11] Think of it as our final exam or job review.

Some Questions the Lord Might Ask

Some of the things in our lives that the Lord will look at to make His determination:

- Did we love Him and love others? (Matthew 22:37–39)
- Did we walk by the Spirit, showing forth His Life, His Love, wisdom, and power? Were we "fruit bearing?" (John 10:10)
- Did we make choices to follow God, regardless of our feelings?
- Did we love our enemies? (Luke 6:35)
- Did we do everything from a heart of love? (1 Corinthians 13:1–3)
- Did we stay yielded, so that He could be strong through us? (2 Corinthians 12:9–10)
- Did we do everything for *His* glory? (Matthew 6:1–6)
- Did we follow the Spirit's leading and feed the poor and visit those in prison? (Matthew 25:35–36, 40)

- Did we seek His will and not our own? (John 5:30)
- Did we always have a servant's heart? (Matthew 20:25–27)
- Did we feed the flock? (1 Peter 5:1–4)
- Did we continually deny ourselves, follow Christ, and put others first? (Titus 2:12; Luke 9:23)
- Did we look for His soon return? (Matthew 24:46; 1 John 2:28)
- Did we witness for Him with our lives? (Daniel 12:3; 2 Peter 1:2–11)
- Did we preach the gospel in and out of season? (Matthew 28:19–20)
- Did the fruit from our lives remain? (John 15:16)

All of God's future blessings will be determined by *our faithfulness* and *our obedience* to do His will here and now. Therefore our inheritance, position, and privileges in the coming kingdom are all still at stake.

Five Books Will Be Opened

The Bible tells us at least five books will be opened at the Bema Seat Judgment: the *Book of the Living* (Psalm 69:28); the *Lamb's Book of Life* (Revelation 3:5; 13:8 Note: there are really two books of Life); the *Book of Tears* (Psalm 56:8; 2 Kings 20:5); the *Book of Deeds* (Daniel 7:10; Revelation 20:12); and the *Book of Remembrance* (Malachi 3:16). These are the books that Christ will use in order to judge our lives fairly (Exodus 32:32–33; Psalm 139:16).

These books will tell the absolute truth about our lives. They will reveal our motives, our doctrine, our works, our stewardship, our service, our accountability, and our sanctification. Each of these areas will be scrutinized.

Matthew 10:26–27 even suggests that this judgment might be visible. In other words, all will see and all will know. It says everything that is covered and hidden *now* will be revealed and out in the open *there* (Luke 12:2–3).

The Quality of Material

The Bema Seat Judgment is the time when we will be judged as to the *quality of materials* that we have used to build our lives here on earth. Our foundation must always be Christ: "For [no] other foundation can man lay than that is [which is] laid, which is Jesus Christ" (1 Corinthians 3:11). The additional building materials ("*our works, our deeds, our fruit, and our actions*") will either be "works of the flesh" *or* "works of the spirit": "Now if any man build upon this foundation [Christ] gold, silver, precious stones [will result], [If not], wood, hay, stubble [will result]" (1 Corinthians 3:12). "*Every man's work shall be made manifest*: for the day shall declare it, because it shall *be revealed by fire;* and the fire shall try every man's work of what sort it is [Spirit-led or fleshly]" (1 Corinthians 3:13).

This is saying that only one set of building materials will withstand the fire; any other material will feed the fire. Any work or fruit that survives the fire of judgment will be rewarded. Any work that burns in the fire will be considered a loss. The test will be conducted as a "baptism of fire." (The Greek word for *test* is *dokimazo,* which means "testing someone to see if they pass the exam; to see if they may be approved or sanctioned.") Kenneth Wuest said in his book *Word Studies in the Greek New Testament*, "The word (testing) has in it the idea of proving a thing whether it's 'worthy' (*axios*) or not to be received."[12]

John talked about this baptism by fire in Matthew 3:11 and Luke 3:16. *Fire doesn't cleanse us, it tries our works!* It will test the superstructure of our lives—what we did with the gifts, the talents, and the calling that God gave us. *What kind of righteous works did we do because of these abilities?* The fleshly things will be burned and the spiritual things will be rewarded. There is only one set of building materials that will withstand the fire—the things that the Holy Spirit not only *prompts* in our lives but also *does* in our lives—*the gold, silver, and precious stones.* The fleshly things—*the wood, hay, and stubble*—will feed the fire.

Every disciple has control over the "building" materials he uses. The foundation in each of our lives, if we are believers, must be Christ—already a "tried" stone. *But the fire is going to test the superstructure we have added to that foundation.* Every idle word, every secret, and every hidden motive will be exposed and tried. The Lord will look at our motives, our hidden secrets,[13] our faithfulness,[14] our words,[15] and then He will test our deeds.[16]

"But I say unto you, that every idle word that men shall speak, they shall give account thereof in the day of judgment. For by thy words thou shalt be justified, and by thy words, thou shalt be condemned" (Matthew 12:36–37).

Thinking about the foundation that our works must be built upon reminds us of the story of the wise man in Matthew 7. When the storm came, his house did not fall because it was built upon the rock (Matthew 7:24–25). But the foolish man built his house upon the sand and when the rains came and the winds blew, it fell and it fell hard (Matthew 7:26–27). *Christ must be the foundation and the source for everything we do!* Otherwise our house will fall, not only in this lifetime, but in the next as well.

Confidence at the Judgment Seat

The believers who have "built their houses upon the Rock" are those who are experientially sanctified, partakers of Christ's Life, and have produced fruit in their lives. They can have confidence and boldness on that day of judgment because they have already judged themselves through prayer, already recognized their sin and dealt with it (1 John 4:17). Thus, their works will be "gold, silver, precious stones." If they have not made proper judgment of themselves *here* (have not applied 1 John 1:9) and their lives have not produced righteous works, then God will be forced to make that judgment for them *there* (1 Corinthians 11:31).

If love for God has been our motive here, then we can have confidence there; if it has not, we have reason to be concerned (1 Corinthians 13:1–8). We will talk about what it means to love God (*agapao*) in chapter eight. Loving God does not refer to an emotional feeling of love for Him, but a total state of yieldedness to Him.

The bottom line is that *all judgment at the Bema Seat will be on the basis of works, either fleshly works or spiritual works* "The Son of man shall come in the glory of His Father with His angels; and then He shall reward every man according to his works" (Matthew 16:27. See also 1 Corinthians 3:12–15; 2 Corinthians 5:10). The result of this judgment either will be to receive the "reward of inheritance" (Colossians 3:24) or to "suffer loss" and eventually be separated from the joy of His fellowship.

Unfaithful Christians whose works are burned will be found spiritually naked and ashamed, but can be certain that even this nakedness will *not* separate them from God's Love (Romans 8:35–39).

Only What's Done for Christ Will Last

Paul Benware in his great book *The Believer's Payday* said: "We can be sure that at the Judgment Seat of Christ there will be a marked difference between the Christian who has lived his life before the Lord, clearly discerning what was for His glory, and a nominal Christian. All will be in heaven, but the differences between them will be eternal. We may be sure that the consequences of our character will survive the grave and that we shall face those consequences at the Judgment Seat of Christ."[17]

And Steve Lawson in his book *Heaven Help Us* said: "One life to live will soon be past. Only what's done for Christ will last!"[18]

Every Christian's position in the Millennial Kingdom will be determined at the Bema Seat.[19] There will be a marked difference—varying degrees of glory—between the nominal Christian and the spiritual Christian.[20] God will faithfully reward those who have sought Him with all their hearts and also recompense those who have left their first love. "In a great house there are not only vessels of gold and of silver, but also of wood and of earth; and some to honour, and some to dishonour" (2 Timothy 2:20). Gold symbolizes sovereignty and eternal things; wood symbolizes earthly and temporal things. In this Scripture believers are likened to vessels in a great house. Some will be there to honour, and some to dishonour. The idea is that in the Millennium we should not presume that we will all be alike. We won't be. It doesn't stand to reason that Paul the apostle, who labored more than many of the others, would receive the same degree of glory or responsibility as the thief on the cross who was saved only one hour before he died.

At the Bema Seat, believers will find out exactly where they will be for the next thousand years. Will they enter the Millennial Kingdom but not receive an "inheritance from the Lord"? Or will they be sovereigns (inheritors) there and receive positions of authority and responsibility? The outcome will be on the basis of their faithfulness, sanctification, and obedience. There will be no equality. All will be "in the kingdom," but some will occupy positions of honor and glory, while others will miss out on positions of responsibility altogether.

This determination will influence our attendance at the Wedding Ceremony and the Marriage Feast. (See Revelation 19:7-9.)

See *Chart 14: Judgment Seat Criteria*

Each of us will "reap what we have sown" at the Bema Seat (Galatians 6:7). The Lord will use the following criteria to judge us: Were our works done by the power of His Spirit or were they done in the flesh? In other words, what was the *source* of our strength and *who* actually produced the work in our lives?

Our labor—our works of righteousness—must be motivated by His Life in our hearts and then produced in our lives by His ability and His power, not our own. If this is the case, then we will be "clothed with

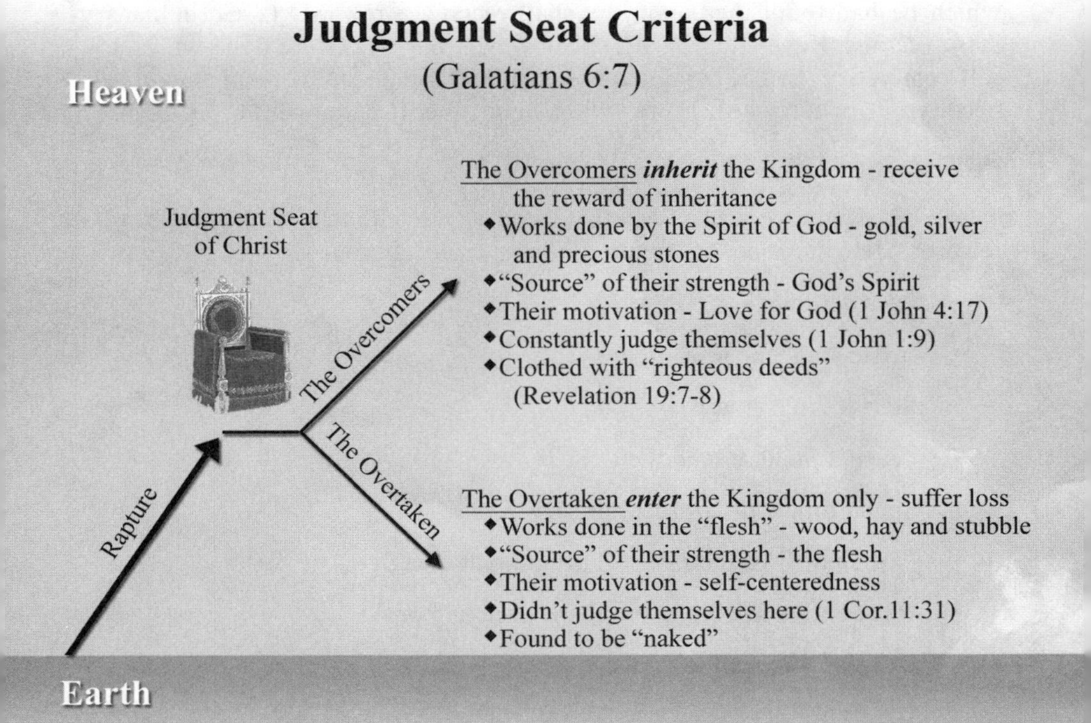

Judgment Seat Criteria

(Galatians 6:7)

The Overcomers *inherit* the Kingdom - receive the reward of inheritance

- Works done by the Spirit of God - gold, silver and precious stones
- "Source" of their strength - God's Spirit
- Their motivation - Love for God (1 John 4:17)
- Constantly judge themselves (1 John 1:9)
- Clothed with "righteous deeds" (Revelation 19:7-8)

The Overtaken *enter* the Kingdom only - suffer loss

- Works done in the "flesh" - wood, hay and stubble
- "Source" of their strength - the flesh
- Their motivation - self-centeredness
- Didn't judge themselves here (1 Cor.11:31)
- Found to be "naked"

Chart 14

righteous deeds" (Revelation 19:8). Whereas, if the flesh is the source of our works, then we will produce unfruitful works and be found naked (See Revelation 3:17; 16:15).

"Good Works"

"Good works" are those words, deeds, and actions that are not only prompted by the Holy Spirit, but also performed through the power of His Spirit. "But he that doeth truth cometh to light, that his deeds may be made manifest, that they are wrought in God" (John 3:21). This is speaking of the good works that are produced by the Spirit through us and not produced by the flesh.

When you mention doing good works, it seems to send shivers down some people's backs. Why is that? It's simple. Many Christians get justification, which is a *free gift* from God and requires *no* works at all, mixed up with experiential sanctification, which results in *doing good works* by the power of God's Spirit. "We are His workmanship, created in Christ Jesus unto good works, which God hath before ordained that we should walk in them" (Ephesians 2:10).

If our "works" are prompted by the Holy Spirit and then performed by Him (even though no one else sees), those works will withstand the fire at the Bema Seat and the believer will be rewarded. "If any man's *work abide* which he hath built thereupon, he shall receive a reward" (1 Corinthians 3:14; see also Revelation 22:12). If, however, our works are done with the self-centered motive of being seen by men and applauded by them, then that becomes its own reward. There will be none other (Matthew 6:1).

A "Sure All" Method

Recently we read a book that listed a "sure all method" for receiving rewards. Here are some of the things it suggested: If you—

- Pass out tracts
- Invite someone to church
- Start a Bible study
- Teach a Sunday school class
- Spend time with a street ministry
- Participate in a recreational program at church
- Have coffee in your home for your neighbors
- Develop a welcome ministry for your street

—then you will be sure to receive a reward

Unfortunately, the author of this book seems to have totally missed the point of what God means by "good works" because every one of the above things can be done in the flesh. What God means by good works or fruit are those things done in the power of *His* Spirit, through *His* Love, and by *His* wisdom, not our own. These are the kind of works that will bring glory to His Name and that's the whole purpose!

Doing good works by the power of the Spirit means that Christ is the Source of the work and His Spirit gives us the strength to perform that work! It's something *He* prompts and then something *He* accomplishes through us. Our part is simply to obey Him and then trust Him to do it through us. If the above list is done by the power of the Holy Spirit in our lives, then, yes, obviously it would be considered good works.

(We will discuss the difference between the "works of the Spirit" and the "works of the flesh" further in chapter eleven.)

"The Terror of the Lord"

The Judgment Seat of Christ is often perceived as "the Fear of the Lord" or "the Terror of the Lord." And rightly so. It will be a fearful thing to stand before the Lord as He scrutinizes our lives. If mercy does not mark our dealings with others here on earth, mercy will probably not mark our personal judgment there either (Colossians 3:25).

Maybe now we can understand a little more clearly why Paul was apprehensive about this and why he said: "For we must all appear before the Judgment seat of Christ; that every one may receive the things done in his body, according to that he hath done, where it be good or bad. Knowing therefore *the terror* [#5401, *phobos*] of the Lord, we persuade men—" (2 Corinthians 5:10–11). And also he said: "It is a fearful thing to fall into the hands of the living God!" (Hebrews 10:31).

Having been declared righteous and justified at our new birth so that we might escape the wrath of God does *not* exempt us from being chastised on judgment day. God will pronounce some very harsh judgments on the unfaithful Christian who has allowed the cares of the world, the temptations of the flesh, and the wiles of the devil to overtake him and lead him into carnality.[21] Just as an unfruitful branch is cut off from the tree, so these Christians will suffer the loss of rewards and the casting out from fellowship.[22] This is why Paul exhorted us to *judge ourselves now*, so that we will not have to be judged then (1 Corinthians 11:31). An honest, daily self-judgment is necessary in order to avoid the penalties of this judgment. In chapter twelve we'll share a few practical ways of doing this.

Sadly, many of us have lost that fear of the Lord. This does *not* mean we are to be fearful *of* Him (because He might punish us). It simply means we should have reverence, respect, and awe toward Him in everything we do, knowing He is watching, knowing He is taking detailed notes, and knowing He will be talking to us about our each and every move if we haven't repented.

Rewards for Works Done in the Spirit

God is not only a loving God, He is also a just God and His justice demands a review of the lives of all of His children (Psalm 89:14; Ecclesiastes 12:14; Romans 2:5–6). That justice will be administered according to the quality of our works (2 Corinthians 5:10; Revelation 2:23). And a prize or a reward will be given for faithful service and for work well done (Matthew 5:12). The dictionary defines a *reward* as "something given or received in return for service, merit, or hardship."[23] Rewards are often called our inheritance, as in Colossians 3:24, "the reward of inheritance."[24] "Christ shall reward every man according to his work" (Matthew 16:27).

Rewards, however, only apply to those works that "abide" and that are "acceptable to Him" (Ephesians 5:9–10). "If any man's work *abide* which he hath built thereupon, he shall receive a reward" (1 Corinthians 3:15). *The "work" that this Scripture is referring to means "that which is done through Christ and by His power."* These are *not* works that we do through our own motives, by our own efforts, or in our own abilities! Works performed under the leadership and direction of the Holy Spirit will result in the praise and honor and glory of God; whereas works performed under the leadership and direction of a man will result in the praise and glory of that man. And, unfortunately, that's all the reward that man will ever receive.

Our exaltation in the age to come will be in the inverse ratio to the lowliness of service we have accomplished in this present age. For example, if we "love our enemies and do good to them that have abused us" our reward shall be great (Luke 6:35). And "whomever will be great among you, shall be your servant" (Mark 10:43) and "the first shall be last and the last first" (Mark 10:43).

Our rewards will depend upon our likeness in character and conduct to our Lord and Savior, Jesus Christ. Everything must be done in His Name, for Scripture tells us that without Him, we can do nothing (John 15:5). There must be a constant dependence upon Him.

Different Facets of God's Rewards

There will be varying degrees and different facets of God's rewards in proportion to our works that have "stood the test of fire."[25]

Charles Stanley, in his wonderful book *Eternal Security,* said, "Some believers will be entrusted with certain privileges; others will not. Some will reign with Christ; others will not (see 2 Timothy 2:12). Some will be rich in the kingdom of God; others will be poor (see Luke 12:21, 33). Some will be given true riches; others will not. Some will be given heavenly treasures of their own; others will not. Some will reign and rule with Christ; others will not (see Revelation 3:21)."

Stanley ends by saying, "*Privilege in the kingdom of God is determined by one's faithfulness in this life* . . . It is true that there will be equality in terms of our inclusion in the kingdom of God but not in our rank and privilege."[26]

Some believers will receive:

- An entrance to the Wedding Ceremony (Matthew 25:10) and the Marriage Feast (Matthew 22:1-14)
- The ability to co-reign with Christ (Revelation 3:21)
- Treasure in heaven (Proverbs 8:21)[27]
- Praise from Christ (1 Peter 1:7)[28]
- A place of honor (Mark 10:40)

Still others will receive:

- Positions of stewardship (Matthew 25:23)
- Spheres of influence (Revelation 2:26)
- Positions of authority (Luke 19:17)
- Different crowns (1 Corinthians 9:25; James 1:12)

Crowns

Erwin Lutzer had much to say about rewards and crowns in his book *Your Eternal Reward*: "The assumption that rewards are nothing more than crowns is false in my opinion. Rewards have more to do with *levels of responsibility* that will be given to us."

So the "crowns" that Scripture speaks about are not necessarily literal crowns, but *symbols of rank, seals of inheritance, or achieved distinction*. All sovereigns in the kingdom will receive crowns. If we lose our crown, it will simply mean we will have lost our rank. "Behold, I come quickly; hold fast that which you have; that no man take your crown" (Revelation 3:11).

A *crown* (Strong's #4735, *stephanos*) is a symbol or a badge of victory. It's a prize that is won in public games, a reward for loyalty.[29] (This crown should not be confused with a *diadema* [Strong's #1238], which means "a kingly crown or a crown of royalty.") The crowns we are speaking of here are conditional and are dependent upon approved service.

At least five crowns are mentioned in Scripture:

The Incorruptible Crown — also called the Victor's Crown — is awarded for self-control and having victory over the flesh (1 Corinthians 9:24–25).

The Crown of Rejoicing—is awarded for fruitful labor for the Lord in the lives of others (1 Thessalonians 2:19). This is the soul winner's crown, the winning of the saved to the kingdom.

The Crown of Life—is for those who have persevered, endured trials, and even faced death, and yet still remain faithful (James 1:12; Revelation 2:10).

The Crown of Glory—is for those who have shepherded and tended the flock and yearned to see them grow (1 Peter 5:4). These have the heart of Christ.

The Crown of Righteousness—is for those who radiate Christ's Life in all they do (2 Timothy 4:8). They live His Life, do His will, and love His appearing.

As believers, we are to strive to obtain *all* of these crowns, not just one. These are God's tangible expressions of His approval. Consequently, our sole ambition should be to labor, strive, and make it our aim to be well pleasing to God. Every seed we sow, every word we speak, and every deed we do is "banked" with God and will one day spring up in a wonderful harvest of works. As we said earlier, every act of the present is registered.

Only those who live faithful and obedient lives *here* will enjoy a special fellowship with the Lord *there*. These are the overcomers who have not only washed their robes in the Blood of Christ, but who have walked according to the Spirit, and who have persevered through the trials. "Blessed are ye, when men shall hate you, and when they shall separate you from their company, and shall reproach you, and cast out your name as evil, for the Son of man's sake. Rejoice ye in that day, and leap for joy; for behold, *your reward is great in heaven*" (Luke 6:22–23). These Christians will enjoy a special intimacy with the Father throughout the Millennium (Revelation 2:7).

"He that overcomes shall inherit *all* things and I will be his God, and he shall be My son" (Revelation 21:7). This Scripture challenges *all* Christians to be overcomers so they might inherit *all* things!

The Wedding Ceremony

The next event that occurs in heaven, after the Rapture and after the Bema Seat Judgment, is the gathering of the "bride" to attend the Marriage Ceremony itself (Revelation 19:7–8). This is an area that is *not* well trodden, so we want you again to be as the Bereans—get into the Word and check out everything that is shared (Acts 17:11).

The word *marriage* in the Greek is *gamos* (Strong's #1062), and can mean either a "wedding ceremony" or a "wedding feast." This is often where the confusion comes in. The word *gamos* can be used for either the "wedding ceremony" itself or for the "wedding feast," which happens at a later date. In a moment we'll explore the entire Jewish wedding celebration, which will help clear up the confusion.

The sequence of future events that will occur after the Bema Seat are: 1) The Wedding Ceremony (or the Marriage of the Lamb), which will occur in the Father's house *in heaven* with only a few in attendance (Revelation

19:7). 2) This event is then followed by Christ's return to earth with His wife. 3) And finally, the Marriage Feast (or the Marriage Supper) which will be held *on earth* with many in attendance just as the Millennium begins. The Marriage Supper includes "the friends of the Groom" (i.e. John the Baptist and other Old Testament saints) who are *not* resurrected until after His Second Coming (John 3:29).

Those believers whose works pass the baptism of fire at the Bema Seat Judgment and who are deemed ready and worthy and prepared will obviously attend *both* the Wedding Ceremony in heaven and the Marriage Feast on earth that follows. It will be the highest honor possible to be a part of the wife of Christ, but also an honor to be one of the King's guests at the Marriage Feast (Matthew 22:1–14; 25:1–13).

The Jewish Wedding Ceremony

To help us understand the sequence of these future events a little more clearly, let's describe a Jewish marriage ceremony, as this is the model that Christ uses. There are many parallels in the Bible to various events in a believer's life, but none more visible than the parallel of the *Christian life* to that of a *Jewish marriage ceremony*.[30]

Their parents normally arranged the marriage between two young Jewish people. Romantic unions were uncommon. This marriage consisted of three parts:

1. The *betrothal* was called the *erusin* or the *kiddashin*. The groom gave his bride-to-be an object of value such as a ring, money, or a deed of intention, which was symbolic of a promise providing a legal tie between the two. The father of the groom usually paid the bridal price. It was a true legal document. This had no immediate effect on their personal stake, it was just a promise for the future (Deuteronomy 20:7).

After this ceremony, the bride remained in her father's home *to prepare for* the day her groom would come back for her, marry her, and take her to his house or some special room he had built. Cohabitation was forbidden at this time and the bride must remain a virgin, using this time to prepare herself for her marriage. In other words, *the bride must make herself ready*. This preparation meant making her own wedding gown, getting ready for her new role, transferring her allegiance from her father to her new husband, going from the familiar to the unfamiliar, from depending on family to depending upon her husband for everything, learning to love him, and setting her mind on how to please him.

During this preparation period, the bride is referred to as "consecrated" or set apart (sanctified). She always wore a veil, so it was apparent to others that she was engaged. This veil was symbolic of a pledge or a commitment.

2. The second part of the ceremony was called the *nissuin* or the *marriage ceremony* itself. The groom often surprised his bride by his

unexpected or early return. All Jewish brides were said to be "stolen, caught up, and snatched up by surprise." The bride was then led to the groom's house by a wedding procession of women carrying lighted lamps, similar to the parable of the ten virgins that we will explore in just a moment. Lamps were a part of the bride's preparation in case her groom came at night. The bride was arrayed in *fine linen, clean and white*.

The wedding ceremony was held at the groom's father's house and usually included only a few invited guests. At this time a series of benedictions are made and the couple is finally made husband and wife.

3. The wedding ceremony was then followed by seven days of celebration, great rejoicing, and finally, *a marriage feast*. This occasion was often held at a different place and many people were invited.

See *Chart 15: The Jewish Wedding and Its Parallels*

Now that we understand a little more about the Jewish marriage celebration, let's compare this to the Christian life.

1. The salvation of our spirit (justification) with the seal of the Holy Spirit is analogous to the *betrothal* of the Jewish bride with the down payment, pledge, or seal of "an object of value" (Ephesians 5:25–27). "I will

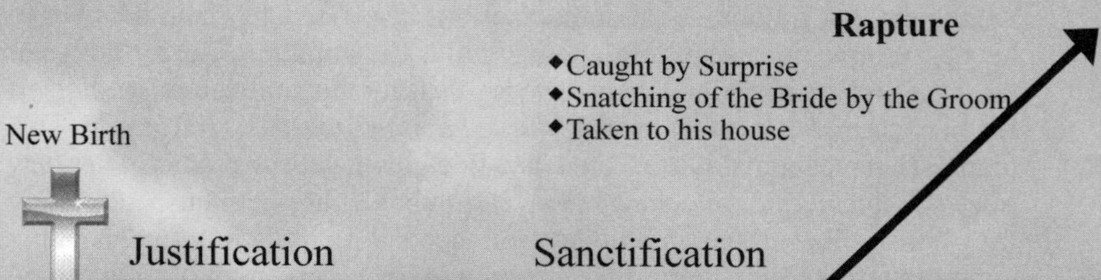

betroth thee unto Me forever; yea, I will *betroth* thee unto Me in righteousness, and in justice, and in loving-kindness, and in mercies. I will even *betroth* thee unto Me in faithfulness; and thou shalt know the Lord" (Hosea 2:19; 2 Corinthians 11:2).

The process of sanctification that we are all in now as we wait for our Lord's return, can be compared to the long wait between the time the groom leaves to prepare a place for his bride and the time he returns for her. Note the importance placed upon the Jewish bride during this waiting period to *prepare herself* for her groom's return—to make her own gown and her own wedding garment. This stresses the significance of the sanctification process—our time of preparation, our time of fitting, and our time of making ourselves ready, worthy, and qualified for our Groom's return.

Sanctification, again, is our bridal preparation! Getting ourselves ready for our new role: Transferring our allegiance from earthly things to heavenly things. Learning to love God rather than self; replacing our preoccupation with our friends and families to making the Lord the most important thing in our lives; and finally, going from depending upon self (and our own abilities) to depending upon Christ for everything (Revelation 19:7). *The bride of Christ must make herself ready to be presented to the Lord without stain or wrinkle*. Inside purity!

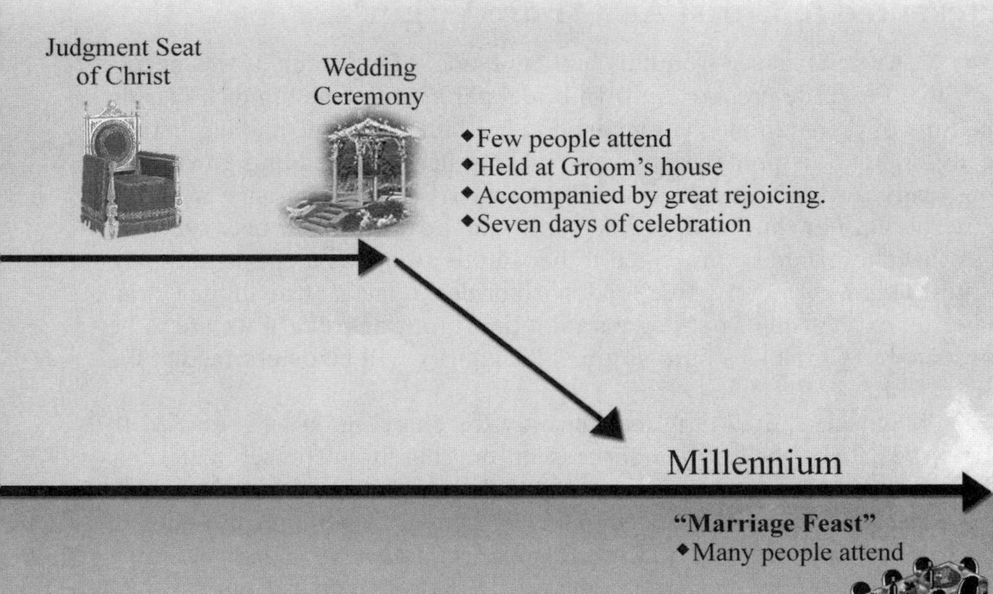

Chart 15

2. The Jewish groom often surprised his bride by coming back early for her. This is analogous to the unexpected return of our Lord at the Rapture (1 Thessalonians 4:13–18). As we said, the procession of women carrying lighted lamps to meet the groom when he returns reminds us of the parable of the ten virgins. The five wise virgins, whose lamps were still burning when the groom returned, were ready and prepared to go into the wedding ceremony; the other five virgins were not prepared and thus, were not allowed to enter. The wedding ceremony is analogous to the Marriage of the Lamb in heaven where Christ will choose His wife.

3. The seven days of Jewish celebration and rejoicing between the wedding ceremony itself and the marriage feast, may be analogous to the rejoicing that will occur first in heaven at the wedding and then at the Marriage Supper on earth where Christ will again drink of the "fruit of the vine" (Luke 22:29–30; Revelation 19:9). Many resurrected Old Testament saints and Tribulation saints will also attend this feast on earth.

In summary: Our "justification" can be compared to the Jewish betrothal. Our "sanctification" can be compared to a Jewish woman preparing herself for her future wedding. Our "glorification" (the Rapture) can be compared to a Jewish groom coming by surprise to carry his bride away. The Marriage of the Lamb in heaven can be compared to the Jewish wedding ceremony. And the Marriage Feast at the beginning of the Millennium can be compared to the Jewish marriage supper.

Presented to Christ As a "Pure Virgin"

As you can see from this biblical model of marriage, it was necessary that the bride prepare her own bridal garment for the big day. During the time of preparation, she remained in her father's home, making herself ready. Again, this preparation meant making her own wedding gown, getting ready for her new role as a wife, transferring her allegiance from her father to her new husband, and so forth. The goal of this in-between time was that she would be presented to her future groom as a chaste and pure virgin. This was not only true for Jewish brides, it is also true in the Christian life. At the end of our "preparation time" (our betrothal), we are to be presented to Christ as a pure virgin.[31] This purity will be determined at the Bema Seat.

Ephesians 5:27 describes the way the church is to be presented to Christ: "That He [the Lord] *might* present [the church] to Himself a glorious church *not having spot or wrinkle* or any such thing; but that it should be holy and *without blemish*." Paul added to this by saying, "That I *may* present you to Christ as a *chaste virgin*" (2 Corinthians 11:2). *Chaste* (#53, *hagnos*) is the root from which *hagiosmos* (#38), the word *sanctified,* comes from.

Notice, however, the words *might* and *may* in these two verses. They indicate that it's God's will to present us "as a chaste and holy virgin, without spot or wrinkle," but it's *not* a given. In other words, it's *not* automatic. Something is required of us! We must participate in the action. We must prepare ourselves—make ourselves fit and ready—just as a Jewish bride does.

So according to the Biblical model, the presentation of the bride to the Lord is *conditional*.[32] She must not only be presented as a "chaste virgin, not having spot or wrinkle" (Ephesians 1:4), she must also be sanctified, holy, and without blemish (Hebrews 12:14). What this is saying is that there is a possibility that while we are waiting for Christ to return, we can defile our garments and prevent this from happening.

We will expand in chapter fourteen upon the two different kinds of garments a believer can wear. The first one is the *Garment of Salvation* which Christ imputes to us at our new birth (Isaiah 61:10). This is our *external* garment without spot or wrinkle. The second garment and the one that Christ requires for the Marriage festivities is the white linen garment made up of the believer's own "righteous works" (Revelation 19:7–8). Overcomers will be clothed in clean, white garments. This speaks of the *internal* sanctification and the moral fitness that Christ requires of His bride (2 Corinthians 7:1; 11:2). This second garment, then, is the one that can get defiled, stained, and blackened through the believer's own negligence.

Remember, God said to the Church at Sardis, "There are a few who have *not* defiled their garments." *Defile* here means "a stain or a blackening of something." It refers to an internal condition, a moral or spiritual transgression. It simply means "unfaithfulness." It's an action that defiles oneself, or as Strong's puts it: "It means dirtying our clothes." As Christians, we dirty our clothes by polluting our souls, not being faithful, and quenching God's Spirit.

The "holy ones without blemish" in Ephesians 5:27 are those believers who have chosen to keep themselves *clean, prepared, and ready.* They are the sanctified ones. They have continued to "put off" their sin and self and "put on" Christ. They are now arrayed in fine linen, clear and white. This garment does *not* refer to the "righteousness of Christ," which has been imputed to them (Isaiah 61:10), but rather to their *own* righteous deeds. "Let us be glad and rejoice, and give honour to Him: for the marriage of the Lamb is come, and *His wife hath made herself ready"* (Revelation 19:7–8). In other words, these believers have chosen to make themselves fit, prepared, and ready. They're sanctified, holy, and chaste virgins.

James 1:27 exhorts us to keep ourselves "unspotted" (See also Revelation 3:4–5; 2 Corinthians 7:1; 11:2–3). "Blessed is he that watcheth and keepeth his garments" (Revelation 16:15). These are the ones who will be deemed worthy to enter the bridal chamber and become Christ's wife because they have on the appropriate *wedding garments*.

God desires to present us to Himself a glorious church, having no defects, holy and without blemish. God calls all of us to be His bride and eventually, if chosen, His wife (Ephesians 5:23–33). But He does not coerce His subjects; He respects our will. We can of our own choosing fall short of the glory of God (Hebrews 12:15).

The million-dollar question is: What happens to those believers who are *not* ready, *not* prepared, *not* fit, *not* holy, and *not* chaste? What happens to them? Are they allowed into the Marriage festivities? Some theologians believe they are; some others believe they are not. Study Ephesians 5:27 for yourself and see what the Spirit shows you.

The Parable of the Ten Virgins (Matthew 25:1–13)

(See Picture.)

Speaking of the importance of being *prepared, fit, and ready* for Christ's soon return, the parable of the ten virgins in Matthew 25 is very appropriate.

The Five Foolish Virgins

There are many interpretations of this parable, so again, be as the Bereans and study the Scripture for yourself. Remember a parable is simply a truth told in story form to help explain a previous truth. The previous truth in Matthew 24 is to watch, be ready, and endure to the end, for you know not what hour the Lord comes.

The parable of the ten virgins follows:

> [1]Then shall the kingdom of heaven be likened unto ten
> virgins, which took their lamps, and went forth to meet the
> bridegroom. [2]And five of them were wise, and five *were*
> foolish. [3]They that *were* foolish took their lamps, and took no
> oil with them: [4]But the wise took oil in their vessels with their
> lamps. [5]While the bridegroom tarried, they all slumbered and
> slept. [6]And at midnight there was a cry made, Behold, the
> bridegroom cometh; go ye out to meet him. [7]Then all those
> virgins arose, and trimmed their lamps. [8]And the foolish said
> unto the wise, Give us of your oil; for our lamps are gone
> out. [9]But the wise answered, saying, *Not so*; lest there be
> not enough for us and you: but go ye rather to them that sell,
> and buy for yourselves. [10]And while they went to buy, the
> bridegroom came; and they that were ready went in with him
> to the marriage: and the door was shut. [11]Afterward came
> also the other virgins, saying, Lord, Lord, open to us. [12]But
> he answered and said, Verily I say unto you, I know you not.
> [13]Watch therefore, for ye know neither the day nor the hour
> wherein the Son of man cometh.

Note that *ten* virgins took their lamps (torches filled with oil) and went out to meet the bridegroom. Five of those virgins were *wise* because they took extra oil. The other five virgins, however, were *foolish* because they didn't bring extra oil.

Vines Complete Expository Dictionary says that the number *10* (Strong's #1176, *deka*) is a very significant number. It's used 248 times in the Bible and means "the measure of human responsibility" and also the number of "completion." *Virgin* (Strong's #3933) means "an unmarried woman." The word *wise* (Strong's 5429, *phromiros)* means "single-minded" (i.e., one life is being lived—God's) and thus, this believer is full of light (Luke 11:34). The word "wise" is from the root word *phren*, which means "to rein in or curb the emotions." These virgins were wise because they allowed God to continually rein in their self-life, which then allowed the Spirit of God (the oil) to come forth and produce fruit in their lives. The word *foolish* (Strong's # 3474, *moros*) means "double-minded" (i.e., two lives are being lived—God's and ours), and thus, these believers were full of darkness (Luke 11:34).

While waiting for the bridegroom, all ten virgins slept. But at midnight a cry was made that the bridegroom was coming and they were to go out and meet him. All the virgins arose and trimmed their lamps (adjusted them), but the foolish found that their lamps had gone out and they had no oil to refill them. They asked the wise if they could have some of their oil, whereupon the wise said, "We cannot let you have some of our oil because there will not be enough for us. Why don't you go and purchase some for yourselves?"

While the five foolish virgins were gone trying to find extra oil, the bridegroom came and those wise virgins who were *ready, worthy,* and *prepared* (who had their lamps lit), went in with him to the wedding festivities *and the door was shut*.

Later when the five foolish virgins came, they said, "Lord, Lord, open the door." But he answered them saying, "*I know you not*" (Matthew 25:12).

"I Know You Not"

The Greek word used here for *know* is *oida* (Strong's #1492), which means to "*know intimately*, to see, or to perceive." The Lord was saying to the five foolish virgins: "*I don't know you intimately;* we don't have a close relationship. If we did, you would have obeyed Me."[33] In other words, He was saying, "You were *not* a partaker or a sharer of My Life—My power, My Love. There was no fellowship between us. *I know you only by observation*."

The five foolish virgins in this parable obviously are *in heaven* i.e. they are believers. But because they *didn't know Him intimately* (they weren't intimately acquainted with His character, His person, His attributes), He didn't let them in to the wedding. They were not qualified or worthy (*axios*) to enter.

The accuracy of the Scriptures continues to amaze us. When you peel back all the details, the Bible is an absolute treasure hunt! For example, Matthew 7:23, where Jesus is talking to those who "professed" to be Christians and who "professed" to have prophesied in His Name, cast out devils in His Name, and done many wonderful works in His Name. Jesus doesn't say, "*I know you not,*" like He does in Matthew 25. He says, "*I never knew you*" (i.e. they are not believers). And the Greek word He uses is *ginosko,* which means "to have knowledge of." In other words, He is saying "*I don't recognize you at all! I never knew you to begin with. I never knew you at all.*" In contrast to Matthew 25 where He says because they were not intimate with Him, He only knew them from a distance.

So "knowing" seems to be the key!

A friend of ours sent us the following quote and it seems so applicable here: "Far above all the *doing* . . . it seems the *knowing* is where we need to focus . . . and let the *doing* spring forth from the *real knowing*." This is so true. If we are sanctified and partaking of His Life, we'll have intimacy (*oida*) with Christ and fruit will result. If we are *not* faithful and we aren't partaking of His Life, then we won't know Him intimately, nor will any fruit be produced.

All Ten Virgins Were Believers

All ten virgins in this parable represent born-again, Bible-believing, *Christian believers* preparing themselves for passage into glory. As we said, *virgin* means "unmarried, undefiled, clean, chaste, and pure."[34] Unbelievers are *not* virgins! This means that all ten virgins had on "Christ's garment of salvation" (Isaiah 61:10). This is the robe of righteousness that got them into heaven in the first place. They were *all* followers of Christ and they *all* went out to meet Him, which showed their belief in the blessed hope. They *all* took their lamps and they *all*, at one time, had oil in them.

But because the five foolish virgins did *not* maintain their faithfulness and their watchfulness to the very end, the oil in their lamps ran out and they ended up with no light. Over a period of time, they quenched God's Spirit in their hearts, which stopped their intimate fellowship with Him and caused the light in their lives to go out. Thus, they became *foolish* and *double-minded* and *they walked in darkness*—

See *Chart 16: Double-mindedness*

We just learned that the definition of *foolish* is "double-minded." A double-minded believer lives two lives: God's Life and "self-life." God's

Double-Mindedness
(Living Two Lives)

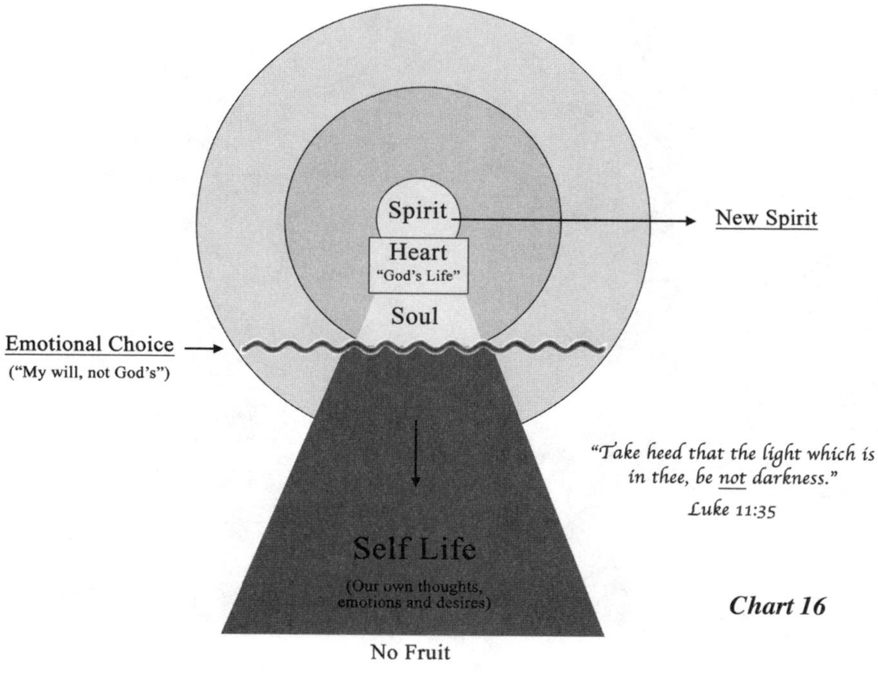

Chart 16

Life (the Light) is still in this believer's heart, but because it has been quenched, "self-life" is ruling in his soul (1 Thessalonians 5:19; James 1:8). Thus, when we are double-minded, it's impossible to partake of Christ's life Consequently, rather than overcoming the world, the flesh, and the devil, this believer is overtaken by the same. This believer does not produce fruit or works of righteousness. As a result this double-minded believer will become foolish.

Because this person did not maintain an intimate relationship with the Lord, the light of God's Spirit is blocked. "No man, when he hath lighted a lamp, putteth it in a secret place, neither under a bushel, but on a lampstand, that they who come in may see the light . . . *Take heed, therefore, that the light which is in thee be not darkness*" (Luke 11:35).

At this point in the Parable of the Ten Virgins, it's *too late* for the five foolish virgins to acquire the character traits and the faithful perseverance that's needed for an entrance to the wedding. They were *not* prepared, *not* fit, and *not* worthy to enter.

See *Chart 17: Single-Mindedness*

If, however, as Luke 11:36 goes on to say, "thy whole body be full of light, having no dark part, [then] the whole shall be full of light."

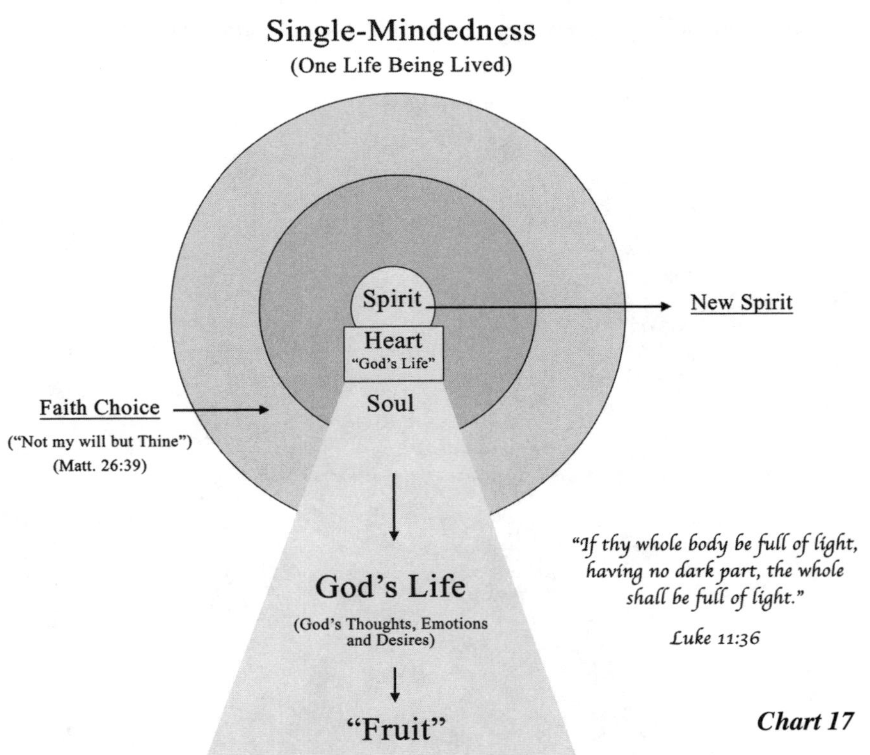

Chart 17

God's Life in this believer's heart has come forth and is now filling his soul with light. This is called "single mindedness"—only one life is being lived, God's. This is a believer who is sanctified, a partaker of Christ, and an overcomer, producing the fruit of righteousness.

The five wise virgins represent single-minded believers who are experiencing an ongoing intimate relationship with the Lord *(oida),* and thus they are able to participate in and pass on His Life by His power. Their lights are burning brightly. Luke 12:35 validates this, we must "let our loins be girded about [with Truth], and [keep] *our lamps burning.*"

Therefore, just having the Holy Spirit (and Christ's Life) in our hearts is not enough. The Spirit must not only indwell us, we must also choose to be filled with the Spirit (be single-minded) in order to produce the "works of the Spirit" that God desires.

See *Parable Chart 3: Matthew 25:1-13*

Look at Parable Chart 3 again in relation to the Ten Virgins.

Who was Jesus talking to? Jesus was talking to His disciples who had just asked, "What are the signs of Your coming again?" *Whom was He talking about?* He was talking about the church in general. *What had part of the church (the five foolish virgins) done wrong?* They had no intimacy and no personal relationship with the Lord. He knew them only by observation. *What was their loss?* They were locked out of the wedding itself and the door was shut. *What occasion does this remind us of?* Possibly, the Marriage of the Lamb in heaven. And finally, *what is the lesson here for us?* We must know the Lord intimately and partake of His Life so that we can be ready and prepared when He comes for us.

The *Pulpit Commentary* says, "The parable of the Talents and the Ten Virgins emphasize only Christian people, those who are the immediate servants of the Lord and those who have gone forth to meet the heavenly bridegroom. The first parable (the ten talents) represents the *judgment of the outer life*—and the lack of obedience and readiness; the second parable (the virgins) represents the *judgment of the inner life of the soul*—and a lack of faithfulness."[35]

Oil Is Symbolic of the Holy Spirit

Oil in Scripture stands for the Holy Spirit, who had become quenched in the "foolish" virgins' hearts.[36] As one commentator put it, these virgins simply had a "burnout." They had no oil to refill their lamps and, thus, they were unable to go out and meet the Lord. *Extra oil means "spiritual preparation."* Because they had none, they had to remain behind. Works done by one person cannot be credited to another. Each of us must personally and daily be filled with God's Spirit, in order to produce our own good work and earn our own reward. An extra oil supply simply means we are spiritually prepared.

PARABLE CHART 3 (MATT. 25: 1-13)

STORY OR PARABLE	TO WHOM IS JESUS SPEAKING	ABOUT WHOM IS HE TALKING	WHAT HAD THEY DONE WRONG	WHAT WAS THEIR LOSS	WHAT EVENT IS BEING PREDICTED	WHAT IS THE LESSON FOR US
Matt. 8:12 Sons of the Kingdom "Story"	Gentile Centurion	"Sons of the Kingdom" - Jewish believers	Lack of Faith	Cast into outer darkness-weeping and gnashing of teeth	Preparation for the Kingdom	Need to have faith
Matt. 24: 45-51 Faithful & Wise Servants "Story"	Disciples ("What are the signs of Your coming?")	Any believer waiting for his Lord's return	Thought the Lord would not come-Mistreated his fellow servants	Cut him asunder & appointed him a place with "hypo-crites"-weeping and gnashing of teeth	The Rapture	Need to always be looking for His soon return
Matt. 25:14-30 10 Talents "Parable"	Disciples ("What are the signs of Your coming?")	His own servants	Wicked servant didn't do anything with his talent	Take talent away Cast into outer darkness-weeping and gnashing of teeth	The Bema Seat	Need to be faithful with the abilities God gives us
Matt. 25:1-13 10 Virgins "Parable"	Disciples ("What are the signs of Your coming?")	The "Church"	They had no intimacy with the Lord. He did not "know" them	Locked out of wedding - The door was shut & they were left out	The Wedding Ceremony	Need to know the Lord intimately
Matt. 22: 1-13 Man without a Wedding Garment "Parable"	Pharisees	Gentile believers at wedding (original ones called were not "worthy")	No wedding garment (no "fruit")	Bind him - cast into outer darkness-weeping and gnashing of teeth	The Marriage Supper	Need to wear the appropriate wedding garment

Do you recall what the third piece of the *Armor of God* is in Ephesians 6:15? "Our feet are to be shod with the *preparation* of the Gospel of Peace." This means we are to "*put off the flesh*" and be "filled with the Spirit." This is the readiness and the preparation that is required for those "clean, white linen garments" necessary for admittance to the Wedding Ceremony (Revelation 19:7–8).

The Foolish Virgins Were Not Prepared

Because these five foolish virgins were *not* prepared for the long wait, they simply ran out of oil. This means they hadn't made the necessary choices to refill their lamps. That extra portion of oil is something only the individual himself can secure. *It comes from an outside place* called "Gethsemane" (the place where Christ submitted all to His Father)—it's a place of crushing, a place of surrender, and a place of emptying so one can be filled with Christ's oil and His Spirit. Gethsemane is the only place where oil for our lamps can be purchased. "Unless a corn of wheat fall to the ground and die, it will abide alone; but if it dies, it will bring forth much fruit" (John 12:24–25).

Proverbs 20:27 says, "The spirit of a man is the lamp of the Lord." The lamps of our human spirits are not meant to burn out; they are designed to run forever by being refilled and refueled by the Holy Spirit. The oil (the Spirit) comes from an external place, outside and beyond ourselves. In other words, our empowerment is to be found in Christ alone. Then we will be single-minded and Spirit filled.

We are to have our lights burning brightly and set on top of a candlestick where all can see it (Luke 8:16).

The Importance of Preparation

At the end of the parable of the ten virgins, Christ turned to those who were listening and said, "Watch [be ready, be prepared], for you know *not* the hour that the Son of man cometh" (Matthew 25:13).

We can see from this parable, and others, the importance God puts on watching, being ready, and being prepared for His soon return. The word *preparation* has two different Greek words. One means internal preparation (Strong's #2090, *hetoimos*) and the other means external preparation (Strong's #2680, *kataskeuazo*).

The first definition (*hetoimos*), which means "internal preparation," is the one we are most interested in, as it means man's self-preparation and readiness. It means "to be morally fit, internally prepared" (Luke 1:17; Titus 3:1; Ephesians 6:15). *The Dictionary of New Testament Theology* says *hetoimos* "refers to something already existing in a state befitting its purpose."[37] *Its use in Scripture seems to always be in association with man's preparation and readiness to meet with his God.* In like manner, in the parable of the ten virgins, those who were ready and prepared went into the Wedding Ceremony (Matthew 25:10). Those who were not ready, did not.

Internal preparation entails continually washing ourselves, putting off our sin and self, being refilled with the Holy Spirit, and producing works of righteousness, which is our white linen wedding garment. It's *not* enough to just put on surface cosmetics, perfumes, and oils; we must also allow the Lord to complete the inward beautification process that will ultimately produce the fruit that He is looking for in each of our lives. God is building us according to His plans, not ours. Our job is to make the appropriate choices to allow Him to construct the temples of our bodies according to His will.

The second Greek word *kataskeuazo,* which has to do with external preparedness, means "human preparation for God's saving act." Paul told the story of Noah, who God warned of future events and how Noah, in obedience then prepared an ark. By so doing, he not only became an heir of righteousness, but also saved his family and members of the animal kingdom (Hebrews 11:7).

Like so many other principles in the Bible, the term "preparation" has two aspects. *God* is preparing a suitable place for us in His kingdom. But in the meantime we are preparing ourselves for His soon return and our subsequent marriage. Our engagement and betrothal are confirmed (sealed by the Holy Spirit when we first were born again) and our future in the kingdom is assured, but until He returns for us, we must continue to remain faithful, steadfast, and obedient, making ourselves ready, fit, and prepared!

The five foolish virgins were shut out of the wedding because they weren't prepared. They weren't experientially sanctified. They weren't partakers *of* Christ's Life and thus, they weren't overcomers. For them, the race was over. They could have earned a place of sovereignty in the coming kingdom, but because of their foolishness, they will end up only being Christ's subjects.

We must remember that the hardships, pain, and trials we are encountering now are simply a corridor to the palace that is our destination. We don't want to slip in the corridor and miss the palace.[38]

David Wilkerson, one of our favorite pastors, said in a newsletter, "The battle you're enduring now is not about this world, not about the flesh, not about the devil. Rather, the warfare you're facing is preparation for your eternal service in glory."[39]

The Bride Is to Make Herself Ready

Sanctification, therefore, is our bridal preparation!

This is how we continue to make ourselves *ready, fit, and prepared.* "Let us be glad and rejoice, and give honor to Him: for the marriage of the Lamb is come, and His wife *hath made herself ready*"(Revelation 19:7–8). *Notice that His wife has made* herself *ready*. She wears the fine linen, white and pure, an attire of her own making. This is *not* the righteousness of Christ that has been imputed to her, but her own "deeds of righteousness." Christ must not only be *on* us as a robe, but also *in* us as a life."[40]

The truth is that we, the body of Christ today, are the *Laodicean church* of Revelation who think they are "rich and in need of nothing," but in reality we are poor, blind, *and naked* (Revelation 3:17). Our robes have not only become defiled, they are often nonexistent!

Look around! Do we see a healthy church? Do we see vibrant Christian marriages? Do we see loving families? No! We see marriages falling apart, churches splitting, all kinds of trouble and hopelessness everywhere. *As Christians, our hope has been deferred and our hearts have become sad, sick and depressed, just as Proverbs 13:12 tells us.*

There is an urgent need for all of us to "put off" our sin and self and to "put on" Christ.

See *Chart 18: Reigning with Christ*

Finally, just saying the sinner's prayer at some time in our lives and going to church occasionally does *not* secure us a place in the wedding celebration as the wife of Christ or a position in the coming Millennial Kingdom. Only obedience, faithfulness, and perseverance do.[41]

Inheriting the Millennial Kingdom from the Lord and co-reigning with Him is *conditional*.[42] It is conditioned upon our personal preparation here on earth. Did we use our talents wisely? Have we been overcomers? Did we produce righteous deeds? Were they done in the power of the Holy Spirit? Did we complete the task Jesus gave us? Did we finish well? Were we faithful?

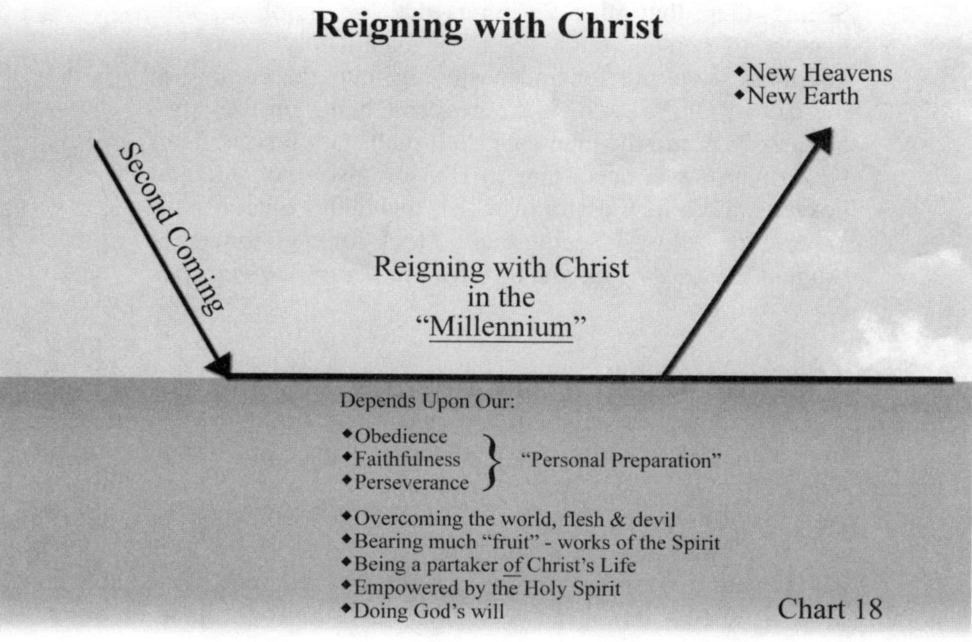

It all boils down to the fact that our diligence *here* on earth determines our rule *there* (1 Corinthians 6:2).

In Conclusion

Is it any wonder then that this doctrine of perseverance and longsuffering hasn't gained more acceptance in the church? Most of us don't want to hear that we are expected to buffet our bodies, run the race, and through much tribulation enter into the kingdom reign. We would much rather hear that we will *all* inherit the kingdom, that we will *all* receive rewards, that we will *all* rule and reign with Christ, and that we will *all* attend both the wedding and the marriage supper of the Lamb. We want to hear that there are *no* consequences to a careless Christian life. Unfortunately, that's just *not* scriptural![43] Even though we like to think of ourselves as rich and in need of nothing, in reality we are poor, blind, and naked (Revelation 3:17).

Many of us have only sprinkled blood on the doorposts of our houses—only been born again (Exodus 12:7), but have *not* totally surrendered our lives to Christ. We have been delivered from *the penalty of sin* (justification), but *not* from *the bondage of sin* (sanctification). And *that's* going to affect our place, our position, and our inheritance in the coming kingdom.

This is why we are so passionate about this message. *Having a kingdom perspective here and now* is of the utmost importance. It will affect every choice we make, determine every decision we come to, and influence every action we take.

Our eternal destiny will depend upon these things!

> Seeing, then, that all these things shall be dissolved, what manner of persons ought ye to be in all holy living and godliness. Looking for and hastening unto the coming of the day of God, in which the heavens, being on fire, shall be dissolved and the elements shall melt with fervent heat? Nevertheless we, according to His promise, look for new heavens and a new earth, in which dwelleth righteousness. Wherefore, beloved, seeing that ye look for such things, be diligent that *ye may be found of Him in peace, without spot, and blameless*.
>
> —2 Peter 3:11–14

A kingdom perspective will continually remind us that we are preparing our wedding garments *now* for what we are going to wear *there*!

Imagine the devastation we would feel if the Lord turned to us at the entrance to the wedding ceremony and said, "I'm sorry, but you are not ready; you are not prepared. You are not qualified to enter. I simply don't know (*oida*) you." And then He would shut the door (Matthew 25:12).

The salvation of our spirits (our justification) is a free gift and there is nothing more we need to do to receive it, other than simply accept it. Entering the Marriage Ceremony, attending the Marriage Feast and inheriting the kingdom, however, is another matter. It comes with endurance, perseverance, suffering, and personal crucifixion.

One of Paul's parting comments to the Philippians was:

> Not as though I had already attained, either were already perfect; but I follow after, if that I may apprehend that for which also I am apprehended of Christ Jesus. Brethren, I count not myself to have apprehended; but this one thing I do, forgetting those things which are behind, and reaching forth unto those things which are before, *I press toward the mark for the prize of the high calling of God in Christ Jesus.*
>
> —Philippians 3:12–14

This must be our motto also!

Chapter Seven

The Millennial Temple

After the Bema Seat Judgment and the Wedding Ceremony in heaven, Christ will return to earth with His armies for His second coming (Revelation 19:7-8,14). At this juncture, there will be a strange seventy-five day interval between His coming and the actual beginning of the Millennium, during which the Tribulation saints and the Old Testament saints will be resurrected, the Sheep and Goat Judgment will occur (which we will discuss in the next chapter), the Marriage Feast will happen and, finally, Christ Himself will build the Millennial Temple in Jerusalem where He will rule and reign for a thousand years.[1]

Let's discuss this temple as it has a tremendous role in the Millennium.

Description of the Millennial Temple

The Millennial Temple is a literal temple that will be built at the beginning of the Millennium where Christ will rule for a thousand years. Many Old Testament prophets, including Isaiah, Daniel, Joel, and Haggai, have all spoken about this temple and its significance.[2]

It's called Ezekiel's Temple because God gave its plans and dimensions to Ezekiel in a vision (Ezekiel 40–48). This temple will function not only as Christ's dwelling place (His Throne Room) for His thousand-year earthly reign, but also it will be the focal point and the worship center for the entire kingdom. At that time Jerusalem will be the center of world government. (Don't get the literal city of Jerusalem, where Christ will reign for a thousand years, confused with the heavenly, eternal state called "the new Jerusalem" that will appear at the end of the Millennium [Revelation 21:1–6].)

The first Jewish temple, Solomon's Temple, was designed not only to house God's presence, but also to illustrate God's plan of personal redemption. Because Israel was rebellious and chose instead to retain their sin, however, God withdrew His presence and His glory (Ezekiel 10). Even after Solomon's Temple was destroyed, the people still remained unchanged. Thus, God stayed absent even during the second temple period (Herod's Temple). Before the final destruction of this temple, however, God came in the person of Jesus Christ, "the temple made without hands" (Matthew

12:6). He then chose "another nation" (the church) to carry out His plan of salvation. By placing His Spirit in believers' hearts, they became living representatives of what God's physical temple was originally designed to do and to communicate. "Know ye not that your body is [now] the *temple* of the Holy Spirit?" (1 Corinthians 6:19).

Since Herod's Temple was destroyed almost two thousand years ago, there has been no physical temple in the city of Jerusalem. Therefore, Ezekiel's Millennial Temple will be very special. It will be more glorious than all the previous temples put together: "The glory of this latter house shall be greater than of the former, saith the Lord of hosts: and in this place will I give peace, saith the Lord of hosts" (Haggai 2:9).

Other prophets have predicted something very similar. For example, Isaiah wrote, "And many people shall go and say, Come ye, and let us go up to the mountain of the Lord, to the house of the God of Jacob; and He will teach us of His ways, and we will walk in His paths: for out of Zion shall go forth the law, and the word of the Lord from Jerusalem" (Isaiah 2:3). Micah wrote, "And many nations shall come, and say, Come, and let us go up to the mountain of the Lord, and to the house of the God of Jacob; and He will teach us of His ways, and we will walk in His paths; for the law shall go forth of Zion, and the word of the Lord from Jerusalem" (Micah 4:2). Zechariah told us that Jesus, Himself, will build the temple of the Lord and that "He shall bear the glory, and shall sit and rule upon His Throne" (Zechariah 6:12–13; Luke 1:32–33).

Ezekiel's Vision

Ezekiel, whose name means "God strengthens," was a prophet and priest and trained for temple ministry. As a "watchman" for the house of Israel, he knew the law and was able to teach it to the people. Ezekiel was a true prophet of God; all of his predictions came true in every detail. For example, he predicted that the city of Tyre would be destroyed (Ezekiel 26:1–14). And it happened just as he said! The Millennial Temple will be no different. It will be built just as he said.

Ezekiel was already exiled to Babylon when he received the vision of the future temple (around April 573 BC). At the time of the vision, Ezekiel was supernaturally transported to a high mountain in Israel where he saw the glorious temple that God would establish in the Millennium. Ezekiel was told to record this vision (in amazing detail) so that he could present it to the Jewish people who were in captivity at the time.[3] God wanted to encourage them through Ezekiel not only about the coming temple, but also about their restoration and their glorious future.

God wanted His hurting people to know that *His judgments are always redemptive* and that His purpose was *not* to destroy them, but to restore and reconcile them. "[God's] judgment [always] returns to righteousness" (Psalm 94:15). *This was God's purpose for them and it's His purpose for us also*. Ezekiel's vision was to convict the Jews of their past unfaithfulness, but also to demonstrate—by this future hope—God's unconditional Love. God wanted Israel to see that He was forced to judge them in the past, but that in the future He will regather them, cleanse them, and ultimately bless them (Ezekiel 36:26–27).

Ezekiel was a very forceful communicator in relating some of his visions and dreams and he often used a great deal of symbolism. In this vision about the temple, however, everything is described in minute detail. It's literal to the last point. Ezekiel 40—44:3 describes the temple complex in unbelievable architectural detail; 44:4—46:24 spells out the return of the Lord to the temple and the new organization that He will establish; and 47:1—48:35 tells of the incredible changes and blessings that will come to the promised land from the temple.

There will be a totally new system of temple service, so that Israel can, once again, prove to be a holy people and can participate in God's blessings, which will flow like a river.[4]

This Millennial Temple will *not* be built on the same site as Solomon's Temple (i.e., the temple mount area in Jerusalem today), because Ezekiel's dimensions require a much, much larger space. Some Hebrew authorities believe it will be built to the north—halfway between the Mediterranean and the Dead Sea. This area will be called a "dedicated area," similar to a national park (Hebrew, *terumah)*.[5] Scripture tells us that at the end of the Tribulation, Jerusalem, as we know it today, will be leveled by a massive earthquake (Zechariah 14:4).

The area earmarked and set aside for the temple and its surrounding buildings will be approximately 50 square miles (Ezekiel 48:8–20). In other words, this temple will be immense!

Many people think that Ezekiel's Temple is the same temple as the Tribulation Temple. It is not. How could Christ set up His kingdom rule in the same place the Antichrist, possessed by Satan, had reigned, especially where holiness and purity is the overall theme of the Millenial Temple? No, Ezekiel's Millennial Temple will be built by Christ at the beginning of the Millennium (Zechariah 6:12–13).

The Purpose of the Temple

Ezekiel's Temple will have two main purposes:

1. The first purpose will be to *provide a throne room for the Lord Jesus Christ* and a place for His glory (Ezekiel 43:7). His glory will be a *visible* sign of God's presence among His people. It will be a constant reminder of His promise to dwell in their midst. The glory of God departed Solomon's Temple in Ezekiel 10–11, after which the structure was destroyed, but the coming Millennial Temple will again house His radiant glory and be a visible sign of God's returned presence.

2. The second purpose for the temple will be *to demonstrate Christ's holiness and purity* (Ezekiel 43:12). Holiness will permeate everything that is connected to this temple. The entire worship service will be designed to emphasize holiness. As Psalm 93:5 says, "Holiness becomes Thine house." It will be a sanctified place, a place apart, a place of God's holiness, where there is to be no human defilement or corruption.[6] This is the time when God's people will learn to worship the Lord "in the beauty of His holiness." In other words, everyone who enters this temple will have to be purified, sanctified, and set apart. Only those "circumcised in heart," only those experientially sanctified, and only those who are clean and pure will be allowed to come into the sanctuary and stand before the Lord.

"Who shall ascend into the hill of the Lord? Or who shall stand in His holy place? He that hath clean hands, and a pure heart; who hath not lifted up his soul unto vanity nor sworn deceitfully. He shall receive the blessing from the Lord [that second inheritance], and righteousness from the God of his salvation" (Psalm 24:3–5).

This temple will be a memorial and a teaching center, not only to instruct men about the awesome holiness of God and about the proper way to worship, but also to remind us of the substitutionary death of Jesus on the Cross some two thousand years ago.

We believe the Millennial Temple will be one of the places where the faithful and obedient believers will be able to participate in positions of authority. Revelation 3:12 tells us that the overcomers in the Church of Philadelphia will be "pillars" in that temple. A *pillar* (Strong's # 4769) means "something or someone who helps to support, who helps to make stand, or who helps to hold up."

Consequently this temple will be a personal object lesson for every believer.[7] It will serve to show them *how* to be pure, *how* to be undefiled, and *how* to be perfect (or complete). *The Millennial Temple will be a place for perfecting the saints and completing what perhaps was* not *accomplished here on earth during the church age.*

See *Chart 19: "The Separate Place"*

With this in mind, one of the most intriguing parts in Ezekiel's Temple is the space directly behind (or west of) the Holy of Holies called the *Gizrah* or *gezerah* (Strong's #1508). According to Strong's, a *gizrah* is a separate place or "a *figure* or a *person* who is cut out." It's a separated enclosure. It comes from the root word *gezer* (Strong's #1506), which means "a portion cut off" and the primitive root *gazar* (Strong's #1504), which means "to exclude." It's a Hebrew noun based on the roots of the Hebrew verb, *gazara*, meaning "to divide, to portion off, or to cut away." It is used in Psalm 136:13 in reference to the dividing of the Red Sea.

Strong's Concordance also says that the *gizrah* is a place for "polishing or making something smooth by friction." It's used eight times

Ezekiel's Temple
(Ezekiel 40-44)

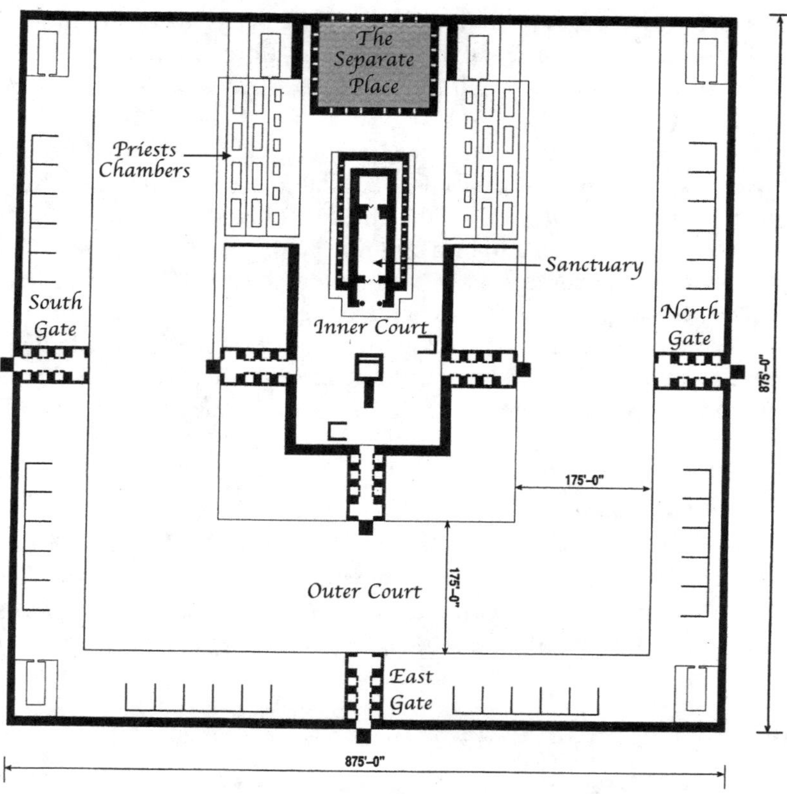

→ Drawing from John W. Schmitt & J. Carl Laney's book "Messiah's Coming Temple."
1 cubit = 21 inches ("royal cubit")

Chart 19

in the Bible (seven in reference to the temple in Ezekiel 41 and 42) and once in reference to the polishing of a godly sect in Lamentations 4:7, who had sinned greatly. This sect, the Nazarenes, had previously been "purer than snow," "whiter than milk," and "polished like lapis lazuli" (precious stones), but they had become "dark," and "blacker than coal." These verses imply that if something is tarnished, it must be excluded, but *not* necessarily destroyed, because in verse 22, God tells them, "I will exile you no longer."

The *gizrah* is a "separate place" for cutting and polishing in order to produce a refined and magnificent finish. If the word *gizrah* contained an *ayin,* then the sound *raw* would have a negative connotation, but it does not, so *this space has some mysterious and yet beneficial purpose*.[8]

The Theological Dictionary of the Old Testament says that the term *gizrah* can be applied to an area where the "excluded man" or the "banished man" is placed. It refers to 2 Chronicles 26:21, when Uzziah was excluded from God's house because (after all the wonderful things he had done for God and for his people) "his heart was lifted up to his destruction" and he transgressed against the Lord, his God. The Lord immediately struck him down with leprosy. As a result he was cut off from the House of the Lord until he died.

(*Gezerah* is also used in Leviticus 16:22 where the scapegoat carried away the sins and guilt of Israel into a separate region. This region, interestingly enough, was called the "unfruitful land.")[9]

The Gizrah then will be a separate place or another building for those objects that have become unclean and unholy as they must be "cut off" from the sanctified things. Such items can later be cleansed and restored.

Any commentary on Ezekiel will show you the following diagram of Ezekiel's Temple, clearly showing the *Gizrah.* Note, however, that none of the previous Jewish temples had a *Gizrah*. It's unique to Ezekiel's. Why?

See *Chart 20: The Gizrah*

The Gizrah will be 122 1/2 feet by 157 feet and its walls will be five feet thick. This wall emphasizes the separation of "the holy" and "the common" (Ezekiel 42:20). This is God's divine intention. *The Gizrah in Ezekiel's Temple will be a place where everything that is excluded from the worship service (because of defilement), will be kept. It is an unsanctified area, separate from the sanctified region.*

The Profane Place

The *Gizrah* is called "*the profane place*" in Ezekiel 42:20. The Hebrew word for *profane* is *chol* (Strong's #2455), which means "something that is exposed and common, opposed to something that is sanctified and holy." *Chol* is from the root *chalal* (Strong's #2490), which means to break one's word, to pollute or *to defile one's inheritance*. Remember the emphasis on *defilement* in chapters four and six of this book. Here again we find this word. Strong's says, "This word is often used to describe the defilement that comes from immorality."

Could this gizrah possibly be the place that is called "the outer darkness" or the "darkness outside," spoken of in the three Matthew parables?[10] Could this be where the Lord in His Love, but out of His justice, casts the unfaithful servants who were *not* prepared for the kingdom? Could this be an expression of His "tough Love" in providing an area for remedial training? Could this be the separate place into which the fruitless and defiled believers are put, while the rest of the body of Christ enjoys fellowship with the Lord in some other area of the temple? Could this be what is called the "darkness outside"?

The Gizrah

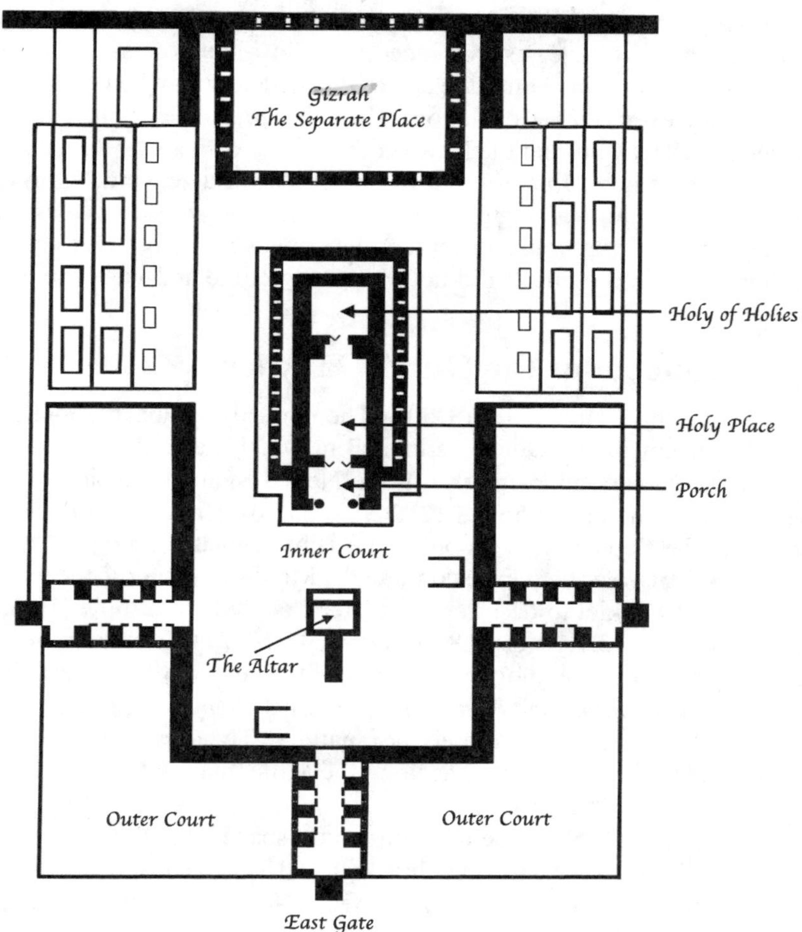

Chart 20

The Darkness Outside

We suggested that the "outer darkness" or the "darkness outside" is a separate place, another room or another region outside the region of Light. This darkness outside is just beyond the brilliant light of Christ's presence in the sanctuary (John 9:5). The believers put here will still be with the Lord, but just not able to see Him. It's an area that is marked by loss of liberty, forfeiture of privileges, decrease of knowledge, and a deprivation of service and rewards. One either *enters in* to the festivities because they are sanctified and wearing the appropriate wedding garment; or one is *cast out* of the festivities and is excluded from fellowship because of defilement and the absence of the proper garment. (Matthew 22:1-14.)

In this darkness outside, believers will experience unimaginable regret, remorse, and a sense of shame as they look back on their lives and all the lost opportunities.[11] And yes, they *will* remember, because at the Judgment Seat, Christ will have just reminded them in minute detail.[12] Past memory evidently will continue until the end of the Millennium when God will finally wipe away every tear (Revelation 21:4). This will occur before the creation of the New Heavens and the New Earth.

In his book *Your Eternal Reward,* Erwin Lutzer said, "Our tears will be those of regret and shame, tears of remorse for lives lived for ourselves rather than for Christ and for others. Perhaps we would never cease crying in heaven if God Himself did not eventually come and wipe the tears from our eyes."

The Concept of the Outer Darkness

Michael Huber from Dallas Theological Seminary wrote an article "The Concept of the Outer Darkness" in which he said: "The term 'outer darkness' appears nowhere else in the New Testament outside of the three verses mentioned (Matthew 8:12; 22:13; 25:30). However, it does occur 20 times in the Septuagint version of the Bible and it's *always in relation to Ezekiel's Temple or God.*" He continued: "Most significantly, the term is used 15 times in Ezekiel to describe the Outer Court of the temple (10:5; 40:19–20; 41:15, 17; 42:1, 3, 6, 7, 8, 9; 44:19; 46:20–21). It may be noteworthy, considering the eschatological imagery of the subject of the parable that the *dominant use of the term is in relation to the Millennial Temple*."

We found this absolutely fascinating: "The dominant use of the term *outer darkness* is in its relationship to the Millennial Temple."

You check it out.

The *Gizrah* may be the entire outer space behind the temple and *not* just the building itself. However, Ezekiel 41:13–14 seems to indicate its exact measurements as 122 1/2 feet by 157 feet. (Note: one cubit = 21 inches.)

See *Chart 21: The Light of Christ's Presence*

The kingdom in view here is a region of light that is encircled by darkness. This darkness, remember, is just beyond the brilliant light of Christ's presence in the sanctuary.

This is what it might look like.

The *temple itself is filled with the light of Christ's presence* (John 9:5). The Source of Light is coming from the actual presence of the Lord in the Throne Room. Those saints closest to Him will be in the brightest (but smallest) rings of light around Him. Those farthest away from Him, will be in the fainter (but larger) rings of light in the outer circle. Those in the *Gizrah* will be like those in the last seat, of the last row, in the last balcony of a huge Music Hall. They know Christ is there. They are "with Him," but they can't quite "see" Him.

Being *with* Him but not able to *see* Him reminds us of Hebrew 12:14: "Follow peace with all men, and holiness, *without which no man shall* see *the Lord.*" The word *to see* here (Strong's # 3700) means "to gaze upon something." *Holiness* (Strong's #38, *hagiasmos*) in this verse refers to being undefiled and set apart. Paul explained in verse 10 the absolute need for believers to be "partakers of His holiness" so we *can* see Him. We do that by "lay[ing] aside every weight [sin] that so easily besets us" (12:1).

The Light of Christ's Presence

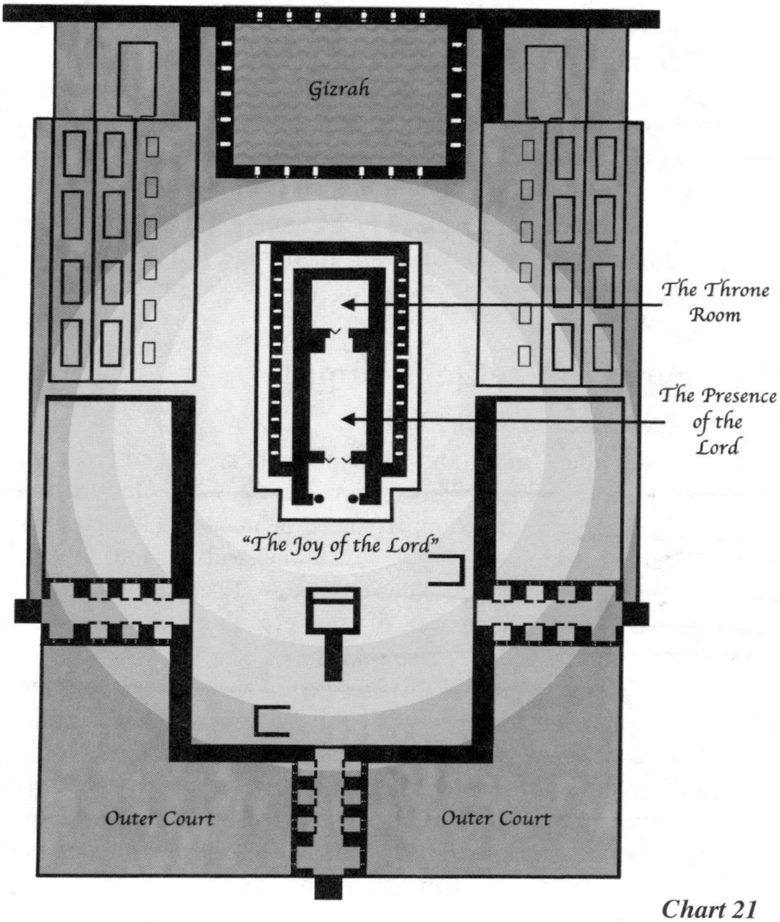

Chart 21

The *Gizrah* Is a Real Place

The whole idea of the Millennial Temple is "separation," a place apart, a holy place. The Gizrah will be a separate place for things that become ritually unclean and unholy. They will have to be separated, so that "such items can later be cleansed and restored." God's plan has always been to show us that His judgment is redemptive. "Judgment returns to righteousness" (Psalm 94:15). Perhaps God will spend the next thousand years lovingly restoring, renewing, and refreshing those believers (His sons) who were unsanctified (defiled) in this life back to holiness. That's what a loving Father would do. What we might have in view here is a place where those who were disqualified from inheriting the kingdom, will have a chance to relearn sanctification so they can produce godly fruit in their lives. How long one would stay there, Scripture does not say. We're sure it varies with each believer.

Remember Philippians 1:6 "He that began a good work in you will perform it until the day of Jesus Christ."

(Recently the National Spelling Bee contest was televised and coincidentally one of its test words was *genizah*. They explained that it was a Hebrew word and came from the root *gezrah*. The definition they gave for *genizah* was "a storeroom where the priests of the temple kept *damaged*, but *sacred* objects.") Again, we thought this fascinating.

The *Gizrah* is a real place in Ezekiel's Temple. But scholars have debated its function for years. We again encourage you to study the Scriptures and see what the Lord shows you (Acts 17:11). We present this supposition for you to investigate.

Differences in Ezekiel's Temple

A few more interesting facts—

Besides the *Gizrah* and its significance, it is interesting to notice the furniture and sacrificial items from previous temples that are *missing* in Ezekiel's Temple. For example, there is no Ark (Jeremiah 3:16)[13]; no Brazen Lavers (Ezekiel 36:24–27), no Lampstands (Isaiah 49:6), no Tables of Shewbread (Micah 5:4), no Altar of Incense (Zechariah 8:20–23), and no gold embellishments. The answer, of course, is that *Jesus' physical presence in this Temple replaces all of these things*.

Jesus replaces the Ark by *His literal presence* on the throne (John 10:30–33). He replaces the Lavers by the *cleansing of His shed Blood* (John 15:3). He replaces the Lampstands because *He is our Light* (John 8:12). He replaces the Tables of Shewbread because *He is our Bread of Life* (John 6:35). And He replaces the Incense Altar because we will have *intimacy with Him* in the future temple as He will hear and answer our prayers personally (John 14:6). And He *is* the gold (the purity) in the temple.

Unlike the previous temples, Ezekiel's Temple or the Millennial Temple will have no wall of partition between the Inner and Outer Courts, nor a separate Women's Court. In the previous temples, there always was a high partition wall between the Inner Court where believing Jews were allowed and the Outer Court where Gentiles were allowed. Gentiles and women were excluded from the Inner Court by penalty of death.

Jesus, through His sacrificial death, made Jewish and Gentile believers (including women), into one body and broke down the barrier between them (Galatians 3:28). "For He is our peace, who hath made both one, and hath broken down the middle wall of partition between us" (Ephesians 2:14).

There are only two pieces of furniture that remain in Ezekiel's Temple: the *Throne* located in the Holy of Holies and the *Altar of Sacrifice* sitting in the middle of the Inner Court, with the most unusual Hebrew name of "*Ariel,*" which means "*Lion of God.*"

Consequently the whole Millennial Temple points to the actual presence of Jesus Christ as the Messiah. Lambert Dolphin said, "This temple will be a 'memorial'—*a teaching center* apparently to instruct men about the holiness of God and proper worship during the coming kingdom of Jesus on the earth . . . this temple is supposed to remind everyone of the substitutionary death of Jesus on the Cross, as the 'Lamb of God,' some two thousand years earlier."[14] Thus, it's *not* a reinstitution of the Mosaic sacrificial system, but a brand-new system that will contain some, but not all, of the historical temple features. The sacrificial system of the Mosaic law did not remove sin, it only "covered" it. It served as a visual picture of what the Messiah would do when He came (Isaiah 53:10–11).

This new Millennial system of worship will be in remembrance of what Christ has done. It will be a means of restoring fellowship for a holy people who have committed an error. It will provide ritual cleansing. Just as the church has been commanded to keep the Lord's Supper as a visual picture of what Christ did for us, so the worship items in Ezekiel's Temple will be a perpetual reminder for the Jews of who Jesus Christ is.

The Zadok Priests

It's also interesting to note that the original line of Levitical priests, who were once in charge of the worship services in Solomon's Temple, will *not* be able to approach the sanctuary in the future Millennium Temple. The reason is because their forefathers did *not* remain faithful to the Lord when they were being conquered, but caved in to the religions of their enemies. An example of God's mercy, however, is that He will allow them to be in charge of the maintenance of the temple structure (Ezekiel 44:15–31).

An example of His justice is that He is going to choose the sons of Zadok to personally serve Him in the Millennial Temple because of their forefather's faithfulness in the past to stand strong for Him. As a reward they will receive access to the presence of the Lord.[15] "And the chamber whose prospect is toward the north is for the priests, the keepers of the charge of the altar: these are the sons of Zadok among the sons of Levi, which come near to the Lord to minister unto Him" (Ezekiel 40:46). Again, showing by their proximity the intimacy they will enjoy with the Lord.

Thus in the Millennium, the distinction between the holy and the profane will even be shown in the selection of the priests.

(See "The Sons of Zadok" in the Supplemental Notes Section of the Appendix for additional fascinating information.)

See *Chart 22: A Millennial Perspective*

Take a look at Chart 22, which is an overview of *some of the events* that will occur in the Millennium. Christ will return with all the church saints; the Old Testament saints and the Tribulation saints will then be resurrected; the mortal believers from the Tribulation will then enter the kingdom; Christ will build the temple from which He will rule the nations with a rod of iron; the nation of Israel will finally be restored; and the Marriage Supper of the Lamb will be held.

Where Will We Be?

The question for all of us to ponder is: *Where will we be for those thousand years?* Will we be rejoicing as a "pillar" (Revelation 3:12) in the

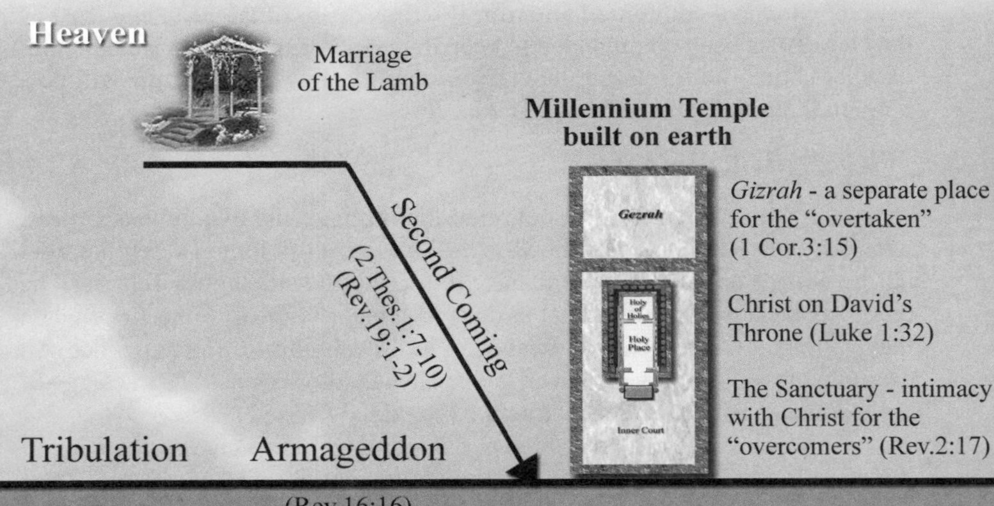

sanctuary in the "light and presence of Christ" never to be moved, or will we be in the darkness outside being retrained in His way of Holiness?

You can see the importance of developing a proper Millennial perspective in everything we do here—in every choice we make, in every action we take, in every decision and in every response. These choices are what will ultimately determine our place and our position in that coming kingdom.

The hope of our salvation is "being able to have some level of responsibility" with Christ in this incredible period of time coming up. It's the reason we were created, the reason we were called, and what we are being trained for *now*.

Ruling and reigning with Christ is not only "the prize" of the high calling, it's also the "mark" we should all be shooting for.

For Thine, O Lord, is the Kingdom—

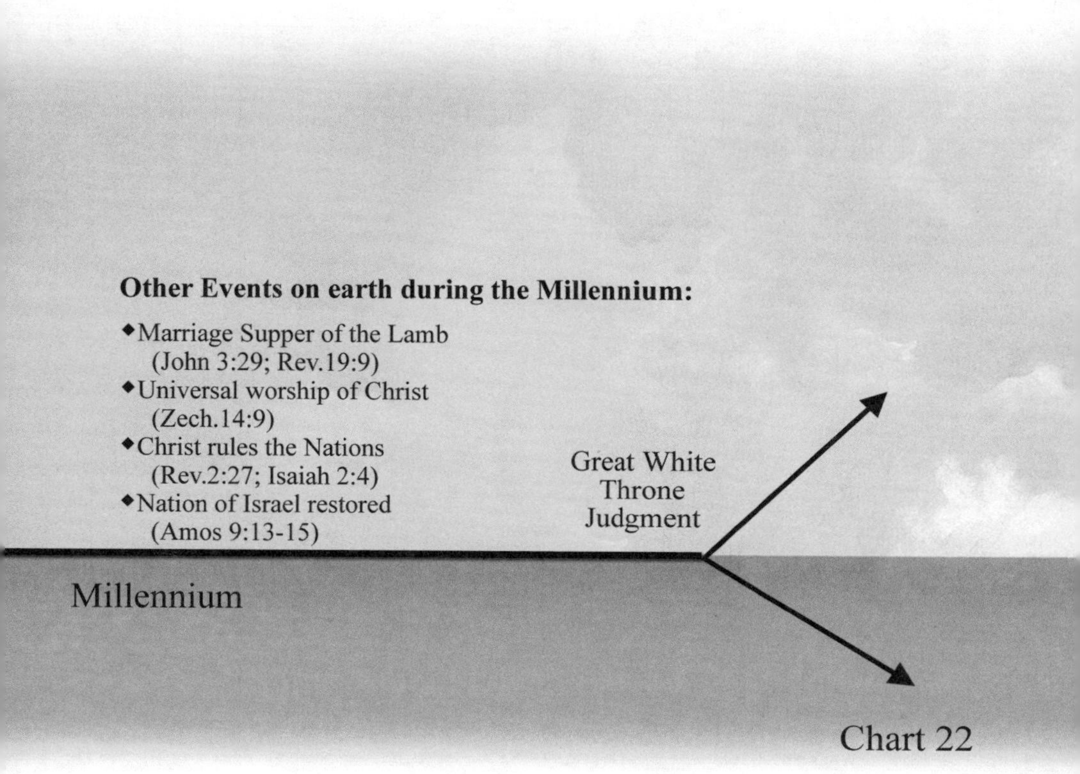

Other Events on earth during the Millennium:

- Marriage Supper of the Lamb (John 3:29; Rev.19:9)
- Universal worship of Christ (Zech.14:9)
- Christ rules the Nations (Rev.2:27; Isaiah 2:4)
- Nation of Israel restored (Amos 9:13-15)

Great White Throne Judgment

Millennium

Chart 22

Section Three

The Power

"That ye might walk worthy of the Lord unto all pleasing, being fruitful in every good work, and increasing in the knowledge of God; *strengthened with all might, according to His glorious power,* unto all patience and longsuffering with joyfulness; Giving thanks unto the Father, which hath made us meet [qualified] to be partakers of the inheritance of the saints in light: Who hath delivered us from the power of darkness, and hath translated us into the kingdom of His dear Son."

—Colossians 1:10–13

Chapter Eight

Partakers *of* Christ's Life

In the Introduction Section (chapters 1–4), we discussed *why we are here and what was God's purpose in calling us.* In the Kingdom Section (chapters 5–7) we talked about *Where we are going and what does the future hold?* This section, the Power Section (chapters 8–12), centers on *What do we have to do to get there?* We believe this is the most important section. In other words, we won't be able to inherit the blessings we have been discussing without knowing *how* to become sanctified, *how* to become a partaker *of* Christ, and *how* to overcome. Section three is the practical application part of this book. This is where we learn the importance of God's empowering. He must be the One enabling us to do all of the above.

It's great to learn new exciting things such as, why we are here and where we are going, but the most important part is *how* these things change our lives. How do they conform us more into the image of Christ? And how do they help us produce more godly fruit for the kingdom? What good is learning new biblical revelation if it doesn't somehow make us more like Jesus?

Again, let's start with the basics.

What Is a "Partaker"?

As we mentioned earlier, this book seeks to integrate the sanctification process here on earth with the reward of inheritance in the Millennial Kingdom. Colossians 1:10–13 (found at the beginning of this section) connects the importance of "walking worthily" and "being qualified"—through sanctification—with becoming a *partaker of the inheritance of Christ* in the future Millennial Kingdom.

What is a partaker?

The word *partake* (Strong's #2844, *koinonos* and #3353, *metochos*) means "to be a participant of something, a sharer in something, or a carrier of something." All believers are *partakers of Christ's divine nature*: "According to His divine power hath given unto us all things that pertain unto life and godliness, through the knowledge of Him that hath called us to glory and virtue: Whereby are given unto us exceeding great and precious promises; that by these *ye might be partakers of the divine nature*" (2 Peter 1:3–4).

Other places that the word *partaker* appears are:

- Partakers *of* His sufferings (1 Peter 4:12–13; 2 Corinthians 1:7)
- Partakers *of* the inheritance of the saints (Colossians 1:12)
- Partakers *of* His holiness (Hebrews 12:10)
- Partakers *of* His promise (Ephesians 3:6)
- Partakers *of* Christ (Hebrews 3:14)

Partaking *of* Christ's Life means not only receiving His Life in our hearts when we are born again, but also living that Life out in our souls. Partaking of His Life is what empowers us to become overcomers — faithful ones who produce "fruit." It means that the Life of Christ is now being lived out through us. His Life has filled us and the Holy Spirit is now empowering us.[1]

Being a partaker *of* Christ is *not* the same thing as being a partaker *in* Christ. The former is "experiential" whereas the latter is "positional." We are placed *in* Christ when we are first born again as a free gift (justification), but we become partakers *of* Christ when His life begins to come forth through us (experiential sanctification). In other words, we have laid our self-life down at the Cross saying, "not my will, but Thine" and thus, His Life is able to come forth.

Partaking *of* His Life results in becoming those overcomers whom Revelation refers to as ruling and reigning in the Millennium. *It is Christ's overcoming Life*—His *Agape* Love, His supernatural power, and His divine wisdom. Overcomers are simply partaking of that Life. They are loving with His Love, depending upon His strength, and making decisions through His wisdom.

These are the faithful believers who will be Christ's co-heirs in His future kingdom.

God's plan is not to repair us, but to absolutely re-create us. He wants our old nature replaced by the release of His new nature in us. This is what the sanctification process is all about—re-creating the image of Christ in us—for the purpose of bringing glory to Him (Romans 8:29).

The Exchanged Life

Partaking of Christ's Life means that our self-life (our own natural self-centered thoughts and emotions) has been set aside and God's Life freed to come forth. Matthew 16:24–26 tells us only when we lose our lives will we be able to find them. When our self-life is replaced with Christ's Life, it is called "the exchanged life," "the shared life," or "the imparted life." We must exchange our love for His Love (Ephesians 3:19), our wisdom for His, our strength for His, our faith for His (Romans 3:22; Galatians 2:16), our joy for His, our peace, and so forth. It is Christ's eternal Life, but because we are open and cleansed vessels, we can now partake of it, share it, and live it.

This is the oneness and the union of spirits that we read about in Galatians 2:20: "I am crucified with Christ; nevertheless I live; yet not I, but Christ liveth in me; and the life which I now live in the flesh I live by the faith of the Son of God, who loved me and gave Himself for me." This is the exchanged Life.

It's also the "treasure" in 2 Corinthians 4:7 and "the mystery of godliness" that 1 Timothy 3:16 talks about.[2]

This exchange of life, however, does *not* happen automatically. In order to live Christ's Life, we must not only be cleansed vessels (sanctified), we must also have childlike faith. By faith, *we* choose to give God our hurts, our bitterness, our insecurities, our unforgiveness (any self-life that has quenched His Spirit in us) and in exchange, He gives us His Life—His power and His Love.

John 12:24–25 also describes this exchange of life perfectly: "Verily, verily, I say unto you, except a corn of wheat fall into the ground and die it abideth alone; but if it die, it bringeth forth much fruit. He that loveth [holds on to] his life shall lose it; and he that hateth [lets go of] his life in this world shall keep it unto life eternal."

This is what exchanging lives with Christ might look like:

See *Chart 23: Exchanging Lives with Christ*

If we have made faith choices to set aside our own thoughts, emotions, and desires (our self life), then God's Life—His Thoughts and His Love—can come forth and produce "fruit." The is called "walking by the Spirit" and can only occur when we are cleansed and sanctified vessels.

If, however, we have quenched God's Spirit in our hearts by making emotional choices (because of our own hurts, fears, resentment and unbelief), it forces us to show forth our own self-life. And, thus, no "fruit" will be produced.

See *Chart 24: No Exchange of Life*

Chart 24 shows us what "walking by the flesh" looks like.

The scary part is that if we keep quenching God's Spirit over a period of time, we will run the risk of becoming those unfaithful, backsliding, nominal Christians who ultimately will miss the inheritance that God has planned. Scripture says we can even go so far as to "sear our conscience"—where we don't even recognize right from wrong, holiness from ungodliness, and kindness from hardness (1 Timothy 4:2).

The substitutionary death of Christ on the Cross solved the problem of sin for us, but only the moment-by-moment surrender of our self-life will empower us to become cleansed vessels producing fruit. Consequently, we must not only be *recipients* of Christ's Life at our new birth, we must also be partakers, vessels, and *carriers* of His Life to others by the power of the Holy Spirit.

Many Christians believe that Christ is the Lifegiver, but they forget that He must also be their "Life." Scripture tells us that if we "live" by the Spirit, we must also "walk" by the Spirit.[3]

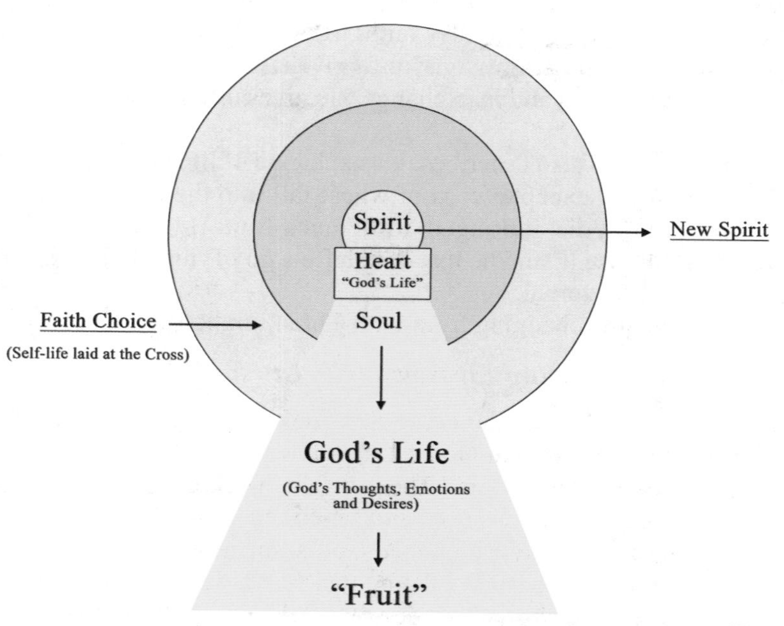

Chart 23

The Purpose of Being a Partaker: "Fruit"

The purpose of being a partaker of Christ's Life is that we might become the overcomers in Revelation 2 and 3 who produce the "fruit of righteousness" in their lives (Philippians 1:10–11). The Greek word for *fruit* is *karpos* (Strong's #2590), which means "that which is produced by the Spirit of God in us."[4] Fruit comes from sanctification, through deliverance from a life of sin and self, and the subsequent filling and empowering of the Holy Spirit. The *Pulpit Commentary* makes an interesting remark: "*Our* work *is our fruit; and our fruit is the product of our lives.*"[5]

From now on when we mention *fruit,* you'll know that we are referring to the "good works"—the righteous deeds and the godly actions—

that are done by the Spirit of God through us (Ephesians 5:9; Philippians 1:11). Without a continual "co-death" with Christ (the crucifixion of self), however, there will be no exchange of Life, and thus, no fruit.

> You shall know them by their fruits . . . every good tree bringeth forth good fruit, but a corrupt tree bringeth forth bad fruit. A good tree cannot bring forth bad fruit, neither can a corrupt tree bring forth good fruit.
>
> —Matthew 7:16–18[6]

In other words, "fruit" is the visible expression of the power of God working in us. However,

> Every branch in Me that beareth not fruit, He taketh away: and every branch that beareth fruit, He purgeth it, that it may bring forth more fruit . . . *Abide in Me,* and I in you. As the branch cannot bear fruit of itself, except it *abide in Me*, and I in him, the same bringeth forth much fruit: *for without Me ye can do nothing.*
>
> —John 15:2–5

(See "Abiding in Christ" in the Supplemental Notes Section of the appendix for more information.)

No Exchange of Life

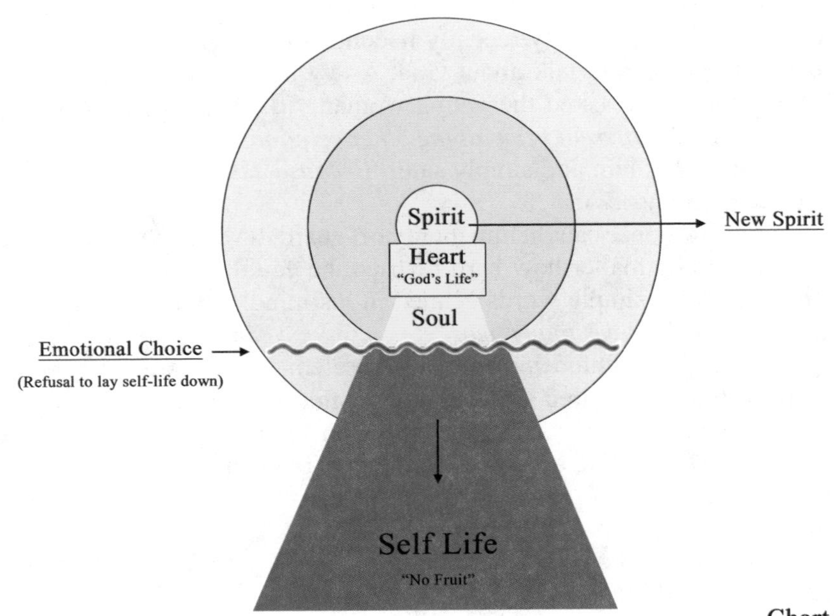

Chart 24

The Fruit of the Spirit Is Love

Of course, the ultimate "fruit" is *Agape*—God's Love. The whole Bible can be summed up in this one word (Mark 12:31). *Agape* Love is poured into our hearts the moment we invite Christ to take control of our lives, the moment our spirits are regenerated. God is that *Agape* Love. It is God Himself who comes into our hearts at that moment! "Everyone that loveth is born of God, and knoweth God. He that loveth not knoweth not God; for *God is Agape*" (1 John 4:7–8).

One of the greatest proofs that we are, indeed, partaking of Christ's Life is when we share God's *Agape* Love. "By this [*Agape*] shall *all* men know that you are My disciples" (John 13:35). *God's presence is shown forth in our lives by His Love, which is implemented and brought about by His power.*

This personal Love is what makes Christianity so totally different from all the other religions in the world. Christianity is the only religion where God, who is Love, comes to dwell within each of our hearts.

An Example: Ben Israel (Arthur Katz)

We would like to share a wonderful story about *Agape* Love and how it drew one hardened and obstinate man to the Lord.

Art Katz, author of *Ben Israel: The Odyssey of a Modern Jew*, was a brilliant Jewish philosopher and teacher at the University of California at Berkeley, who decided to go on his own quest to find God. He literally traveled all over the world, investigating every religion, in search of Him.

While riding on a train in Germany, he happened to sit next to a young Christian girl who had only recently become a believer (three or four days before). They began to talk about God. A few minutes into the discussion, Mr. Katz arrogantly asked the young woman, "*What makes you think that your Jesus is any different from all the other religions in the world?*" The girl lovingly looked at him and simply said: *"Because Jesus is God. He is Love, and He lives in my heart."*

This response caught him totally off guard. It was not one that Art had expected. And no matter how hard he tried, he could not refute her answer. For months those simple words echoed in his mind: *Because Jesus is God. He is Love and He lives in my heart.*

Finally Art found himself in Jerusalem, Israel. A Jewish believer befriended him and shared his testimony. After experiencing so much love and compassion from this Israeli, the Holy Spirit finally broke down the walls of Arthur's heart and he accepted Christ as his personal Messiah. The God of the Universe, who is *Agape* Love just as the young woman said, came to live in his heart.

We love this story because it shows that God *does* use "the foolish things of the world to confound the wise."

God's (*Agape*) Love

Agape represents something far greater than any of us can ever imagine. We often think of *Agape* as just another type of love. It is not! As Arthur Katz discovered, *Agape is God Himself.* Thus, it is something *totally opposite* to our own human, natural self-centered love.

Agape is an *unconditional, one-sided, and freeing Love,* in contrast to human love, which is a *conditional, two-sided* (meaning it has to be returned in order to be kept alive), *and bondage love. Agape* is part of the eternal Life that God gives us at our new birth, but this Love can only be passed on when we are clean, open, and sanctified. (That beam of light!)

The only way we are ever going to experience *Agape* Love, not only for ourselves, but also for others, is by experiencing a co-death with Christ and exchanging lives with Him (Ephesians 3:16–19). We give Him our lives—our fears, doubts, insecurities, etc.—at the Cross; then He gives us His Life—His Love, wisdom, and power.

Many Christians have trusted God for salvation, but they have failed to declare war on their flesh. As a result they have quenched God's pure Love in their hearts, which has caused them not only to be loveless toward others, but also unable to experience God's Love for themselves. He is still in their hearts, but when they continue to make emotional choices that allow fear, doubt, insecurities, and so forth, to consume them, they not only block God's Love from pouring forth through them to others, they also prevent God from personally showing them how much He loves them.

The Importance of Knowing God Loves Us

This brings up a critical point: the importance of *knowing first-hand that God loves us* with this same kind of unconditional, one-sided, and freeing *Agape* Love.

If we don't really know that God loves us, it will be very difficult for us to lay our lives down to Him and trust Him in our present trials and tribulations. We can't lay our lives down to someone, even if it is God, if we're not sure that person loves us. In order to truly embrace the message of *Agape*, we must personally know how much God loves us. Only *then* will we be able to totally relinquish our lives back to Him and trust Him not only with our present circumstances, but also with our future.

Life is the classroom; Love is the lesson. This is the bottom line. And, this is the missing ingredient in so many of our lives!

The essence of *Agape* Love is the giving of ourselves for another. Jesus did this for us and this is the example He has left for us to follow. "Greater love has no man but to lay his life down for his friend" (John 15:13). Love is not only essential for this life, it also seems to be the criteria for the future kingdom.

If you happen to be one of those people who does not really know that God loves you and who may also be fearful of what the future holds, the place you need to start is by asking God to show you His personal Love. *This is a prayer He delights in answering*.

(You might also want to see page 326, "Knowing God Loves Me" and page 328, "Who We Are in Christ" in the Supplemental Notes Section of this book. Additionally, you might also want to pick up the book *The Way of Agape*—Understanding God's Love.)

The Good Samaritan (Luke 10:25–37) *(See picture)*

Let's examine a biblical example of how God desires us to love.

Jesus told the story of a lawyer who asked Him, "What shall I do to inherit eternal life?"

Jesus answered, "What does the law say?"

The lawyer responded, "*Love the Lord thy God with all thy heart, and with all thy soul, and with all thy strength, and with all thy mind, and thy neighbor as thyself*." (Note the order here: We must love God first; then we'll be able to love others.)

Jesus said to the lawyer, "You have answered correctly. Do this and you will live."

But the lawyer, trying to justify himself, asked Jesus, "*Who is my neighbor?*"

Whereupon Jesus answered him with this story:

> A certain man went down to Jericho. On the way some thieves caught him, stripped him of his clothes, wounded him, and left him half dead. (The road from Jerusalem to Jericho where this might have taken place passes through twenty miles of very rugged and rocky terrain that is perfect for a bandit's hideout.)
>
> First a priest came by. He saw the wounded man, but he chose to pass by on the other side of the road. Then a Levite came by, looked at him, but again chose to pass him by. Both of these men shrank from trouble, the time and the expense of helping a stranger.
>
> Finally a certain Samaritan came by and when he saw the man in trouble, he had compassion on him. Samaritans had no dealings with the Jews at that time. They were almost enemies (John 4:9). That's what makes this story so touching. This Samaritan chose to stay by the wounded man and do what he could to help, regardless of what this would do to his reputation, his family, and his business. He bound the man's wounds, poured oil and wine over him, put him on his

donkey, brought him to the nearest inn, and took care of him. The next day he paid the innkeeper what he owed, told him to continue to take care of him and that he would return and pay any further costs.

The good Samaritan did what Jesus would have done.

THE STORY OF THE GOOD SAMARITAN

Comments on the Good Samaritan Parable

This Samaritan inconvenienced himself to take care of this injured man and provide lodging for him. He unconditionally chose to take care of not only a stranger, but also someone who was an enemy. And he did it without the hope of recompense, without thinking of his reputation, and without a thought as to what it would cost him in time and effort. He chose to do it because it was the right thing to do.

This is the way God desires us to love one another. This is the fruit of the Spirit that God delights in and an example of the "fruit of righteousness" that God will reward at the Judgment Seat.

This story also answered the lawyer's question, "Who is my neighbor?" Our neighbor is anyone who needs help and whom we have the power and opportunity to help, no matter what race, what income, or what religion (Galatians 6:10).

Keep in mind, however, that God's *Agape* Love has two sides to it. It's not only a long-suffering Love, it's also a tough or a disciplining Love. In other words, we don't become doormats when we love with God's Love. On the contrary, God's wisdom will show us which type of Love to use in our particular situation and then God's power will implement that Love in our lives.

Loving Our Neighbor

"Loving our neighbor" as the good Samaritan did, however, cannot be done in the flesh. See Charts 23 and 24 again. Genuinely loving our neighbor can only be done through the Spirit and with the pure motive of giving glory to God. This story of the good Samaritan is just as applicable today as it was in Jesus' time. And it begs the same questions: *Where are the good Samaritans today? Where are the Christians who are laying their lives down for their neighbors? And where are the living examples of Jesus' Love?*

What we see and hear in our ministries, unfortunately, are just the opposite of the good Samaritan story. Here are a couple of shocking examples:

We recently received a letter from a young woman who said she was desperately searching for real love. Her letter said: "*I have searched and searched for someone to show me genuine love and I haven't found it anywhere.*" Then she said something absolutely shocking: *"I grew up in the church. In fact, my family are the pastors!"*

She grew up in the church! And her parents are the pastors! Yet she has *never* experienced real love. This is outrageous! What a commentary on Christianity today. This is the daughter of Christian pastors who has never experienced real love. This should hit a chord with all of us.

How about our children, would they say the same thing about us?

Here's another example: a woman we know, whose marriage was totally falling apart, called her pastor in desperation for counseling and was told: *"I'm sorry, but I don't have time to counsel you. Besides, it makes me think poorly of my parishioners."*

What on earth is church for, if not to help with the sick, the wounded, and the hurt?

Agape Is Growing Cold

Where are the good Samaritans today? Matthew 24:12 gives us the answer. It says that in the end-times "the *Agape* Love of many will grow cold." *And, yes, this Scripture is talking about Christians*. Matthew told us that *the Agape Love of many will grow cold because it will be quenched by our carnality and our self-centered ways.*

This is certainly true with the family of the young woman and the pastor who was too busy to counsel her. The "*Agape* Love of many *has* grown cold" and many believers are not producing the fruit that God desires. This is because they are not partaking of Christ's Life.

Christ told us we are to love others *as He loved us* (John 15:12–14). How did He love us? *He laid down His Life for us*. Our goal should be to do the same for others (John 13:35). We do this by denying ourselves and exchanging lives with Him (Matthew 16:24).

The "fruit of the Spirit" means God's *Agape* Love. If there is *Agape Love*, then *all* the fruit of the Spirit will be included. "The fruit of the Spirit is Love, joy, peace, longsuffering, gentleness, goodness, faith, meekness, [and] temperance. Against such there is no law" (Galatians 5:22–23). 1 Corinthians 13:1–8 adds specifics to Love's characteristics.

The only way we can ever pass along this kind of fruit, however, is if we are cleansed and sanctified vessels, which allows us to exchange lives with Christ. These believers can have confidence on judgment day because God's Love has been made perfect and complete in them (1 John 4:17).

Loving God

God gave us two great commandments and He gave them to us in a very important order. *First* we are to learn to love Him, *then* we are to learn to love our neighbors. If we don't learn to love Him first, we won't be able to love others at all. Many of us have tried to do it the other way around. And as we have quickly found out, it hasn't worked.

What does loving God really mean? Is it just an emotional type of love?

According to the Bible, loving God means *totally surrendering ourselves to Him*. It's exchanging lives with Him. We are to "Love the Lord [our] God *with all [our] heart* and *with all [our] soul* and *with all [our] mind"* (Matthew 22:37). The Greek word for the verb *love* in this Scripture is *agapao,* which means "to totally give ourselves over to something."

Agapao is not just an emotional feeling but what we surrender our lives to or what we relinquish ourselves to. It's what we put first in our lives. It's a total commitment of ourselves to something. Loving God means recognizing our choices, dealing with our sin and self, and becoming open and cleansed vessels so *He* can then love others through us. Loving God simply means becoming sanctified so we *can* partake of His Life—His Love.

Agapao is *not* a "feeling" kind of love, but a complete surrendering of ourselves. It's that to which we continually submit our wills and our lives.

Loving God means no longer living for ourselves. Loving Him is a demonstration of complete selflessness. In other words, *we live for the godly edification of others rather than for ourselves*—as the good Samaritan did. Our motive in doing acts of kindness is *not* to earn God's approval, but simply because we love Him and want to please Him.[7] Consequently, we must continually set aside our own plans, our own agendas, and our own ambitions, and out of love seek His will.

Keep in mind that the Greek verb *agapao* can also have a negative connotation. In other words, we can *agapao*—totally give ourselves over to—bad things like "darkness" (John 3:19); "the praise of men" (John 12:43); "this present world,"[8] as well as "good things like loving God and others." So don't confuse the verb *agapao* with the noun *Agape*, because they mean totally different things. *Agapao* is what we totally commit ourselves to and what we surrender our lives to, which can be good or bad. Whereas *Agape* is the supernatural, one-sided, other-centered, and unconditional Love of God. *Agape* never has a negative usage, so do not confuse the noun *Agape* (God's Love) with the verb *agapao* (what we give ourselves over to).

The Bible gives incredible promises to those who love God. For example, "Hearken My beloved brethren, Hath not God chosen the poor of this world [the humble, the receptive and the yielded] to be rich in faith, *to be heirs of the kingdom which He hath promised to them that love Him*" (James 2:5). *If* we love God—*if* we totally give ourselves over to Him—then He will make us *heirs of His kingdom*. This is that "inheritance *from the Lord"* that we talked about in chapter three. It's a conditional type of inheritance. *If* we love Him, then He will give us an inheritance in the coming kingdom.

(If you are interested in learning more about loving God and loving others, we recommend the book *The Way of Agape.*)

The Greatest Commandment of All

Loving God and loving others is God's supreme will (Mark 12:30–31). *The Bible is summed up in these two verses*:

> "Thou shalt *love* the Lord thy God with all thy heart, and with all thy soul, and with all thy mind, and with all thy strength; this is the first commandment. And the second is

this: Thou shalt love thy neighbor as thyself. *There is no other commandment greater than these."*

—Deuteronomy 6:4–5; Leviticus 19:18

Learning to love God and learning to love others is the sum and substance of God's will. These two commandments summarize the sanctification process in a nutshell. People who actually *live* and *keep* these two commandments, will be the ones who will inherit the kingdom.

Some Christians protest that it is wrong to be motivated by the reward of inheritance in the future kingdom. They believe we should be motivated only by our love for God. We agree wholeheartedly. The truth is we will be eligible for the reward of inheritance by loving God and by totally giving ourselves over to Him.[9] By doing this, we *will* produce the fruit that will allow us to inherit the kingdom and gain rewards. Either way—as a motive or a by-product—we'll end up being the partakers of Christ's Life and the overcomers whom God is looking for.

Here are some of the questions Christ might ask us about His Love at the Bema Seat:

"I gave you My Love at your new birth, what did you do with it?"

"Did you love Me?"

"Did you love others as I told you to do?"

"Did you multiply My Love or did you bury it as the unprofitable servant did?"

"Was I your life? Or was I just your crutch?"

The deadness in today's churches has two causes: 1) a lack of God's *Agape* Love and 2) the absence of God's power working in and through Christians' lives. These two are linked. *We have no Love because we have no power*. Many Christians are following the truth only with their minds, not with their hearts or with their lives. And the sobering part of all of this is that we will be judged at the Bema Seat of Christ, not for justification but for not exhibiting His Love in our lives by His power (sanctification).

Sheep and Goat Judgment (Matthew 25:32–46)

Loving God and loving others is going to be the criteria that God will use for the Sheep and Goat Judgment at the beginning of the Millennium.

Jesus described what His second coming will be like when He returns with all His glory and the angels with Him (Matthew 25:31). He will then sit upon His Throne and all the Gentile nations of the world will be gathered before Him.

He will then proceed to separate the sheep from the goats as a shepherd divides his herd. He will put the sheep on His right hand and the goats on His left. He will then say to the sheep, "Come, blessed of My Father, *inherit the kingdom* prepared for you from the foundation of the world. *For I was hungry, and ye gave Me food; I was thirsty, and ye gave Me drink; I was a stranger, and ye took Me in; naked, and ye clothed Me; I was sick, and ye visited Me; I was in prison, and ye came unto Me.*" (verses 34-36).

Jesus was talking to the Tribulation saints who helped, shielded, and protected the Jews (Christ's brethren) during their most difficult times. These Gentiles gave the Jews special treatment during the Tribulation. Notice how God defined *loving one's neighbor:* giving them food, drink, housing, clothes, visiting them when they were sick or in prison, and so forth. He was saying that actions speak louder than words.

Then the sheep will say to Him, "Lord, *when* did we see You hungry and fed You; or thirsty and gave You a drink? *When* did we see You a stranger and took You in; or naked and clothed You? Or saw You sick or in prison and came to You?" (verses 37–39).

The King will answer and say unto them, "*Verily I say unto you inasmuch as ye have done it unto one of the least of these My brethren, ye have done it unto Me*" (verse 40).

Jesus is saying to these sheep, because you loved [gave yourself over to] these My brethren [you will] "inherit the kingdom."

But to the goats Jesus will say, "Depart from Me" (verse 41).

Loving God and loving others is of the utmost importance to God.

In Conclusion

Believers in Christ really have two lives: One is called our *self-life,* which is our soulish life and is made up of our natural thoughts, emotions, and desires that are usually contrary to God's Life. (The life we had *before* becoming believers.) The other life we enjoy as believers is called *God's Life,* which is made up of His supernatural Love, wisdom, and power. (The Life we received *after* we were born again.)

In order for God's Life to come forth from our hearts, we must continually choose to put off our sin and self. In other words, we must choose to stay clean and sanctified. In chapter twelve we will address exactly how we do this in a practical way. Putting off our sin and self on a daily basis is how we become *partakers* of Christ's Life, not just *recipients* of His Life. God's Life is always in our hearts if we are born again, but it's our choice whether or not we share it.

The purpose of being a partaker of Christ's Life is to produce fruit. The ultimate fruit is God's Love. When we make choices to exchange lives with Christ, we will experience His Love; when we don't, His Love will grow cold in our hearts (Matthew 24:12). This, of course, will affect our place, our position, and our status in the coming kingdom.

Therefore, the Bible can be summed up in three words: *Learn to love.*

Chapter Nine

God's *Dunamis* Power

All Christians are eternally secure and will be involved in the Rapture and *entering* the Millennial Kingdom. However, only those Christians who are deemed *worthy, fit,* and *qualified* at the Bema Seat Judgment will be able to *inherit* that kingdom. These will be the overcomers whose works will withstand the test of fire. The deciding factors will be: Were they partakers *of* Christ's Life? What was the *source* of their works? Were these works done by the power of the Holy Spirit or were they done in the flesh?

In chapter eight we talked about God's eternal Life and the importance of exchanging lives with Him, which means we give Him our hurts, our anger, our insecurities, our resentments, our doubts, our guilt, and so forth; and in exchange, He gives us His Life, His Love, wisdom, and power.

God's supernatural power is a part of that Life; it enables us to be sanctified, to become partakers of Christ's Life, and empowers us to overcome the world, the flesh, and the devil.

Let's delve into *the empowering aspect* of God's Life. What it is, how we get it, and how we must learn to depend upon it.

God Is the Source of All Power

Scripture tells us that God upholds *all* things by the Word of His power (Hebrews 1:3). Just think about what this is really saying. God sustains everything in the universe by His Hand of power. In other words, all He has to do is speak His will and His power will then accomplish it (Psalm 33:9). For example, He formed the mountains by His power. He divided the seas by His power. He divided the light from the darkness by His power (Genesis 1:4). He created man by His power (Genesis 1:26). And He will quicken the dead and call them to life by His power (Romans 4:17).

The source of *all* power, therefore, is God.[1] It is *His* saving power, *His* pardoning power (Matthew 9:6), *His* infinite power (Matthew 28:18), *His* power over nature (Luke 8:24), and *His* life-giving power (John 17:2; John 10:10). "For there is no power but of God" (Romans 13:1).

The term "Lord of Hosts" in the Bible means *Lord of Power* (2 Samuel 6:2; Psalm 89:8). He is the One who removes rulers from their positions, and

He is the One who places rulers in positions of power. In other words, He is the One who controls our lives and our destinies by His power.

God is unequaled in power (Jude 25). He has no rivals.

It is amazing that if we believe in Him, He promises to instill a small portion of that same immense power in our hearts (Deuteronomy 8:18). And through that power, He will give us the ability to execute the impossible.[2] Remember Abraham and Sarah? God promised them a son (Genesis 17:16–19). According to the laws of nature, it was impossible for them to conceive. Yet the Lord said to them, "Is anything too hard for Me? At the time appointed I will return unto thee and Sarah shall have a son" (Genesis 18:14). Something totally impossible was about to be made possible by the power of God (Luke 1:37). And of course, Sarah ended up conceiving and bringing forth a son who would play a major role in God's plan for mankind.

Scripturally there are hundreds of examples of God's power in action. We immediately think of His mighty acts such as the parting of the Red Sea (Exodus 14:21–23), the giving of the Ten Commandments on Mt. Sinai (Exodus 19:16–18), and the ten plagues of Egypt.[3] These are fabulous examples of God's power that shapes and fashions history. This type of divine power is true all the way through the Scriptures and it's true in our lives as well. Christianity is simply the manifestation of divine power in the presence of human weakness.

What Is God's Supernatural Power?

What exactly is God's supernatural power and how does it manifest itself in our lives? God's power is demonstrated in many different ways, but the following are two of the most important.

1. God's divine power was manifested in the Old Testament by miraculous deeds. A special and sometimes temporary anointing often accompanied these miracles, for example, as with Moses, Sampson, Elijah, Elisha, and so on. Today we read about the incredible outpouring of the Spirit and the miracles happening in China, Africa, and other countries. But as great as these supernatural gifts may be, these believers still may not be the overcomers the Bible talks about who go on to inherit the kingdom in the Millennium. (Remember Moses.)

2. The second aspect of God's divine power is called "*the power of Christ's resurrection*": "That I may know Him and the power of His resurrection and the fellowship of His sufferings, being made conformable unto His death" (Philippians 3:10). This power is given to every believer by the Holy Spirit at his new birth—it is part of the Life of God that He has instilled and sealed in our hearts. Consequently, this supernatural power resides in *every* Christian, but it requires a submitted and sanctified life in order to partake of it. Just like God's Love; it can be quenched and blocked by emotional choices.

This second type of divine power—God's resurrection power—is what we want to focus our attention on in this book. Because only those believers who rely upon the resurrection power of Christ to produce works of righteousness will be allowed to inherit the kingdom. It's *His* power, but as we learn to be sanctified, we too, can partake of it.

Paul prayed for the saints at Ephesus to know this kind of resurrection power: "That the eyes of your understanding [may] be enlightened; that ye may know [1] what is the hope of His calling, and [2] what the riches of the glory of His inheritance in the saints, and [3] *what is the exceeding greatness of His power towards us who believe"* (Ephesians 1:18–19).

The "hope of His calling" (our inheritance in Christ) and "the riches of His inheritance" (our future blessings in the kingdom) are linked here with the "exceeding greatness of His power." The first two promises in this Scripture cannot become a reality in our lives, however, without the third promise of the "exceeding greatness of His power."

God's challenge to all of us is that we must learn to partake of, rely upon, and be controlled by the exceeding greatness of His power. And, by so doing, we'll not only apprehend the hope of His calling, but also the riches of His future inheritance.

What Is the Purpose of God's Supernatural Power?

The purpose of God's power in our lives is to come alongside us and help us learn three things: 1) *how to be sanctified*, 2) *how to partake of Christ's Life*, and 3) h*ow to become those overcomers* (faithful ones) who bear righteous fruit. As we said earlier, *sanctification* leads to partaking, *partaking* to overcoming, and *overcoming* to *inheriting*. God's resurrection power accomplishes all three. His power not only gives us a *new spirit* when we are born again, but His power also produces a *transformed life* through the sanctification process (1 Peter 1:5).

God not only teaches us *how to live* through His Word, He also gives us the *power to live* through His Spirit. "For this cause I bow my knees unto the Father of our Lord Jesus Christ, of whom the whole family in heaven and earth is named, that He would grant you, according to the riches of His glory, *to be strengthened with might by His spirit in the inner man"* (Ephesians 3:14–16).

What good is knowing God's will, if we don't have the power to perform it? *His power enables us to do what His Word demands.*

The Holy Spirit is the enabler, the executor, and the implementor of God's will being accomplished in our lives. Our responsibility is simply to make the choice to let Him do so! It's really *a partnership*. *We* offer our bodies as a "living sacrifice," *God* then fills us with His Spirit and accomplishes His will through us (Romans 12:1–2).

> "Blessed be the God and Father of our Lord Jesus Christ, which, according to His abundant mercy, hath begotten us

> again unto a living hope by the resurrection of Jesus Christ from the dead, to an inheritance incorruptible, and undefiled, and that fadeth not away, reserved in heaven for you, *who are kept by the power of God through faith unto salvation ready to be revealed in the last time."*
>
> —1 Peter 1:3–5

Christ not only came to save us, but also to reveal His Life in us. He has given us the Holy Spirit of Power to do just that. God's purpose is that we might first personally experience His imparted Life and then pass it along to others (2 Corinthians 4:7–12). This transcendent resurrection power belongs to God, not us. "For God, who commanded the light to shine out of darkness, hath shone in our hearts, to give the light of the knowledge of the glory of God in the face of Jesus Christ. But we have this "treasure" in earthen vessels, *that the excellency of the power may be of God, and not of us*" (2 Corinthians 4:6–7).

The people who depend upon this power, partake of it, share it, and allow it to produce fruit are the people who not only will be able to *enter into* the Millennial Kingdom, but also to *rule and reign* there.

Our Example Is Christ

Christ is the perfect example of the manifestation of God's power. He lived His entire life depending upon this power.[4] The Holy Spirit empowered Him to do all His miraculous acts and, of course, the Resurrection was the supreme manifestation of that power (Acts 2:24). The purpose of Christ's incarnation was to nullify the power of the devil and to free those held in bondage (Hebrews 2:14).

The Lord first passed along this resurrection power to His disciples in order that they might accomplish the work He called them to do. "He called His twelve disciples together and gave them power and authority over all devils and to cure diseases . . . Behold, I give unto you power to tread on serpents and scorpions, and over all the power of the enemy: and nothing shall by any means hurt you" (Luke 9:1; 10:19). The power the disciples received is called "the resurrection power of Christ."

Christ then passed this same life-giving power on to us. This endowment took place at Pentecost when the Holy Spirit came upon thousands of believers and bestowed upon them a new and divine power (Acts 2:1–4).

God Equips Believers with His Power

Personal union with Christ gives believers this same divine power (Hebrews 6:5). "According as *His divine Power* hath given unto us *all things that pertain unto life and godliness*, through the knowledge of Him that hath called us to glory and virtue" (2 Peter 1:3). He imparts His resurrection power to each of us the moment we believe so that we, too, can *overcome* the enemy, proclaim the message of the gospel, and persevere to the end.

This saving power will also *deliver* us from the power of sin, from the draw of the world, and from demonic attacks.[5] It will protect us, preserve us, guard us, and keep us from falling.[6] "God strengthens our soul with His strength"[7] (Psalm 138:3). Our responsibility is to learn to walk by His Spirit of power, not our flesh. A true disciple can only minister in the power of the Spirit, just as Jesus did (Luke 4:14). The Spirit must always be the power source of our lives, or everything we do will end up being "wood, hay, and stubble" (Acts 1:8).

Jesus is the perfect example of an overcomer. Everything He did, He accomplished by depending upon the Spirit of God in Him. We, too, can learn to become overcomers by yielding to the same supernatural power that sustained Christ. The outworking of that power—the fruit that is produced—is the hallmark of a true disciple.

An Example: Christine

Here's a wonderful example. On one of our trips to Israel, a woman named Christine was a powerful example of an overcomer. Not only did the other people on the trip acknowledge her life as totally supernatural, but many of them yearned to have just a small portion of the empowering that she possessed.

Christine suffers from a debilitating disease that has stunted her growth. It's a form of juvenile osteoporosis where the skeletal bones are unable to sustain weight. They constantly fracture and break. Christine was very small—about three feet tall—and permanently confined to a wheelchair. But, that didn't seem to matter to her. This incredible woman had been married for twenty-five years. She had been a missionary in India and won several scholarships for her artwork, including one to the Louvre in Paris. She scuba dives, para-sails, and is a gymnast who works out daily on the trampoline. No self-pity here. Just pressing on to be all God wants her to be!

When you talk to Christine, the light of Jesus absolutely exudes from her face, the joy of the Lord radiates from her eyes, and her enthusiasm about everything is contagious. She truly is a living example of Christ and His empowering. Others are not only drawn to her, they also want what she has. Here is a beautiful woman who not only has been born of the Spirit, but who is also depending upon God's power for everything. Metaphorically speaking, she is "walking in the Spirit."

A disciple is not just someone who has been born again (justified), but someone who is a participant, a partaker, and a sharer of God's resurrection power (1 Corinthians 9:12).

The Ministry of God's Supernatural Power

Let's briefly review the ministry of God's divine power. How does God's supernatural power work in a believer?

Before we become believers, God's Spirit of power works *with us* (*para*), leading and drawing us to Himself (Acts 19:2). We can all remember how God wooed, courted, and pursued us.

See *Chart 25: Indwelling of the Holy Spirit*

In response to our personal invitation, God's Spirit of power comes *in us* (*en*) and indwells us. At this time, He unites our spirit with His and gives us a brand-new spirit and heart.[8] This is called "the new birth" or being "born again" or "justification." This is the time when Christ implants His eternal Life—His Love, His wisdom, and His power—in our spirit and heart, and we become the temple of the Holy Spirit.

Chart 25 is what this might look like.

Indwelling of the Spirit

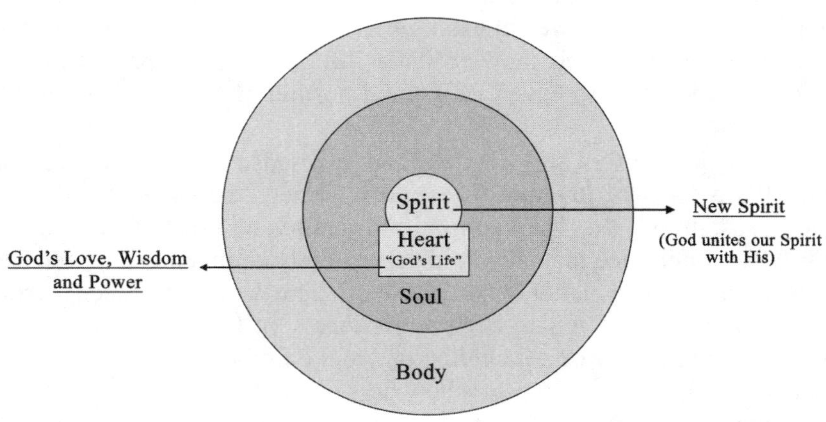

Spirit Comes *In Us*

(The New Birth)

Chart 25

See *Chart 26: Empowering of the Holy Spirit*

This is also the time that the Spirit is supposed to come *upon us* (*epi*) for the sake of empowering.

This is called the *"baptism of the Spirit"* or the initial infilling of the Spirit (Acts 1:8). Jesus told His disciples: "And behold, I send the promise of My Father upon you. But tarry in the city of Jerusalem until ye *be endued with power* from on high" (Luke 24:49. See also Matthew 3:11; Acts 1:5). The baptism of the Spirit is God breaking through the soulish and physical realm. It's the *beginning* of our "outer man" (our soul) being subjected to our "spirit man" (our spirit). It's God's power to become a genuine witness of Christ, not just in our words, but also in our lives.

Chart 26 is what this might look like.

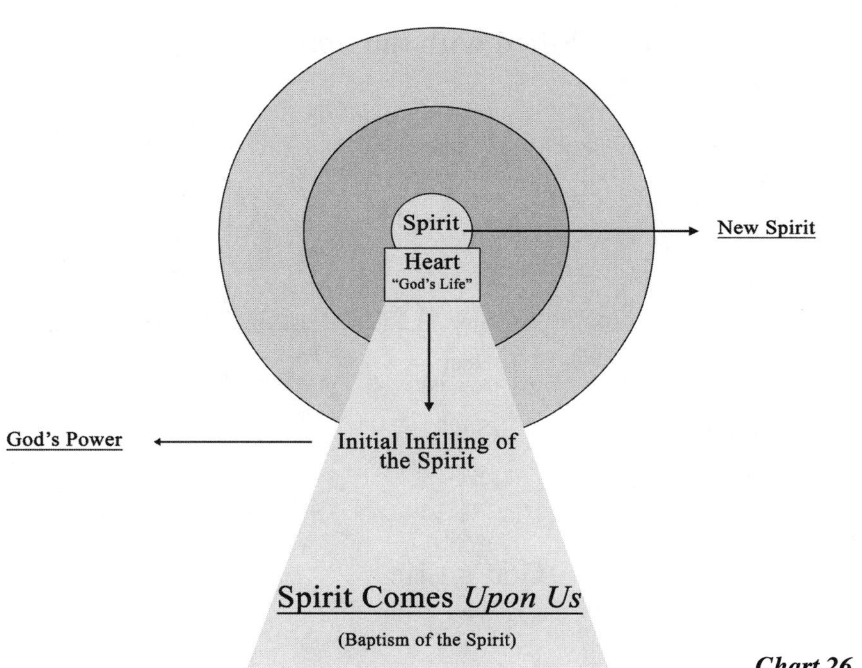

Chart 26

Without this initial empowering, however, we will be just like believers who have a "form of godliness," but who "deny the power within" (2 Timothy 3:5). In other words, they know the Scriptures in their heads, but they don't allow the power of God to come forth and transform their lives.

(The *indwelling* and the *empowering* of the Holy Spirit should happen at the very same time. But for many of us, because we didn't know enough to ask for the empowering, they occurred on two separate occasions, many years apart.)

See *Chart 27: Refilled with the Holy Spirit*

After we have been indwelt and empowered by God's resurrection power, we must daily be *refilled* (*pleroo*) with His Spirit of power from the inside out. "Wherefore be ye not unwise, but understanding what the will of the Lord is, and be not drunk with wine, wherein is excess; but *be filled with the Spirit"* (Ephesians 5:17–18). The verb *be filled* here means "to be *continually* filled and empowered, not allowing the Spirit to be quenched." This step differs from the first two steps in that it's now *our* responsibility (*our* choice) to stay cleansed and sanctified, so we *can* be refilled and empowered. This does not happen automatically. It is God's will, but it is our choice whether or not we do it.

Chart 27 is what it might look like.

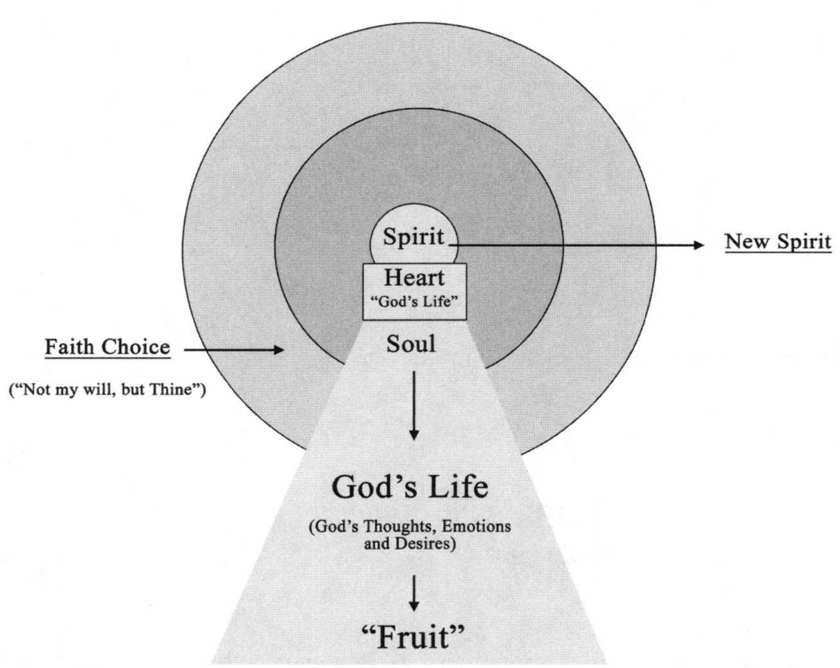

Chart 27

This last step is the beginning of the process called sanctification. "Having, therefore, these promises, dearly beloved, let us *cleanse ourselves* from all filthiness of the flesh and spirit, perfecting holiness in the fear of God" (2 Corinthians 7:1). *Our* job is to make the right faith choices. God is the One who empowers us to accomplish His will.

Consequently, it's imperative that we *not* stop at the first step of salvation—our justification—but that we go on to the next phase, which is our sanctification. "If we *live* in the Spirit [if we are born-again], [we must learn to] also *walk* in the Spirit" (Galatians 5:25. See also Ephesians 5:18). It's the Spirit of Christ's resurrection power that not only renews our minds and transforms our lives, but also enables us to walk by His Spirit.

The Spirit brings us to Christ and gives us His Life, then He empowers us to reflect Him in all we do. Our job, then, is to stay cleansed and filled so we can be empowered.

> "But we have this treasure in earthen vessels, that *the excellency of the power may be of God*, and not of us. We are troubled on every side, yet not distressed; we are perplexed, but not in despair; Persecuted, but not forsaken, cast down, but not destroyed; *Always bearing about in the body the dying of the Lord Jesus, [so] that the Life also of Jesus might be made manifest in our body.*"

—2 Corinthians 4:7–10

The excellency of the power *must* be of God and not ourselves.

God promises us that in the end, He will raise us up by this same power as He did Christ. "God hath both raised up the Lord, and *will also* raise up us by His own power" (1 Corinthians 6:14. See also Romans 8:11).

The Three Functions of God's Supernatural Power

There are three aspects or functions to God's supernatural power. In the Greek these three functions are: 1) God's *dunamis* power, which we receive in our spirits when we are born again and that strengthens us spiritually, 2) His *kratos* might, which operates in our souls and strengthens us emotionally, and 3) His *ischus* strength which operates in our bodies and strengthens us physically. These three functions are very important for us to understand because as you will see in a moment, *they make up the process by which God's resurrection power works in each of our lives.*

The Greeks were very precise with their language. They had a specific word to describe every facet of living. English, on the other hand, can be quite sloppy and general with its use of words. For example, we say, "I love my husband / wife." Then we use the very same word to describe our fondness for desserts and for fast cars. The Greek language, however, is much more specific. It has a special word to describe each of the aspects of God's power. Once you understand the intended meaning of these words, it will help explain the value of God's spiritual, emotional, and physical power in your life.

There are several Scriptures that mention all three of these aspects of God's power—His spiritual, emotional, and physical power—in the same verse:

> "...that ye may know what is the hope of His calling, and what the riches of the glory of His inheritance in the saints, and what is the exceeding greatness of *His power* [*dunamis*] towards us who believe, according to the working of His *mighty* [*kratos*] *power* [*ischus*]."

—Ephesians 1:18–19

> "Be *strong* [*endunamoo*] in the Lord and in the *power* [*kratos*] of His *might* [*ischus*] so that you can stand against the wiles of the enemy."
>
> —Ephesians 6:10–11

> "Being strengthened [*dunamoo*] with all power [*dunamis*] according to His glorious power [*kratos*] unto all patience and joyfully giving thanks to the Father."
>
> —Colossians 1:11

All three of these words represent some part, some function, or some aspect of God's resurrection power. They are not the same thing at all. Together they make up the process by which God's power works in each of our lives. *However, if we don't personally understand this process, it will be very easy to quench God's Spirit in one of these areas and block His Life from coming forth.*

Let's explore each of these Greek words and try to understand their exact functions.

1. God's *Dunamis* Power (*Strong's* #1411) (in our spirit and heart)

We'll start with God's *dunamis* power. In the English language, *dunamis* means "divine ability" or "divine empowerment." It is a source of dependable and continuous power. It is *inherent power*—meaning power that belongs to the essential nature of something. *Dunamis* almost always points to a new and higher force that has entered and is now working through us.

Dunamis means having the capacity to carry something out—the strength to implement an idea or to take a thought and make it an action.

The watchword for *dunamis* is "Spirit *Source*" (or the origin of divine power).

When we become born again, we receive God's *dunamis* power in our spirits. This power cannot be released in our lives, however, until our own spirits and hearts are cleansed (Psalm 51:10). In other words, God doesn't give supernatural power to the "old man," but only to the "new one." One of the reasons we lack power in the Christian body is because we have quenched God's Spirit in our hearts. Rather than cleanse ourselves, we often choose to follow our own self-centered ways and end up not only blocking God's Love, but also His resurrection power.

God's resurrection power can only grow stronger in us when our "outer man" (our soulish man—our own self-centered thoughts, emotions, and desires) is totally submitted and yielded to God. Even though we receive God's power in our spirit at our new birth, *we'll be unable to use it until we learn to relinquish and surrender ourselves daily.*

An Example: Tortured for Christ

Richard Wurmbrand, a Romanian pastor who spent fourteen years in a Communist prison, is an incredible example of total relinquishment.

Pastor Wurmbrand was involved in the Christian Romanian underground movement. He met with groups of Christians in homes, basements, army barracks, and in woods, knowing full well what the cost of his actions could be. The Communists were determined to stamp out the Christians so that they could control the churches for their own purposes. Eventually the pastor and his Christian brothers and sisters were exposed and captured.

Taken from his wife and son in 1948, Pastor Wurmbrand spent three years in slave labor, three years in solitary confinement, and five more years in a mass cell. He was finally released after many years, only to be arrested two years later and sentenced to twenty-five more years. He was released for good in 1964. His wife was confined to another prison where the women were repeatedly raped, made to work at hard labor, forced to eat grass, rats and snakes, and required to stand alone for hours at a time. At the time of their arrest, their son was only nine years old. He was left to roam the streets of their city.

Many of the Christians who were arrested at the same time lost their faith as they were brainwashed by the Communists. Some even joined the party and denounced their brothers and sisters. It was a tragic and horrendous time. The human torture was beyond anything one could ever imagine or describe. One prisoner said, "All the biblical descriptions of hell and the pain of *Dante's Inferno* are nothing compared with the torture in the Communist prisons."

Loving God with his whole being, Pastor Wurmbrand would not let any circumstance or any emotion separate him from his Beloved. Someone asked him, "How did you resist the brainwashing?"

The pastor replied, "If your heart is truly cleansed by the Love of Christ and your heart loves Him back, you can resist any torture . . . *God will judge us, not on how much we had to endure, but on how much we loved.*"

Wurmbrand said he was not frustrated by all the years that he lost in prison because he also saw beautiful things happen there. He saw great saints and heroes of all kinds, much like the first-century church. "Christians could be happy even there," he said. The reason they could be happy was that they "saw the Savior in the midst of everything."[9] This exemplifies Isaiah 24:15: "Wherefore glorify ye the Lord in the fires."

The lesson is that if the Spirit is truly the *master* of the body, then God's power is always with us, no matter what is occurring in our lives. The enemy, of course, wants to kill, steal, and destroy our faith by the things that happen in our lives. But as we saw in the above example, God wants to use our circumstances, no matter how difficult, for His glory. That is only possible through His supernatural empowering.

After his release from prison, Wurmbrand wrote numerous books and became the head of an international ministry called *the Voice of the Martyrs*, which serves the persecuted church.

Once we allow the sanctifying process to go unheeded, just like Pastor Wurmbrand, we can draw near to God and rely upon His *dunamis* power, regardless of the trials that surround us.

We are endowed with God's *dunamis* power—His divine empowerment—when we are born again. It becomes the source of God's power in us. It's the higher force that has entered us and is now working through us.

2. God's *Kratos* Might (*Strong's* #2904) (in our soul)

The second aspect or function of God's resurrection power is called *kratos* in the Greek and is absolutely fascinating.

Kratos means "mastery over self, self-control or power to rein in" (like the reins of a horse). God not only has given us His *dunamis* power—His divine ability—to do "the impossible," He has also given us the ability to rein in our self-life so that He can freely work in and through us. *Kratos* comes from the Greek word *katria,* which literally means "to rein in." God's *kratos* power reins in our self-life (soulish life) and brings it into captivity so that God's Life (from our hearts) can come forth. "In your patience *rein in your souls*" (Luke 21:19). In other words, keep your souls under control so that God's Life can come forth. Reins are often associated with our minds and with our choices. Scripture tells us we have a constant decision as to what we will choose: either "reins or cords of Love" that are held by the Lord *or* "reins or cords of sin" that are held by our flesh and even sometimes the enemy.[10]

The watchword for *kratos* is Spirit-*control.*

Kratos means God's supernatural might to take what He has told us in His Word and then implement it in our lives, no matter how we feel, what we think, or what we want. When we make the faith choice to do His will, God's "*kratos* might" will rein in our self-life and accomplish that will in our lives regardless of everything else (Romans 6:12–14). *Kratos* is power to "put off" our sin and self, and then power to "put on" Christ.

Kratos is often associated with the Greek word *exousia,* which means "authority." God gives us the authority (*exousia*) not only to choose His will, but also His power (*kratos*) to perform that will! What good is it to know God's will if we don't have the strength or the power to carry it out? "For it is God which worketh in you both *to will* and *to do* of His good pleasure" (Philippians 2:13). This is saying that when we choose by faith to do God's will; He will enable us to accomplish it, regardless of what we think or how we feel. In other words, He gives us His supernatural *kratos* might to "rein in our souls" and to act out of His Life—His Love and His wisdom.

Do you remember the parable of the ten virgins in chapter six? Remember that five of the virgins were wise because they took oil. The word *wise* in this Scripture is the Greek word *phromeros* (Strong's 5429), which literally means "single-minded," meaning only one life is being lived. *Phromeros* is from the Greek root word *phren,* which means *"to rein in or curb the emotions*." These five virgins were wise because they allowed the *kratos* power of God to rein in their self-life. The other five virgins were "double-minded" because they had quenched God's Life in their hearts and thus, self-life was showing forth in their souls.

Kratos basically means "Spirit-control." It's the power to rein in our emotions, knowing that in God's timing and way, He will align our feelings to match the "faith choices" we have made. God not only gives us the emotional strength to say "not my will, but Thine," He also aligns our feelings with the choices we have made. Simply put, He makes us genuine.

If we are a cleansed vessel, the *kratos* power of God can overcome whatever our flesh desires and instead, enable us to do what God wants.

God has not only given us the authority to choose His will, He has also given us the power to do His will!

Kratos Means "To Overcome"

One of the definitions of the word *power* in the Old Testament is "to overcome." It's the Hebrew word *gibbor* (*Strong's* #1368), which speaks of David's "mighty men," who were "mighty men of valor." Regardless of how they really felt or what they wanted, they were willing to *choose God's will* and then willing to *trust God* to perform that will in their lives.[11] These mighty men were, indeed, "overcomers."

An overcomer is simply one who is free from self to serve God. He is one who has appropriated the *kratos* might of the Lord in order to overcome sin, self, and the devil.

3. God's *Ischus* Strength (*Strong's* #2479) (in our bodies)

The third and final function of God's resurrection power is called in the Greek *ischus*, which means the *physical* strength or ability needed to actually do His will. It's manifested or expressed energy, being superior in the physical sense (Judges 16:5).

Ischus (physical power) and *kratos* (self-control power) often work together. God gives us the authority and the ability to choose His will (*exousia* and *kratos*) and then the ability and the strength to perform that will in our lives (*ischus*). He wants us to yield our natural strength and ability to Him and depend totally upon His supernatural strength to accomplish His will (Mark 12:30). (Next chapter we're going to talk about how we can be strong in His might in our very weakest moments.)

The watchword for *ischus* is Spirit-*empowerment.*

In summary, God's resurrection power consists of three elements or aspects: His *dunamis* power, which gives us the spiritual strength or the divine ability to do the impossible; His *kratos* might, which gives us the ability to go against our flesh and choose to do His will regardless of how we feel or what we want; and His *ischus* strength, which empowers our physical bodies to accomplish His will. Spirit-source, Spirit-control, and Spirit-empowerment.

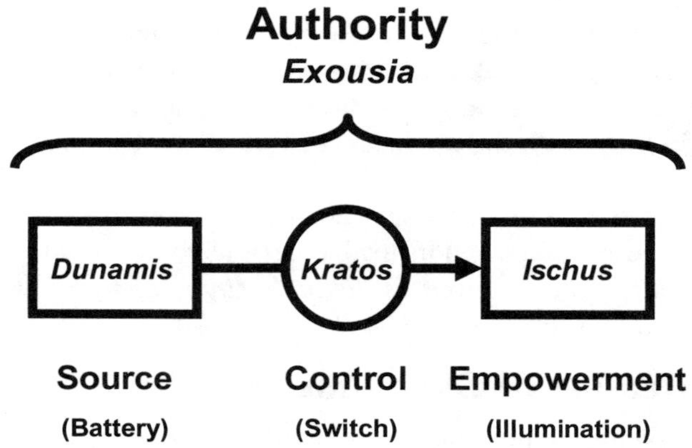

We will continue our discussion of these three elements of God's power in chapter twelve when we focus on overcoming the world, the flesh, and the devil.

Personally Knowing His Power

God's resurrection power is a steady flow of energy that is not dependent upon our understanding, our emotions, or our circumstances, but simply upon our choice to believe God's Word and then trust Him to implement His will in our lives. In order to overcome the world, the flesh, and the devil, to proclaim the message of Christ, and to have the assurance of a place in the future kingdom, it's critical that we personally know the power of His resurrection: His *dunamis force*, His *kratos control,* and His *ischus empowerment*.

God's will is that His *Agape* Love and His resurrection power function in every segment of our lives. Then we can become overcomers who produce "fruit" by the power of God's Spirit and thus, are deemed worthy and fit to inherit the Millennial Kingdom.

This again raises a couple of important questions: Where is the resurrection power of God among Christians today? And what are we doing wrong that we have totally missed it?

The answer is that just like God's Love, God's supernatural power has been quenched in many of our hearts by our own emotional and self-centered choices. Consequently, God has not been able to make us partakers of His Life. We have chosen to hang on to our own sin and self, rather than confess it, repent of it, and lay it at the Cross. God's *dunamis* power is still in our hearts, but like His Love, it's unable to come forth in our lives. Once our sin and self is exposed and dealt with by His *kratos* might, then His supernatural power can, once again, operate in our lives through His *ischus* strength.

Love Is the Sign of God's Empowering

God's Love in our lives is the sign that the sanctification process is in progress and that God's Spirit is empowering us. "By this shall all men know that ye are My disciples, if ye have love [*Agape*] one to another" (John 13:35). Then, as 1 John 4:17 says "*We can have boldness in the day of judgment*, because as He is [*Agape*], so are we in this world."

Those who genuinely love God and love others will inherit the kingdom. These are the ones who have acquired righteous deeds (fruit) done by the power of the Holy Spirit through them. These believers will not only be approved at the Bema Seat Judgment, they will also have on the appropriate wedding garment that qualifies them for the marriage festivities.

The salvation of our spirit—our being born again—is only the beginning of our walk with the Lord. This must be followed by a lifelong process of change called sanctification, which is shown forth by God's Love and implemented by His resurrection power.

Christ has *already* delivered us from the power of darkness and has *already* translated us into the kingdom of His Son (Colossians 1:13). But it is our own choice that will make these things a reality in our lives. The Kingdom of God is not one of words, but one of power (Mark 9:1).

The power of God's Spirit is usually the first power we experience after becoming a believer, but it is often the last power we really come to understand. This has certainly been true in our own experience. We've been Christians for more than fifty years and we are only now beginning to understand the full ramification of the power and authority that God has bestowed upon us.

The goal of Christian ministry is not eloquence, charm, or human wisdom, but personally exhibiting Christ's saving power so that His Name might be declared throughout the earth. Revival is simply the return of God's people to an obedient love of God and to being genuine representatives of His power. Christians, who evidence God's power, are people who continually allow Him to renew their minds and transform their lives (Romans 12:1–2).

Chapter Ten

Strength in Weakness

Let's Recap

In the Introduction Section of this book, we talked about "Why we are here" and "What's the reason for our salvation?" The conclusion we came to is that *the hope of our salvation* is to rule and reign with Christ in the coming kingdom. That's the prize; that's the goal; and that's the mark of the high calling. Our life now is just the training ground and the proving ground for that purpose. Therefore the way we live our lives here and now does have eternal consequences.

In the Kingdom Section we shared that all Christians are eternally secure and will *enter* the Millennial Kingdom. However, only those Christians who have chosen to stay sanctified (clean and open) for God's use, will be deemed *worthy*, *fit,* and *qualified* to *inherit* that kingdom and enjoy levels of responsibilities there. These believers are not perfect or good or religious, but simply those who have recognized their choices and who have chosen to remain partakers of Christ's Life. These are the believers whose works will stand the test of fire at the Bema Seat.

The Power Section of this book is designed to help with the practical application of what *we* must do in order to become sanctified, partakers of His Life, overcomers, and eventually inheritors. This process is God's will, but we are the ones who must make the appropriate choices that allow Him to accomplish it in our lives. Often, however, it seems that He brings about His will in a *completely illogical way*.

> "For My thoughts are not your thoughts, neither are your ways My ways, saith the Lord. For as the heavens are higher than the earth, so are My ways higher than your ways and My thoughts than your thoughts."
>
> —Isaiah 55:8–9

The way God works out His will in our lives often seems contrary not only to the way *we* would do things, but contrary to the way *the world* does things (1 Corinthians 1:19).

Our Yielding Imparts God's Strength

One example is found in 2 Corinthians 12:9–10: "For My [God's] strength is made perfect [or complete] in weakness."

The world sees natural strength as a formidable asset and as a demonstration of a strong character. In the above Scripture, God is saying just the opposite. Only when we are *weak*, can we be made strong. Only when we are yielded vessels can His *dunamis, kratos,* and *ischus* strength work in our lives.

Another example is found in 1 Corinthians 1:27, "God has chosen the foolish things of the world to confound the wise; and . . . the weak things of the world to confound the things which are mighty."

You will see throughout the Bible that God does use "the weak things of the world in order to confound the things that are mighty" and the "foolish things to confound the wise." Here are a few more examples:

- Moses used a staff to command the hand of the Lord. (Exodus 4:20)
- Samson used a jawbone to kill a thousand men. (Judges 15:15)
- David used a smooth stone to kill the giant Goliath. (1 Samuel 17:40)
- Jesus fed the five thousand with only five barley loaves. (John 6:9–11)
- The widow baked a handful of flour and oil that fed Elijah and her family for weeks. (1 Kings 17:12)

According to the Bible, it is through *the weakness of man and the foolish things of the world that God's power can be seen* (Zechariah 4:6). This is saying that God's power will work through us only when we reach *the end of ourselves* and only when we realize that we cannot depend upon our own natural strength. In others words, only when we are yielded to Him will God be able to fill us with His power and accomplish His will through us.

"Not by [your own] might, nor by [your own] power, but by My Spirit, saith the Lord of hosts" (Zechariah 4:6). It is not by our own power or our own might, but by God's Spirit that His will can be done. Suffice it to say that only when we die to our self-life (relinquish and surrender it), can we be empowered to live by God's Life.

> "Verily, verily, I say unto you, Except a corn of wheat fall into the ground and die, it abideth alone: but if it die, it bringeth forth much fruit. He that loveth [hangs on to] his life shall

lose it and he that hateth [is willing to surrender] his life in this world shall keep it unto life eternal."

—John 12:24–25

This process of being emptied of self and filled with God—strength through weakness—is what the sanctification process is all about.

Jesus Is Our Example

Jesus, of course, is the supreme example of "strength through weakness." He was born in a stable in a small, unknown town called Bethlehem. He was the son of a humble and uneducated carpenter. And He was raised in the nondescript town of Nazareth—"Can anything good come out of Nazareth?" (John 1:46). Jesus wasn't from royalty, He wasn't raised in a well-known family, and He wasn't brought up in an important city or country, and yet He was the King of kings, the King of the universe, and the Creator of all things! Jesus ultimately demonstrated that God's power can be seen through the foolish and weak things of the world.

Not only is Jesus' birth an example of humility, but also His entire Life is an example of yielding and strength through weakness. Even though He was the Son of God and the King of kings and could in an instant bring down all the legions of heaven, everything He did in His ministry was by the direction of the Holy Spirit. He was a willing vessel through which God could implement His *dunamis* power.

Even in His crucifixion, this principle is shown forth. "*Christ was crucified through weakness*" (2 Corinthians 13:4). The key is that "weakness" in this context does *not* mean feebleness or inability, but rather a total relinquishment to God, a total yielding and openness to His will. According to the Bible "weakness" means freedom from self, freedom from what others think, freedom from our circumstances—allowing a total reliance upon Christ. It means being cleansed of all known sin and self, so that He can be strong through us.[1] This is how He is glorified (Psalm 89:17).

Jesus lived His whole life in obedience to this principle. Even though He was the Son of God, everything He did in His ministry was *by the power of the Holy Spirit working through Him.* At any time He could have called upon all the heavenly angels to do His *own* will, but He loved the Father—and us—so much that He chose to lay aside His own strength and ability and do only His Father's will by the power of the Holy Spirit.

We must do the same. "For this very cause have I raised thee up, to shew in thee My power . . . that My Name may be declared throughout all the earth" (Exodus 9:16). Jesus is to be glorified, not us!

Consequently, it's only through weakness that God's divine empowerment can be experienced.

Life Comes Only from Death

God's *dunamis* power, if allowed to accomplish its mission, would lead us first to repentance, then to surrender, and ultimately to being an overcomer bearing fruit. As a result of this total yieldedness to God, we will be able to handle situations we never thought possible, endure circumstances we never could have withstood in the natural, and fight the enemy in ways we never dreamed attainable.

Thus, God is *not* looking for capable and self-sufficient believers; He is looking for *broken, submissive, and humble believers*. Remember Christ's example. He was rejected, betrayed, and then killed. But His humiliation led to His exaltation. The more we allow Him to break and mold us, the more open and pliable we'll become for His use.

Until our souls are broken of their own natural strength through the Cross, they will continue to influence, lead, and direct us. *Once our souls are submitted to the Cross, however, and our natural strength broken, we'll be able to serve God as He desires, in* His *power and in* His *strength.* The best executives are those who have experienced catastrophic failures. And the best pilots are those who have made a forced landing. Brokenness is God's path to blessings and His *high* way to the kingdom.

> "We are *troubled* on every side, yet not distressed; we are *perplexed*, but not in despair; *Persecuted*, but not forsaken; cast down, but not destroyed; Always bearing about in the body the *dying of the Lord Jesus*, [so] that the *Life of Jesus* might be made manifest in our body. For we which live are always delivered unto *death* for Jesus' sake, [so] that the *Life* also of Jesus might be made manifest in our mortal flesh. So then *death* [death of self-life] worketh in us, but *Life* [God's Life] in you."
>
> —2 Corinthians 4:8–12

In God's economy, Life comes from death.

It is only through yielding and through brokenness that God's *dunamis* power can be seen (John 15:5). All self-confidence and self-dependence must be exposed, confessed, repented of, put at the Cross, and then replaced with God-confidence and God-dependence. "I can do all things [only] through Christ who strengthens me" (Philippians 4:13). All self-esteem (*I like what I do and what I am*) must be yielded and replaced with God-esteem (*I like what God does through me and what He makes me*). We must always remember it's not what *we* can do for God, but *what God will do through us*—if we are clean.

True life only comes through brokenness and death of self-life. "I am crucified with Christ; nevertheless I live; yet not I, but Christ liveth in me; and the life which I now live in the flesh I live by the faith of the Son of God, who loved me and gave Himself for me" (Galatians 2:20).

"We Have Forsaken All" (Matthew 19:16–30)

We, again, are reminded of the importance of total submission when Jesus tells His disciples in Matthew 19 how difficult it is for a rich man to enter the Kingdom from Heaven.

Jesus had turned His attention from Israel (who had rejected Him) to His disciples and the future church. He told them that in order to enter the Kingdom of Heaven (verse 23), they must go and sell *all* they had, give to the poor, and come and follow Him (Matthew 19:21). In other words, *they must surrender, relinquish, and give up everything for Him!*

The disciples were floored by His answer and they asked Him, "Who then *can* be saved?"

Jesus responded, "With men this is impossible; but with God all things are possible" (Matthew 19:26).

Then Peter said to the Lord: "*Behold, we have forsaken all, and followed Thee;* what shall we have therefore?" (Matthew 19:27).

Jesus answered, "Verily I say unto you, that ye who have *followed* Me, in the regeneration [next life] when the Son of man shall sit on the Throne of His glory, ye also shall sit upon twelve thrones, judging the twelve tribes of Israel. And every one that hath *forsaken* houses, or brethren, or sisters, or father, or mother, or wife, or children, or lands, for My name's sake, shall receive an hundredfold, and *shall inherit everlasting life*" (Matthew 19:28–29).

The word *follow* (Strong's #190, *akoloutheo*) means "union, or in the same way or in the same likeness." The word *forsaken* (Strong's #863, *aphiemi*) means "to lay aside, to yield up, to let go or to give up." Jesus does *not* necessarily mean we are to go and sell everything we own. It's not our possessions that He is talking about. *It's our heart attitude*. It's our own desires, our own will, and our own plans that often stand in the way of God's leading. These are the things that He is pointing out here in this story. Anything that is more important to us than Christ needs to be dealt with and disposed of. Christ needs to be first in our lives. Then all the things we desire will be added to us (Matthew 6:33). Remember Matthew 22:37, which tells us we are to love (*agapao*) Him first!

> "If any man come to Me, and hate not [is willing to set aside] his father, and mother, and wife, and children, and brethren, and sisters, yea, and his own life also, he cannot be My disciple. And whosoever doth not bear his cross and come after Me, cannot be My disciple"
>
> —Luke 14:26–27

Matthew 19 concludes with Christ's words: "Many that are first [here] shall be last [there]; and the last [here] shall be first [there]" (Matthew 19:30).

Jesus was reiterating that in order to receive abundant Life, we must be willing to surrender anything and everything that stands in the way of God's Spirit working freely through us. Then, and only then, will we inherit the blessings of the future kingdom. We are to "deny ourselves, pick up our crosses, and follow Him" (Matthew 16:24). Then as He said, we will be blessed to sit with Him on His throne in the coming Millennium.

Scripture tells us that the "last days" just before Christ returns will be difficult because "men will be lovers of themselves . . . boastful, proud, and unholy" (2 Timothy 3:2). They will not serve God for *His* will to be done, but rather for their own needs to be met, for their own benefit, and for their own glory (Matthew 7:22). Unless we let the power of God's Spirit freely point out our own sin and self, the truth we possess in our heads will just remain a theory. We won't be able to genuinely pass along any godly principles. We can only give out what we possess.

Waiting on the Lord

The central purpose of the Christian life is to be totally surrendered to Him so that His Spirit of power can direct our lives. This will ultimately make us overcomers who will inherit His kingdom. The secret is God's power freely working through us. It's the key. God will give power to the faint and to them that have no might He will increase their strength (Isaiah 40:29). In other words, if we are open and yielded ("weak"), God will pour His Spirit and His power through us. He told us that "those who *wait upon the Lord* will renew their strength" (Isaiah 40:31).

The word *wait* (Strong's #2442) is a very interesting word. It not only means "to abide and adhere to over time," it also means "to carve or etch an image into." In other words, *only* those who have Christ's image "carved or etched into them" will be able to renew their strength. Only those who are "conformed into *His* image" (Romans 8:29) will experience Christ's empowering. Isaiah 64:4 carries this a little further: "For since the beginning of the world, men have not heard, nor perceived by the ear, neither hath eye seen, O God, beside Thee, what He hath prepared for him that *waiteth* for Him." (For those who have been "conformed into His image" by carving or etching.)

Receiving Christ's Spirit into our spirits and being born-again (justification) is an absolutely free gift. We are beginning to see and understand that. But what we sometimes neglect to understand about sanctification is that it's *not* free. It will cost us our lives (John 12:24–25). "Believing" in the gospel (justification) is essential. Yes, this is what saves us. But a lifestyle alongside that belief (sanctification) is the only thing that proves we are!

What Is a True Disciple?

"A lifestyle alongside one's belief" describes a *true disciple.*

A *true* disciple of Christ is one who not only has "partaken *in* Christ," meaning he has received God's Spirit, but one who has also "partaken *of* Christ," meaning he is living Christ's Life, His Love, and His power. In other words, he is not only following Christ around, listening to His sermons, he is also obeying and doing what he hears. Just because we are learners or followers of Christ does not necessarily mean we are "true disciples." Remember Judas? He was a follower of Christ, but not a true disciple (John 12:4). Being a disciple indicates that a *life action* is accompanying our belief. A true disciple not only proclaims the message of Christ with his words, he also shows forth Christ's Life in his actions (Galatians 5:25).

A true disciple is one who *does* the will of God. He is one who denies himself, picks up his cross, and follows Christ (Mark 8:34). He is one who has forsaken *all* in order to follow Him (Luke 14:33).

Everything that Paul *taught* in his epistles, he actually lived out daily. He daily walked by faith and not by sight (2 Corinthians 5:7). He preached the gospel and taught all the counsel of God, "not in the letter that kills" but in the power of the "Spirit who gives life" (Romans 1:16; 2 Corinthians 3:6). He suffered every sort of persecution there is for his Lord's sake (2 Corinthians 11:23–27; Romans 8:17–18). Everything he did, he did so that he might share Christ's glory. His life was, in every sense, a pattern for all to follow. Paul also told us that if we need to boast, we are to do so only in our infirmities. That way the Lord will be glorified, not us.[3]

Paul saw weakness *not* as a liability, but rather as a way of being totally surrendered to the Lord. "I take pleasure in infirmities, in reproaches, in necessities, in persecutions, in distresses for Christ's sake: *for when I am weak, then am I strong*" (2 Corinthians 12:10).

A true disciple of Christ, therefore, is one who has done a complete *reordering* of his life. He constantly relinquishes his self-life to the Lord and in exchange, Christ gives him His. He is one who not only spends time in the Word, but he also lives what he preaches. Divine power seems to be the mark of a true disciple of Christ (2 Corinthians 12:9). *Weakness (or yielding to Him) is the prerequisite for this kind of divine power.*

A real disciple is always concerned with the personal application of truth first. Then he becomes willing to share what he has learned. "For I will not dare to speak of any of those things which Christ *hath not wrought by me* [first], to make the Gentiles obedient, by word and deed" (Romans 15:18). God's truth must first be personalized in a disciple's life, *before* it can be shared. It's one thing to know God's principles in your head, but it's something totally different to walk out those principles in your everyday life.

Christ told us that our mission is to go out and make disciples of all nations, baptizing them in the name of the Father, Son, and Holy Spirit and teaching them to observe all that the Lord has told us in His Word (Matthew 28:18–20). *In summary, not just talking to them about the gospel, but actually showing them how to live it.*

Characteristics of a True Disciple

Let's contrast the characteristics of a true disciple or a faithful Christian with a nominal or unfaithful Christian. As we describe these two types of believers, see if you can identify yourself.

A spiritual or a faithful Christian is a person who not only has been born again, but who is also abiding in and walking by the power of the Holy Spirit, thereby producing fruit (Galatians 5:22; John 15:2, 5, 8). He has allowed the *kratos* strength of God to rein in his emotions and will, so that his works are done through God's empowering, not the flesh (1 Peter 1:2; 1 Thessalonians 5:23). His motive for speaking, his strength for working, and his reason for living is simply the Love of God (1 Timothy 1:5). He is more concerned about what Christ thinks of him, than what others think. Christ's presence in this believer brings about "a peace that passes all understanding" (John 16:33; 2 Corinthians 2:14).

Some of the main characteristics that this spiritual Christian should display are presented in Galatians 5:22. He should be filled with "the fruit of the Spirit" as evidenced by Love (*Agape*), joy, peace, long-suffering, gentleness, goodness, faith, meekness, temperance. These characteristics all manifest themselves in humility (Luke 14:11).

> "Love suffereth long, and is kind; Love envieth not; it vaunteth not itself, is not puffed up, doth not behave itself unseemly, seeketh not [its] own, is not easily provoked, thinketh no evil; rejoiceth not in iniquity, but rejoiceth in the truth; beareth all things, believeth all things, hopeth all things, endureth all things. Love never fails."
>
> —1 Corinthians 13:4–8

> "And beside this . . . add to your *faith virtue; and to virtue knowledge; and to knowledge temperance; and to temperance patience; and to patience godliness; and to godliness brotherly kindness; and to brotherly kindness, charity.*"
>
> —2 Peter 1:5–7

This believer radiates God's holiness. Consequently, the world hates him[4] (John 17:11–14; 15:19–20).

Do any of these characteristics describe you? "*If* ye do these things, ye shall never fall. For so an entrance shall be ministered unto you abundantly into the everlasting kingdom of our Lord and Savior, Jesus Christ" (2 Peter 1:11).

Characteristics of a Carnal (or secular or nominal) Christian

Conversely, a "carnal, unfaithful or nominal Christian" is one in whom the flesh is in control, not the Spirit of God (Hebrews 5:12–13). He is a saved believer, but he loves the world and himself more than he loves Christ. Thus, he operates out of his own desires rather than God's will. He does not apply the *kratos* power of God to rein in his own thoughts and emotions. He can't, because the Spirit of God is quenched. Because of this, there is *no* life transformation in his soul (Romans 12:1–2), no *Agape* Love, no resurrection power, and no fruit (Romans 7:22–24; Galatians 5:17).

This type of carnal Christian professes to be born-again, and yet has not allowed the Cross to slay his self-life (2 Timothy 3:5). He claims to know God, but in truth he actually denies Him by the way he lives. Galatians 5:19–21 tells us those who live by the flesh will not inherit the coming kingdom.

Instead of overcoming the flesh, the world, and the enemy by the power of God, these unfaithful Christians have been overtaken by the same. The flesh rules *over* them, the world has a hold *on* them, and the enemy has acquired a stronghold *in* them.

Some of the characteristics that a carnal or unfaithful Christian displays are a bad temper, anger, fretting, murmuring, pride, selfishness, malice, worldliness, evil speaking, bitterness, jealousy, envy, quarrelling and hatred. They also portray self-confidence, self-centeredness, self-exaltation, self-reliance, self-importance, self-love, and self-ambition. On the other end of the spectrum, they can also be *totally consumed with* themselves (*agapao*) through self-pity, self-condemnation, and self-doubt. Either way, they are pridefully consumed with themselves and not God (Romans 7:18; 1 John 2:16).

A carnal Christian often makes himself the center of attention and values his own will above God's. He is a "soulish" Christian, which means his own self-life rules. He can do righteous deeds and do them well. However, any good deed that the flesh does is an abomination in the sight of God.[5]

Carnal Christians say one thing, but often do another. They are also often talkative and flippant. They tend to use many words and have the attitude that they are more advanced than others. As a result, they are often faultfinders. Working for the Lord is also of the utmost importance to them; however, they feel that everything must be done in a hurry and all must be done to attain the glory for themselves. They do not wait on the Lord for His direction and His answers. Thus, they are *not* "carved into His image." They walk by sight not by faith. They are often uncommonly gifted, have great talent and magnetic personalities, but at the same time are worldly, ambitious, and self-pleasing (1 Corinthians 3:1–3). In the

Old Testament, Saul, Solomon, Lot, and Uzziah have similar profiles and could be called carnal believers (Ezekiel 18:24).

Many carnal Christians try to satisfy their curiosity by studying. They believe that knowing something mentally is the same thing as possessing it experientially. Consequently, they are often double-minded, living two lives. They have an abundance of *acquired knowledge*, but very little *Spirit-revealed* knowledge. They don't realize that *increased spiritual head knowledge can often become a trap*. Head knowledge can strengthen our carnality and deceive us into thinking we are spiritual. The danger is that because God's Spirit is suppressed, the soulish and bodily realm will rule. God designed the sanctification process to remove all hindrances such as these, so that the Holy Spirit can control and direct us.

To summarize, much of what a carnal Christian does, he does for show and to gain something for himself, even if it's just the praise of men (Isaiah 29:13). He does these things for the love of self, not for the glory of God. Remember, a lack of Love for others, no supernatural power, and no godly wisdom shows a denial of Christ's character (1 Corinthians 13:1–4).

Galatians 5:19-20 sheds further light on the "works of the flesh": "Adultery, fornication, uncleanness, lasciviousness, idolatry, witchcraft, hatred, variance, emulations, wrath, strife, seditions, heresies, envyings, murders, drunkenness, revelings, and the like." Obviously, this is not the "fruit of the Spirit" that God desires (Hebrews 5:12–13).

(A portion of the preceding description is from *The Spiritual Man,* by Watchman Nee.)

Dangers of Being Carnal or Lukewarm

It is impossible for us to really know who is carnal and who is spiritual. Only God knows the truth. We are not to judge! That's God's business at the Bema Seat. We are told to be "fruit pickers." Our lives will either show forth the fruit of the Spirit manifested by God's Love or we will display rotten fruit showing forth our carnality (Luke 8:14).

We will be discussing carnal Christians as this book progresses, because these Christians will *not* inherit the Millennial Kingdom.[6] The danger of being carnal is that we can be born-again by God's Spirit (justified) and yet spend 90 percent of our time in the soulish or fleshly realm. If this is the case, our ministry, our teaching, and our preaching will not produce any real godly fruit. "It is the Spirit that quickeneth; the *flesh* profiteth nothing" (John 6:63).

Carnal Christians not only quench the power of God from coming forth through them, thereby hindering their own salvation (their own sanctification), they also hinder salvation in others. They give a false impression of what a true Christian is really like. They can actually become stumbling blocks to passing along the true gospel because nonbelievers look at them and say, "Hey! If that's a Christian, I want no part of it."

Unfortunately, we were stumbling blocks for our children twenty years ago when we were going through our own marital trials. We were all smiles when we were out in public, but behind closed doors we argued, screamed, and yelled at each other. Sadly, our children experienced this and said to us, "Why would we want what you have? You're no different from the people down the street who don't even know God."

This broke our hearts, but we knew it was true.

If we want the gospel to be passed on, especially to our families, our friends, and our associates, we must become spiritual Christians. There's no such thing as fence-sitter Christians. As we get closer to Christ's coming, we'll be pushed one way or the other.

If a carnal Christian persists in doing things his own way, he will never grow to full maturity. This results in spiritual dullness, with no possibility of sparking a revival in himself, much less in anyone else. By living this way, he discredits Christ in all his actions. The sobering part of this is that Matthew 10:33 says that: "If we *deny* Christ [in our actions], He will deny us before the Father."[7] "Denying Christ" in this Scripture not only refers to our words, it also refers to not reflecting (showing forth) His Life. If there is no fruit of the Spirit, it doesn't matter how many verses of Scripture we know, we still will be denying Christ in our actions. The Lord told us that if we deny Him here, He will be forced to deny us there.

God's will is that we *deny ourselves*—totally disavow our self-life, pick up our cross, and *follow Him* (Matthew 16:24).

What is also scary is that carnal and unfaithful Christians are no longer moved by a sense of urgency or watchfulness for Christ's soon coming. They have been lulled to sleep by a sense of complacency and they are not concerned about being prepared or ready or qualified to inherit the kingdom.

Parable of the Faithful and Wise Servants (Matthew 24:42–51)

Jesus described both the spiritual Christian and the carnal Christian in His story or narrative about the "faithful and wise servants" (Matthew 24:42–51).

After finishing with the parable of the fig tree, Jesus warned His disciples and His followers:

> 42Watch therefore: for ye know not what hour your Lord doth
> come. 43But know this, that if the goodman of the house had
> known in what watch the thief would come, he would have

> watched, and would not have suffered his house to be broken
> up. [44]Therefore be ye also ready: for in such an hour as ye
> think not the Son of man cometh. [45]Who then is a faithful
> and wise servant, whom his lord hath made ruler over his
> household, to give them meat in due season? [46]Blessed *is* that
> servant, whom his lord when he cometh shall find so doing.
> [47]Verily I say unto you, That he shall make him ruler over all
> his goods. [48]But and if that evil servant shall say in his heart,
> My lord delayeth his coming; [49]And shall begin to smite *his*
> fellowservants, and to eat and drink with the drunken; [50]The
> lord of that servant shall come in a day when he looketh
> not for *him*, and in an hour that he is not aware of, [51]And
> shall cut him asunder, and appoint *him* his portion with the
> hypocrites: there shall be weeping and gnashing of teeth.

There are many interpretations of this Scripture, so study like Bereans and see what the Holy Spirit reveals to you.

Who Was Jesus Talking To?

First of all, *who* was Jesus addressing?

He was addressing His own disciples, those who had just asked Him, "What are the signs of Your coming again?"[8] He began by telling them some of the many signs and events that would occur. One of those signs is that "iniquity shall abound, the Love (*Agape*) of many will wax [grow] cold" (Matthew 24:12). This is a very interesting verse to us because it validates that Christ was talking about His body of believers, the church. Only believers (the church) have God's *Agape* in their hearts and only they will experience it growing cold in the end times. Even the disciples did not have the indwelling Spirit of God at this time. This all occurs after the Resurrection.

Jesus was addressing not only His disciples, but also the future church. "Watch therefore, for you know not when *your* Lord will return" (Matthew 24:42). The usage of "your Lord" validates that He was talking to believers. Christ was not talking about unbelievers here. Why would an unbeliever even care about being faithful or waiting for the Lord's return? Christ was talking about believers.

The Jewish people and their Pharisaical leaders had hardened their hearts against Christ and His message (Matthew 23:1–39). Christ had now turned His attention to His own followers and was speaking directly to them in these parables so they could understand, but those with hardened hearts would not (Matthew 13:11). The disciples listened with eager minds, the unbelievers with opposition. The Matthew parables were part of the "mysteries of the kingdom," meaning things that had been hidden and never before revealed (Psalm 78:2).

Romans 9 and 11 were written specifically about a time when God will have no more mercy on His own people and will turn His attention to "another nation," meaning the church. By cutting off His own people, Christ creates a new people for Himself—Jews and Gentiles merged together into one "new man."[9]

Comments About the Faithful and Wise Servants

The faithful and wise servant in this story, of course, is equivalent to a true disciple or a spiritual Christian. This faithful servant placed the desires of the lord of the house *above* his own and was an obedient steward who provided for his family. He did what he was required to do and he steadfastly awaited his lord's return. In the same way, God entrusts us to do His will, to feed His spiritual family, and to await His return. Our reward for doing so, will be the privilege of greater service in the kingdom.

The special pleasures, honors, and splendors, which are to accompany the return of the Lord from heaven and the setting up of His kingdom are to be a reward for fidelity and faithful service in His absence. Without this, future blessings will be forfeited.

The unfaithful and disobedient servant, however, is the equivalent of a carnal and nominal Christian.

Note that the word *evil* in Matthew 24:48, is the Greek word *kakos* (Strong's #2556), which means "someone who has been disqualified." It means "a worthless or injurious person." It means *he lacks the qualities that he should possess*. Simply put, he is "not worthy." This servant thought his lord would delay his coming. And this, of course, affected how he lived his life. He was lazy, untrustworthy, and cruel. He abused his position by being ill tempered and self-indulgent to those who worked with him. He thought he would never be called into account for these things because he secretly believed his lord would not come.

Jesus then replaces the term "cast out" here with the term "cut asunder" (Strong's #1371), which metaphorically means "to be cut open so all can see." It means "to expose and scrutinize the thoughts and motives of a person's heart." It is simply an analogy for what will happen at the Judgment Seat. Hebrews 4:12 talks about a sharp two-edged sword that will bring to light not only the motives of our hearts, but also all the things of darkness.

Jesus also replaces the term "outer darkness" here with the term "a portion with the hypocrites." *Hypocrite* refers to believers who have lived a double life, the "foolish ones."[10] The word *hypocrite* can be used of nonbelievers (Matthew 15:7–8; 23:13), but *it also can be used of Christians who judge others while ignoring their own sin.* In this Scripture, *hypocrisy* simply means "unfaithful" (*apistion*). It is referring to one who assumes the role of a servant, but doesn't live like one.[11] It is someone who says one thing, but lives something totally different.

The Pharisees were a perfect example of hypocrites. They pretended that they were spiritual and holy, and yet in action they were insincere, pretentious, self-righteous, and they stumbled many. Jesus called them on it many times. "Woe unto you, scribes and pharisees, hypocrites! For you are like unto whited sepulchres, which indeed appear beautiful outwardly, but are within full of dead men's bones and all uncleanness" (Matthew 23:27).

Like the disobedient servant in the parable of the ten talents, this unfaithful and unfruitful servant will be thrown into a specific place—a place with all the other hypocrites, who said they were Christians, but really didn't live it—and there will be weeping and gnashing of teeth.[12] We believe this refers to a dark space outside the light and company of the spiritual saints and the blessings provided to them.

A Christian who refuses to avail himself of the moment-by-moment cleansing that God provides is seen as walking in darkness. He has not been cleansed by the washing of the water of the Word, therefore he can only remain in the darkened courtyard outside the light of the Holy Place.

Weeping and Gnashing of Teeth

In this "outer darkness" there is going to be much "weeping and gnashing of teeth." This particular phrase occurs three times in the Bible describing believers: Matthew 8:12; 22:13; and 25:30. It's interesting to note that all three of these passages use the very same phrases: They are *in the kingdom*, but they will be *cast out* from experiencing the joy of the Lord, thrown into the *outer darkness* (or the darkness outside) where they will experience *weeping and gnashing of teeth*.

"Weeping and gnashing of teeth" occurs when carnal believers reflect remorsefully on their lives and all the missed opportunities. Scripture says they will remember their past because God will just have reminded them of every detail at the Bema Seat Judgment.[13]

In his book *Your Eternal Reward,* Erwin Lutzer said that "our tears will be those of regret and shame, tears of remorse for lives lived for ourselves rather than for Christ and for others. Perhaps we would never cease crying in heaven if God Himself did not eventually come and wipe the tears from our eyes" (Revelation 21:4).

The Pulpit Commentary says:

> Rewards and punishments will be allotted in the coming world with strict justice. To some, great knowledge of the Divine will be given and a high place in the city of God will be allotted. But for those that fail, their portion will be many stripes . . . They will occupy a lower grade in the hierarchy of heaven, but still have friendship with God . . . This shows that admission to the church is not all that is required [to enter the Marriage of the Lamb]. There is a scrutiny to be undergone and an award to be made.[14]

There are *four* passages that talk about "weeping and gnashing of teeth," which remorseful *Christians* will experience in the "outer darkness"—or the "place of the hypocrites"—in the Kingdom from Heaven.[15] *But, again, there is nothing inherent in the terminology of "weeping and gnashing of teeth" that automatically associates it with unbelievers or with hell. Again, we jump to that conclusion because of our own preconceived ideas.*

The term *weeping* is used in reference to Judah in Genesis 45:2; 46:29; and in Deuteronomy 34:8 of the Israelites who wept over Moses when he died. It is used over Hezekiah in 2 Kings 20:3; and over Job in Job 30:31; and over David in Psalm 6:8; and even over Jesus in Luke 13:27. *The term "gnashing of teeth" occurs in Job 16:9.*

It's the context of the Scripture that defines the meaning of the words. Just as the word *darkness* can refer to *spiritual darkness* for believers or *physical darkness* for unbelievers, so "weeping and gnashing of teeth" can refer to either extreme sadness or remorse for believers in the darkness outside Christ's throne room or the anguish and hopelessness unbelievers will experience in hell. It all depends upon the context of the particular passage.

See *Parable Chart # 4: Matthew 24:42-51*

Let's sum this up as best we can.

Note that this story is different in several ways from the other parables. First of all, it's not a parable, but simply a narrative, as is Matthew 8:12. Also, it does not say that it "takes place in" or "is like" the Kingdom from Heaven, but it occurs *at the Lord's return*, which would be the beginning of the Kingdom from Heaven.

To whom was Christ speaking? His disciples. *About whom was He speaking?* Any believer waiting for his Lord's return. *What had they done wrong?* They thought the Lord would not come and so they mistreated their fellow servants. *What was their loss?* They were cut asunder and appointed a place with the other hypocrites where there will be weeping and gnashing of teeth. *What future event is this referring to?* Possibly, the Rapture. And *what is the lesson for us?* We must always be looking for Christ's return.

Consequences of an Unfaithful and Carnal Lifestyle

In review then, unfaithful Christians are those believers who are disobedient, self-consumed, and self-indulgent. They have hardened their hearts, they walk by the flesh, and they are dull of hearing.[16] According to the Scriptures, here are some of the consequences that they may encounter:

- They may receive a stinging rebuke from the Lord because they denied Him in their actions and failed to persevere to the end. (Matthew 10:33; 25:3, 10, 12)
- They may be called wicked servants. (Matthew 18:32; 25:26)

PARABLE CHART 4 (MATT. 24: 45-51)

STORY OR PARABLE	TO WHOM IS JESUS SPEAKING	ABOUT WHOM IS HE TALKING	WHAT HAD THEY DONE WRONG	WHAT WAS THEIR LOSS	WHAT EVENT IS BEING PREDICTED	WHAT IS THE LESSON FOR US
Matt. 8:12 Sons of the Kingdom "Story"	Gentile Centurion	"Sons of the Kingdom" - Jewish believers	Lack of Faith	Cast into outer darkness-weeping and gnashing of teeth	Preparation for the Kingdom	Need to have faith
Matt. 24: 45-51 Faithful & Wise Servants "Story"	Disciples ("What are the signs of Your coming?")	Any believer waiting for his Lord's return	Thought the Lord would not come-Mistreated his fellow servants	Cut him asunder & appointed him a place with "hypo-crites"-weeping and gnashing of teeth	The Rapture	Need to always be looking for His soon return
Matt. 25:14-30 10 Talents "Parable"	Disciples ("What are the signs of Your coming?")	His own servants	Wicked servant didn't do anything with his talent	Take talent away Cast into outer darkness-weeping and gnashing of teeth	The Bema Seat	Need to be faithful with the abilities God gives us
Matt. 25:1-13 10 Virgins "Parable"	Disciples ("What are the signs of Your coming?")	The "Church"	They had no intimacy with the Lord. He did not "know" them	Locked out of wedding - The door was shut & they were left out	The Wedding Ceremony	Need to know the Lord intimately
Matt. 22: 1-13 Man without a Wedding Garment "Parable"	Pharisees	Gentile believers at wedding (original ones called were not "worthy")	No wedding garment (no "fruit")	Bind him - cast into outer darkness-weeping and gnashing of teeth	The Marriage Supper	Need to wear the appropriate wedding garment

- They may be cast out of fellowship. (Matthew 8:12; 22:13; 25:30)
- They may be "cut in pieces," that is, their secret motivations exposed. (Matthew 24:51)
- They may receive a Millennial disinheritance, the loss of rewards, and be disqualified for the prize. (1 Corinthians 3:8; 9:27; 2 Corinthians 5:10; Revelation 3:11; Matthew 25:28–29)
- They may be excluded from the joy of the wedding celebration, the marriage feast, and from ruling and reigning with Christ. (Matthew 22:13–14; 25:10–12, 26–30)
- They may even experience "gnashing of teeth"—despair, regret, and remorse. (Matthew 24:51; 8:12; 25:30)

God does not punish believers, but in His Love He does discipline and chastise them and He may do so in the coming kingdom also.

Carnal Christians will be in heaven, at the Bema Seat, and will enter the Millennial Kingdom, but Scripture tells us they will not inherit it *unless they repent and turn around* now.[17] This should make all of us wake up and begin to take our walk with the Lord very seriously. What we do in this lifetime does matter. It does count! Someone is watching and taking detailed notes. This life is the testing ground and the proving ground for the coming kingdom.

Just as in the Old Testament where only a few entered the promised land, so only a small remnant will enter into God's Millennial rest.[18] One of the ways that *rest* is used in Scripture is in association with the coming kingdom. Rest symbolizes the reward that comes from successfully completing divinely assigned tasks given to us here.

> "For if Jesus had given them rest, then would he not afterward have spoken of *another day*. There remaineth, therefore, a rest to the people of God. For he that is entered into his rest, he also hath ceased from his own works, as God did from His. *Let us labor, therefore, to enter into that rest, lest any man fall after the same example of unbelief.*"
>
> —Hebrews 4:8–11

Hebrews also warns us about not entering God's "rest" because of our failure to partake *of* Christ's Life up till the very end. It says we are made "partakers of Christ, *if* we hold the beginning of our confidence steadfast unto the end" (Hebrews 3:7–14).

(See chapter fourteen for a more detailed explanation of "laboring to enter in" to His rest and the possibility of forfeiting our inheritance.)

All of this is saying that if we don't learn how to have our souls experientially sanctified *here*, we will lose incredible opportunities *there*.[19] We will end up being subjects in Christ's kingdom, rather than sovereigns.

As we hear these somber warnings again, don't let the enemy put fear or condemnation upon you. Instead, let the Spirit of God convict you to turn around and begin to live as God desires. There is still time! Even if you have not been faithful, you can still learn to be. Even if you have not been obedient, there's still time to confess and repent. And even if you've not been watchful, you can learn to be. Remember our friend in prison. If he can become a faithful overcomer in his situation, then any of us can. All that's required is an unconditional choice to follow Christ. Yes, you will trip; yes, you will fall. And yes, you will blow it, but Christ will be there to catch you, to help you stand up, and to encourage you to begin to walk again.

We share these warnings to "provoke one another unto love and good works" (Hebrews 10:24).

The Importance of Being Ready

Jesus' exhortation in the Matthew 24 example, "*Be ye ready; for in such an hour as ye think not the Son of man will come*" is critical for all of us to hear (Matthew 24:44).[20]

This means that we all must be watchful, ready, and prepared for Christ's return at any moment. This means that we all must make ourselves equipped, fit, and suitable to co-reign—to have levels of responsibility—with Christ. This is the preparation and the readiness that Revelation 19:7 refers to: "Let us be glad and rejoice and give honor to Him. For the marriage of the Lamb is come and *His wife hath made herself ready.*"

Making ourselves ready means we must make ourselves qualified and worthy to inherit the blessings of the kingdom. We must be: 1) cleansed and sanctified; 2) partakers of Christ's Life; 3) faithful overcomers; and 4) producing good work [fruit]. As a result we'll be walking by the Spirit, loving one another, and making disciples of all nations.

We must be daily prepared and ready so that when He taps us on the shoulders and says, "Let's go!" we won't be surprised. *Constancy* and *perseverance* are key words in this process. "Take ye heed, watch and pray: for ye know not when the time is . . . Watch ye therefore: for ye know not when the master of the house cometh, at even, or at midnight, or at the cock-crowing, or in the morning: lest coming suddenly he find you sleeping. And what I say unto you I say unto all, *Watch*!"[21] "Watch ye, therefore, and pray always, that ye may be accounted worthy to escape all these things that shall come to pass, and to stand before the Son of man" (Luke 21:36; 2 Thessalonians 1:5, 11).

"Forgetting those things which are behind and reaching forth unto those things which are before. [We must] press toward the mark for the prize of the high calling of God in Christ Jesus."

—Philippians 3:13

Chapter Eleven

Faith—the Means of God's Power

We saw last chapter that choosing to stay "weak" —open, yielded, and cleansed—so God can be "strong" through us is of the utmost importance. This is how the Spirit of God can not only *motivat*e our actions, but also *implement* them in our lives. The critically important ingredient in this scenario, however, is our faith. We must provide faith in order for God's will to be done.

Faith is the means by which God's divine power works in us. In other words, *God* provides the power and the Love, but *we* must choose to believe and receive it. This is called *faith.* Without faith it is impossible to please God (Hebrews 11:6).

His Power: Our Faith

God's responsibility is to perform what He promises in His Word (Romans 4:20–21). Our responsibility is to believe and trust that He will. *Power* is the supernatural ability that God gives us to do His will, but *faith* is the means by which that power is appropriated. God's power is only made visible by our faith.

This answers the question we posed in chapter nine, Where is the resurrection power of God today? The answer is that many of us have lost faith.

There's a parallel between the Exodus generation of the Old Testament and believers of today. The Old Testament generation had God's promises, but they failed to claim them because they didn't mix His promises with faith (Hebrews 4:2). *God's promises are only profitable if they are implemented by faith. That was true then, and it's also true today!*

God waits to reveal Himself—His Love, His power—until we take the first step of faith.

What Is Faith?

The Greek word for *faith* is *pisteuo* (Strong's #4100), which means "to put trust in, to be committed to, to be persuaded of, to place confidence in, and to rely upon." As Christians we are to put our trust in, be committed to, be persuaded of, have confidence in, and rely upon Christ as our Savior and Lord and Master.

Faith is not only the assurance that Christ *is* who He professes to be, but also the trust that He will *do* all that He promises to do. Faith is not only *believing* His promises intellectually, it is also *trusting* our lives to Him.

Faith is "the substance [the assurance and confidence] of things hoped for and the evidence [the proof] of things not yet seen" (Hebrews 11:1). Faith is the means by which God's will becomes a reality in our life experience.

Real faith is *not* feeling, *not* seeing, *not* understanding, and *not* knowing but still choosing to trust and rely upon Him. It's being convinced that no matter what we see happening in our lives, no matter what we understand to be true, and no matter how we feel, *God will be faithful to His Word and perform His promises to us in His timing and in His way!*

Our faith is never stronger than when what we are experiencing in our spirits totally contradicts what our senses are telling us. Faith is trusting that God loves us even then, and believing He will still work out every detail of our lives for His glory.

An Example of an Overcoming Faith: George Mueller

We can't talk about the subject of faith without expounding on the life and ministry of George Mueller, the famous English teacher of the 1800s. By faith alone, he overcame obstacles and established orphanages in England that fed and housed many thousands of orphans.

Mr. Mueller believed that faith rested upon the Word of God. He said, "When sight ceases, then faith has a chance to work." As long as there was any possibility of human success, he felt that faith could accomplish nothing. His motto was "God is able to do this; I cannot." His greatest desire was to live a public life of faith so that other people's trust in God would be strengthened. He felt it would be living proof that faith works if he, a poor man, without asking the aid or finances of anyone, could simply by prayer and faith have all the needs of the orphanage met. When there was no money, as happened often, he would simply say, "The Lord in His wisdom and love has not sent help, but I believe, in due time He will." He didn't know how God would do it, but he trusted He would. And God always did! These are called *faith choices* or non-feeling choices. They are choices to believe God in the midst of huge obstacles, barriers, and roadblocks.

As a result of George Mueller's life of prayer and faith, he was given the necessary money to build three orphanages that housed and fed more than two thousand children at a time, buy all the furniture and supplies to furnish and run the homes, and hire all the needed personnel to manage the facilities. Mueller expected God to answer his prayers and he expected God's blessings on his labor of love. And He always received both! Mr. Mueller epitomized Galatians 3:11: "The just shall live by faith."

Faith is the key that opens the door to our spiritual victory and what will enable us to walk triumphantly. We need *faith* in order to choose God's will. We need *faith* in order to trust God's power to implement His will. And we need *faith* in order to become overcomers who do His will.[1]

The Lord provides us with His power to overcome the world, the flesh, and the devil. Our responsibility is to have the faith that He will.

Don't Give Up the Fight

We see so many believers today ready to give up the fight because they don't see how God is going to provide for them or how He is going to help them in their tough situations. They have become weary and unable to persevere in faith.

Just yesterday, a friend called and said he was "checking out" because his life situation was too overwhelming. Rather than trying any longer to be an overcomer in his situation, he was "throwing in the towel" and going to allow the situation to overtake him.

There seems to be such an atmosphere of *hopelessness* among Christians today. Many have become discouraged and depressed and despondent because their situations just don't change or improve. They pray, they believe, and they trust God, but nothing happens; then they pray, believe, and trust God again, *but the situation still remains the same*. Finally, they just stop praying, stop believing, and give up. As a consequence, they not only lose sight of God's personal Love, they also lose the "hope of their salvation"—the reason they were called. "Hope deferred makes the heart sick" (Proverbs 13:12). You could say it this way: Hopelessness causes discouragement, depression, and lack of purpose, making our hearts sick.

The end of Proverbs 13:12, however, tells us that our hope is realized when *by faith* we *embrace God's purpose for our lives—our inheritance in Christ in the coming kingdom.* (See Ephesians 1:18.) Then our "hope" becomes a tree of Life. *This, along with God's Love, is what will sustain us through the difficult times*.

We understand how difficult it is to continue to have faith and continue to choose to trust God, especially when we don't see any change in our situation. We know, because we've been there! But the truth is, *we really don't have another choice.* That's what faith is all about. If we stop choosing, if we stop having faith, and if we stop trusting, the situation will be doomed to failure and the enemy will rejoice.

We must take our eyes off the temporal situations and focus on God's eternal plan. That's our hope! That's our destiny! And that's our future! We cannot find that hope—that tree of Life—in any other way but the way God planned it. He created us, He called us, and He has instilled that purpose in our hearts. And only by aligning ourselves with *His* purpose and *His* plan can that hope ever be realized in our lives. *Faith is the means to that hope!*

Faith Is Trusting God

Faith comes in the form of a constant choice and it's a choice we can never stop making, no matter how hard the situation. It's a choice to follow God and do what He asks, regardless of how we feel, what we think, or what we want. Just as God loves us unconditionally, we must trust Him unconditionally.

Faith is trusting God even when we've been stripped of our position, our finances, our reputation, our comfort, our family, and even our last ounce of understanding. It's getting to the place where we can say and mean, "I won't let any of these things move me," even if that means letting go of all that we hold dear (Acts 20:24). As Job exclaimed, "Though You slay me, yet will I trust You" (Job 13:15). This must be our commitment also.

Here's our personal story:

Back in the late eighties, the development company where Chuck was CEO went bankrupt. We lost *our position* in the community as we went from being well respected and millionaires to not having enough money to buy our next meal. We lost *our finances* as the situation forced us to declare personal bankruptcy as well as corporate bankruptcy. We lost *our reputation* when, as a result of the corporate bankruptcy, some people felt that we had hidden the money away in an offshore account and they falsely accused us in public. We lost *our comfort,* when as a result of the personal bankruptcy we lost our cars, our insurance, and our dream home—the one we had just spent two years remodeling and planned to retire in. On top of this, we lost *our last bit of understanding* when, after receiving many wonderful promises from the Lord of complete restoration of all the things, all our belongings were subsequently destroyed by a 6.8 earthquake that hit our rented house. Several years later we lost one of the most beloved members of *our family* when our son, Chip, died unexpectedly at the age of thirty-nine of a massive heart attack while out jogging one afternoon.

So when we say we understand how hard it is to have faith when things only seem to get worse, we really *do* understand!

Faith means laying aside all of our circumstances and getting to the place where we can say and really mean, "I won't let any of these things move me" (Acts 20:24). The real test of faith comes when we can trust God in the depths of the trial, even *before* the victory is realized, and even before the promises are revealed.

Faith has to pass the test of disappointment and the urge to want to quit. The enemy will set up every roadblock he can think of to entice us to just give up. We must do just the opposite! When we experience the opposition, we must shout our unconditional love for God from the housetops and be assured in our hearts that the victory *will* come.

Here's what the Lord did for us. He reestablished *our positions*, not in the corporate world as before, but in a much better world (the spiritual world), ministering through *Koinonia House* and *the King's High Way Ministries*. He restored *our finances* to the point where it seemed as if the more we gave away in His Name, the more He returned. He renewed *our reputation,* again not in the corporate world as before, but in the spiritual world. He restored our comfort through a series of miracles. We now have a beautiful home, cars, and insurance. He rebuilt *our understanding* as to why He allowed these devastating things to come into our lives, much of which is explained in our book *Faith in the Night Seasons*. And, He revived *our family,* even though our son Chip can never be replaced, our daughter Lisa and her husband and their four kids live on the same property as we do, our other daughter Meshell lives very close by, and our son Mark and his family have experienced miraculous healings. All of our children know and love the Lord.

If He can do these things for us, He will be faithful to do the same in your life also.

Faith is the principle by which we obtain Christ's Life and the means to God's power. Obedience and trust, however, are the principles by which we live that Life out. In other words, faith must be the foundation of our walk with the Lord. Then we can add to that faith—obedience, trust, and experience, which will give us the victory that overcomes (2 Peter 1:5–7). God is faithful—we are living proof! He brought us through the trials. And He will do that for you, as well.

Faithful Perseverance

The goal of our faith is the salvation of our souls (1 Peter 1:9). Notice that this "salvation of our souls" happens at the *end* of our faith, not the beginning. When God talks about "saving our souls," He's not referring to the new birth. He's talking about the sanctification process—the cleansing, renewing, and transforming—of those who already believe, which occurs at the end of our faith. (See also Hebrews 10:36–39.)

Perseverance (endurance) is one of the most important characteristics of faith. The words *endure* and *persevere* (Strong's #5278, *hupomeno*) mean "to stay under, to undergo, to hold up under [suffering], to be patient, to tarry or to abide under."[2] *Perseverance* is "resigned submission to a situation that is out of our control." *It means not to be overtaken by it, but to overcome it. Perseverance* is another word for patience and forbearance. Colossians 3:12–13 exhorts us to "put it on," along with compassion, kindness, lowliness and meekness (Ephesians 4:2). Endurance and perseverance are characteristics of God's Love. His Love "endures all things, bears all things, believes all things and hopes all things" (1 Corinthians 13:7).

The purpose of our lives *here* on earth—including our trials—is to train us to rule and reign with Christ *there* in the kingdom. He is constantly testing us to see if we are worthy of such a great responsibility. Endurance and perseverance are two major parts of this testing. "To him that overcomes and does my will *to the very end*, I will give power over the nations" (Revelation 2:26–27).

It's not that we persevere in faith because we are being forced to, we endure because it's what God expects of us and we want to please Him (Luke 19:17). We want to finish well.[3]

Christ wants us to be longsuffering, patient, and forbearing toward others—even toward those who have used us, misused us, and despised us. God even goes so far as to say we are to "love our enemies"—we are to totally give ourselves over to them—be open vessels of Christ's Life and His Love toward them (Matthew 5:44). When forbearance and perseverance are exercised, virtue is no longer self-centered, but is of necessity other-centered.

It's not enough to just *enter* the race, we must *persevere* to the very end of the race in order to win. 2 Timothy 2:11–12 tells us if we endure while suffering, we will reign with Him.

An Example: Cindy

A perfect example of someone who has had tremendous faith and who has persevered through more trials than anyone we know is a dear friend of ours, named Cindy Scinto. Cindy is in her forties, married, and has one son. She is also a complete miracle, having survived almost fifty heart surgeries and, most recently, a complete heart transplant—all in the last five years.

Two years ago, before her heart transplant, she went back east for an experimental procedure in which they grew new arteries to replace the ones that had become clogged. Cindy was so excited to have this procedure done. And when she began to experience the new arteries giving her strength and vitality that she had not felt for months, she was ecstatic. Cindy came to our ministry and enthusiastically shared how, for the first time in more than two years, she was able to shovel snow off her sidewalk. This was a huge achievement for her. *She was so sure God was going to heal her totally that she offered to become a poster child for this new artery procedure.* She was convinced God would not have taken her that far, only to let her get sick again.

But eight weeks later her main arteries, were 98 percent clogged again.

She was very confused, as any of us would be. What was God thinking? What was He doing? She could not logically reason it out in her own mind; nor could any of us who had been praying for her.

Earlier in Cindy's sickness, God had spoken these words to her: "*I cannot heal you until you are ready to accept how I choose to heal you. And I am not finished yet!*" This affirmation that the Lord was orchestrating the entire process, has kept her strong. It wasn't the promise she would have liked, but it *was* a promise that God knew exactly what He was doing, even if she didn't.

Even though the outcome of her procedure made no sense to Cindy, she chose by faith to fully surrender herself to the Lord, trusting that He loved her and that He was totally in control. This is where "faith choices" or non-feeling choices come in. *When what we see happening makes no sense to us, when it's the opposite of what we had hoped for, and when it's a blow to all our expectations, that's when we must choose by faith to trust God's hand anyway.*

Two years ago she had a total heart transplant.

The transplanted heart that Cindy received, however, was damaged. The doctor knew about it, but without that heart she would have died. Her new heart has what is called the CMV virus, which is a cancer-type virus. In a normal heart the immune system would kick in and it wouldn't be so dangerous, but in a transplanted heart (without the help of a good immune system) that cancer can become fatal. After several months at the hospital because of the original heart transplant, Cindy spent another two months in the ICU unit going through one of the most aggressive chemotherapy treatments possible. (Most people have a chemo treatment two times a week and that makes them sick. Cindy had her treatment two times a day, every day for two months. That's 14 sessions a week and 104 sessions in all!)

After recovering from that ordeal, Cindy took a trip to a relative's wedding where, unfortunately, she tripped and fell and broke her right leg in two places. Again she was down for the count. It took almost three and a half months before she was able to walk.

This precious child of God has withstood more in the last six years than most people do in an entire lifetime. Yet she always comes back smiling and praising God every time. *She has her down days (she's human), but I know of no one who has made more "faith choices" to stay in the race and endure than Cindy.* When we think of perseverance, Cindy is at the top of our list as an example.

She has just written a book, *A Heart Like Mine*, about her trials and triumphs and how God has sustained her through it all. We know God will use it to encourage and restore hope to hundreds of patients suffering through many of the trials that Cindy has endured.

The way we endure and persevere in difficult times is by "seeing Him who is invisible" in the middle of the situation (Hebrews 11:27) and by remembering Isaiah 55:8–9: "For My thoughts are not your thoughts, neither are your ways My ways, saith the Lord. For as the heavens are higher than the earth, so are My ways higher than your ways, and My thoughts than your thoughts."

Cindy certainly has done both.

It's not enough to just *enter* the race (be justified), we must *persevere* and endure to the very end in order to win the prize. And the way we do that is by faith. If we persevere and endure, then we will reign with Him.

Faithful Obedience

Like Cindy, we must not only *claim God's promises*, we must also *have the faith* to walk them out.

For more than forty years God provided everything the Old Testament Israelites needed. He provided guidance by the Pillar of Fire, the tabernacle for their worship, their daily clothing, their shoes, their deliverance from their enemies, and even a day of rest for them. But the Israelites still turned against Him, forgot His promises and impugned (reproached) His faithfulness. As a result, they encountered forty years of misery, discouragement, and death, primarily because of a lack of faith to enter His rest. It is imperative that we, as New Testament believers, learn from their mistakes. We must wait upon the Lord (be carved into His image), knowing in our hearts that *in His timing* and *in His way*, He will be faithful to *all* His promises.

Faith really comes in the form of a constant choice. A choice to follow God and do what He asks, regardless of how we feel, what we think, or what we want (Romans 4:20–21). God's reward for this kind of faith and obedience is more of His Love, more of His overcoming power, and a position of responsibility in the coming kingdom beside Him.

Our usefulness to God, therefore, is not determined by how much we have suffered or by how much we have lost, but by how much faith and obedience we have learned through that suffering and that loss. We must continually examine ourselves and see if we are in the faith, because it's very easy to get derailed, sidetracked, and ultimately shipwrecked.[4] I'm sure you've seen examples in your own circle of friends.

Remember the unfaithful and disobedient servants in the parables in Matthew 24 and 25. When the Lord finally returned, He reprimanded the carnal Christians: "Where was your faith? Where was your obedience? Where was your perseverance? Because you didn't endure to the end, I can't let you in!" Then He cast them into the "darkness outside" where there was weeping and gnashing of teeth. But to the spiritual Christians He said: "Well done, good and faithful servants [because you endured to the end], I will make you a ruler over many. *Enter into* the joy of the Lord."

We should follow their examples. "Be not slothful, but followers of them who *through faith and patience inherit the promises*" (Hebrew 6:12).

(See "The Difference Between Obeyers and Followers" in the Supplemental Notes Section of the appendix.)

Two Extremes—"Faith or Works"

Because so much of our kingdom perspective seems to depend upon our "righteous works"—*fruit* resulting from God's Spirit of power working through us—we need to understand exactly what God means when He says "by faith" in Galatians 2:16 and what He means when He says "by works" in Matthew 16:27.

There seem to be *two extremes* in the Christian body in the way we view "faith and works" and they both have a tremendous impact on our kingdom perspective. Let's "rightly divide" the truth and see if we can sort this out (2 Timothy 2:15).

1. First of all, there are those Christians who believe that we *enter* and *inherit* the kingdom totally by faith and grace alone. The Reformation is what brought to light this doctrine of *salvation by grace through faith, not as a result of works*. As a consequence of an overemphasis on grace and the confusion between justification and sanctification, however, the encouragement of works in the life of a believer has been almost held in disdain by some saints. With this perspective, faith takes on a sort of "sacred aura," which demands *nothing* of us, except to "rest in it."[5]

2. On the other hand, there are those Christians who believe we get into the kingdom only by doing good works. They teach that if you don't bring forth fruit, if you don't produce works of righteousness, there's a chance you're really not saved.

Following are Scriptures that show how this confusion occurs:

> "For by grace are ye saved *through faith*; and that not of yourselves; it is the gift of God: *not of works*, lest any man should boast."
>
> —Ephesians 2:8–9

> "Let your light so shine before men, that they may *see your good works and glorify your Father* which is in heaven."
>
> —Matthew 5:16

> "For the Son of man shall come in the glory of His Father with His angels; and then *He shall reward every man according to his works*."
>
> — Matthew 16:27

You can see why there is such a huge misunderstanding in this area. We believe the first Scripture (Ephesians 2:8–9) is talking about *justification,* which requires absolutely *no* works at all. It's totally by faith and the grace of God. However, the last two verses (Matthew 5:16 and 16:27) are talking about the righteous works that result from *sanctification*. In this context *"works" refer to the fruit of the Spirit that faithful believers produce.* They are still produced by faith and God's grace, but they totally depend upon our own moment-by-moment choice to let the Spirit of God minister through us. James said, "I will show you my faith by my works" (James 2:18). Or you could say it another way: "I will show you my *justification* (that I am born again) by my *sanctification* (by producing fruit in my life).

The confusion over faith and works has caused untold misunderstanding in the body of Christ. In fact, we heard an entire sermon on the importance of *resting in faith* and in what God has already done. And, of course, that's very true, but the point the pastor was emphasizing was that it's all been done. *We are to simply relax and our future will be assured.* What would he say about verses such as Luke 13:24, which tell us to "*Strive* to enter in at the strait gate: for many, I say unto you, will seek to enter in and shall *not* be able," and Hebrews 4:11, which says, "Let us *labor*, therefore, to enter into that rest, lest any man fall after the same example of unbelief." The confusion occurs because, yes, we are to rest in our justification, but we are also to strive and labor in our sanctification to produce the "fruit of the Spirit," which will assure our future. As Christians, we continually get these two concepts confused.

Understanding the difference between *justification*, which is a free gift and requires no works, and *sanctification*, which requires effort and works of the Spirit, is absolutely critical.

The Difference Between Works of the Spirit and Works of the Flesh

The Pulpit Commentary says, "*Work is our fruit*. It is the product of our very being . . . All real work is a growth from a man's life. The worker will be judged by his work . . . Just as the tree exists for the sake of its fruit. It must bear fruit or it is useless. God's test of the great judgment will ignore the fame of popular preaching, the glitter of daring thinkers and the honor of exalted positions. All will be judged on the quality of their work."[6]

Works (Strong's #2041, *ergon*), which means "toil or labor," can have either a good connotation or a bad one. The works that God refers to as "good" in the Bible are those deeds, actions, and fruit that the Holy Spirit directs and produces through us by His *dunamis* power. The "bad works" that the Bible refers to are those things that the flesh directs and that are accomplished by our own power and ability. The difference between them is not only the *motive* behind the action, but also the *one* accomplishing the work (Romans 12:9–18).

"Works of the Spirit" are those actions prompted, directed, and produced by the Holy Spirit and that, ultimately, will bring glory to Christ. In contrast, "works of the flesh" are those deeds done in our own power and ability and that elevate us. The Bible tells us that everything we do is to magnify Christ, not ourselves.

We don't do "good works" to *earn* God's Love or to earn ourselves a place in the Millennium. Doing good works is simply the outgrowth of "walking by the Spirit." Here's a perfect example:

> The pastor of a small fundamental church in Wisconsin had in his congregation an elderly couple who lived on a farm, but who were unable to milk their cows anymore. Because of their advanced age, it was too difficult for them. The pastor of this small church, got up at three every morning, went over to their farm—many miles

> away from his own home—and milked their cows for them, then returned home to his young family. No one in the congregation knew about this. Some friends of the elderly couple, who were personally acquainted with the situation, told us the story. This pastor didn't do this to earn God's Love, but it was simply a natural outflow of the Life of God in his heart. The Spirit of God prompted him to do it and he just obeyed. *This is a work of the Spirit that God will reward.*

"Yea, a man may say, Thou hast faith, and I have works; show me thy faith without thy works, and *I will show thee my faith by my works*" (James 2:18). Our faith will be demonstrated by our "good and righteous works" (James 2:14–26).

Works of the Spirit

What are some of the other works of the Spirit, the righteous deeds, or the fruit of the Spirit that God desires in our lives? It might be doing something godly for someone who has betrayed us, belittled us, or used us. It might be praying for someone who has told lies about us. It might be reaching out to someone who in the past has ignored us or snubbed us. Works of the Spirit would be responding in a godly way and *doing what Jesus would do.*

In the flesh, these kinds of reactions are totally impossible. Only through God's Spirit of Love and power can we respond in this way (John 3:6). Remember that God's Love has two sides to it. It's a long-suffering Love, but it's also a tough Love. We want to emphasize that we're not talking about being "doormats," but about reacting as Jesus would (1 Peter 3:8).

Scripture tells us that God created us "unto good works, which He ordained that we should walk in them" (Ephesians 2:10).

Again, our motive in doing good works is not trying to *earn* or *work* our way to heaven, but simply allowing God to have His way in us. As a result, we become *partakers of His Life*, and fruit will result.

Following is an example of Spirit-led works:

> Andrea, a real-estate friend of ours, had just listed a home for sale by a family with two young children and a mom who was eight months pregnant. The home was adorable but the yard was totally trashed, obviously because the mom was unable to pick anything up in her condition. Her hands were full just keeping up with her two young children and expecting a baby in just one month.
>
> As Andrea left the home with the signed contract in hand, she saw the yard and briefly thought about hiring a gardener. But

realizing the suggestion could possibly offend the owners and that they probably couldn't afford one, she quickly rejected the idea.

When she got to the car, she felt the Lord say to her "I want *you* to help them." Andrea was also stressed financially, so she quickly thought "no way!" God, however, would not give her peace until she finally said, "Okay, Lord, what do you want me to do?" In her heart, she knew immediately. She went straight home, changed her clothes, and out of obedience to the Lord went back to the little home and spent the rest of the afternoon picking up the fallen tree branches, the weeds, and overgrown bushes, and renting a U-Haul to take it all to the dump. She even bought and planted flowers to replace the old dead ones. That night she experienced the "peace that passes all understanding" (Philippians 4:7).

So, "works of the Spirit" are not things we do to earn God's approval or our sanctification, but simply things we do out of obedience when His Spirit moves us. Our motive is not to try to *earn* our way to heaven or to earn rewards, but comes from our love of God and our desire to do His Will.

See *Chart 28: Works of the Spirit*

As we said earlier, the defining line between "works of the Spirit" and "works of the flesh" is not only the *motive* or source behind the deed, but also *who* accomplishes the work—*i.e.* who prompts it and then who performs it.

When we make "faith choices" to do God's will no matter how we feel or what we think, then God's Love and His Life will be freed to flow. This is what will then produce those "good works" (fruit of the Spirit) that we were created for. These works will be classified as gold, silver, and precious stones at the Bema Seat of Christ (1 Corinthians 3).

Works of the Flesh

See *Chart 29: Works of the Flesh*

If, however, our motive is our *own will* and the deed is performed through our *own power* and strength, it's going to be a "work of the flesh." In this case, we will have quenched God's Spirit in our hearts by sin and self, and the source of our works will be our own will and desires, performed by our own strength and abilities. As a result "unfruitful works" will be manifested. The Bible calls these "works of the flesh." They are the wood, hay, and stubble that will be burned at the Judgment Seat of Christ (1 Corinthians 3:12).

Works of the Spirit

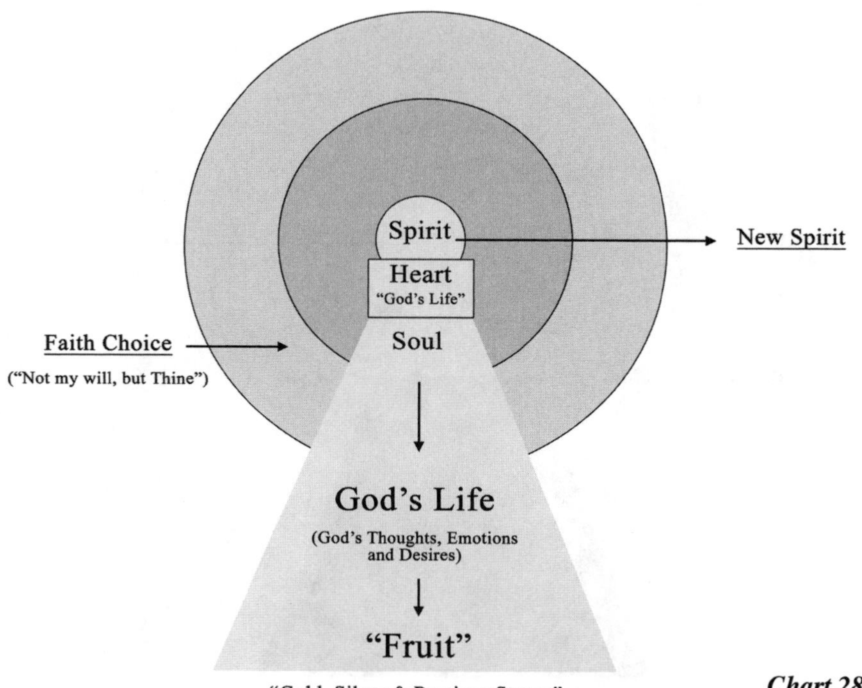

Chart 28

Galatians 5:19–21 names a few of these works of the flesh: adultery, fornication, uncleanness, lasciviousness, idolatry, hatred, jealousy, strife, wrath, seditions, heresies, envyings, murders, drunkenness, revelings, and so forth. These are things we choose to do in our *own* strength, by our *own* ability (John 3:19).

Remember the example we gave in chapter six about the "sure-all method" for receiving kingdom rewards? It suggested that if we pass out tracts, teach a Sunday school class, and so forth, we will be sure to inherit the kingdom and receive a reward. Now, of course, all of the things *can* be done in the Spirit and please God. But unfortunately with a list like this, many will miss the whole point of what righteous deeds really are, because every one of the things on the list can also be motivated by the flesh and accomplished by our own natural abilities. We can easily pass out tracts *in the flesh* and teach a Sunday school class *in the flesh* without ever having heard from the Lord . . . without ever participating in God's imparted Life at all . . . and without ever exchanging lives with Christ. Titus 1:16 talks about these kinds of believers: "They profess to know God; but *in works they deny Him*" (Titus 1:16).

Works of the Flesh

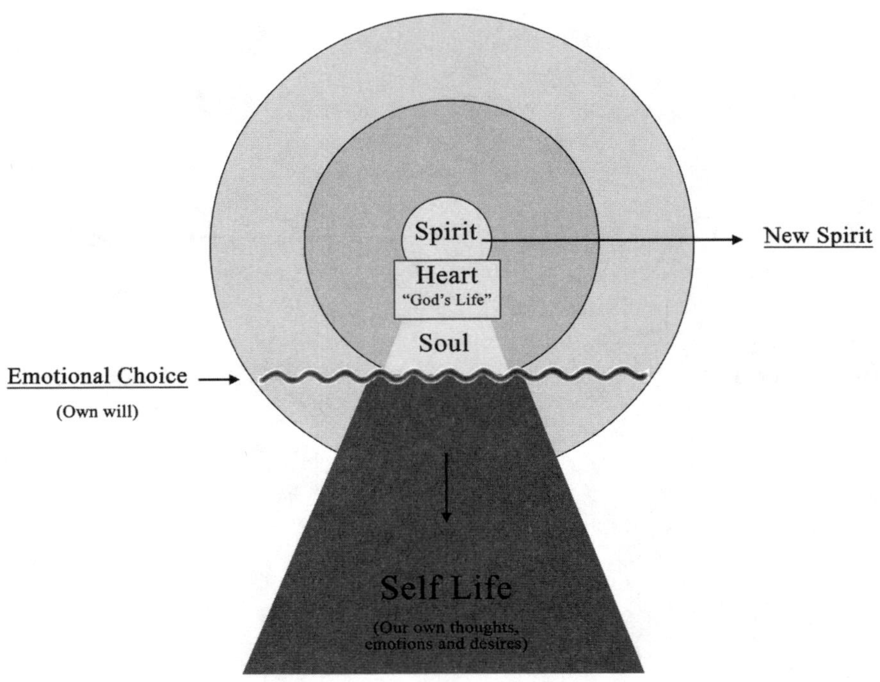

Chart 29

With works of the flesh, *we* decide for ourselves what we are going to do. And then we set about doing the action in our own strength and ability. We don't pray about it or consult with the Lord, but we depend totally upon our own love, our own wisdom, and our own power to do the action. We strive, we work, and we labor, but we really never know whether God is behind the work or not. Instead we do the work to please men, to show our spirituality, and to feel good about ourselves. Down deep, however, we never enjoy that peace that passes all understanding. Peace is the barometer that lets us know whether God is involved or not.

God's rewards will be given out at the Bema Seat in perfect proportion to what we did in the Spirit (gold, silver, and precious stones) here on earth.

Law versus Faith

This brings us to another confusing area. What about those Christians who try to keep the law *after* they become believers? Is this *faith* or is this *works*?

The Law (the five books of Moses) is good and it's pure, and it shows us our sin and tells us what God's will is. But the law *never* will lead anyone to salvation. *The law never made anything perfect* (Hebrews 7:19). The law is not the remedy. Faith is!

The Old Testament saints had *the law* (Strong's #8451). The problem was that they didn't have the "indwelling power of God" to help them keep it. In the New Testament we not only have the law (God's Word), we also have the *dunamis* power of God enabling us to keep it. And that's what will lead others to salvation. We don't keep the law to earn our way to heaven or to convince people about Christ; we yield by faith to the Spirit of God to produce His Life through us and *that's* what will convince others about the reality of Christ.

So, the remedy is faith in the power of God, which will accomplish His will in our lives and at the same time, be shown forth in Agape Love! This is what not only will lead others to Christ, but also bring about the good works that God is looking for.

Legalism—trying to keep the law by good works—actually renders Christians powerless. The Bible validates this: "Stand fast in the liberty wherewith Christ hath made [you] free, and be not entangled again with the yoke of bondage" (Galatians 5:1). Romans 7:1-4 tells us anyone who tries to keep the law *after* he has the Spirit of God in him is really an "adulterer" (Galatians 3:12a). In other words, their attempt at keeping the law indicates they have not really died to themselves, nor have they surrendered themselves completely to Christ (Galatians 3:19–24). They are still trying to work their way to salvation. However, the Word of God makes it clear that "by the flesh shall no man be justified" (Galatians 2:16).

The salvation of our *spirit* is a free gift. Nothing is required of us but faith in Christ. The salvation of our *soul* (or sanctification), however, is a different matter. *It requires obedience, not to the law, but to the Spirit of God so that we might walk in His righteousness and His Love.* Any attempt at keeping the law in our own strength after we become believers indicates that we have not really relinquished ourselves to Christ (Galatians 5:4).

Yes, it's true that knowledge of sin comes by the law, and that it is our schoolmaster to show us our need of a Savior (Galatians 3:24–25). This is the fruit of the law. But the law does not set us free from sinful things—sinful thoughts, emotions, or desires, lust of the flesh, pride of life, and so forth. It merely points them out. (Hebrews 7:19) So, the law is not the remedy! *The remedy is faith in the dunamis power of God, which not only points out our sin and self, but also helps us deal with it and get rid of it* (1 John 1:9).

This is what sets us free (Galatians 5:1).

"For all the law is fulfilled in one word, even in this: thou shalt love thy neighbor as thyself" (Galatians 5:14). In other words, by Love we are to serve one another. Trying to keep the law does just the opposite of this,

it often turns people off and pushes them away from the Lord. They sense the absence of Love. Remember, "They will know we are Christians by our *Love*" (John 13:35). It doesn't say they will know we are Christians *by our keeping the law*.

What we need in the body of Christ now are more living examples of Christ's Love, not more legalism! "Love is what fulfills the Law" (Romans 13:10).

Grace

In contrast to the law, *grace* (Strong's #5485, *charis*) means "to give something unconditionally without the expectation of any return." In Christian terminology, *grace* means "divine favor," favor that has been bestowed upon us by the Lord and then prompts thanksgiving, praise, and rejoicing on our part. *Grace is an undeserved, free gift from God that cannot be earned. It's unmerited favor from the Lord.*[7]

"For by grace you are saved, through faith and that not of yourself, it is a *gift of God*" (Ephesians 2:8).

Grace is what brings us to God and grace is what enables us to stay there. By grace we are saved and by grace we are justified. *These are things that the law could never do* (Romans 3:21–31). In fact, if righteousness came by the law, then Christ died in vain (Galatians 2:21). The truth is His righteousness came by "grace." *Grace is really the antithesis to the law* (John 1:17).

The Christian life, therefore, from beginning to end, is really one of grace. *Faith is simply our response to God's grace.*[8] If we attempt in any way to earn God's favor by any other means besides faith, we have fallen away from the grace that He has already supplied (Galatians 5:4). Consequently, it is imperative that we make a clear distinction between *justification*—free by God's grace—and *sanctification*—earned by faith—because our future inheritance depends upon it (1 Corinthians 3:14–15).

In Conclusion

The salvation of our *spirit,* then, is a free gift. Nothing is required of us but *faith* in Christ. The salvation of our *soul* (sanctification), however, is a different matter. It requires obedience, *not* to the law, but to the Spirit of God so that we might genuinely walk in *His* righteousness, *His* Love, and *His* power, thereby producing fruit. *Faith is simply the means by which all of this is accomplished. It is the vehicle by which God's Spirit and His Love works in us. Without faith, it is impossible to please God.* Faith, however, comes in the form of a constant choice and it's a choice we can never stop making. It is not automatic. *Just as God loves us unconditionally, we must constantly choose to trust Him unconditionally.*

Having unconditional faith and trust in God and the future He has planned for us leads us to hope that will become a "tree of Life." Losing faith in God and the heritage He has planned for us, however, leads to despair, hopelessness, and a broken heart.

Faith, Hope, and Love are essential ingredients in our walk with the Lord. But the greatest of these is *Love*.

Chapter Twelve

What Is an Overcomer?

Longing to Be an Overcomer

This probably is one of the most important chapters of the entire book because it contains the practical application of sanctification. It will cover *how* we say no to the world, the flesh, and the devil, and *how* we say yes to the Spirit of God. It's easy to verbally agree "we must overcome the world, the flesh, and the devil," but it's very difficult to do in practice.

If we are honest with ourselves, most of us long to be overcomers in every area of our lives. It's what we are called for, what we are being trained for, and the purpose of our lives. In other words, it's what the Christian life is all about. But, in actual practice, many of us stumble and fall continually.

An overcomer is someone who faces all of the challenges in his life with one attitude—God will be faithful no matter what. This believer will possess that "peace that passes all understanding." He is a person who knows in his heart that if he calls upon the Lord and seeks His face, he *will* be delivered.[1] And even though he doesn't understand all that God has allowed, he still chooses to rely upon Him anyway. He knows that God will be faithful to His Word and that He *will* perform His promises in His timing.

Learning to be an overcomer, therefore, is absolutely essential to our Christian walk. Otherwise, why would God emphasize *overcoming* as the key to inheriting His kingdom? (See Revelation 2 and 3.)

As mentioned in the Introduction, many Christians have been taught that if we are believers, we are automatically overcomers. The Scripture used as proof text is 1 John 5:4: "For whatsoever is born of God overcomes the world: and this is the victory that overcometh the world, even our faith. Who is he that overcometh the world, but he that believeth that Jesus is the Son of God."

Positionally, it's absolutely true that we *are* overcomers the moment we believe, because Jesus Christ is in us and *He* is the true overcomer (John 16:33). But *experientially,* (in actual fact), how many of us are actually overcoming in our everyday lives? In truth, most of us haven't the slightest idea how to really gain victory over the world, the flesh, and the devil. That's what this chapter is all about.

Definition of an Overcomer

In chapter four we discussed *who* the overcomers are in Revelation 2 and 3 and we recounted some of the incredible promises God makes to these overcomers. In this chapter we want to explore exactly *what* an overcomer is and just *how* we can become one. This is the practical application part of 1 John 5:4.

The Greek word for *overcome* is *nikao* (Strong's #3528), which means "to subdue, conquer, or gain the victory over something." It occurs almost fifteen times in Revelation alone and means "to have victory over hostile powers." Overcomers are those believers who have learned how to *refuse* the world, *forbid* the flesh, and *bind* the enemy. They have learned how to deny themselves, relinquish their self-life regardless of how they feel, what they think, or what they want, and have chosen by faith to trust God's indwelling *dunamis* power. They are the genuine conquerors because they have learned how to depend upon Christ's power to bring about His will. These are the believers who have survived the furnace of affliction and have come forth as pure gold. They are not perfect, but they are always willing to try again. That's why they are called overcomers. They know that *God will be faithful to cleanse and wipe away their sin and self, and give them a new, fresh start* (1 John 1:9).

The definition of *overcoming* is simply "freedom from the *world*"—our circumstances and other's responses (Galatians 1:4); "freedom from our *flesh*"—our natural thoughts and emotions; and "freedom from the *enemy*"—Satan and all his hordes (Revelation 12:11). God has given believers the authority and the power to overcome all three of these hostile powers.

Overcoming Is God's Will for All Believers

In our extensive research for this project, we came across a book that stated: "Overcomers are a special category of Christians." In other words, not all Christians are meant to be overcomers, *nor should they even try to be.* This is the kind of Christian thinking that has kept the body of Christ anemic, weak, and failing. If we are all *not* supposed to be overcomers, then how are we supposed to win the war against the world, the flesh, and the devil? How are we supposed to overcome all things as Revelation 21 instructs us? And how are we supposed to gain the blessings that Revelation 2 and 3 talk about? What kind of a special category are they talking about here? *This kind of Christian philosophy, plus an ignorance of the kingdom perspective, has allowed the enemy to gain huge inroads in our lives. Experience tells us that we have not overcome him; he has overcome us!*

Being an overcomer is God's will for every believer (Revelation 2:7, 11, 17, 26; 3:5, 12, 21; 21:7). We are "not to be overcome with evil, but we are to overcome evil with good" (Romans 12:21). God wants every believer to be sanctified, a partaker of His Life, and thus, an overcomer (1 Thessalonians 4:3). Whether a believer does so or not, however, is their own choice.

"Religious" people often try to overcome the world, the flesh, and the devil by *removing themselves* from them. Spiritual believers, on the other hand, do so by experiencing a co-death with Christ and then allowing His Life to overcome these things through them.

Overcoming Is Not Automatic

Despite what some believers say about 1 John 5:4, *the ability to overcome is* not *automatic!* Just because we are believers and Christ lives in us, does not mean we're going to instantaneously overcome. We won't! This is the striving and laboring part of sanctification that Hebrews 4:11 and Luke 13:24 talk about. We are *all* meant to be overcomers because Christ, who is the *real* overcomer, lives in us (Revelation 17:14). Not *all* of us, however, choose to lay our lives down so that He *can* overcome through us. It would be like saying *all of us who have God's Love in our hearts always show forth that Love in our lives.* Unfortunately, we don't. A personal choice is always involved. In the same way, we are not automatically overcomers. *It all depends upon our continuing moment-by-moment faith choice to let Christ live His Life out through us by the power of His Holy Spirit.* It's the daily release of His Life in us that will give us that victory.

Most of us in difficult situations, unfortunately, do just the opposite. When we are hurting, we make emotional choices that end up quenching God's Life in our hearts; *or* we depend upon our own will and desires and make our own plans; *or* we devise our own rules and regulations; *or* we try to overcome the world, the flesh, and the devil by removing ourselves totally from them. It's easy to be spiritual when there is no one else around. Unfortunately, life is just not like that. Life is full of conflicts, challenges, and obstacles that we must learn to overcome, not run from.

Thus, the theory that we are all overcomers no matter what we do in our Christian life has robbed the church of the truth and clouded its perspective of grace.

If we want to have peace and joy and purpose in our lives *now* and have positions of responsibility in the coming kingdom, we need to learn how God designed us to overcome. Faith is the bridge between God's promises and our overcoming. In other words, overcoming will not work without faith.

The Authority of Believers to Overcome

The question becomes: How can we develop the kind of faith that will lead us to victory and to becoming overcomers?

At our new birth God not only gives us His strength (*His power*) to do His will, as we talked about in chapter nine with the *dunamis, kratos,* and *ischus* power of God, He also gives us *His authority* to choose His will *regardless of how we feel or what we think.* As mentioned in chapter

9, the Greek word for this kind of authority is *exousia* (Strong's #1849), which means "the right to exercise power or the right of the person in charge" (Matthew 26:39). *This authority originates with God's Life, because, obviously, He is the Person in charge.* He is also the ultimate source of all authority.[2] The Father passed that authority on to Christ, and through Christ, to us.[3] Because Christ lives in us, we, too, can be bearers of that authority. In other words, *exousia* belongs to God Himself, but because He has commissioned us as His representatives, we, too, can call upon His authority.

The Word of God is what gives us this authority and the Spirit of God is what gives us the power. These two phenomenal gifts—the authority and power of Christ—are not only the keys to overcoming the world, the flesh, and the devil (all the challenges in this life), but they are also the keys to the future Millennial Kingdom.

If we didn't have God's permission to make non-emotional, non-feeling choices to do His will, His power would really be of no use to us. But God knows that and He has given us not only His authority to choose something we don't feel or even want to do, but also His power to perform that choice in our lives. Philippians 2:13 confirms this: "For it is God which worketh in you *both to will and to do* of His good pleasure."

Ignorance of this incredible authority and power from God has caused untold grief for the body of Christ. There are more severed relationships, more hopelessness, more substance abuse, more mental breakdowns, and more emotional issues than at any other time in history. *Rather than overcoming, we are being overtaken.*

Our lack of understanding in this critical area of authority is one of the reasons Satan is making such headway in so many of our lives. It's also why he hates this message so much. He can't let us connect the dots and find a pathway to victory. He has to keep us mentally, emotionally, and spiritually in the dark. He is devoted to keeping us "infants" and "spiritual babes." He can't let us progress to spiritual maturity and to develop a kingdom perspective. And unfortunately he is doing a good job at *all* of the above!

Many ask: Do we really have the authority to choose to *do* something we don't feel, don't want to do, or don't think will work? Is this a legitimate choice? Can we override our real thoughts and emotions in order to do this?

The answer is absolutely yes! We can't, but *He* can!

We not only have God's authority (*exousia*) to make choices we don't feel, we also have His strength (*kratos*) to implement those choices in our lives.[4] John 10:18 gives us Christ's example of having the authority and power not only to lay His Life down, but also the authority and power to pick it back up again. John 1:12 confirms that we, too, have this same spiritual authority: "As many as received Him, to them gave He power [*exousia*] to become the sons of God, even to them that believe on His Name."[5]

The Dictionary of New Testament Theology says, "Our authority is founded in the rule of Christ."[6] We exercise that power only by the authority that *God* has given us. Again, it's the *Word of God* that gives us the authority and the *Spirit of God* that gives us the power.

(For more information on the "Power and Authority of the Believer," be sure to see the Supplemental Study Notes Section of the appendix.)

"Faith Choices"—The Way to Overcome

Making a choice to do God's will by God's authority, regardless of how we feel, is called a "faith choice." It's a choice that is usually contrary to what we think, what we feel, and what we want to do. *It's a choice to do God's will regardless of our negative thoughts and emotions.*

Faith choices—contrary choices, or non-feeling choices—are the means by which we exercise God's authority and power. It's simply saying, "Not as I will, but as Thou wilt" (Matthew 26:39). In other words, *we* make the choice to do God's will, *He* then implements that choice in our lives. As 2 Corinthians 8:11 says, "As there was a readiness to will, so there may be a performance also."

Faith choices are how we initiate (energize, trigger, start) God's Spirit of power to work in our lives, and also how His promises are then realized.

Nonbelievers can make all the non-feeling choices they want to, but it will never do them any good, because they don't have another power source (another spirit) within them to perform *anything different* than what they naturally think or feel. Christians, however, do! *Because we have Christ's divine nature—His Life in us—we have His authority not only to choose His will (regardless of how we feel or what we think) but also His power to perform His will in our lives no matter how we feel* (1 John 4:4; Mark 6:7).

Our responsibility is simply to choose to "put off" our sin and self by God's authority and allow Him to accomplish His will in our lives by His power and might.

Let me give you an example of how He can make us overcomers in the middle of the most difficult situations.

An Example: "Your Will, Not Mine"

The following story describes the power and authority God has given us to overcome the flesh. A woman named Sheri wrote an incredible letter to us.

> It was the last day of our trip home to Florida to visit our family and I was at my husband's parents' house where we'd always stayed, packing alone. All the kids were at the beach and Ken, my husband, was out fishing with two brothers-in-law.

The Lord had me stay home alone and soon I would find out why. As I was packing, the Holy Spirit led me to Ken's suitcase and had me lift up the bottom of the inside of it to find an address book with over two pages of women's names and their descriptions. At first I froze, as tears of unbelief welled up deep inside of me. I wanted to run (I felt like I had finally found my ticket out of a very unhappy marriage), but the still, small voice of the Spirit of God within constrained me. *"Remember, I'm in control,"* He said. *"How you handle this and the choices you make are critical. Choose to walk by faith, not your feelings, and your life will change."*

I called a friend and placed myself under her accountability and received some wise counsel as to how to proceed. My husband arrived home shortly after that and with the book in my hand. I asked him if this was happening all over again. He said, "Yes." He just looked at me and said, "I am going to hell. You know Jesus. Will you please pray for me!"

Those were perhaps the most honest words I have ever heard him say. So I did pray and I asked God, "May Your will and not mine be done. I give this to You and it is now in Your hands." (My own feelings inside were screaming, "Run, get out, this is your chance!" But I chose, by faith, to really mean what I had just said in my prayer.)

Immediately, Ken began to confess everything. He took the book from my hands, ran into the adjoining bathroom and lit it on fire. When he came back he said, "It is time to expose my sin."

A dear pastor that we know came over that night and spent three hours with Ken out in the street. Later, the pastor asked me to come out and told me that "Ken has just had a Damascus Road experience." I wouldn't have believed him, except that I had prayed those very same words for my husband many times. And in a prayer meeting just a month earlier, someone gave me a word for my husband, using "the Damascus Road" analogy. Then the pastor said to me, "God has heard your prayer. Ken was saved tonight and baptized out in that street." Well, you can imagine the extreme feelings I was experiencing!

> The next few weeks involved a lot of pain, but an unfolding of the glory of God like I have never seen before. Ken confessed to all his close friends. He confessed to our four teenage children, my mom, sisters and two pastor friends that he was a false convert living a life headed for hell. He even named all his sins sparing the grossness of the details to protect their imaginations. Telling the children was the hardest of all. They each began to cry. They thought their dad *was* a Christian. But God's glory shined, even through this, and He began to heal all of our hearts.
>
> Eventually, Ken asked me to marry him again [renew our vows] and our lives have never been the same. He now calls me from his car and holds the phone up to the marriage tapes he is listening to, so I can hear. For the first time in 19 years, we are experiencing the oneness in the Spirit that God so desires. We are continually in the Word and praying together. We have had more conversation in the past year than we've had in all our 19 years put together. Our children are alive as never before. I didn't realize till now that they, too, were dying.
>
> There is so much more to share, but God has given me a heart filled with the joy that is born out of pain, a great new love for my Savior and a hunger to know God's Love in an even deeper way. Isn't He wonderful!

Faith choices, by God's authority, are the only ones that unleash all of *God's power* to come to our aid and free us from ourselves, our circumstances, and other's reactions.

(For more information, see "*Faith Choices*" in the Supplemental Note Section of the appendix.)

God's Authority and Power

The Bible emphasizes the fact that *before* God can entrust us with authority in the kingdom to come, He wants to see the manner in which we personally multiply the authority and power He has entrusted to us here on earth. This will determine just how much power and authority we will have in the Millennial Kingdom. This godly authority and power are really the "keys to the kingdom" because they allow us to stay *sanctified*, which in turn leads us to *partaking* of Christ's Life, *overcoming,* and ultimately *to inheriting the kingdom*.

Jesus is the true Overcomer (Revelation 17:14). He said, "In the world ye shall have tribulation: but be of good cheer; *I have overcome the world*" (John 16:33). Jesus is the victor, the winner, and the conqueror, but as we allow Him to live His Life out in us, we, too, can become victors and overcomers. *It's the daily release of His Life in us that gives us that victory*. He has already given us all that we need—the authority, the power, the Love, and the wisdom; we simply must choose to let Him accomplish His will in our lives. Then we, too, will be partakers of His victory.

There are three specific areas that God wants us to overcome: the world, the flesh, and the devil.[7]

Overcoming the World

Let's first explore the "world" and see just how He tells us to overcome.

When Scripture speaks of "the world," what exactly does it mean? The Greek word for *world* is *kosmos* (Strong's #2889) and it denotes "the earth in contrast to the heavens." "The world" is often referred to as "mankind in general," "the human race," or "the sum and total of temporal possessions." It essentially means the present conditions of human affairs in opposition to God's affairs (John 7:7). It includes worldly riches, endowments, advantages, and pleasures. The main thing to remember is that the world operates by the *senses*.

1 John 2:15 tells us that we are <u>not</u> to love (*agapao*) the world, i.e. we are <u>not</u> to "totally give ourselves over to it." If we do, this Scripture says "the *Agape* Love of the Father is *not* in us." The meaning of the verb *to love* (*agapao)* here is "what we put first in our lives" and "what we commit ourselves to." We are <u>not</u> to commit ourselves to the world or put the world first. If we do, we'll quench God's *Agape* Love in our hearts, miss out on the abundant Life He has for us here, and forfeit the blessings He has planned for us in the future. (See 1 John.)

The Rich Young Ruler (Matthew 19:16-22)

A perfect example of this is the rich young ruler who asked Jesus what he had to do to have eternal life. Jesus said, "If you will be perfect [complete], go and *sell what thou hast, and give to the poor, and thou shalt have treasure in heaven*; and come and follow Me" (Matthew 19:21). When the young man heard this, he went away sorrowful for he had a great many possessions. This rich young ruler lacked the *faith* to surrender everything in which he trusted. In other words, He loved the world first.

Then Jesus said to His disciples, "It is very difficult for a rich man to enter the kingdom from heaven" (Matthew 19:23). In fact, He said, "It's easier for a camel to go through the eye of a needle, than for a rich man to enter the kingdom." (See also Mark 10:17–22.)

As Christians we have Christ's authority and His power to choose *not* to love the world and the things in it. We have Christ's authority to make faith choices to refuse the world, and then His power to implement those choices in our lives.

Things of the World to Overcome

There are three specific things of the world that *we* are to overcome (1 John 2:15–16):

1. The *lust of flesh*— a strong and sometimes uncontrollable desire for fleshly pleasures: sex, drugs, alcohol, gluttony, or any other physical pleasure. The lust of the flesh is an ungodly passion that tends toward evil. These are some of the things that we "naturally" desire and love *before the Lord.*[8]
2. The *lust of eyes*—a strong and often uncontrollable desire for: wealth, possessions, fame, position, control, vanity, or beauty. It's the love of material things. Again, these are things we naturally desire *before the Lord.*
3. The *pride of life*—a total inability to see beyond oneself. It's the height of arrogance and self-sufficiency. This is a person who is totally into himself: what he does, the money he makes and the people he influences—no one else is important. It refers to someone who is *totally consumed with self* and puts his own cares, his own career, and his own future *before God* and others.

Paul wrote that "the world is crucified unto me; *and I unto the world*" (Galatians 6:14). This needs to be our attitude toward the lust of the flesh, the lust of the eyes, and the pride of life. Scripture says we are *positionally* "dead" to these things, but *experientially* we must be the ones who constantly choose not to succumb to them. This means that we must not only rely upon the power of God in us to overcome, we must also have the faith that He will. *Our part is to make faith choices to refuse these things; His part is to bring it to pass.* "Whatever is born of God overcometh the world; and this is the victory that overcometh the world, even our *faith*" (1 John 5:4).

Remedy to Overcoming the World: *Faith*

How do we overcome these "worldly things" and love God first? We do this by making constant "faith choices" to trust God and what He promises in His Word.

As believers this has got to be our mind-set. We are to love (*agapao*) God first, by being crucified to the world—the lust of the flesh, the lust of the eyes, and the pride of life. Otherwise we will not experience any victory, peace, or joy in our lives and will end up frantically searching for meaning and purpose in all the wrong places.

Faith, then, is the watchword to overcoming the world.[9]

We must, however, constantly choose to apply that faith. It's not automatic! Faith comes in the form of a constant choice.

Only Christians can overcome the present world system, which is dominated by Satan.[10] And we do so by being willing to part with whatever belongs to us "of the world." Again, we are not saying sell everything you have that is worldly, but just be willing to do so *if God requires you to*. It's our faith in God and His Word that's going to give us the victory over the world.

Overcoming the Flesh

What Is "the Flesh"?

Next we must learn how to overcome the flesh and the power of sin that dwells therein. What exactly is meant by the "flesh"?

As Christians we glibly toss around the term "the flesh," and yet many of us don't really understand what it means. Simply put, the flesh is our old human nature—our earthly nature apart from God's divine influence; it's our "old man"—our "natural" thoughts, emotions, and desires that are usually contrary to God's. This "old man" does not go away when we become Christians. It will always be with us. It will always be prone to sin and opposed to God.

The term "flesh" can also include our "body," our natural physical being. It simply means depending upon our own strength and our own ability to accomplish God's will, rather than depending on His Spirit.

As shown on our chart, page 41, when we are first born again, God's Spirit (that gold dot) comes into our spirits and gives us a new power source. The "flesh," then, is the area that remains unredeemed. It's our "soulish" or natural thoughts, emotions, and desires, plus the motions of our bodies. This is the seat of the power of sin. The flesh is continually at war with God's Spirit.

The flesh includes things like pride, arrogance, spite, revenge, cruelty, foolishness, egotism, possessiveness, and all the other *works of the flesh* that Galatians 5:19–21 mentions. Some of us can look at this list and feel pretty good about ourselves and say, "Hey, I don't do those things! I'm okay." But what about doubt, resentment, insecurity, and selfishness? And then there's self-confidence, self-importance, self-love, self-reliance, self-trust, self-pity, self-grasping, self-seeking, self-preservation, and self-esteem. We *all* experience these things! And then there's fear. Again, we all experience fear in one way or another. *Fear is the absence of faith and fear is what cripples us*. Listen to what Scripture says about fear. "For God hath not given us the spirit of fear, but of power, and of love and of a sound mind" (2 Timothy 1:7).

These are some of the things of the flesh that we must constantly take to the Cross and deal with in order to stay clean and sanctified. The

Bible confirms this: "Dearly beloved, *let us cleanse ourselves from all filthiness of the flesh and spirit, perfecting holiness in the fear of God*" (2 Corinthians 7:1. See also Ephesians 4:22–24). *So it's our faith in the Word of God that helps us refuse the world, but it's the Cross of Christ that crucifies our flesh with its innate power.*

> "I am crucified with Christ: nevertheless I live; yet not I, but Christ liveth in me: and the life which I now live in the flesh I live by the faith of the Son of God, who loved me, and gave Himself for me."
>
> —Galatians 2:20

Consequently the way we overcome the flesh is by continually mortifying the deeds of the flesh,[11] placing ourselves on the altar as a "living sacrifice," and leaving ourselves there, *never to be removed* (Romans 12:1–2).

This is where the *kratos* power of God (Spirit-control) comes into view. God's *kratos* power helps us to rein in our fleshly thoughts and emotions, so that God's Life can come forth.

(See "The Power of Sin" in the Supplemental Study Notes Section of the Appendix for more information on the war that rages in us between the power of sin and the power of God [Galatians 5:16–17].)

Overcoming the Flesh Involves Suffering

The purpose of the Cross is to bring an end to the domination of our flesh, so that the Life of God (from our hearts) can come forth. Unfortunately it's very painful when the Cross is applied. But pain is an integral part of the sanctification process. That's what "dying to self" really means. 2 Timothy 3:12 says *all who live godly in Christ Jesus will suffer.*

Sharing in His sufferings *now* is our training for sharing in His glory *there*.[12]

We heard a pastor recently ask his congregation if anyone had ever suffered. We were shocked when only *one* person raised their hand. The rest of the church seemed to think that suffering meant physical pain, torture, or persecution in some far off country. Scripture, however, tells us that when we choose to *deny ourself, pick up our cross, and follow Christ,* we often will suffer (Matthew 16:24). Suffering is simply the result of denying ourselves and choosing to follow Christ. It is interesting that the definition of the word *deny* means to "*bar ourselves from following what our sin and self are telling us.*" When we do this it often does hurt and it is painful.[13]

Scripture tells us that the way Jesus was made "complete" (or perfect) was through suffering (Hebrews 2:10; 5:8).

Consequently when we read statements like, "The Spirit Himself beareth witness with our spirit, that we are the children of God; and if children, then heirs—heirs of God, and joint heirs with Christ . . . *if so be that we suffer with Him*," we can understand a little more clearly what is really meant (Romans 8:16–17). It's saying that if we want to be joint heirs with Him in the coming kingdom, we must constantly choose to bar (deny) ourselves from following what *we think*, what *we feel,* and what *we want*, and choose instead to follow what *He* wants.

God's plan is that we arrive at the future kingdom by the road of suffering and sanctification. "If we suffer [if we bar ourselves from following our flesh], we shall also reign with Him" (2 Timothy 2:12). And Paul wrote, "It is given unto [us] on behalf of Christ, not only to believe on Him, *but also to suffer for His sake*" (Philippians 1:29). Suffering with Christ is a way of growing like Him in holiness (1 Peter 4:1). As we ask God not only to deal with our sinful acts, but also our self-centered ways, we will suffer.

We often pray and quote Philippians 3:10: "That I may know Him, and the power of His resurrection." But what we fail to see is the rest of this Scripture, which says: "*and [to know] the fellowship of His sufferings, being made conformable unto His death.*" These principles all go together. We can't "know Him or the power of His resurrection," *without knowing* "the fellowship of His sufferings." In other words, in order to experience the power of His resurrection, we must also allow Him to conform us to His death. In order to experience *His Life*, we must first experience *His death* and resurrection.

But here's the best part. "*If we are partakers of [His] suffering, [then] shall we be also of [His] consolation*" (2 Corinthians 1:7).

Throughout Scripture "suffering" and "glory" seem to go hand in hand. The path of suffering is not the meriting of the prize, but the preparation for being glorified. Suffering always precedes glory. Romans 8, which we quoted a moment ago, ends by saying: "And if children, then heirs; heirs of God and joint heirs with Christ; if so be that we suffer with Him, *that we may also be glorified together*" (verse 17).

Through the Cross, God will give us His authority and His power to "put off" our sin and self, and then to "put on" Christ. This is what overcoming really means. We already possess Christ's Life in our hearts; we simply must make sure that is what's showing in our lives. Then He can become our comforter, our defender, and our deliverer.

Jesus' Example

Jesus gave us the ultimate demonstration of how we are to deny ourselves, pick up our cross, and follow Him (Matthew 16:24–25). Even though He didn't have a sinful human nature like our own, He nevertheless chose to go to the Cross and die so that you and I could obtain eternal life and be set free. He chose to totally lay Himself down (body, soul, and spirit) so that we could partake of His nature. He was crucified so that you and I could inherit the kingdom and one day rule and reign with Him. "For He [the Father] hath made Him [Jesus], who knew no sin, to be sin for us, that we [you and I] might be made the righteousness of God in Him" (2 Corinthians 5:21).

That's ultimate Love!

The Cross is the heart of all Love and Love is the heart of the Cross. The Cross is the only way to rise *above* all that imprisons our souls. His example shows us that "life" comes only from the Cross. Its purpose is to purge our self-life, so that God's Life can come forth from our hearts.

Christ not only suffered *before* He entered His glory, Scripture tells us that He *continues to suffer* as His "body" suffers here on earth.[14]

Remedy to Overcoming the Flesh: *Flight*

The solution to overcoming the flesh is by making faith choices—by the authority and power of God—to flee the temptations of the flesh.

Flight, then is the watchword to overcoming the flesh.[15] This is accomplished by continually choosing to "put off" the old man and "put on" Christ (Ephesians 4:22–24).

There are four practical application steps to doing this. These steps are patterned after the four steps that the priests of Solomon's Temple took in the Inner Court in order to deal with sin. We'll go over these steps very quickly here, but if you want more details, you might check out "Putting off Sin and Putting on Christ" in the *Supplemental Notes Section* of this book.

Very briefly, the priests washed their hands and feet in the Lavers of Bronze, which symbolizes our confessing and repenting of sin. Then they went to the Brazen Altar where they sacrificed their offerings, which symbolizes our giving God our sin and self and then letting His Blood atone for them. Finally, the priests bodily washed in the Molten Sea, which symbolizes being washed by the water of the Word. After the priests had done all three of these steps, they then entered the Holy Place and worshiped the Lord, which symbolizes our being reconciled with God and able to, once again, have fellowship with Him.

We call these four steps of the priests the "Steps to Sanctification." They are how we deal with our sin, give it to God, and then exchange lives with Him. This is how we overcome the flesh.

The four steps are as follows:

1. The first step is to *acknowledge our own sin and self, not try to hide or justify it*. We are simply to admit to God when we blow it. Admit when we are angry, bitter, resentful, doubtful or fearful, and so forth. Admit when we are wrong, when we fail, and when we do things in our own strength.

There is such freedom in "owning" our own sin. Because we are human, we *are* going to fail at times. We *are* going to do wrong and we *are* going to sin. But when we do, if we can be honest with God about it, confess it, and repent of it and choose by faith to bring it to the Cross, we'll be forgiven, cleansed, and sanctified (1 John 1:9). This freedom to fail and yet be forgiven allows us to be who we really are and *not* have to wear masks or facades or coverups. By doing this we will also give others with whom we are interacting the freedom to be themselves.

Freedom is one of the definitions for "overcoming." It's freedom from the *world,* which includes our circumstances and other's responses; freedom from our *flesh,* our own natural thoughts and emotions; and freedom from the *enemy,* Satan and all his demons (Revelation 12:11; Galatians 1:4).

2. Once we acknowledge what we have done wrong, the next step is to *confess it and repent of it,* which simply means to acknowledge it to God—He knows it anyway, He just wants us to admit it. *Repent* simply means "to turn around from following what our sin and self are telling us and choose to follow His Will."

A part of this second step is that we must *not only* ask God for His forgiveness for our own sins, but we must also *choose to unconditionally forgive anyone who has wronged us.* This releases that person into God's hands. It's not that we pardon that person. That's God's business. But by forgiving them we release them into His hands so that He can do what He knows is best. By doing this, we also free ourselves from Satan's arrows. If we don't forgive, we give Satan huge inroads and end up "walking in darkness" (1 John 2:10–11).

3. The third step in overcoming the flesh is that we must *now* lay everything that the Lord has shown us—all our sin and self-centeredness––down at the Cross. Only the shed Blood of Christ can atone for our sins. They have already been paid for, we are just appropriating what Christ has already done (1 John 1:9).

Hebrews tell us: "How much more shall the *Blood of Christ,* who through the eternal Spirit offered Himself without spot to God, purge your conscience from dead works to serve the living God?" (9:14). In other words, God is the only One who can free us from our sin and fill us with His Spirit.[16]

4. Finally, we must *replace the lies that we have believed with the truth of God's Word.* We must put Scripture back into our minds where the lies have been. This is why it's so important to memorize Scripture. That way even when we are out on the road, we can renew our minds.

These are the four steps to "putting off" the old man and to "putting on" the new (Ephesians 4:22–24). All of the steps can be done by making "faith choices" or non-feeling choices to do God's will regardless of what we think or feel. This is how God cleanses us of our sin and self and how we are able to stay sanctified. Jesus said, "If you don't allow Me to wash you, you will have no part of Me" (John 13:8).

Daily confession, repentance, and forgiveness will bring an incredible sense of peace and joy into our lives (Philippians 4:7). These blessings can be found nowhere else.

After personally doing these four steps of sanctification *by the power and authority of God* every day for the past twenty-five years, and sometimes many times a day, we truly believe they are the keys to the Christian walk. Only by staying a cleansed and open vessel are we able to overcome not only the flesh, but also the world and the devil. We must be sanctified before we can partake and before we can overcome.

(Be sure to see "The Steps to Sanctification" in the Supplemental Study Notes Section of the Appendix of this book for more information. Here you will find a whole section on *how to* "put off" our sin and self and *how to* "put on" Christ. Also be sure to see the "Overcoming the Flesh" prayer in the Prayer Section of the appendix. If you want even more information on renewing your mind and giving things to God, we would also recommend the little book *The Key* and the larger textbook *Be Ye Transformed.*)

Overcoming the Enemy

We overcome the *world* by making "faith choices" to apply *His Word*; we overcome the *flesh* by running to *the Cross* and fleeing temptations. What about the enemy of our souls? How do we overcome him? (See Ephesians 6:12.)

First of all, we must recognize that we are living in the enemy's territory. He is the prince of this world.[17] In other words, this world belongs to him. D. L. Moody said, "The reason so many Christians fail all through life is that they underestimate the strength of the enemy . . . The nearer you get to the Cross, the fiercer the battle."[18]

The reason Jesus came was to bring an end to Satan's rule and to free those held by it.[19] The victory that overcomes the enemy is really *the victory of Christ*. He is the One who overcomes the devil, not us. But because He lives in us, we have His authority and His power to overcome. His Word gives us the authority to choose by faith and His power gives us the ability to perform His Word in our lives.

His Word says that the way we overcome the enemy is by "the blood of the Lamb, the word of our testimony and loving not our lives unto death"[20] (Revelation 12:11). Simply put, this means we overcome the enemy *by applying Christ's Blood*, *by speaking forth His Word,* and by *experiencing a co-death with Christ on the Cross* (1 John 2:14). *Because the devil is a spirit, however, we can only overcome him when we, too, are in the spirit (i.e. cleansed of sin and self)*. We are to *first* "submit ourselves to God, *then* the enemy will flee from us (James 4:7). Only when we do this, can Christ's authority and His power function properly. Christ's Life is always in our hearts, but in order to experience it in our lives, we must be spiritually clean.

Christ came to give us "life" and that more abundantly (John 10:10). The enemy of our souls, on the other hand, wants to kill, steal, and destroy that life in us. The way we overcome him is by fighting against him in the authority and power of the Lord and by having on the "whole armor of God" (Luke 11:22–23; Matthew 12:29).

The Armor of God

In light of the intense warfare we are in and the need to know how to fight, understanding Ephesians 6:11–19 is critical. We must be strong in the power (*kratos*) of *His* might (*ischus*). Then and only then, will we "be able to stand against the wiles of the devil" (verse 11).

We are to:

- Gird our waist with *His Truth*—His Word and His Spirit.
- Put on the *Breastplate of Righteousness*—the righteousness of Christ.
- Have our feet (our souls) shod with the preparation of the *Gospel of Peace*— "putting off" the flesh and "putting on" Christ. This is the "preparation" that Christ requires for those "clean garments."
- Take the *Shield of Faith* by which we can quench the fiery darts—our choice to unconditionally trust what God has promised us in His Word.
- Put on the *Helmet of Salvation*—showing forth God's Life instead of our own.
- Pick up the *Sword of the Spirit*—the Word of God. We are to use the Word of God as our "battle axe." That's the only way we are able to stand (Jeremiah 51:20).
- *Praying always* for all saints. We are to be constantly praying to God on behalf of all the saints.
- Praying *that utterance may be given to us* to make known by "living example" the mystery of the gospel.

Perhaps now you are beginning to understand a little more clearly why the enemy hates this message of overcoming. It highlights his total inability to defeat Christ. When we begin to grasp this message, we truly will have found the keys to the kingdom.

(For a more in-depth study of the Armor of God, see *Be Ye Transformed*, chapter sixteen.)

The Keys to the Kingdom (Binding and Loosing)

The *authority* to make a "faith choice" and the *power* to implement that choice in our lives are the "keys to the kingdom." Keys open prison doors; keys release the prisoners; and keys set the prisoners free.

Jesus said: "And I will give unto thee the *keys of the kingdom of heaven;* and whatsoever thou shalt *bind* on earth shall be bound in heaven; and whatsoever thou shalt *loose* on earth shall be loosed in heaven" (Matthew 16:19. See also Matthew 18:18).

The word *bind* (Strong's #1210, *deo*) in this Scripture actually means "*to forbid, to refuse*, to shut the door or to bring into subjection." The word *overcome* is often used interchangeably with the word *bind* found in passages like Matthew 12:29: "How can one enter into a strong man's house, and spoil his goods, except he first bind [*overcome*] the strong man? And then he will spoil his house." (See also Mark 3:27.)

The New International Dictionary of New Testament Theology explains, "Here the stronger man overcomes the armed strong man, by disarming and despoiling him. The metaphor simply explains Jesus' superiority over demonic powers. *He*, again, is the victor over all the forces opposed to God."[21]

The word *loose* (Strong's #3089, *luo*) in the above Matthew 16 passage means "to *permit, to open, to allow or to release.*" To loose means to release the captive—let him go (John 11:44; Matthew 12:29).

Binding and loosing are simply Hebrew idioms for exercising the Lord's authority (*exousia*) and His power (*kratos*).[22] It is Christ's authority and His power, but because we belong to Him and He lives in us, we have His authority to *bind* the enemy, forbid the flesh, and refuse the world.

Binding and loosing have in the past been applied primarily to fighting the enemy. But we believe it can also be applied to all three areas—the world, the flesh, and the devil! What we are doing is simply saying "no" to the world, the flesh, and the enemy and "yes" to the Spirit of God.

How Are These the Keys to the Kingdom?

The basic issue in spiritual warfare is *authority*.[23]

Down through the ages, God has given His authority and His power not only to Jesus and His disciples, but also to various anointed prophets and chosen men of God. These men had God's authority to *say what was permitted* and to *say what was forbidden.* Adam Clark in his commentary on Matthew 16:19 said that when the Jews confirmed a man as a doctor of the Law, they actually put into his hands the keys to the closet in the temple where the sacred books were kept, signifying that they were giving him the authority to teach *what was to be permitted* and *what was to be forbidden*. These keys were a symbol of the delegated authority and the badge of the office.

As sanctified believers, we have that same personal authority over the temples of our bodies. We have God's authority to forbid or bind what we know is *against* His will and we have His authority to permit or loose what we know *is* His will.

This authority and power truly are the keys to the kingdom because of the chain reaction that results: "Binding" (forbidding and refusing) either the enemy, the flesh, or the world and "loosing" (releasing) their hold on us leads to *sanctification*; sanctification leads to *partaking of His Life*; partaking of His Life leads to *overcoming* the world, the flesh, and the devil; overcoming leads to *inheriting*; and inheriting leads to *ruling and reigning in the future kingdom*.

Remedy to Overcoming the Enemy: *Fight*

Binding and loosing (forbidding and permitting), therefore, are not only God's way of overcoming the world and the flesh, but *also a way of personally equipping the believer to overcome and fight the enemy.*

"Fight," then is the watchword to overcoming the devil.[24]

Again, because the devil is a spirit, we can only fight him in the spiritual dimension. Consequently, if we are not cleansed of sin and self, then God's authority and power will not operate. Only if we are sanctified can we "bind" the enemy in Jesus' Name and "loose" the strongholds and ask the power of God to come forth.

Notice, first of all, that we are speaking only about *personal* application here. We don't believe we can bind the enemy or loose the strongholds in someone else's life. Each of us must choose to do this for ourselves. We can pray and ask that *Jesus* would *bind the enemy* in that other person's life, release them from the enemies grip, and pour out His Spirit upon them, but in order for that individual to be totally freed, he must make those choices for himself.

Jesus should always be considered as our example. In regard to binding and loosing the enemy, He *bound* the enemy in the spirit—forbid him from speaking, He rebuked him, and then He commanded him to flee. By doing so, Jesus pulled down, broke up, and dissolved many fortified hideouts and other walled defenses the enemy had erected. Christ is the only One who has the overcoming power to destroy the evil one (Hebrews 2:14). But because Jesus lives in us and if we are clean, we, too, have the authority to *bind the enemy* and *ask the power of God* into the difficult situations that we face.

This brings us to another reason why we don't see more victories for Christ in the area of overcoming. The answer is obvious. We haven't really understood the delegated authority and power of Christ that we possess as children of God and that these are the Keys to the Kingdom. Many of us have seen the abuses in the area of binding and loosing, and as a result *we've "thrown the baby out with the bath water" and have missed a major truth.*

Consequently we've not been able to overcome the enemy in our personal lives, let alone help others to do so. As a result, *instead of overcoming, many of us have been overcome.*

(See the Supplemental Study Notes Section of this book for more information on the "Power of the Enemy.")

Specific Scriptures on Overcoming

With this in mind, let's return to Revelation 12:11: "And they overcame him [the devil] by the blood of the Lamb, and by the word of their testimony; and they loved not their lives unto death." What does it mean to overcome the devil by "the Blood of the Lamb," "the word of our testimony," and "loving not our lives unto death"?

The *Blood of the Lamb* means that we must not only be "born again" (justified by Christ's Blood), we must also have personally applied His Blood to our own sin and self and have become experientially sanctified. In other words, we must have already "submitted ourselves to God" (James 4:7).

The word of our testimony means we must know how to use the delegated authority (*exousia*) and power (*kratos*) that God has given us through His Word to bind, forbid, and prevent the enemy entrance into our souls. We also must know how to use that authority to loose and pull down (cast down) any strongholds that have already been established. It's essential we know God's Word in order to speak it forth in power!

And finally, *loving not our lives unto death* simply means we must be willing to surrender, relinquish, and lay down any self-life that God reveals to us, so that His Life can come forth. It's imperative that we exchange lives with Christ, remembering that *He* is the overcomer, not us.

This clarifies 1 Peter 5:8–9 and James 4:7: "Be sober, be vigilant; because your adversary the devil, as a roaring lion, walketh about, seeking whom he may devour; whom resist steadfast in the faith" and "*submit yourselves therefore to God. Resist the devil,* and he will flee from you." (See Psalm 144:1.)

Resist simply means "to stand against" or "to oppose." The way we stand against or oppose the devil is by doing the same above three things: 1) using our authority in Christ *to forbid him entrance* into our lives, 2) *pleading the Blood of Christ* over us, and then 3) *asking the dunamis power of God to fill us* and cause the enemy to flee.[25] In essence, we are saying the very same thing as "binding and loosing."

Satan's greatest fear is not a "carnal" Christian, but an "experientially sanctified" Christian who understands this kind of authority and power in Christ.

Again, the reason we don't see more victories for Christ in this area is because many of us don't understand the "Keys to the Kingdom" that

He has given us. And as a result *instead of overcoming the enemy, he has overtaken us.*

(See End Note #25 for a very interesting fact about binding and loosing.)

Pulling Down the Strongholds

In addition to binding, forbidding, and preventing the enemy's entrance to our soul by the power of Christ, we also have His authority and power to dissolve, break up, and cast down any strongholds that have already been established. "For the weapons of our warfare are not carnal, but mighty through God to the pulling down of strongholds" (2 Corinthians 10:4).

Strongholds can be old hurtful memories, past rejections, lifelong insecurities, crippling fears, and many other things that we have simply pushed down and chosen not to deal with. We must, therefore, ask the Lord *to expose* these strongholds, acknowledge them, confess them, repent of them, give them to the Lord, and then replace them with His Word—those same four sanctification steps.

2 Corinthians 10:5 tells us we are to: "[Cast] down imagination, and every high thing that exalteth itself against the knowledge of God, and [bring] into captivity every thought to the obedience of Christ." *Casting down* (Strong's 2507) means "demolishing, taking down for oneself, putting down with force and destroying." *Imaginations* (Strong's #3053, *logismos*) means "thoughts of evil intent." 2 Corinthians 10:6 continues: "And [have] in *a readiness to revenge all disobedience*, when your obedience is fulfilled." This part of 2 Corinthians 10, "having a readiness to revenge all disobedience," is our own responsibility and is referring to the four sanctification steps as the way we pull down any strongholds (Colossians 3:5–11).

Christ has given us His supernatural authority and power not only to remove the surface issues in our lives, but also to remove the root issues. "Surface issues" are current thoughts, emotions, and desires that quench God's Spirit. "Root issues" are things that have occurred previously and that we have never dealt with but simply pushed down and buried, mainly because we didn't know what else to do with them. They are issues that have not been dealt with, such as resentment, discouragement, and unforgiveness that have become root issues or strongholds of bitterness, depression, and hatred (Hebrews 12:15). And if we don't understand the power and authority that we have in Christ to dissolve these hideouts of the enemy and replace them with God's Spirit, we become perfect targets for more of the enemy's deceit, lies, and traps.

There's a huge difference between simply defining the sin and actually pulling down the strongholds of the enemy that helped produce that sin in the first place. By doing the latter, we will destroy any deception around which the strongholds are built. Isaiah 44:20 talks about "*a deceived heart that makes us unable to deliver our own soul.*" In other words, if our spirit is quenched and our heart covered, we'll not be able to recognize the lies that are keeping us captive—meaning, we'll continue to be open to deception! Scripture tells us: "If we say we have no sin, we lie and the truth is not in us" (1 John 1:8). We must acknowledge the real truth, not our perception of the truth. The real truth is what sets us free (John 8:32).

If we have missed the root causes—the strongholds—of our sin, Nahum 3:19 tells us: "There is no healing of thy bruise." Then what often happens is that we erect our *own* "walls of protection," our own "truth," to cover these vulnerabilities. *These self-erected defenses can actually assist the enemy, rather than defeating him* (Nahum 3:17). That's why they are called "snares of the devil" in 2 Timothy 2:26 and "snares in our sides" in Judges 2:2–3. The result is that "*there is no healing of [our] bruise.*"

By asking the Lord to expose these strongholds, and by confessing and repenting of them, we will destroy any deception around which the strongholds are built. *God* is the One who must expose these breaches, but *we are the ones who must lay them at the Cross by the authority and power of Christ.* Then Christ can cleanse us, refill us, and once again empower us with His Spirit.

This is where the overcoming *dunamis* power of God—that "spiritual strength" of God—comes in.

It's imperative that we surrender every negative emotion, every self-centered thought, every selfish desire, every attitude, every fear, and every stronghold—inside and out—that might create opportunities for the enemy. We do this by recognizing our sin, by confessing and repenting of it, by giving it to God, and by replacing it with the Word.

The bottom line is: *We cannot inherit the Millennial Kingdom without being continually sanctified; and we cannot be sanctified without making faith choices; and we cannot make faith choices without knowing the power and authority of Christ.*

We spoke about the importance of preparation in chapter six. Now you can see how it determines our victory or defeat (Revelation 19:7–8).

Satan does not fear intellectual understanding of spiritual things; what he does fear is a Christian overcomer. When our life begins to change from self-centeredness to other-centeredness, from human love to God's Love, and from human understanding to God's wisdom, the enemy becomes ferocious. He doesn't fear doctrine; he fears Christ-likeness and the results of sanctification.

Three Stages of Warfare

In conclusion, there are three stages of warfare that we must be aware of in order to overcome the world, the flesh, and the devil:

1. FAITH: In the *physical realm*, we must learn to wage war against the world and all its temptations by not loving it, but by having *faith* to apply His Word. *Faith* is the watchword to overcoming the world (1 John

2:15).

2. FLIGHT: In the *soulish realm*, we must learn to do warfare against the flesh and the power of sin that dwells therein by making choices to *flee* the temptations of the flesh. *Flight* is the watchword to overcoming the flesh (Romans 8:2).

3. FIGHT: And finally, in the *spiritual realm*, we must *fight* the enemy by applying the Blood of Christ, the power and authority that God has given us to speak forth His Word, and by loving *not* our lives unto death. *Fight* is the watchword to overcoming the devil (Revelation 12:11).

Thus, you can see the critical importance of surrendering every negative emotion, every self-centered thought, every selfish desire, every attitude, every fear, and every stronghold—inside and out—that might prevent us from becoming overcomers in any of these three areas.

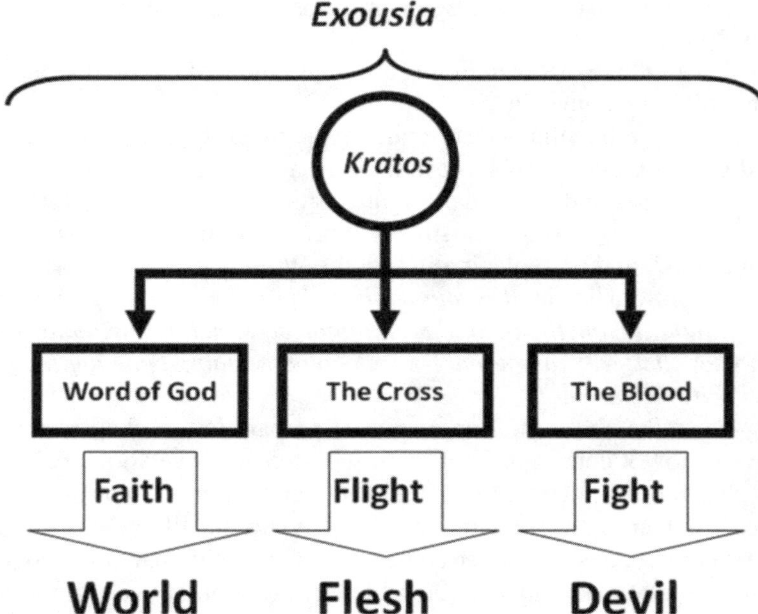

The Victory of Christ

The victory of Christ is not only that He defeated and *overcame* Satan, but that He *overcame* the world and the power of sin as well. As believers, because Christ lives in us, we have that same personal authority and power to overcome. "For though He was crucified through weakness, yet He liveth by the *dunamis* power of God. *For we shall live with Him by the [same] dunamis power of God*" (2 Corinthians 13:4). This is the key not only to our lives here on earth, but also the key to reigning with Him in the future kingdom as well (Luke 12:33–37).

Overcomers will possess the wedding garment that is recognized as the necessary attire for inheriting the kingdom. They will also receive special rewards and blessings and the prize of the high calling of God—not only an entrance to the kingdom, but also the possibility of ruling and reigning with Him (Revelation 2–3; Philippians 3:14). "Brethren, give diligence to make your calling and election sure: for if ye do these things, ye shall never fall: for so an entrance shall be ministered unto you abundantly into the everlasting kingdom of our Lord and Saviour Jesus Christ" (2 Peter 1:10–11). Nearness to Christ is the privilege afforded the overcomers, not only in this lifetime, but also in the Millennium.

This is the *preparation* that God wants each of us to incorporate into our lives so we can be ready for His soon return.

For Thine, O Lord, is the Kingdom and the Power—

Section Four

The Glory

"For Thine is the Kingdom, the Power and the Glory."

—Matthew 6:13

Chapter Thirteen

The Return of His Glory

God's Glory Departs

"God's glory" is a theme that runs throughout the book of Ezekiel. It's an aspect of God's character that seems to be featured more prominently in the book of Ezekiel than any other of the prophetic books. Like Isaiah before him, Ezekiel was called to prophesy to the Jews, many of whom had already been exiled to Babylon and who were still in shock over the destruction of Jerusalem.

One of Ezekiel's visions was of the destruction of Jerusalem in 586 BC and how the Glory of God left Solomon's Temple as the Babylonians besieged the city (Ezekiel 10:18). This signaled the end of a relationship between God and His people that had existed for four centuries.[1] Because His people had been stubborn, obstinate, and rebellious, the divine King had finally abandoned His residence.

God's chosen people had despised His laws, turned aside from worshiping Him, filled the land with violence, and persecuted His prophets. Thus, His glory departed and God withdrew His presence.

Ezekiel had been appointed by God to be a "watchman" for the Jews, not only to warn them about the possibility of divine judgment, but also to encourage them about the incredible blessings that lay ahead. He was to tell them that another glorious kingdom was coming and that *this* kingdom would *never* be destroyed.

God told Ezekiel not to fear how the Jews responded, but to speak *His* words and *His* words only (Ezekiel 2:6–7). Success, God told him, would be measured by his faithfulness to proclaim the message, not by Israel's response. (A good lesson for us to remember also.)

The highlight of the book of Ezekiel is his detailed description of the Millennial Temple in chapters 40 to 46. God gave the vision of the temple to Ezekiel not only to give hope and encouragement to the house of Israel and to make them realize that God is always faithful to His promises, but also to make them ashamed of their previous sins.

God's Glory Returns and Fills the Temple

The climax of Ezekiel's prophetic vision of the Millennial Temple occurs when the glory of God returns from the East, over the Mount of Olives, and once again, enters the temple (Ezekiel 43:1–5). Isaiah wrote that when the Shekinah Glory returns, it will cover Mount Zion entirely (Isaiah 4:5–6). When the glory of the Lord takes possession of the temple and fills it with His radiance, it will highlight God's presence among His people again and the restoration of their fellowship. Haggai tells us that Christ Himself will dwell in this Millennial Temple, and thus, "the glory of this house shall exceed the glory of the former" (Haggai 2:9). Scripture also tells us that once God's Glory returns, it will never again depart (Ezekiel 43:6–9)!

So Ezekiel's vision validates a literal temple that will be built just before the Millennium begins. Many Old Testament prophets envisioned this very same future temple in their writings.[2] In fact, the Bible says all the nations will see the Shekinah Glory in the midst of the temple, and they will know that it is the visible manifestation of God (Zechariah 8:20–23).

Some theologians believe that Ezekiel's Temple will be the temple built during the Tribulation and ultimately will be desecrated by the Antichrist. They don't believe another temple will be built during the Millennium. The Bible tells us, however, that there will be *two* different temples. The first one will probably be built on the existing Temple Mount area in Jerusalem and is foretold to be desecrated during the Tribulation. Christ will build the second temple just as the Millennium begins. This temple will be built to the north of the existing Temple Mount area. Scripture validates this, as it says that there will be *huge* topographical changes in Israel at the end of the Tribulation. A massive earthquake will flatten the Temple Mount as we know it today and this will cause the Millennial Temple to be erected many miles to the north. Zechariah 14:4 refers to this earthquake when it talks about Jesus coming back the second time and putting His foot on the Mount of Olives, which will then split in two, leaving a huge mountain plateau in its place. This is where the future temple and city of Jerusalem will be rebuilt (Zechariah 2:4–5).

It's also interesting that "the glory of the Lord returns to this temple only *after* the separation between the sanctuary and the profane place is accomplished."[3] In other words, God's Spirit returns to the temple only when its purification is completed. God's return to Ezekiel's Temple heralds the beginning of His great redemption of Israel and His blessing on their land.

The message of Ezekiel's Temple is not only a future hope for believing Jews, it is also the Christians' "call to holiness."[4] Holiness is emphasized throughout Ezekiel's Temple, as we discussed in chapter seven. Holiness is what this future temple is all about.

The Waters from the Temple

One of the most profound aspects of Ezekiel's vision in chapter 47 is his description of the waters that will issue out from under the threshold of the Millennial Temple on the east side (verses 1–12). Specifically, these waters flow from under the East Gate of the temple downward toward the Kidron Valley. Even though these waters begin as a very small stream, they quickly flow down the side of the mountain until they actually become a raging river, which then splits into two. One stream will flow eastward toward the Dead Sea, and the other will flow westward toward the Mediterranean (Zechariah 14:8). Both will cleanse and renew everything in their path. Thousands of trees on either side of this river suddenly will come alive, bear fruit, and never lose their leaves. These waters will wash away all impurities and transform and heal as they flow. They are "living waters," reminding us that the Lord is the only One who can turn death into life!

This "river of life" is identical to the one described in Isaiah 35:6–7 and Joel 3:18. It's also reminiscent of the river in the Garden of Eden (Genesis 2:10).

Just as Ezekiel refers to a *literal* temple in Jerusalem at this time, so he is referring here to a *literal* river, as well as the *literal* healing and blessings it brings to the land of Israel. The Source of the water is, of course, the Lord. *He* is the One who sends forth this Life-giving flood.[5] Water is a symbol of spiritual life. The water is called the "River of Life," symbolizing God's redeeming power and the universal knowledge of Him.[6] *It's not only a symbol of cleansing and refreshment, it also stands for fruitfulness and beauty.*

In the first temple, Solomon's Temple, the Molten Sea and the Brazen Lavers were the only sources of water (2 Chronicles 4). In Ezekiel's Temple, however, they will be replaced by this "river of living waters" issuing out from "under the threshold of the house eastward" (Ezekiel 47:1). Christ Himself will be the fountain of living water. This river of living water will issue out from the temple in the most natural way, and end up flowing out over much of the earth. This is as if to say, the blessings of the messianic era will be like waters flowing to the ends of the earth, causing everything in its way to become green and fruitful.[7] Scripture says: "There is a river, the streams whereof shall make glad the city of God, the holy place of the tabernacles of the Most High"(Psalm 46:4). His Love, His mercy, His salvation, His healing, His forgiveness, His redemption, His grace, His pardon, His peace, His strength, and His abundant Life will *all* flow from these waters.

The climax of the book of Ezekiel is that the Lord divides the land of Israel according to the inheritance of the twelve tribes and then He establishes a new city of Jerusalem called *Jehovah-shammah,* "The Lord is here" (Ezekiel 48:35). This new city will be established on a plateau of the highest mountain. It will be fifty square miles on top with the temple to the north. Christ will rule and reign from this temple for a thousand years.

At the very end of the Millennium, after Christ has put down all satanic power and authority (1 Corinthians 15:24), He will finally unite His *earthly* kingdom with the Father's *eternal* kingdom. And there will be a *new* heaven and a *new* earth. God finally will become the "*all and in all*" which has been His plan and His purpose all along (1 Corinthians 15:28). This future heavenly kingdom will also have a river proceeding out from the throne of God and the Lamb. (See Revelation 22:1.) In this case, it will only be one river, not two.

Christ's River of Life

Ezekiel's vision is a picture of the Glory of God flowing out from the temple, filling all the earth, and making everything that it touches come alive. What can we make of this "river of Life"? What lessons are here for us personally?

Number one, are we partakers of God's glorious river of Life? Is He our salvation, our Healer, and our Life-giver? Do we possess His "river of Life" in our hearts? Are we passing it on to all those we come in contact with?

The whole event in Ezekiel—the refilling of the temple with God's glory and then, the waters of life flowing out from His presence—is analogous to a believer being filled with the Spirit and then letting the "rivers of living water" flow from his life.[8] In order for this to happen, however, we must continually stay clean and sanctified so God's Spirit *can* manifest Himself through us.

Next, we must allow that "river of Life" in our hearts to flow through us to others so they, too, can experience God's Love, His wisdom, His peace, and His joy. When we quench that river of Life, bitter water will flow from our lives instead of sweet water.

See ***Charts 30 and 31: Sweet Water or Bitter Water***

This reminds us of James 3:11–12: "Does a fountain send forth at the same place sweet water and bitter? Can the fig tree, my brethren, bear olive berries? Either a vine, figs? *No fountain can yield both salt water and fresh.*"

We must be wells and fountains of "sweet," fresh, living water, meaning that Christ's imparted Life must be able to freely come forth from our hearts, fill our souls, and permeate all our relationships. Isaiah 12:3 calls this "wells of salvation."[9] If, however, we are clogged vessels, no "sweet" water will flow from our lives, only "bitter" water.

Ye Are the Salt of the Earth

With this in mind there is one area that Ezekiel's river does *not* cleanse and does *not* heal. In fact, Ezekiel says this area is given over to "salt": "But the miry places thereof and the marishes thereof shall *not* be

"Sweet Water"

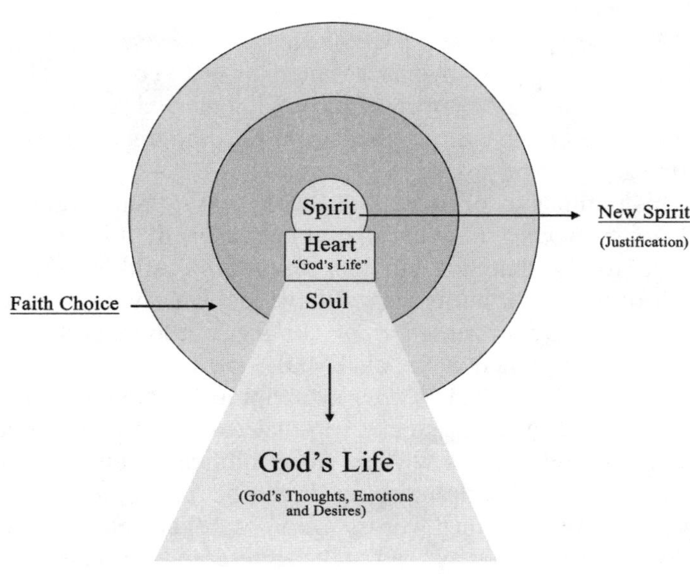

"River of Life"

Chart 30

"Bitter Water"

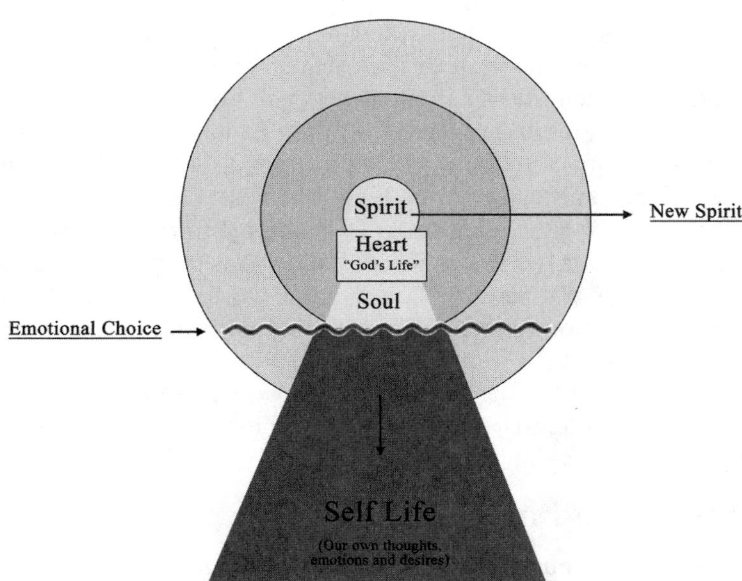

"No River of Life"

Chart 31

healed; *they shall be given to salt*" (Ezekiel 47:11). This is fascinating to us. Every place this river flows, it heals and renews and makes alive, *except the miry places and the marishes*.

Miry places (Strong's #1207) means "soil over white fine linen." *Marishes* (Strong's #1360) means a "reservoir or to collect." This Scripture says these places are "given over to salt." What the Hebrew word *salt* means here is "to pulverize, to turn to powder, to become dissolved or barren." It means no "fruit" can be produced.

This reminds us of Luke 14:34 which says: "Salt is good; but if the salt has lost its *savour*, with what shall it be seasoned? It is neither fit for the land, nor yet for the dunghill, but *men cast it out*." And Matthew 5:13: "Ye are the salt of the earth: but if the salt have lost his savour, wherewith shall it be salted? It is thenceforth *good for nothing*, but to be cast out, and to be trodden under foot of men." (See also Mark 9:50.)

Salt (Strong's # 251, *halas*) in Scripture metaphorically refers to a believer. It is used of a Christian's spiritual condition. It is emblematic of the holiness of God. But as with so many biblical terms we have studied in this book, it has a double meaning. It can be used in a positive sense or in a negative sense. In other words, "good" salt can refer to a "wise" and Spirit-filled believer, whereas "bad" salt can refer to a "foolish" believer who has quenched the Spirit and thus lost his savour. Salt is supposed to purify, preserve, and season, but if it loses its ability to do so, it will be thrown out. Christians are supposed to be the "salt of the earth," spreading the gospel and being living examples of Christ's Life. But what happens if they "lose their savour" (lose their witness)?

The Greek word for *savour* here is *moraino* (Strong's #3471), which means "to become foolish," tasteless, and unable to "give thirst." As believers we are supposed to be the "salt of the earth" and we can be so, if we are sanctified, because then Christ's living waters will flow. If, however, we have quenched His Spirit, the living waters will not be able to flow and we will be unable to give "thirst" to the world. At that point, like salt that has lost its savour, we will become "good for nothing" and "cast out."

The word for *cast out* in Luke 14 is *ballo* (Strong's #906), which is from the same root word (*Exballo*, Strong's #1544) as the "casting out" of the unfaithful servant in Matthew 25:30. This same word is also used for people who were *excluded* from the church: "He casts them out of the church" (3 John 10).

In order to inherit the kingdom, we must "give thirst" to the world by being "wise" and letting Christ's living waters flow from our lives and reflecting His image in all we do.

Christ Is All and in All

The ultimate purpose of the theocratic kingdom is that Christ ultimately might unite His *earthly* kingdom with God's *eternal* kingdom, thereby literally become our "*all and in all.*" "*And when all things shall be subdued unto Him, then shall the Son also Himself be subject unto Him that put all things under Him, that God may be all and in all*" (1 Corinthians 15:28).

This is the time that the eternal state—the new heavens, new earth, and new Jerusalem—will be formed. (See also Revelation 21:1–2.) But until that time–until "all things are subdued unto Him"—Christ must *spiritually* be our all and all (Colossians 3:11). He must not only be our "river of Life," our sweet water, but also our Source, our Standard, our Fountain, our Overcomer and the sum of all that we know and desire. He is everything we need for justification, for sanctification, and for glorification (1 Corinthians 1:30).

He must be our life itself (Galatians 2:20). He is the sole and the substance of all we experience as Christians. He is the Center and Circumference of truth, the Alpha and the Omega. He is the Author and Finisher of our faith, the Savior in whom dwelleth all the fullness of the Godhead. His blood cleanses us from sin, His Love surpasses knowledge, and His Life offers us eternity. By His indwelling us, all distinctions, separations, and divisions are negated.

Just as the glory of God emanated from Solomon's and Ezekiel's Temples, so Christ's Life and His glory are to exude from our lives. The practical application of how this happens is what the next chapter is all about.

Chapter Fourteen

Personally Reflecting His Glory

Showing Forth His Life

In the Old Testament the Shekinah Glory was the visible manifestation of God shown forth by light, fire, or a cloud. The word *glory* simply symbolizes the "presence of God."

We see in Ezekiel how the Glory of God slowly left Solomon's Temple by first standing over the threshold, then over the cherubim, then over the East Gate and finally, upon the mountains above the city of Jerusalem.[1] As believers, however, we are promised that the Holy Spirit (God's Glory) will *never* leave us, because we are stamped, sealed, and confirmed by Him (2 Corinthians 1:22). It is possible, however, to quench and block His Spirit from coming forth through us, which will then prevent the manifestation of the presence of God in our lives.

God's purpose in calling us is to glorify Him in everything we do: "If any man speak, let him speak as the oracles of God (God's Word); if any man minister, let him do it as of the ability which God giveth; that God *in all things may be glorified*" (1 Peter 4:11).

We Are to Glorify God

To glorify God means to personally reflect His presence, to manifest and show forth His Life and His radiance. Glorifying God means displaying His character and all the fruits of the Spirit to the world (Romans 15:6). God's glory is seen by the transformation of a believer's life.

> Ye are the light of the world. A city that is set on an hill cannot be hid. Neither do men light a candle, and put it under a bushel, but on a candlestick; and it giveth light unto all that are in the house. Let your light so shine before men, that they may see your good works, and glorify your Father which is in heaven.
>
> —Matthew 5:14–16

Glory is the "vehicle" or the instrument God uses to convey and reveal His presence.

Part of the "sanctification process" is learning to be "conformed into Christ's Image" so that we *can* reflect, glorify, and mirror Him in all we do (Romans 8:29). To *mirror* something simply means "to exhibit its likeness, its characteristics, and to physically declare it or manifest it. It means to set forth the same image.

Christ wants us to mirror His image to all we come in contact with—to our spouses, our children, other family members, our friends, our co-workers, and so forth. "But *we all*, with open face beholding as in a glass the glory of the Lord, are changed into the same image from glory to glory, even as by the Spirit of the Lord" (2 Corinthians 3:18).

An Example: The Refiner's Fire

A Bible study group studying "Reflecting Christ's Image" came across Malachi 3:3 which says: "He will sit as a refiner and purifier of silver." This verse puzzled them. The leader of the group offered to find out more about the process of refining silver and would get back to them at their next meeting.

That week he called a silversmith and asked if he could come and watch him work. The next day, as the leader was observing the refining process, he saw the silversmith hold up a piece of silver over the fire and let it heat up. The refiner explained that *one needs to hold the silver in the middle of the fire where the flames are the hottest so as to burn away all the impurities*.

The leader asked the silversmith if he had to watch the piece of silver the whole time it was being refined. The refiner answered yes, he not only had to hold the silver the entire time, but he also had to keep his eyes continually on it, because if left too long in the flames, it would be destroyed.

The leader asked, "How do you know when the silver is fully refined?" The refiner smiled at him and answered, *"Oh, that's easy. It's done when I see my own image in it!"*

Jesus does the same thing with us. He keeps His eyes upon us the entire time we are in the "fire"—the sanctification process—and He knows exactly when we are perfected because *He, too, will be able to see His own image in us*.

God wants us all to be mirrors of *His* image, revealing the light of *His* presence, *His* character, and *His* nature in everything we do. "Not unto us, but unto [Your] Name give glory" (Psalm 115:1). "To the end that my glory may sing praise unto Him" (Psalm 30:12).

This is what it means to glorify, reflect, and mirror Christ's image.

Do They Know We Are Christians?

The question is: Do others know we are Christians by our behavior, our words, and our Love? Without even saying anything, do they know we are believers? If we asked our families, our spouses, our children, and our coworkers if they see Christ in us, what would they say?

Do we show them God's compassion and His gentleness when they do something wrong, or do we get angry and condemn them? Are we able to forgive them with God's help when they hurt and betray us, or do we hold a grudge? Do we take the time to reach out in God's Love, comfort, and encourage them in their difficult times or are we too busy, unconcerned, and preoccupied?

Just as the glory of the Lord emanated from Ezekiel's temple, so Christ's Life—His Love and His Wisdom—is supposed to exude from our lives.

When Christ walked the earth, He wasn't a "doormat" or a pushover. People didn't walk all over Him. When needed, He knew exactly how to take a strong stand in Love. He knew that *perfect balance* between longsuffering Love and tough Love, between grace and righteousness and between mercy and judgment. He gave us an example of how we are to love others and even how to love our enemies. When we become "partaker's *of* His Life," we, too, will be able to love wisely. And this is how the gospel will be passed on.

The Link to Revival

When Christ Jesus walked the earth, He was a "living illustration" of the invisible God. By constantly glorifying His Father, He not only honored Him, He also gave the world a reason to believe in His reality. We are to do the same.

We are to partake *of* the actual Life of Jesus so that others may see and know what He is like. And hopefully they will want what we have! *The gospel can never be understood by precept alone. It must have a corresponding example*! Our lives need to be genuine living examples of Christ's character and His Love. We need to be fountains of "living water"—sweet water and fresh water! When others experience Christ's real Love through us, hear His godly wisdom, and see His divine power working in our lives, they are going to be drawn to the Lord through us. Our words alone are not enough to communicate the Gospel. Our actions must go alongside. No other illustration is as effectual as the lives of spiritual Christians. It's difficult for the gospel to take real effect or be understood without a living illustration alongside. *Thus, there can be no bitter or salt water* (John 7:18).

God's Love is supposed to flow out of our lives like that "river of water" in Ezekiel's Temple, refreshing the dry parched lives of all those around us.

Reflecting God's glory in our lives is the key to revival. No words need to be shared. All that's needed to convey the message of Christ is our life. That's contagious enough; everyone is hungry to see the genuine article!

An Example: German Pastor

Here's a perfect example: In the mid-1930's, a dear, sweet German pastor was abducted from his church. He was suspected of harboring and aiding the Jews. He was immediately taken to prison and put in a five-foot cell. There was no hearing, no trial, not even time to let him make a phone call to his family to tell them what had happened.

For weeks this gentle pastor asked the prison guard outside his cell door if he could use the pay phone at the end of the hall to call his wife. The guard, however, was a contemptible man who hated anyone and everyone who had anything to do with Jewry. He not only wouldn't let him use the phone, he determined to make this pastor's life miserable.

This sadistic guard purposefully skipped the pastor's cell when meals were handed out; he made the pastor go for weeks without a shower; he kept lights burning in the pastor's cell so he couldn't sleep; he blasted his shortwave radio so the pastor couldn't think clearly; he used filthy language; he shoved him and pushed him and gave him the most difficult job on the labor gang.

The pastor, on the other hand, prayed over and over again to avoid allowing hate to consume him. He prayed instead to love this guard unconditionally with God's Love. As the months went by, whenever he could, the pastor smiled at him; he thanked him when his meals did come; when the guard was near his cell, the pastor told him about his wife and his children; he even questioned the guard about his own family and his own goals, ideas, visions, and so for; and for one quick moment, he had a chance to tell him about God's Love.

The guard never answered a word, but he obviously heard everything.

After months of unconditionally loving this guard, real Love finally broke through. One night as the pastor was talking to him, the guard cracked a smile; the next day, instead of being skipped for dinner, the pastor got two; the following evening, he was allowed not only to go to the showers, but also to stay as long as he wanted; the lights began going off at night and the radio noise ceased.

Finally one afternoon the guard came into the pastor's cell, asked him for his home phone number, and he personally made that long awaited call to the pastor's family. A few months later, the pastor was released—without any explanation.

The Real Gospel

Being a living example of Christ's Life, is the key to "revival." Words alone are not enough! Life actions are what carry the message we want to convey. People need to see the reality of Christ manifested in our lives.

This is the *real* gospel that needs to be preached around the world—a changed life—a living example, genuineness, transparency, genuine openness, and the freedom to be ourselves. Nonbelievers have seen enough religion, rules, regulations, law, phoniness, and hypocrisy to turn them off. They want to see the real thing!

"Soul winning," therefore, means "saving someone's life" and this really has more to do with "sanctification" than it does with "justification." "Soul winning" is more than just preaching the Word of God to those who are *not* saved, it's reflecting Christ's Life to those who are already saved. Actions always speak louder than words!

All people have some knowledge of God from His witness in their hearts, but what they need to see for *real revival* is the reality of His Life manifested in others. Being a true reflection of Him—glorifying Him—is just as important today as it was in the Old Testament. Just as the Shekinah Glory revealed God's Glory in Solomon's Temple in the past and as it will in Ezekiel's Temple in the future, that glory is to be shown forth through us in the present.

How desperately our families, our friends, and our children need to see this kind of genuine example. If this occurred on a regular basis, it would revolutionize our communities, our state, and our entire country. This is the "gospel" that needs to be preached around the world. It's not the gospel of "free grace," but the gospel of *everlasting Life*, the gospel of the kingdom (Romans 1:16).

How Should We Then Live?

In light of all we have learned so far—Why are we here? Where are we going? How do we get there?—the question now becomes: *how, then, should we live?* What personal changes should we make in our private lives? What should we focus our attention on first? What should be our priority?

One of the first Scripture exhortations that caught our eye was Revelation 3:18. Here Jesus counseled the Church at Laodicea to go and "buy of Him gold tried in the fire" so they may be "clothed with white raiment" and "the shame of their nakedness will not appear."

This Scripture is exhorting us to do whatever is necessary to be prepared and to reflect Christ in all we do. Scripture says *God wants each of us to be "conformed into His Image"* (Romans 8:29). Since *sanctification* is the initial step in this process, *this* is where we need to begin. If we learn to stay clean, holy, and righteous, by making "faith choices" to put off the sin and self, the rest will follow pretty easily. We'll be able to partake of Christ's Life, which will allow us to become overcomers and produce fruit that will eventually lead us to inheriting the kingdom.

The Rest of God

When we become partakers *of* Christ's Life and allow the glory of God to come forth from our lives, we will enter a stage that is called "the rest of God." We read about this kind of "rest" throughout Scripture. For example:

> Come unto Me, all ye that labor and are heavy laden and I will give you rest. Take My yoke upon you, and learn of Me; for I am meek and lowly in heart, and ye shall find rest unto your souls.
>
> —Matthew 11:28–29

The "rest of God" is another one of those confusing terms because, again, there are really *two kinds* of rest:

1. One type of *rest* refers to the present (as in the above Matthew Scripture) and it means "to rest by allowing Christ to live his Life out through us." Most of us are familiar with this kind of rest.
2. However, there is another kind of *rest* that refers to the future. This *rest* implies participation with Christ in His Millennial Kingdom rule. This is where we truly will rest from all our labor. So, *rest* can point to a place as well as an experience.

The third and fourth chapters of Hebrews emphasize this second type of rest. The writer to the Hebrews was warning us that just as the Israelites forfeited their inheritance—the *Canaan rest*—because of unfaithfulness and disobedience, we too, can forfeit our Millennial Kingdom rest for the same reasons. Just as Canaan was the object lesson for the Israelites, so obtaining and possessing the Millennial Kingdom's future blessings is the object lesson for us. Hebrews 4:8–9 says: "For if Jesus had given them rest, then would He not afterward have spoken of *another day* (a coming kingdom). *There remaineth, therefore, a rest to the people of God.* For he that is entered into his rest, he also hath ceased from his own works, as God did from His" (See also Hebrews 4:1).

Hebrews is *not* talking about an "earthly" rest here, but about a future ownership in the Millennial Kingdom. *This kind of* rest *is the reward for finishing well the task that was assigned to us here.* It's the "reward of inheritance." It's speaking about having *finished* the work God gave us to complete here on earth. In other words, *rest* comes *after* the battle is over, not before. Just as the Lord rested on the seventh day from all His work, we, too, are to rest in our finished work—the completion of our sanctification and our battles to overcome the world, the flesh, and the enemy (Hebrews 4:3; Genesis 2:2–3). This second type of "rest" symbolizes the pattern that God set down—the completion of our earthly battles and the ceasing of our own labors (Exodus 20:11).

The Exodus generation, unfortunately, *never entered that rest* because they *never* finished their task or the job assigned to them. Therefore they lost their promised inheritance. We don't want to make the same mistake!

We are encouraged to make every effort to "prepare ourselves"—to make ourselves ready, fit, and qualified—in order to enter into that rest.

Laboring to Enter In

Scripture tells us this second type of "rest" does *not* come easily and that we must work hard for it, labor to achieve it, and strive to enter into it. It entails unremitting toil and continued effort in order to achieve it (Colossians 1:23). The difficulties encountered in order to inherit the Millennial Kingdom permeates the book of Hebrews.[2]

The book of Hebrews also talks extensively about the dangers of falling away and of not entering His rest.[3] In fact, according to Hebrews 4:11 we, too, can fail to enter: "Let us *labor* therefore *to enter into that rest*, lest any man fall after the same example of unbelief [of the Exodus generation]."

The concept of *laboring to enter in* (to God's rest) is further developed in Luke 13:24: "Strive (agonize) to enter in at the narrow gate; *for many, I say unto you, will seek to enter in, and shall not be able*." This confirms what we have been saying throughout this book. *Only those who obediently fulfill the conditions set down by the Father* (obedience, faithfulness, and endurance) *will be able to inherit the Kingdom from Heaven.* And this will entail laboring, struggling, and striving. The "narrow" (strait) gate actually means a gate *beset with difficulties*.[4]

Now, these passages about "laboring to enter into His rest" and "striving to enter the narrow gate" cannot be talking about justification because there is no striving or agonizing or laboring necessary to become a believer. *Justification* is simply a "free gift." This gift comes by faith and rests totally in Christ's completed work on the Cross, but sanctification is an entirely different step. It is something we must labor to achieve and strive to attain. Consequently these passages in Hebrews and Luke must be speaking about the sanctification process, because laboring, striving, and agonizing is definitely a part of staying clean, obedient, and faithful. *Agonizing* means "exerting every possible effort."[5] Remember Acts 14:22, which tells us that "through much tribulation [we] enter into the kingdom."

This second type of rest is entered into by making "faith choices," by diligent effort, and by obedient living.[6] It is forfeited by disobedience, doubt, and unbelief. We discussed the dangers of falling away and losing our inheritance in chapter three.[7]

Inheriting the Millennial Kingdom rule is a very "narrow gate."

Two Different Gates

What puts this all into perspective is that *there are really* two *different gates for believers to enter the kingdom*! One gate is at the *entrance* to the Kingdom from God—justification (Matthew 7:13). The other gate is at the *end of our walk* of sanctification (Luke 13:24). It's called the "Bema Seat Judgment."

1. *The first gate is* described in Matthew 7:13 as being "strait" for believers and the gate for nonbelievers as being "broad." It says, "*Enter ye in at the strait gate; for wide is the gate, and broad is the way, that leadeth to destruction, and many there be which go in there at.*" The strait gate is the entrance to the Kingdom from God, which is a free gift and requires no effort on our part, other than to believe. "Whosoever believeth in Him should not perish, but have eternal Life" (John 3:15).

2. But *Luke 13:24: "Strive to enter in at the narrow gate; for many, I say unto you, will seek to enter in, and shall not be able*" is referring to the second gate for believers—called the "narrow gate" or the Bema Judgment Seat. This gate determines who will inherit the Millennial Kingdom and who will not. As we have previously noted, inheriting this kingdom includes striving, agonizing, and perseverance.[8]

Strive (Strong's #75) means "to give diligence to, to be in hot pursuit of, to earnestly fight for, to struggle, to agonize, to wrestle, to contend with an adversary and to put forth every effort (for a prize)." Striving for passage through that second gate means straining every muscle of our body, casting aside every weight and pressing toward *the mark of the high calling of God.*[9]

See ***Chart 32: Laboring to Enter In***

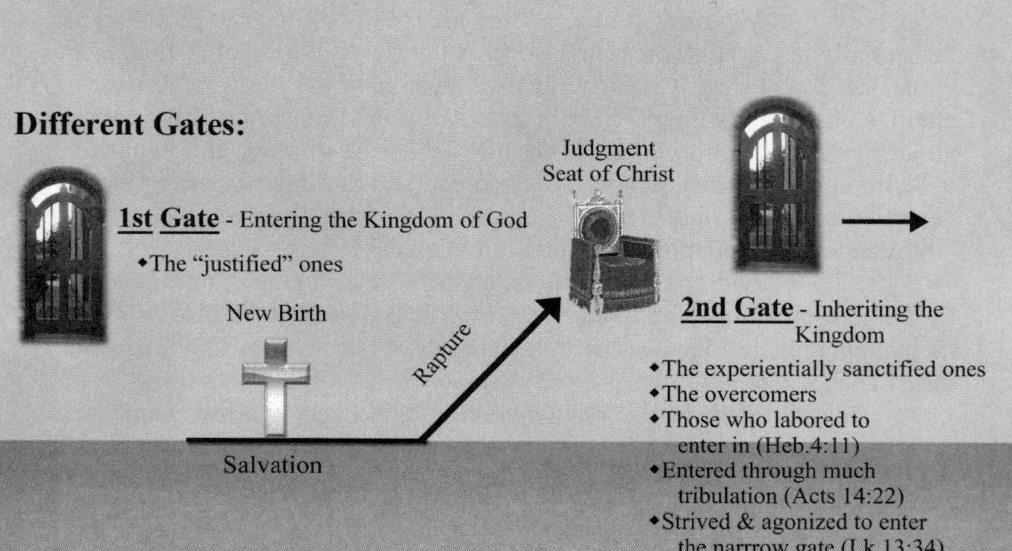
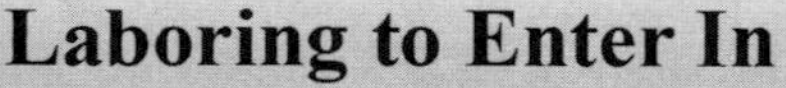

Consequently, there's one gate at the *beginning of the road of faith* (called "justification") that allows believers to *enter* the Kingdom of God, (Matthew 7:14). And there's another gate at the *end of the road of faith* (called "sanctification") that allows believers to inherit the Millennial Kingdom by faithfulness, obedience, and endurance (Luke 13:34).

This second "narrow gate" is entered through sorrow, carefulness, confession, watchfulness, and humility. It is one of toil and labor, struggling and striving; it is long and steep and it is rough and difficult, as many of us know (2 Corinthians 1:8).

Remember Paul's testimony:

> Thrice was I beaten with rods, once was I stoned, thrice I suffered shipwreck, a night and a day I have been in the deep; in journeyings often, in perils of waters, in perils of robbers, in perils by mine own countrymen, in perils by the Gentiles, in perils in the city, in perils in the wilderness, in perils in the sea, in perils among false brethren; in weariness and painfulness, in watchings often, in hunger and thirst, in fastings often, in cold and nakedness.
>
> —2 Corinthians 11:25–27

But then he makes an amazing statement that these things were nothing compared to "winning the prize of the high calling" (Philippians 3:8–14).

Like Paul, we must be steadfast, intent, unshaken, and unswerving in our mission *to press toward the "mark" of the high calling of God,* which is the kingdom rule. We are called to "wrestle and run." The future prize is to be sought after through many difficulties.

If we can't recall any of the struggles and hardships we have endured to get where we are today, then we probably have diverted from the path. Again, *The Pulpit Commentary* confirms that our struggles and our hardships are "what constitutes the straightness of the gate and the narrowness of the way."[10]

Prerequisites for Entering

Self-denial is an absolute prerequisite for an entrance to this second gate. There must be a true submission to Christ and a renunciation of self in all things. And unfortunately there is no middle road. We are either on one side of that gate or the other side. "Fence sitters" (gate sitters) are going to get ripped up the middle. *Justification* is easy because *Jesus* did it all for us—there is no striving or agonizing on our part; but *sanctification* is very difficult, because *we* are the ones who must continually strive and agonize to make the appropriate faith choices.

Those who are true *partakers* of Christ's Life must hold their confidence to the very end by fortitude and effort, through perseverance and longsuffering. "We are made partakers of Christ, *if we hold the beginning of our confidence steadfast unto the end"* (Hebrews 3:14; see also 2 Corinthians 5:9). These believers have proved their title to the kingdom by their faithfulness and their obedience. The testing will be severe, but the reward will be well worth it all (1 Corinthians 3:13).

The wedding party is not going to be made up of believers who are religious, legalistic or hypocritical, but believers who have labored to genuinely partake of Christ's Life, become overcomers, and thus, produce the "fruit of righteousness." Again, these believers are not perfect, but they will be "qualified"(axios) to enter that second gate.

As we said earlier, the Bema Seat Judgment is the gateway (or the second gate) to inheritance in the Millennial Kingdom. It's here that we will discover if we are prepared, fit, and "worthy" of entering. Remember the Greek word *axios* that we studied in chapter 3? Our Spirit-led works of righteousness are what will make us "worthy" of the wonderful blessings God has for us there.

Parable of the Man Without a Wedding Garment (Matthew 22:1–14)

The thought of being *disqualified* from entering, leads us to another parable about "a man without a wedding garment" who was cast out into the outer darkness where he encountered weeping and gnashing of teeth. It is found in Matthew 22:1–14.

This is the third Matthew parable that speaks about being "cast out," "outer darkness," and "weeping and gnashing of teeth." Jesus, again, is the One talking and He is telling the story of the king who arranged a marriage for his son.

> 2The kingdom of heaven is like unto a certain king, which
> made a marriage for his son, 3and sent forth his servants to
> call them that were bidden to the wedding: and they would
> not come. 4Again, he sent forth other servants, saying, Tell
> them which are bidden, behold, I have prepared my dinner:
> my oxen and *my* fatlings *are* killed, and all things *are* ready:
> come unto the marriage. 5But they made light of *it*, and went
> their ways, one to his farm, another to his merchandise: 6And
> the remnant took his servants, and entreated *them* spitefully,
> and slew *them*.
>
> 7But when the king heard *thereof*, he was wroth: and he sent
> forth his armies, and destroyed those murderers, and burned
> up their city. 8Then saith he to his servants, The wedding is
> ready, but they which were bidden were not worthy. 9Go ye

> therefore into the highways, and as many as ye shall find, bid to the marriage. [10]So those servants went out into the highways, and gathered together all as many as they found, both bad and good: and the wedding was furnished with guests.
>
> [11]And when the king came in to see the guests, he saw there a man which had not on a wedding garment: [12]And he saith unto him, Friend, how camest thou in hither not having a wedding garment? And he was speechless. [13]Then said the king to the servants, Bind him hand and foot, and take him away, and cast *him* into outer darkness; there shall be weeping and gnashing of teeth. [14]For many are called, but few *are* chosen.

In verses 8–10, the king tells a third group of servants, "*The wedding festivities are ready*. Go, therefore, into the highways and as many as ye shall find bid to the marriage." And the servants went out and gathered together all they found, both good and *bad* (Strong's #4190, *poneros*), meaning "hurtful in influence but not in character" (it's the same word as "wicked" in the Parable of the Talents). It means a person who lacks the qualities he *should* possess, *i.e.* he is *not* worthy.

Verses 12–14 describe how the king came to the feast, saw a man who did not have on a wedding garment, and said to him: "*Friend*, how did you come in here without a wedding garment?" The man was speechless. He had no excuse. Then the king said to his servants, "*Bind this man hand and foot and take him away and cast him into the outer darkness where there will be weeping and gnashing of teeth.*"

Where Is This Taking Place and Who Is Jesus Speaking To?

First of all, *where* is this incident supposed to be taking place and *who* is Jesus speaking to here?

This parable is talking about what the *kingdom from heaven* will be like. (Note Matthew 22:2.) It was originally *intended for the Jews* (see Matthew 21:45), but because they had stopped listening to Him and stopped believing in Him, they had obviously become "unworthy" of the kingdom message. "For this people's heart is waxed gross, and their ears are dull of hearing, and their eyes they have closed" (Matthew 13:15). Therefore, this parable explains why *Jesus turned His attention to the Gentiles*—those from "the highways and the by ways"—and bids as many as would to come. Like Jesus, the king in this parable tells his servants to bid all to come to the feast. All who were invited not only responded, but also came and the feast was furnished with guests. (This wedding feast may refer to the Marriage Supper of the Lamb that occurs on earth at the beginning of the Millennium (Revelation 19:9).)

Was This Man a Believer?

One of the Gentiles who came to the wedding feast, however, did not have on the appropriate wedding garment.

The first question is: *Was this man a believer or not?* We believe he was a believer because of three things: 1) First of all, *he had received an invitation to the festivities*, he had responded to that invitation, and he had come to the feast. This means 2) *He was already in the kingdom.* John 3:3 tells us that no one can even "see" the kingdom of God, let alone be "in" it, unless they have been "born again." And 3) The *Lord addressed him as "a friend."* In other words, He knew him as a "comrade," a fellow participant, or a follower.

The reason the king had come to the wedding feast in the first place was to examine the guests to see if they were fit for the high honor accorded them. The man without the wedding garment was a Gentile believer, part of the body of Christ, but he was *not* part of the bride, as he didn't have on the appropriate wedding garment. We'll talk more about this garment in a moment. This man had not strived nor labored for good works, nor had he become an overcomer. He had not been faithful, obedient, or enduring. He had not persevered in a life of Spirit-led good works. Therefore he was "cast out" and thrown into the "outer darkness."

Being placed into the "outer darkness" is something that results from the Bema Seat Judgment. But it actually occurs on earth at the beginning of the Millennial reign, perhaps just before the Marriage Feast.

"The Darkness Outside"

Here, again, we run into this explosive term the "outer darkness" or the "darkness outside," which only appears three times in Scripture, always having to do with "the Kingdom from Heaven," "being cast out," and "weeping and gnashing of teeth" (Matthew 8:12; Matthew 22:13; Matthew 25:30).

The "darkness outside" is specifying the location of the darkness. It's *not* general darkness, it's the darkness outside. "Outer darkness" does *not* mean eternal condemnation, hell, or Hades, but simply *exclusion* from the realm (Strong's #932, *basillis*) in which the faithful enter. In this verse, it means a region of darkness *outside* a region of light. It's an area immediately outside the festivities attendant to the King's presence.

Again, the meaning of the word *darkness* comes from the context of the passage (Psalm 105:28). A believer refusing to avail himself of the cleansing that God provides is seen as "walking in darkness." Luke 11:33–34:

> No man when he hath lighted a candle, putteth it in a secret place, neither under a bushel, but on a candlestick, that they which come in may see the light. The light of the body is the eye: therefore when thine eye is single (entwined with God),

thy whole body also is full of light; but *when thine eye is evil, thy body also is full of darkness.*

Other Scriptures that mention Christians "walking in darkness" are: Isaiah 50:10; Matthew 6:23; John 8:12; Acts 13:11; and 1 John 1:6; 2:9, 11.

Charles Stanley commented on the outer darkness in his book *Eternal Security*:

> Many commentators assume it (the outer darkness) is a description of hell. *It is not!* Keep in mind that this is a parable. A parable makes one central point. The point of this parable is that in God's future kingdom, *those who were faithful in this life will be rewarded, and those who were not, will lose any potential reward.* Some will be given more privileges and responsibility while others will have none . . . The outer darkness refers to "being thrown outside a building into the dark" and in that place there shall be weeping and gnashing of teeth" [emphasis added].[11]

So, again, this "outer darkness" is not a dark place of suffering, but possibly a place where God in His Love will retrain believers in His way of holiness (Psalm 94:15).

The Different Kinds of Garments

This parable illustrates that we must not only receive "an invitation" to the wedding festivities, we must also wear the proper attire—*the appropriate wedding garment*. Revelation 19:7–8 calls this garment "the righteous acts of the saints." *The Pulpit Commentary* says, "The righteous acts of the saints symbolize at once a pure spirit and the faithful services and righteous acts of the saints."[12] The man in the parable was a believer and thus, had the proper clothing to be saved and to be "with the Lord," but he wasn't clothed properly for the privilege of attending the wedding festivities. Why? What was he lacking?

The answer is there are again *two* different kinds of "garments" in Scripture. *Garment* means a "symbol of righteousness."

1. First there is the "*garment of salvation,*" Christ's imputed righteousness that God puts on us at our new birth—our *justification garment* (Isaiah 61:10; Romans 4:6). This is Christ's righteousness that has been imputed to us and thus, the garment that gets us into heaven in the first place. This is an "outward" garment.

After we "put on" Christ's righteousness—once it is imputed to us—it is irreversible. It gives us eternal security. In other words, the "justified" cannot be ejected from that status of Christ's righteousness. It would be called "double jeopardy."

2. However, Revelation 19:8 speaks of another kind of garment called the "*garment of fine linen*." These are the "*righteous acts or deeds of the saints*"—our sanctification garment. And *this is the "inward" garment that we must have on in order to enter the marriage festivities.* No other bridal attire will do!

Kenton Beshore said in his book, *The Millennial Apocalypse:* "Christ must not only be *on us* as a robe, but He must be *in us* as a life."[13]

This garment refers to those Spirit-led deeds that are performed *after* we are born again. They are "works of godliness," "deeds of righteousness" that the Holy Spirit produces through us. These "good works" are why we were created in the first place (Ephesians 2:10). They are called the "fruits of righteousness" in Philippians 1:11. We will find out if we are clothed with this "garment of fine linen" or not at the Bema Seat.

Only "overcomers" will possess this wedding garment. Without this garment, Scripture says, a believer will be found "naked." (Revelation 3:17-18).

Appropriate Wedding Garments

If our "works" abide the testing of fire at the Bema Seat, we'll have on the "garment of fine linen" (Revelation 3:4). If our works are burned, we'll be found to be "naked". The Bible tells us that Adam and Eve were still found to be "naked" in the wilderness, even after they had applied the blood (Genesis 2:25—3:6–10). *Naked* (Strong's # 1131) means "nude." It means we once were in a position to array ourselves, but we chose not to.[14]

Remember the Laodicean church and what God said about them? "Because thou sayest, I am rich, and increased with goods, and have need of nothing, and knowest not that thou art wretched, and miserable, and poor, and blind, and *naked*" (Revelation 3:17).

This means that our garments *can* become soiled, tainted, and defiled (James 5:2). Therefore, we must constantly guard, maintain, and watch over our garments, lest they become defiled and blackened. "Blessed is he that watches and keeps his garments (meaning guards, watches over and maintains them), *lest he walk naked* and they see his shame" (Revelation 16:15).

The Pulpit Commentary comments about this garment of fine linen. It says: "This garment is *moral fitness*. We really must be who we profess to be."[15] This is the garment that Revelation 19:7–8 refers to when it says "*His wife prepared herself*" for the wedding. In other words, she chose to stay morally fit, "holy," and without blemish. She didn't do this perfectly, but moment-by-moment she recognized her choices and chose to turn around and follow Christ.

The man without the wedding garment in this Matthew 22 parable was *not* clothed with the *complete* garments of salvation. He had on Christ's "garment of righteousness" (justification garment) which got him into heaven "with Christ," but He scoffed at the idea that it makes a difference how a

Christian lives here and now, and thus he was found *naked* before the Lord at the Bema Seat.

Joseph Dillow, in his book *The Reign of the Servant Kings*, wrote: "The wedding garment consists not of the imputed righteousness of Christ, but of deeds suitable to qualify to participate in the King's banquet. These righteous acts refer not to the act of the Son of God in declaring us righteous [justified]. They refer instead to our faithfulness in this life."[16]

Sanctification, therefore, is our bridal preparation.

God's righteousness must be expressed in our actions and our deeds, without which none of us will "see" the Lord. The Bible urges us to "follow peace with all men, and holiness, without which no man shall *see* the Lord" (Hebrews 12:14). Remember in chapter seven, we referred to "see" as meaning "to gaze upon." Only those "partakers of His holiness" will be able to "gaze upon" Him. The unfaithful will simply be "with Him."

Filthy Garments

Joshua, the High Priest, was barred from ministering to the Lord because he had on "filthy garments" (Zechariah 3:3–4). The Old Testament stresses that in order for the priests to stand before the Lord, they had to have on "holy" garments (Exodus 28:1, 36–38). These garments meant that the priest reflected God's holiness. Without this garment of holiness, however, the priest was forbidden to come into God's presence (Leviticus 21:6–8). Filthy garments were associated with defilement and revealed that the priest no longer reflected holiness. At that point, they not only had to be ceremonially cleansed, but also morally cleansed (Exodus 30:19–21).

In the same manner, we must be "partakers of Christ's holiness" in order to come into His presence, see Him, and minister to Him.

The priest in filthy garments is a perfect picture of a "carnal believer" who has on "blackened" garments, but is nevertheless trying to stand before the Lord (Leviticus 16:23–24, 32). Like Joshua, the high priest who defiled his garmets, we too can become defiled by unfaithfulness, disobedience, and moral unfitness.

Absence of a Wedding Garment

Because the man in this parable did not have on the proper attire, he was denied admittance to the wedding festivities and *the king cast him out*. "Cast out," if you remember, simply means he was rejected, sent away, and thrown out of his original location. He was put into another room, a separate area outside of the place where the wedding celebration was going on. (See also Matthew 8:12; 25:30.)

The absence of a wedding garment does *not* prevent a believer from being in the area of the kingdom, but it does prevent him from taking part in the Marriage festivities and forces him to view it from a darkened area outside—from the darkness just beyond the brilliant light of God's presence.

Because the man in this parable was found naked, he was bound while his brothers participated in the rejoicing of the celebration. *Binding* here simply means that he was excluded and prohibited from fellowshiping with the Lord.

This man was not only cast out of the banqueting hall—like the unprofitable servant in Matthew 25—he was also excluded from the joy of inheriting the kingdom. And in this separate place, both will experience unbearable remorse and sorrow, weeping and gnashing of teeth.

Matthew 22:14 closes with this statement: "For many are called, but few are chosen." *Chosen* (Strong's #1588) means "selected, picked-out ones, or favorite ones." God already knows exactly whom He will choose. He is intimately acquainted with everything we have done with our lives here on earth and is keeping a close account. He also knows that at the Bema Seat, many will be surprised when they finally understand what He meant when He said, "Many that are first shall be last and the last shall be first" (Matthew 19:30).

See *Parable Chart 5: Matthew 22:1–14*

Take a look at our Parable Chart again. *To whom is Jesus speaking?* Originally He addressed the Pharisees. *About whom is He speaking?* The Gentile believers, because the Jews had rejected His message. *What had these Gentile believers done wrong?* They did not have on the appropriate wedding garments. *What was their loss?* They were bound and cast into the darkness outside the light of God's presence at the marriage supper. *When did this take place?* In the Kingdom from Heaven. *What occasion does this reminds us of?* Possibly, the Marriage Supper of the Lamb back on earth. *And, what is our lesson from this parable?* We, as the church, need to have on the appropriate wedding garments—that white linen garment composed of the saints' own works of righteousness, not only for the wedding in heaven, but also for the marriage feast on earth.

In all of the parables that we have been talking about on this chart, Jesus has *not* been talking to "strangers," but to His own: First, He speaks to "the sons of the kingdom;" next, "faithful and wise servants;" next "to the personal servants" of the Master of the house; next to "the bridesmaids" at the wedding; and finally, to the "friend who didn't have on a wedding garment." These are all children of God, some of whom had forfeited—through disobedience—liberties they had once enjoyed.

Notice the chronological order of events in these parables in reference to the future: The Millenial Kingdom, the Rapture, the Bema Seat, the Wedding Supper, and finally, the Marriage Feast. Coincidence? We don't think so.

Treasure in Heaven

In light of all of this, you can see why it's so very important to develop a "kingdom perspective," a kingdom outlook, and a kingdom

Parable Chart 5 (Matt. 22:1-13)

Story or Parable	To Whom is Jesus Speaking	About Whom is He Talking	What had They Done Wrong	What was Their Loss	What Event is Being Predicted	What is the Lesson for Us
Matt. 8:12 Sons of the Kingdom "Story"	Gentile Centurion	"Sons of the Kingdom" - Jewish believers	Lack of Faith	Cast into outer darkness-weeping and gnashing of teeth	Preparation for the Kingdom	Need to have faith
Matt. 24: 45-51 Faithful & Wise Servants "Story"	Disciples ("What are the signs of Your coming?")	Any believer waiting for his Lord's return	Thought the Lord would not come-Mistreated his fellow servants	Cut him asunder & appointed him a place with "hypo-crites"-weeping and gnashing of teeth	The Rapture	Need to always be looking for His soon return
Matt. 25:14-30 10 Talents "Parable"	Disciples ("What are the signs of Your coming?")	His own servants	Wicked servant didn't do anything with his talent	Take talent away Cast into outer darkness-weeping and gnashing of teeth	The Bema Seat	Need to be faithful with the abilities God gives us
Matt. 25:1-13 10 Virgins "Parable"	Disciples ("What are the signs of Your coming?")	The "Church"	They had no intimacy with the Lord. He did not "know" them	Locked out of wedding - The door was shut & they were left out	The Wedding Ceremony	Need to know the Lord intimately
Matt. 22: 1-13 Man without a Wedding Garment "Parable"	Pharisees	Gentile believers at wedding (original ones called were not "worthy")	No wedding garment (no "fruit")	Bind him - cast into outer darkness-weeping and gnashing of teeth	The Marriage Supper	Need to wear the appropriate wedding garment

viewpoint in everything we do *now*, since it will all count *later*. In other words, we must put all our efforts toward responding in each circumstance as God would have us, because it will all affect our position in the future kingdom (Luke 12:33).

We want to be like the man in Matthew 13:44, who when he found a treasure hidden in a field, he went and *sold all he had* in order to buy the whole field. Receiving Christ's eternal Life is that "treasure." But being a partaker *of* Christ's eternal Life here and now so that we might one day rule and reign with Him, is a way of maximizing that treasure.

The word *treasure* in the Greek is *thesauros* (Strong's #2344), which means "a deposit of wealth, a place of safekeeping or a storehouse." The ancients had a "precious jewel casket" in which they kept all their treasures. They didn't have safety deposit boxes in those days, so they just buried their treasures in little caskets. Building on this same theme, Matthew 6:20–21 encourages us to lay up for ourselves *treasures in heaven* where moth, nor rust, nor harm, nor thieves will be able to destroy them. Because *"where our treasure is, there our heart will be also."*

The "treasure" itself is a free gift—justification and eternal Life. But like the man in Matthew, in order to purchase the whole field, it will cost us everything—sanctification (Matthew 19:29).

Jesus said to the rich man, "If you will be perfect [or complete], *go and sell what you have* . . . and [then] you will have treasure in heaven" (Matthew 19:21). It's the same with us. We must be willing to surrender and relinquish *all that we have*, so that we might gain our inheritance in heaven. This attitude should affect every choice we make.

See *Chart 33: A Complete Kingdom Perspective (after page 296)*

This is why it's so important to have a complete "kingdom perspective" by understanding:

- What the Judgment Seat of Christ is all about—what is gained or lost there
- Who attends the Marriage of the Lamb in heaven. Who is the Lamb's wife. And what is the difference between the garment of salvation and the white linen wedding garment
- What the Millennial Temple is and who the overcomers are who will rule and reign with Christ there
- What the Marriage Feast is all about and why it is so important

Once we understand these events, we can look forward to them with hope and anticipation.

When Our Hope Is Realized

The "hope of our salvation" in Christ is, again, the ability to co-reign with Him in the Millennium and forever. It's the mark of the High Calling! It's our goal. And it's the prize (Philippians 3:14). This prospect is open to all of us, but is contingent upon our becoming faithful overcomers.

Remember Proverbs 13:12, which says that *only when our hope is realized (apprehended and taken hold of), can it become a tree of Life. This tree of Life reminds us of Ezekiel's vision and the trees on either side of the river of Life that suddenly become alive, bear fruit and never lose their leaves* (Ezekiel 47:9-12).

When our hope is personally realized, it will become a tree of Life in our hearts. However, also remember, the second part of Proverbs 13:12 which says, when we don't understand the purpose of our salvation—our inheritance in Christ and we don't have that "hope" to look forward to—our hearts will remain sick, sad, and depressed.

Having a "kingdom perspective" will affect every choice we make; every decision we come to, and every action we take. *What we end up choosing and deciding* here *will ultimately determine our place and position* there.

May "the eyes of your understanding being enlightened; that ye may *know* what is the hope of His calling, and what the riches of the glory of His inheritance in the saints and what is the exceeding greatness of His power to us-ward who believe" (Ephesians 1:18). Hopefully, after reading and rereading this book, these three things will be clearer in your mind.

In Summary

The process of full salvation goes something like this: Our *spirits* are saved when we are born again. Our *souls* are in the process of being saved through the sanctification process. And our *bodies* will be saved when Christ comes for us at the Rapture. These are the three different aspects of salvation. As you can see, the salvation of our spirits is very different from the salvation of our souls, which, in turn, is also different from the salvation of our bodies.

Receiving a brand-new spirit at our new birth is just the *beginning* of our faith. It's called *justification* and it is a free "gift" from God, whereas, *our souls are saved on the basis of following a lifelong journey of sanctification*––which allows us *to be partakers of Christ's imparted Life* and thus, *overcomers*. This process is done in cooperation with the divine resurrection power of God. It doesn't happen automatically. It's our own responsibility to make the appropriate faith choices that allows God's Spirit to work in and through us (1 Peter 1:9).

Receiving Christ as Savior (justification) only touches our spirit—it does *not* affect the realm of our soul or our body. Whereas, sanctification is intended to transform our soul back into the image of Christ. Justification relies upon the substitutionary death of Christ *for us*, whereas, sanctification relies upon our moment-by-moment *co-death with Christ* (Galatians 5:24).

The first step—justification—gives us peace, satisfaction, and joy, whereas, the next step—sanctification—gives us *power* to overcome sin and self, *Love* to embrace the poor and the needy, and *wisdom* to understand God's will. The final step— glorification—will manifest the reason why we were created.

When our spirit is saved, we receive forgiveness of past sins and deliverance from the *penalty of sin* through Christ's blood. When our soul is transformed (saved), we receive deliverance from the *power of sin* that operates through the world, the flesh, and the devil. And when Christ returns, our body will be saved from the *presence of sin*.

All Christians *live* by the Spirit, but not all Christians *walk* by the Spirit (being "partakers *of* His Life" and producing fruit). To walk by the Spirit means to put to death the things of the "flesh," to overcome the temptations of the world and the devil, to be led along the path of sanctification, and to produce fruit (Romans 6:11–14).

"Complete" salvation then entails not only a new life brought on by a new Spirit, but also the renewal of every part of our souls as well.[17] This *sanctification process* is absolutely necessary in order to participate in and inherit the Millennial Kingdom (Matthew 25:21).

Remember the ones who were *not* able to inherit:

- Some of the *children of the kingdom* (Matthew 8:11–12)
- The *disobedient servant* (Matthew 24:50)
- The *five foolish virgins* (Matthew 25:12)
- The *unfaithful servant* (Matthew 25:30)
- The *man without the wedding garment* (Matthew 22:12)

These passages are all talking about believers! And yet none of these believers "inherited" the kingdom. They were all *in the kingdom*, but in some other region, some other place—*the darkness outside*—and thus, separated from the light of the Lord's presence.

The purpose of this book is to challenge each of us to establish a renewed recognition of our own accountability before the Lord. Hopefully it has stimulated you to strive to be a faithful overcomer in your personal, as well as, your professional life. We realize that much of what we have shared in this book is very controversial. We realize there are many varying and different viewpoints. We suggest you do your own homework, check out all the Scriptures, pray and see what the Lord confirms to your heart. You have the same Teacher as we do!

We trust that God has ministered to you that "it is not too late!" Even if you are not an overcomer now, you can learn to be. There's still time (Hebrews 10:24). God is a loving and merciful God, full of grace. He has allowed us to enter the Kingdom from God as a free gift, just for believing upon Him. *But* He also is a just and righteous God who will hold us accountable for the gifts and talents that He has given us here (*after* we became believers). At the Bema Seat He will ask what we did with these gifts. Did we use them wisely? Did we use them to love others? Did we produce "fruit" from them? He doesn't expect perfection, but He does expect faithfulness, obedience, and perseverance.[18]

Eternal life is obtained by faith and can never be lost. But the Millennial Kingdom reign, is prepared for those who through Christ continue to make the appropriate choices to overcome. Our eternal destiny depends upon it! Revelation 21:7 says: "He that overcometh shall inherit all things, and I will be his God, and he shall be My son." *God* is the One who gives us the authority and power to become overcomers, but *we* are the ones who must constantly choose to implement that power and authority in our lives.[19]

God's original purpose for man is that he was created in God's image and likeness so that he might be able to co-reign with Christ over the earth (Genesis 1:26–28). *That purpose is still forthcoming. It's the hope of our salvation and a tree of Life to those who find it* (Proverbs 3:18).

The question is: Will you be one who finds it?

***For Thine, O Lord, is* the Kingdom, Power and Glory!**

* * *

Our Father, which art in heaven,

Hallowed be Thy Name.

Thy kingdom come,

Thy will be done in earth, as it is in heaven.

Give us this day our daily bread.

And forgive us our debts, as we forgive our debtors.

And lead us not into temptation, but deliver us from evil:

For Thine is the Kingdom, and the power, and the glory,

Forever.

Amen.

Matthew 6:9–13

Appendices

Prayer Section

Who shall ascend into the hill of the LORD?
Or who shall stand in His Holy Place?
He that hath clean hands, and a pure heart . . .
He shall receive the blessing from the Lord,
and righteousness from the God of his salvation.
This is the generation of them that seek Him,
that seek Thy face.

—Psalm 24:3–6

Prayer Section

Table of Contents

Different Types of Prayers

Overcomers are those who, by faith and the supernatural power of God, learn to "move mountains" by prayer (1 Corinthians 13:2). They know their authority and power in Christ and, thereby, are able to attack any difficulty that is blocking God's will from being accomplished.

Scripture tells us that if we pray according to His will, He *will* hear us, and He *will* answer our prayers. We must remember, however, that His ways are not our ways and the way He might answer our prayers and the way He might "remove the mountains" (remove the hindrances before us) are not necessarily how we would do it. In fact, He probably will answer our prayers in a totally opposite manner from what we expected. Our responsibility is simply to pray and leave the results with Him. The Lord will answer our prayers in *His* way and in *His* timing.

There are several different kinds of prayers of faith that we can pray:

- *Prayer for Salvation* (for justification). This is the prayer we pray to be justified, declared righteous, and not guilty before the Lord. This is our prayer when we choose to believe in all that Christ has done for us—in dying for our sins and reconciling us to God. It is at this time that we receive a new spirit and a new heart.

- *Prayers for Sanctification* are prayers we pray when we choose to "put off" our sin and self and "put on" Christ. If we want God to hear and answer our prayers, we must be cleansed (Psalm 66:18). If not, our prayers will remain in the realm of the *physical*, and do absolutely no good in the *spiritual* area.

- *Spiritual Warfare Prayer*s, praying against the enemy, are prayers of faith that use God's authority and power to bind (prohibit) the enemy's entrance and work, and loose (free) the Holy Spirit to permeate the situation. We unleash God's divine power over unclean spirits through these prayers (Mark 6:7). When we pray authoritative prayers, we must be particularly sensitive to the leading of the Holy Spirit; otherwise, the Spirit can easily become quenched. We must *first* be willing to *submit to Christ's authority* (become clean vessels and willing to do His will) *before* we can exercise *the rights of His authority.*

- *Prayers for Others* are prayers asking God to bless, heal, restore, or protect someone else.

* * *

If you are like us, when you pray, especially, if it's a new prayer, it's always helpful to have a rough example to follow. Yes, the Holy Spirit must always lead, but it's nice to have a guideline when you are just beginning. The following, then, are some ideas as to how you might pray.

Prayer for Salvation (Justification)

It is very important to understand that unless we have asked Jesus Christ into our hearts to be our Savior and have been *born again* by His Spirit (justified), all that we have read in this book about the importance of sanctification will be of no use. The Bible tells us that *without Christ's blood there is no remission of sin nor access to His presence.* In order for God to cleanse us, we must *first* have a new spirit (power source or life source) within us that will produce something *different* from what we naturally think, feel, or want to do. We need the Holy Spirit in our hearts in order for there to be a true cleansing and change of heart.

> Except a man be born of water and of the Spirit, he *cannot* enter into the kingdom of God. That which is born of the flesh is flesh; and that which is born of the Spirit is spirit.
>
> —John 3:5–6

If you are not sure where you stand with the Lord, the following four steps to take and the Prayer for Salvation will help you to make your position with Him certain.

Steps to take:

1. *Recognize God's plan: peace and Life.* God wants us to know that He loves us. And He wants us to experience His Love and to know His peace. John 3:16: "For God so loved the world, that He gave His only begotten Son, that whosoever believeth in Him should not perish, but have everlasting Life."

2. *Realize our problem: separation from God.* People choose to disobey God and go their own way. And this results in separation from Him. Romans 3:23: "For all have sinned, and come short of the glory of God."

3. *Respond to God's remedy: the Cross of Christ.* God sent His Son to bridge the gap. Christ did this by paying the penalty of our sins when He died on the cross and rose from the grave. Romans 5:8: "But God commendeth His Love towards us, in that, while we were yet sinners, Christ died for us."

4. *Receive God's Son—as Lord and Savior.* You cross the bridge into God's family when you ask Christ to come into your heart. Acts 16:30–31: "What must I do to be saved?" Answer: *Simply believe.* John 1:12: "But as many as received him, to them gave He power to become the sons of God, even to them that *believe* on His Name."

Prayer for Salvation (Justification)

Lord Jesus,

I know that I am a sinner. But I believe that You died for my sins. I understand that only by believing in You and what You did for me, am I able to receive eternal life. And so, right now, I turn from my sins and I open the door of my heart and life to You and receive You as my personal Lord and Savior.

I renounce all demonic activity or involvement that I have had in the past. And in Jesus Name, I bind them and cast them out. I plead the blood of Christ over me. And I pray that the Holy Spirit would be poured out upon my life.

I now give You my will and my life. Thank you for saving me, for making me Your child, and for Your gift of Life.

Amen.

Read the following Scriptures to confirm what you just prayed: John 1:12; 4:10.

Prayer for Sanctification

The following steps are not a procedure or technique that we have made up or found in some psychology book, but they are the cleansing and purifying steps the priests went through in Solomon's Temple to be reconciled to God.

God has laid these out for us in Scripture in order that we might deal with our own sin and be reconciled to Him.

Throughout Scripture we are exhorted to "put off" the flesh and "put on" Christ. Following is the practical application of how to do this. This is how God desires for us to moment-by-moment deal with our sin and self, renew our minds, and partake of Christ's Life.

Steps to take:

1. Recognize and acknowledge the sin or the self-centeredness that has just occurred. Don't *vent* these thoughts or feelings and don't *push them down*. Get alone with God and give them to Him. Try to describe to God how you are feeling and what you are thinking. Ask Him to expose any root causes for your ungodly thoughts, emotions, or actions. In this step it's imperative to experience your emotions (your humanness) so you'll know exactly what to confess and what to give over to God.

This step occurred at the "Lavers of Bronze" in the Inner Court of Solomon's Temple.

2. Confess and repent of everything that God shows you is unholy, unrighteous, and not of faith and choose to turn around from following these things (1 John 1:9). *Confessing* simply means acknowledging your sin and self. *Repenting* means choosing to turn around from following that sin and self and choosing instead to follow what God is telling you to do. Asking God to forgive you is not enough; you must *first* confess that you have sinned and then repent of it. *This is your responsibility*. A part of this second step is that you must also unconditionally forgive any others involved. You have asked God to forgive you for your sins; you must now forgive others.

Psalm 32:5: "I acknowledged my sin unto Thee, and mine iniquity have I not hid . . . I will confess my transgressions unto the Lord; and Thou forgavest the iniquity of my sin."

This step also occurred at the "Lavers of Bronze."

3. Give over to God all that He has shown you—not only your specific sin, but also any of your self-centered ways. Present your body to God as a "living sacrifice" (Romans 12:1) and ask Him to continue to expose, cut away, and divide the soulish things in your life from the spiritual.

At this point, offer God the sacrifice of *praise* (Hebrews 13:15), the sacrifice of *righteousness* (Psalm 4:5), the sacrifice of *joy* (Psalm 27:6) and the sacrifice of *thanksgiving* (Psalm 116:17; 107:22). These are "sacrifices" because at this point we usually don't feel much like praising, being thankful or joyful.

This step occurred at the "Brazen Altar."

4. Read God's Word and replace the lies you have believed with the Truth. As you read God's Word, He will cleanse and heal your soul with the "washing of water by the Word" (Ephesians 5:26). Only God's Word can totally restore you at this point. Only God can wash you *in His Love*, minister to you, and heal you with His Word.

At this point, whether you feel like it or not, you have been "renewed in the *spirit* of your mind" and Christ's Life is, once again, freed to come forth. You are now a cleansed and sanctified vessel able to pray not only for yourself, but also for others (Ephesians 4:23).

This step occurred at the "Molten Sea."

(If you want a more in-depth explanation of these four essential steps and how they apply to us, please see the *Supplemental Notes* in this appendix.)

Prayer for Sanctification (Cleansing)

Dearest Lord,

Thank You for Your authority to make choices I don't feel like making and Your power to accomplish those choices in my life. This is the way I am able to overcome the flesh and the world. In Your Name, I choose by faith to "order my behavior aright."

First, I choose to "take every thought captive" and acknowledge my sin and self. I acknowledge my self-centeredness, expectations, disappointments, critical and judgmental spirit, frustrations, hurt, anger, doubts, confusion, fears, etc. May none of these things move me. Psalm 32:5

says, "I acknowledged my sin unto Thee and mine iniquity have I not hid."

I confess my sin and self and anything else that is not of faith. Psalm 32:5 also says, "I will confess my transgressions unto the Lord; and Thou forgavest the iniquity of my sin."

I choose to repent of these things and I also choose to unconditionally forgive others of their wrong doings against me, as I ask You to forgive me of my sins.

I choose to present my body as a living sacrifice and give over to You all that You have shown me. Romans 12:1 says, "I beseech you therefore, brethren, by the mercies of God, that ye present your bodies a living sacrifice, holy, acceptable unto God, which is your reasonable service." I, therefore, offer You the sacrifice of *praise*, the sacrifice of righteousness, the sacrifice of *joy,* and the sacrifice of *thanksgiving*. I desire to be controlled by Your Spirit. I willingly surrender *my will* and *my life* to You. May all that pleases You and all that You wish, and *only* that which You wish, happen today.

I choose to read the Word and replace the lies I have believed with the Truth. I pray I would be cleansed by the washing of the water of the Word.

By faith I am now cleansed and sanctified and can once again partake of Your Life.

Amen.

Read the following Scriptures to confirm what you have just prayed: Psalm 50:23; 2 Corinthians 10:5; Hebrews 13:15; Psalm 4:5; 27:6; 116:17; Ephesians 5:26; Psalm 32:1–6; Psalm 51; Psalm 65:3–4; 2 Corinthians 7:1.

Scriptures to pray:

Following are some paraphrased Scriptures you also might pray for cleansing:

Search me and know my heart and my thoughts. See if there be any wicked way in me and lead me in Your way. (Psalm 139:23–24)

Please teach me that which I cannot see. (Job 34:32)

I desire to make Your Name be remembered in all generations. (Psalm 45:17)

Let my sentence come forth only from Your presence. (Psalm 17:2)

Let no corrupt communication proceed out of my mouth, but that which is good to the use of edifying, that it may minister grace to the hearer. Let me not grieve the Holy Spirit, whereby I am sealed. Let all bitterness and wrath and anger and clamor and evil speaking be put away from me with all malice. (Ephesians 4:29–31)

Help me be kind, tenderhearted, and forgiving, just as Christ has forgiven me. (Ephesians 4:32)

Let me come boldly to Your Throne in time of need and find mercy. (Hebrews 4:16)

Order my steps in Your Word. Don't let sin or self have dominion over me. (Psalm 119:133)

I choose to be fully persuaded that what You have promised me, You will perform. (Romans 4:21)

I pray that I would know nothing but "Christ crucified." (1 Corinthians 2:2)

Please supply all my needs according to Your riches in glory. (Philippians 4:19)

I desire to love You with all my heart, with all my will and with all my soul, so that I can then love my neighbor as myself. (Matthew 22:37)

I offer my body as a living sacrifice, holy and acceptable which is my reasonable service, and I choose not to be conformed to this world, but to be transformed into Your Image and show forth Your Life, by the renewing of my mind, so that I can then prove in my actions what is the good, the acceptable, and the perfect will of God. (Romans 12:1–2)

Make me bold with Your strength in my soul. (Psalm 138:3)

May You reveal Yourself in me, so that I might speak as You would have me. (Galatians 1:16)

I am in Your hands, do what You will with me. Have Your way in me. (Joshua 9:25)

I will do nothing without asking Your opinion. (Philemon 14)

Make me full of joy with Your countenance. (Acts 2:28)

Christ, You are my life. (Colossians 3:4)

For me to live is Christ. (Philippians 1:21)

Spiritual Warfare Prayers

Before praying the following prayer, we recommend going through the Sanctification Prayer. The Word warns us that "If [we] regard iniquity in [our] hearts, the Lord will not hear [us]." (Psalm 66:18)

Personal Deliverance Prayer

Father,

You are my defender and the lifter of my soul. You tell me in Your Word that if I am Your child, "greater is He that is in me, than he who is in the world." Thus, because You live in me, You have given me Your authority and Your power to make faith choices to rebuke the enemy and to cast him out. I ask You to expose him, his deceptions, and the tactics he is employing against me. Open my eyes that I may see and understand the battle that is raging.

I ask You in the Name of Jesus Christ to break any and all assignments that the enemy has to "kill, steal, and destroy" me. In Jesus Name, I ask You to bind the enemy and loose any bands of wickedness that I have consciously or unconsciously given to him—any root of bitterness, any anger, unforgiveness, resentment, pride, or iniquity. I have now openly repented of these and am washed and cleansed by Your blood.

Father, I ask You now to pour out your Spirit upon me—your wisdom, power, and Love—and to release me from the enemy's grip. Let me not take my stand alone, but please send Your mighty angels to defend me. Shoot Your arrows at the enemy and scatter him to the outermost parts. I trust in You, Jehovah-jireh, my Provider, and I will not be disappointed for You are a shield about me.

Amen.

Read the following Scriptures to confirm what you've just prayed: 1 John 4:4; Luke 10:19; Matthew 28:18-20; John 10:10; Psalm 18:14; Romans 8:37.

Scriptures to pray for deliverance:

The following are some other Scriptures to pray for personal deliverance. Again, we must depend completely upon the Holy Spirit for direction. (Some of these Scriptures are paraphrased.)

I come boldly before Your Throne in my time of need. (Hebrews 4:16)

The Spirit knows how to pray. (Romans 8:26)

The god of this world has blinded the eyes of those who don't believe. (2 Corinthians 4:4)

We must forgive so that Satan doesn't get an advantage in us. (2 Corinthians 2:10–11)

You, Jesus, give us the authority over the power of the enemy so that nothing shall hurt us. (Luke 10:19)

You deliver me from this present evil world. (Galatians 1:4)

You have delivered me from the authority of darkness. (Colossians 1:13)

Jesus, You were manifested to destroy the works of the devil. (1 John 3:8)

I will not be afraid, the battle is not mine, but God's. (2 Chronicles 20:15)

God has defeated principalities and powers. (Colossians 2:15)

I can not enter a strong man's house (the enemy's house), unless I first bind him, and then I can spoil his goods. (Matthew 12:29)

Whatever I bind on earth, will be bound in heaven. And whatever I loose on earth will be loosed in heaven. (Matthew 18:18)

I will submit myself to God, resist the devil, and then the devil will flee from me. (James 4:7; 1 Peter 5:9)

Let the high praises of God be in my mouth, and a two-edged sword in my hands, and may You, Jesus, bind the enemy's kings with chains. (Psalm 149:6–8)

Armor of God Scriptures (Ephesians 6:10–19)

The Word of God exhorts us to daily "put on" the armor of God. Then we will be strong in the power of *His* might and be able to withstand the wiles of the enemy. We are to:

> Gird our waist with *God's Truth*
>
> Put on the *Breastplate of Righteousness and Love* (1 Thessalonians 5:8)
>
> Shod our feet (our souls) with the *Gospel of Peace*. (We wash our feet by putting off the "flesh" and putting on Christ. This is how we prepare ourselves for the kingdom.)
>
> Take the *Shield of Faith* by which we can quench the fiery darts. (This is one of the most important parts of our armor because it refers to our choice to trust what God has promised us in His Word.)

Take the *Helmet of Salvation*. (This is showing forth God's Life instead of our own. It's His light that is shining forth. Isaiah 62:1 says, "Salvation [is] a lamp that burneth.")

Take the *Sword of the Spirit,* which is the Word of God. (The Word of God is our "battle ax" and the only way we are able to stand [Jeremiah 51:20].)

Pray always for all the saints.

Pray that *utterance* may be given to us *to make known the mystery of the gospel* in everything we say and do.

Spiritual Warfare Prayer for Others

Here is a sample prayer to help you pray for others who are involved in warfare:

Father,

In the Name of Jesus Christ, I come before You with _________. I ask that [his / her] steps would be steady and sure today and that Jesus' work on the Cross, with all of its mercy, grace, love, forgiveness, and dying to self, would be accomplished.

By Your authority and power, I ask You to *bind* [shackle, tie, cuff] all enemy infiltration, principalities, powers, rulers of spiritual wickedness and demonic forces, the spirit of heaviness, the spirit of discouragement, obscenity, the spirit of criticism, disloyalty, exclusiveness, cowardness, delusion, gossip, divisiveness, anger, apathy, fear, deceit, lust, etc. from every part of _________'s body and soul.

Reveal every *ungodly* pattern of thinking in _________, every attitude, idea, desire, belief, motivation, and behavior that is not of faith and any ungodly soul ties so that [he / she] might see these things, be able to renounce them, and by Your authority and power cast them out and be set free.

Pour out Your Spirit into the situation and may Your perfect will be done in ________'s life.

I pray all these things in Jesus' Name.

Amen.

Scriptures to pray for others:

Following are some paraphrased Scriptures that we can pray for others:

I pray that ________ will resist the devil, who is a roaring lion, knowing that all Christians are in the same battle. You promise us, God, that after we have "barred ourselves from sin," You will make us perfect, established, and strengthened. (1 Peter 5:8–9)

I pray that ________ will submit to God, resist the devil, and that the devil will flee from _________. Let __________ draw close to You and then You have promised that You will draw close to _________. I pray you might cleanse __________'s hands (body) and purify [his / her] heart (spirit). I pray that __________ will humble [himself / herself] in Your sight and You will lift [him / her] up. (James 4:7–10)

The way we overcome the enemy is by the blood of Christ, the Word of our testimony and by "death to self." (Revelation 12:11)

Greater is He (Jesus) that is in us than he that is in the world. Even the spirits are subject to us. (1 John 4:4. See also Luke 10:20.)

Blessed be God, who teaches my hands to war. (Psalm 144:1. See also Psalm 18:34.)

Let the high praises of God be in my mouth, and a two-edged sword in my hand. (Psalm 149:6)

Loose the bands of wickedness. (Isaiah 58:6)

Whatever we bind (forbid) on earth will be bound (forbidden) in heaven. (Matthew 18:18)

Supplemental Study Notes

"Study to show thyself approved unto God,

a workman that needeth not to be ashamed,

rightly dividing the word of truth."

—2 Timothy 2:15

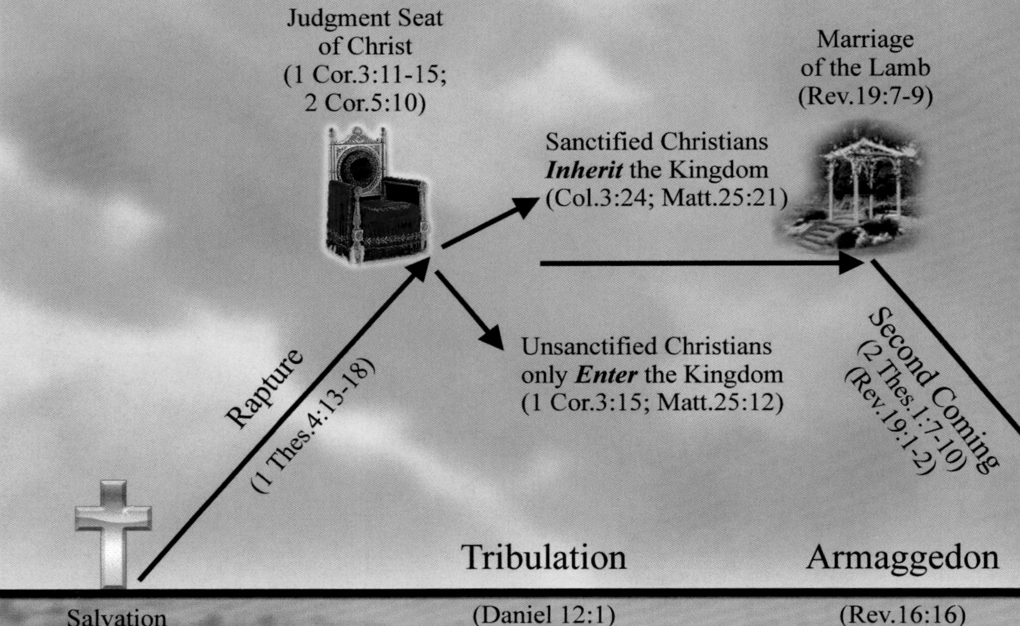
Heaven
Judgment Seat
of Christ
(1 Cor.3:11-15;
2 Cor.5:10)
Marriage
of the Lamb
(Rev.19:7-9)
Sanctified Christians
Inherit the Kingdom
(Col.3:24; Matt.25:21)
Unsanctified Christians
only Enter the Kingdom
(1 Cor.3:15; Matt.25:12)
Rapture
(1 Thes.4:13-18)
Second Coming
(2 Thes.1:7-10)
(Rev.19:1-2)
Tribulation
Armaggedon
Salvation
(Daniel 12:1)
(Rev.16:16)
Earth

Supplemental Study Notes

Table of Contents

The Boundaries of Our Reality

We take our physical reality for granted. And as we begin to explore any domains beyond our own, we make a mistake to transpose our myopic presuppositions to these new vistas. Let's reexamine what we actually do know about reality and see if we can offset the limitations of our immediate personal horizons.

The Macrocosm

Anyone who has pondered the heavens through a telescope has experienced the overwhelming awesome glory of the heavens. The Bible describes it beautifully:

> The heavens declare the glory of God; and the firmament sheweth his handywork. Day unto day uttereth speech, and night unto night sheweth knowledge. There is no speech nor language, where their voice is not heard. Their line is gone out through all the earth, and their words to the end of the world.
>
> —Psalm 19:1–4

The expanse and majesty of the universe never ceases to overwhelm all who study it. The incomprehensible sizes and distances never become comfortable, even to the well informed. They are simply breathtaking.

And yet the great discovery of twentieth-century science is that the universe is *finite*, not infinite! It has a determinable size. It may be expanding, but it is not infinite. It is also now recognized that it had a *beginning*. That is what leads to the conjectures collected under the banner of "the Big Bang." First there was nothing. Then it exploded.

It is profoundly disturbing to come to grips with the reality that the universe is not infinite; it has not always been here; and the day will come when it will end. (Scientists acknowledge that an eventual "heat death" appears to be inevitable, eventually, thermodynamically speaking.)

Our consideration of the macrocosm, however, is the least of these disturbing discoveries. Let's exchange our telescope for a microscope: let's examine the *microcosm* of our universe.

A Model of the Atom

In our modern world we can talk glibly about an atom as the basic building block of physical reality. One way we visualize an atom—a hydrogen atom, for example—is as a nucleus with an electron encircling it:

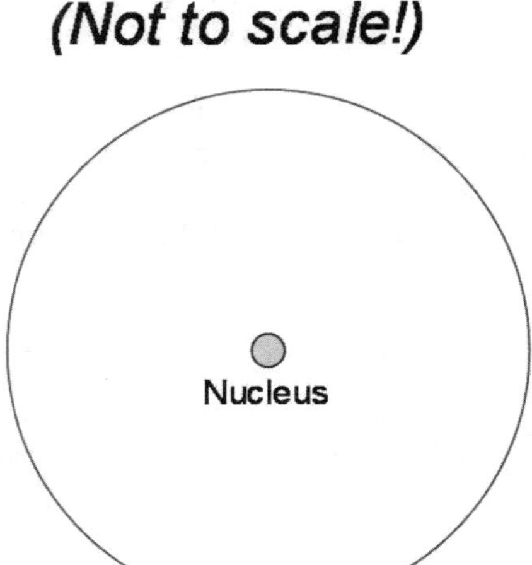

Sketches that are often found in our textbooks usually fail to communicate the sizes involved. (Bear with me to get a grasp of the relative scales.) The nucleus is about 10^{-13} centimeters. The ostensible orbit of the electron is about 10^{-8} centimeters, that is, 10^5 larger—100,000 times larger. If you were to build a scale model, using a golf ball for a nucleus, the electron would be several football-field lengths away.

But 10^5 is just the *linear* relationship. The *area* covered would be $(10^5)^2$. The *volume* involved would be $(10^5)^3$ or 10^{15}! That is a really huge number—larger than most of us can possibly imagine. That is the same ratio one second has to 30 million years!

If we suggested that this table is solid, and you insisted that it was mostly empty space, you would be more correct—by that same ratio: one second to 30 million years! The only reason it *seems* to be solid is due to the collisions of the electrons of the molecules of our bodies with the molecules of the table: it is, in effect, *an electronic simulation* creating the apparent "solidness" we encounter. It's an illusion, of sorts.

But it gets worse.

The Microcosm

As we begin to explore *subatomic* particles, we encounter behavior that is absolutely astonishing. If I take a piece of string, I can cut it in half. If I take one of the two remaining pieces, I can cut that in half again. One would assume that I could do this indefinitely—in concept, at least. It turns out that it is not possible: when I reach beyond the length of 10^{-33} centimeters, it loses "*locality*"; it becomes everywhere at once! These peculiar properties have been validated in laboratory experiments. Every proton in the universe is "directly connected" to every other one in the universe!

It turns out that everything we would seek to measure—length, mass, energy, time—are all composed of *indivisible* units, called "quanta." The study of quanta is called "Quantum Physics."

The peculiar behavior of quanta shatters all of the presuppositions we have drawn from classical physics. We now discover that we actually live within a *digital simulation* that is but a subset, or shadow, of a larger reality.[20]

Using Leonardo da Vinci's "Vitruvian Man" to represent humanity, our finite boundaries can be summarized as below:

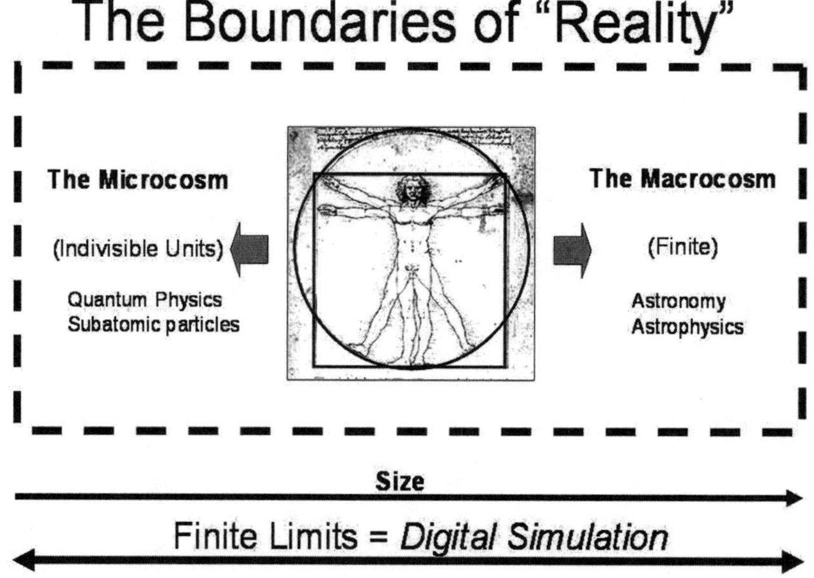

This is what the Bible has declared all along (Hebrews 11:3, et al). We talk of the "Spiritual Universe" which is the larger reality. Our "physical reality" is but a shadow of a larger context. We are in possession of a message from that larger reality and we need to take it more seriously.

A brilliant mind has gone to a lot of trouble to establish this simulated enterprise for a purpose. We find ourselves as participants and it becomes crucial for us to recognize our situation and to discover what is expected of us and what we can anticipate as our destiny. It becomes the greatest adventure of our lifetime!

Fortunately, we are in possession of a message—in fact, a handbook that holds His intended instructions to guide us through this adventure. It details those occasions in which He enters what we call the physical universe to accomplish certain purposes, and we are to prepare for His arrival! It's time we do our homework, as it increasingly appears that time is at hand.

Good hunting! Praise His Name!

(These notes were excerpted from Briefing Packages and DVDs available from Koinonia House, www.khouse.org.)

The Nature of Time

A Discussion of Fate versus Free Will

One of the many revolutionary discoveries of the twentieth century was the realization that time is a *physical* property. Time varies with mass, acceleration, and gravity—among other factors.

The atomic clock located at the Royal Observatory at Greenwich, England, and the virtually identical one located at the National Institute of Standards and Technology at Boulder, Colorado, are each accurate to within a millionth of second in a million years. Yet they need continual correction of 5 microseconds per year due to their difference in *altitudes*: the one at Greenwich is at 80 feet above sea level; the one at Boulder is 5400 feet above sea level. The difference in gravity causes time itself to run at different rates!

We now understand that if two identical astronauts were to participate in an experiment in which one was to be sent to the nearest star—at, say, half the speed of light—he would return more than two years *younger* than his twin brother! (If that doesn't bother you, you weren't reading carefully.)

The key point is this: time is a *physical* property. Once we grasp the implications of that discovery, it resolves some of the most puzzling paradoxes in the universe.

The Nature of Eternity

In our songs and poetry, we imagine that "eternity" is having lots of time—time in unlimited amounts. That makes colorful literature, but it is bad physics.

Is God limited to the restrictions of mass, acceleration, or gravity? Hardly. He is *outside* the dimensionality of time altogether (Isaiah 57:15). And He, alone, being outside the restrictions of time, can see the end from the beginning (Isaiah 46:10). It is this unique capability of God Himself that He uses to *authenticate* His message to us. He writes history *before* it happens.

We are indebted to Dr. Albert Einstein for one of the most revolutionary insights of our lifetime. One of my favorite Einstein quotes is: "People like us, who believe in physics, know that the distinction between the past, the present, and the future, is only a stubbornly persistent illusion."

This also unravels one of the greatest enigmas of the ages. But first, a classic riddle.

The Seven Bridges of Königsburg

> *In the town of Königsburg there is an island called Kneiphof, with two branches of the River Pregel flowing around it. There are seven bridges crossing the two branches. The question is whether a person can plan a walk in such a way that he will cross each of the bridges once but not more than once.* —Euler, 1735

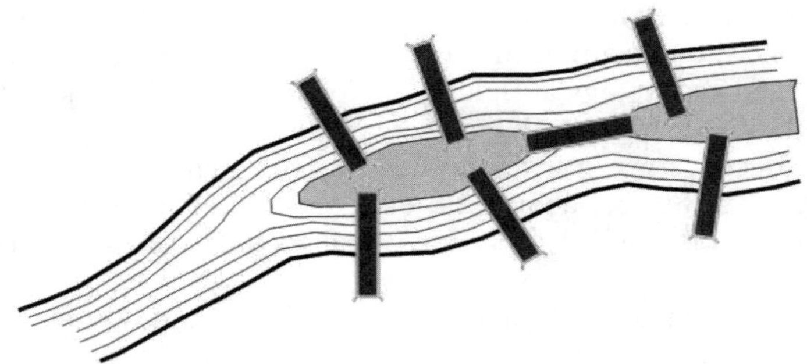

Before you go on, take Euler's challenge. Can you plot a path that crosses each bridge once and only once? (After you give up, you can sneak a peek at the solution at the end of this article; and *then* resume reading.)

- - - -

Predestination versus Free Will

The ostensible paradox of predestination ("fate") versus free will has plagued philosophers and theologians since the beginning of recorded time. However, it appears as a paradox only when viewed from *within the time domain*. Once we recognize God's vantage point, the paradox dissolves.

Consider observing a parade from curbside. The sequence of bands, marching units, floats, and other units composing the parade pass in sequence before us. However, to a helicopter hovering *above the plane of the parade's existence,* one could see the beginning and end simultaneously. (A clumsy analogy, but it is illustrative.)

One of the major challenges in biblical perspectives is the portrayal of divine volition in respect of the believer throughout the epistles:

His foreknowledge determines election. Election looks back to foreknowledge and establishes predestination, which looks forward to destiny. Once God's perspective from outside the constraints of time—a physical property—is recognized, then the paradox dissolves. It is only a paradox when viewed *from within* the constraints of time.

The Geometry of Eternity

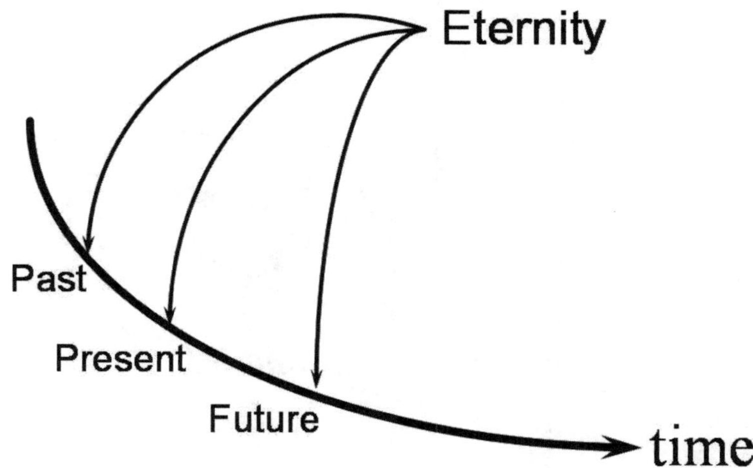

We are caught in the physical dimension of time. The *past* is only a memory. The *future* is a hope. The *present* is a gift! (Perhaps that's why we call it the "present.")

God, seated outside the physical restrictions of time, can observe "the end from the beginning"—and uses that unique capability to authenticate His message to us. We are in possession of a comprehensive "message system"—66 books penned by more than 40 men over almost 2,000 years—that has been handed to us from the Designer of the Universe. Once we comprehend the source and scope of this message system, it eclipses all other sources and priorities!

We are told that nothing in His universe is accidental. You are reading this by His divine appointment. When did He first begin to deal with you personally? *Before the foundation of the earth* (Ephesians 1:4)! And He has an inheritance for you that is beyond imagination.

And He always rewards the diligent. How is this going to impact *your* priorities?

(These notes were excerpted from Briefing Packages and DVDs available from Koinonia House, www.khouse.org.)

— — — — — — — — — — — — — —

Addenda: Solution to the Seven Bridges of Königsburg

The solution to Euler's riddle is to not fall victim to any self-imposed restrictions or boundaries. Every river has a source, and the solution involves a route around the source. This is where the idiom "to think outside the box" comes from. Most paradoxes result from the tyranny of self-imposed constraints that can be relieved, penetrated, or dissolved.

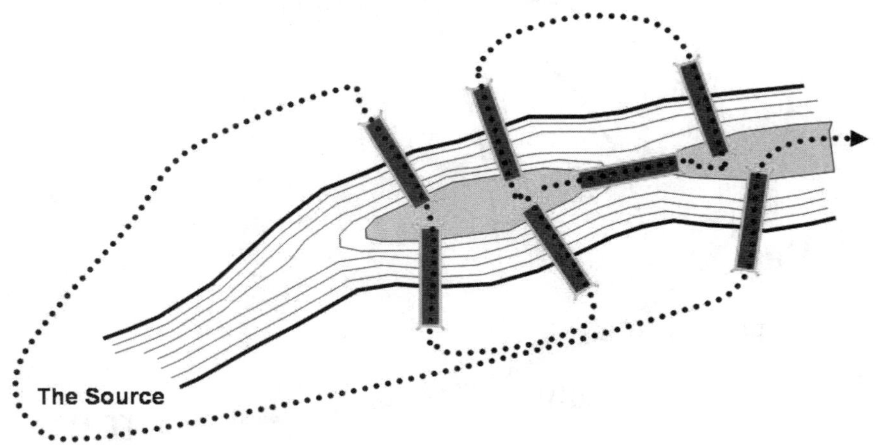

Our Epistemological Cycle

Epistemology is "the study of knowledge, its scope, and its limits." It attempts to answer the question, How do we *know*? What are the tools to facilitate our understanding?

At the elemental level, we discover that the Word of God, even though it was compiled in 66 separate books, by more than 40 penmen (who didn't even know each other), it is an intricate, skillfully crafted *integrated* whole, in which each word, number, and other details, are included deliberately to complete a composite design. The integrity of this design is overwhelming once it is perceived.

A second discovery, which accompanies the first, is that the *origin* of the entire composite had to come from *outside our time domain!* It details history before it happens. It challenges all of our presuppositions about space and time. Its origin is provably extraterrestrial.

This collection of specifications details the arrival of the Creator Himself, personally entering His creation to accomplish a mission planned before the foundation of Planet Earth. His accomplishment of that mission thus validates the entire message to all of us. This epistemological approach is summarized below:

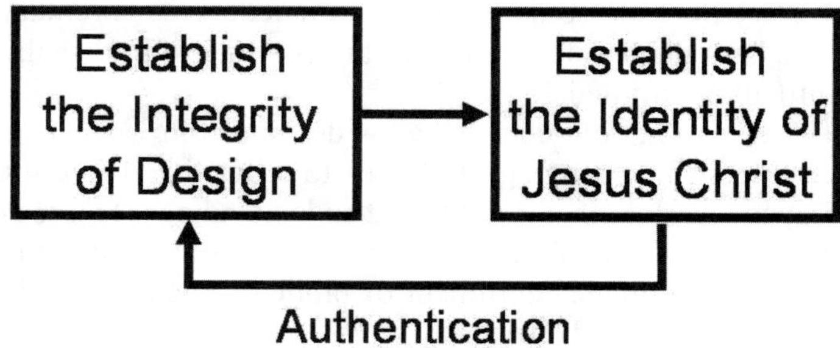

(Some would call this a form of circular reasoning; however, the distribution of these 66 parts, more than 40 authors, over a period of almost 2,000 years, shreds that argument.)

To explore further aspects of an epistemological approach for our biblical understanding, we will explore three basic aspects of theological study:

1. Hermeneutics (our theory of interpreting the text)

2. Eschatology (the study of "last things")

3. Ecclesiology (the study of the church)

Hermeneutics

There are numerous approaches to interpret the Bible. Throughout history the scholars who took the text very literally were in the minority. The more popular approaches have been continual attempts to regard it metaphorically, or allegorically, and to regard it only as an approximate guide for human affairs.

Those who adopted a stricter regard were typically among a small minority. The text itself maintains that the Word of God is pure and without deceit (Psalm 119:140; Proverbs 30:5). These scholars regard an allegory as a license to invent: it is useful for illustration, but hazardous to establish doctrine.

The testimony of Jesus Christ Himself instructed us to take the text *very* seriously:

> Think not that I am come to destroy the law, or the prophets: I am not come to destroy, but to fulfill. For verily I say unto you, till heaven and earth pass, one jot or one tittle shall in no wise pass from the law, till all be fulfilled.
>
> —Matthew 5:17–18

(A "jot" is the tiniest letter of the Hebrew alphabet that you and I might mistake for an apostrophe, or a blemish on the paper. A "tittle" is the little decorative hook on some of the Hebrew letters. This remark could be paraphrased, "not the doting of an 'i' or the crossing of a 't' shall pass from the law until all be fulfilled.")

There exists, of course, a wide spectrum of hermeneutical approaches—from free ranging allegories to strict literal interpretations—that will impact our doctrinal insights and understandings. This is never more evident than in the study of what the Bible says about the end times. In the final analysis, the ultimate fulfillment of biblical prophecies will vindicate the proper hermeneutical doctrines.

Eschatology

One of the most conspicuous areas that will be impacted by our hermeneutical approach is the study of "last things," or end times, called *eschatology*. The first fork in this road to understanding is the issue of the Millennium (Revelation 20), which traditional Protestant denominations emerging from the Reformation have only regarded allegorically. (See our summary of the history of these views in the Supplemental Note on "The History of Amillennialism," which follows.)

It is significant to note that a person's eschatological perspectives will derive directly from his hermeneutical disciplines, as summarized below:

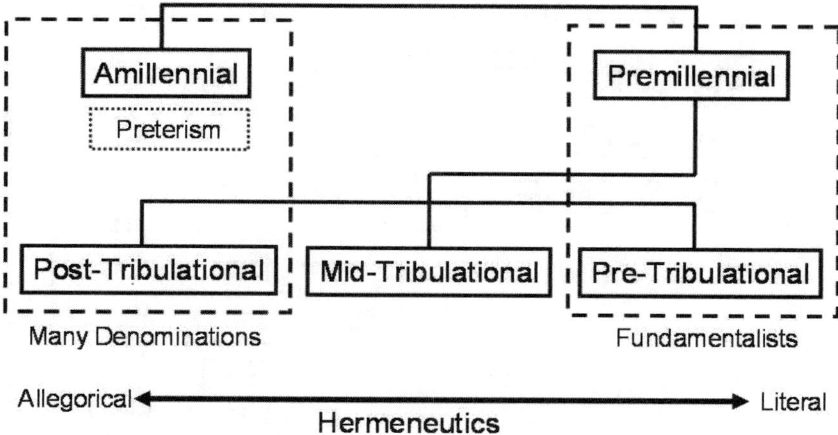

Preterism—the view that prophecies have already been fulfilled—has gained popularity among certain liberal theologians. In the nineteenth century, a *post-millennial* view—that we were already in the Millennium—was popular when some thought the world was destined to keep getting better and better. The conspicuous and continuing decay toward paganism in the twentieth century has substantially refuted those viewpoints.

Those who take the Millennium literally—*premillennialists*—are also divided in their views regarding the church's participation (if any) in the Great Tribulation (as predicted by Jesus, quoting Daniel 12:1 in Matthew 24:21, 22). A review of some of these views has been included in our discussion of the *Harpazo*, commonly known as the Rapture.

Ecclesiology

Many Christians do not fully apprehend the mystical nature of the *Ecclesia*—the called-out body of Christ. It was Paul's unique privilege to reveal this remarkable parenthesis in God's program and its distinctive privileges and responsibilities. Many of the most critical aspects of the church gain particular emphasis from a careful study of prophecies of the church, particularly in the seven letters to the Seven Churches in Revelation 2 and 3:

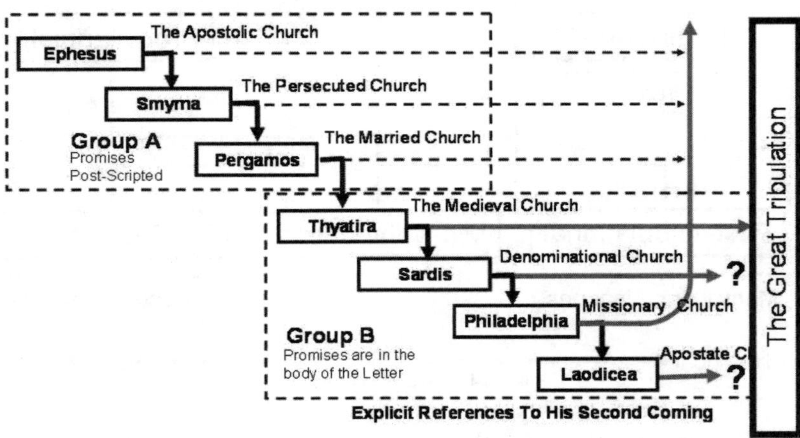

A person's church environment clearly impacts their attitude toward the Word of God and clearly determines their hermeneutical perspectives. Independent Bible churches tend to take the Bible *very* seriously. Traditional denominational churches tend to regard the Scriptures rather "liberally." They seek recourse in modern paraphrases rather than insisting on strict translations, and so forth.

The Epistemological Cycle

It is interesting to see how these three basic elements of theology reinforce themselves to the diligent student:

A person's hermeneutics will determine their eschatological views.

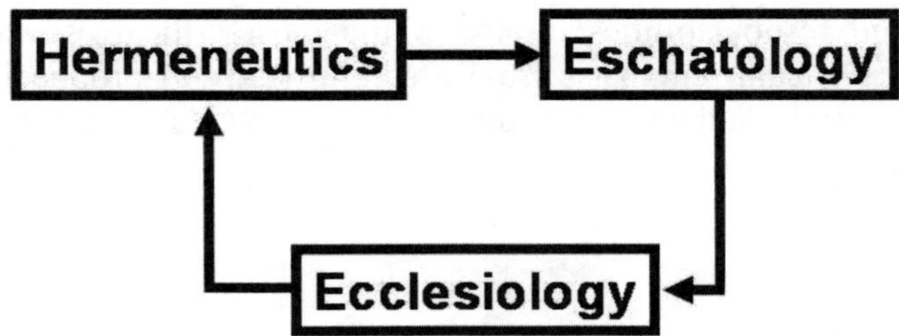

These perspectives, in turn, will impact their understanding of the mystical church and its destiny. These perspectives, in turn, will influence their very approach to the Word of God. Each of these studies will profoundly impact the other.

These are exciting times, particularly in view of the astonishing resources that are now available to anyone: personal, portable information appliances that feature the ability to penetrate the original Hebrew or Greek texts (without having to know Hebrew or Greek). It is now possible for a layman—without special language training—to accomplish in a few minutes what used to take a trained pastor weeks of study!

The Word of God is now more available than ever before in history, which should sharpen our insights into the expectations of the great climax that is now looming before us.

There are no excuses for any of us to fail to do our homework for the days ahead.

Baruch HaShem! Praise His Name, indeed!

(These notes were excerpted from Briefing Packages and DVDs available from Koinonia House, www.khouse.org.)

History of Amillennialism

It is tragic that most of the major denominations—Roman Catholic and Protestant—embrace an eschatology (study of last things) that is *amillennial:* a view that does not envision a literal rule of Christ on the Throne of David on Planet Earth.

While there are many different, yet defendable, views regarding many aspects of end-time prophecies, this basic divergence—denying a literal Millennium—is particularly hazardous since it would appear to be an attack on the very character of God. It does violence to His numerous and explicit promises and commitments that pervade both the Old and New Testaments.

The Old Testament is replete with commitments for a literal Messiah ultimately ruling the world through Israel from His throne in Jerusalem. There are at least 1,845 references in the Old Testament and 17 books give prominence to the event. The ancient rabbinical aspirations were dominated by it. In fact, this obsession obscured their recognizing the Messiah when He made His initial appearance.

There are at least 318 references in 216 chapters of the New Testament and 23 of its 27 books give prominence to the event. The early church looked longingly for His promised return as their "Blessed Hope" to rid a desperate world of its evil rulers. How and where did this form of skepticism known as "Amillennialism" begin?

Origen

Pious, popular, and persuasive, Origen stands out as one of the great figures of the third-century church. Even at the age of eighteen, he stood out spectacularly as a teacher in Alexandria. (In misguided obedience to Matthew 19:12, he emasculated himself, which he later regretted.) Later, as a prolific writer based in Caesarea, his *De Principiis* systematically laid out Christian doctrine in terms of Hellenic thinking and set the pattern for most subsequent theological thought for many years. His numerous sermons and commentaries, however, tragically also established an extreme pattern of allegorizing Scripture, which was to strongly influence Augustine in subsequent years.

Augustine

Augustine, the Bishop of Hippo (AD 354–430), was one of the most influential leaders of the Western church, living during the turbulent days of the disintegration of the Roman Empire.

He initially lived a sensuous, dissolute life, but following a dramatic conversion he experienced a total change of character. In 391 he was ordained as a priest in North Africa and four years later was elevated to the Bishop of

Hippo. He embarked on a writing career and his extensive doctrinal writings deeply affected the Medieval Roman Catholic Church. Augustine's most elaborate writing, *The City of God,* was written as the Empire lay crumbling under a siege by half-civilized tribes. It portrayed the Church as a new civic order in the midst of the ruins of the Roman Empire. Augustine died while the Vandals were besieging the very gates of Hippo in AD 430.

Although his writings effectively defeated a number of heresies emerging in those turbulent times, the allegorizing influences of Origen left an amillennial eschatology in their wake. As the Church had increasingly become an instrument of the state, it wasn't politically expedient for state-supported clergy to point toward a literal return of Christ to rid the world of its evil rulers! The allegorical reposturing of those passages was more "politically correct."

The Reformation Shortfall

A thousand years later, under the influences of Martin Luther and others, the Reformation brought an intensive return to the authority of the Scriptures that, in turn, resulted in the subsequent reform in soteriology (the study of salvation) with its emphasis on salvation by faith alone. Many were willingly burned at the stake for their commitment to a Biblical perspective. However, one of the unfortunate shortcomings of the Reformation was that it failed to also reexamine the *eschatology* of the Medieval Church in the light of Scripture. Thus, the allegorizing alchemy of Origen, institutionalized by Augustine, left a denial of the Millennium that still continues today to pervade the doctrines of most Protestant denominations.

From Augustine to Auschwitz

In addition to forcing an allegorization of many key passages of Scripture, this also led to the tragedy of the Holocaust in Europe. The responsibility for the six million Jews who were systematically murdered in the concentration camps has to include the silent pulpits who had embraced this heretical eschatology and its attendant anti-Semitism.

This tragedy is even more poignant in that it is destined to be repeated: Jesus predicted that, in the period He labeled "the Great Tribulation," there would be "a time of trouble, such as never was since there was a nation even to that same time," (quoting Daniel 12:1). The Holocaust in Europe killed one Jew in three. The next one will apparently kill *two out of three* (Zechariah 13:8).

"Replacement Theology"

One of the derivative aspects of an amillennial perspective is that it denies Israel's future role in God's plans. This also leads to a "replacement theology," a heresy in which the church is viewed as replacing Israel in God's program for mankind. Paul, in his distinctive treatise on the doctrines of

Christianity we call the book of Romans, hammers away for three chapters—9, 10, and 11—on the future destiny of Israel in God's plan for humankind.

It is sobering to recognize the world's attack on the Abrahamic Covenant, Islam's attack on the Land Covenant, and the denominational church's attack on the Davidic Covenant.

It is time for the diligent student of God's Word to take God seriously and realize that He means what He says and says what He means. And we will be held accountable for our response to His Word.

(These notes were excerpted from Briefing Packages and DVDs available from Koinonia House, www.khouse.org.)

The Rapture

The *Harpazo*—commonly called "the Rapture" (from the Latin translation)—is undoubtedly the most preposterous doctrine of biblical Christianity. The only thing it has going for it is that it is an event clearly indicated in the text.

Two Messiahs?

When one examines the numerous Old Testament predictions of the appearance of the Messiah of Israel, we find two ostensibly contradictory presentations. Many passages portray a suffering servant; others clearly emphasize a ruling king. These manifold passages resulted in a view anticipating *two* Messiahs: Messiah Ben Joseph, the suffering servant; and Messiah Ben David, the ruling King, respectively.

When Jesus made His appearance, the overriding expectation of the Messiah Ben David—the reigning King who was to deliver Israel from the world's evil rulers—was so prevalent that they did not recognize Him! The recognition of *one* Messiah in *two* distinct "comings" is now clearly acknowledged among conservative scholars.

(Even the most highly venerated orthodox rabbi, Rabbi Itzak Kaduri, left his bombshell note declaring that the "two Messiah's are one" and His name is *Yehoshuah*! He ordered that it was to be sealed until one year after his death, to block any rebuttal in accordance with orthodox traditions and practice. It is reported that more than two hundred thousand attended his funeral in February, 2006. His note, then unsealed, has caused the orthodox community in Israel considerable consternation.[21])

Just as the Jewish community was misled by confusing the two accounts, there now appears to be a similar—but inverted—parallel among many Christian expositors regarding the Second Coming of Christ. We need to anticipate *two* returns rather than just one.

Two Comings?

When we assemble all of the manifold passages having to do with the return of Jesus Christ, we discover they also seem to fall into two contradictory, mutually exclusive categories:

Group A:

Daniel 2:44–45

Daniel 7:9–14

Daniel 12:1–3

Zechariah 14:1–15

Matthew 13:41

Matthew 24:15–31

Matthew 26:64

Mark 13:14–27

Mark 14:62

Luke 21:25–28

Acts 1:9–11

Acts 3:19–21

1 Thessalonians 3:13

2 Thessalonians 1:6–10

2 Thessalonians 2:8

2 Peter 3:1–14

Jude 14—15

Revelation 1:7

Revelation 19:11—20:6

Revelation 22:7, 12, 20

Group B:

John 14:1–3

1 Corinthians 15:1–53

1 Thessalonians 4:13–18

Romans 8:19

1 Corinthians 1:7–8

1 Corinthians 16:22

Philippians 3:20–21

Colossians 3:4

1 Thessalonians 1:10

1 Thessalonians 2:19

1 Thessalonians 5:9

1 Thessalonians 5:23

2 Thessalonians 2:1, (3)

1 Timothy 6:14

2 Timothy 4:1

Titus 2:13

Hebrews 9:28

James 5:7–9

1 Peter 1:7, 13

1 John 2:28—3:2

Jude 21

Revelation 2:25

Revelation 3:10

As we attempt to compile the distinctive characteristics of these two groups, we encounter mutually contradictory aspects between them.

In Group A, all people on the earth are affected: "every eye shall see Him."
In Group B, only believers are affected.

Group A is preceded by a definite series of precedent events.
Group B is imminent, we are instructed to expect Him at any moment.

Group A does not reference any translation of saints or resurrection.
Group B specifically involves the resurrection of believers.

In Group A, translated saints accompany Him to the earth.
In Group B, saints are gathered from the earth—both live and resurrected dead.

In Group A, the earth is judged.
In Group B, the earth is not judged.

Group A concludes the "Day of wrath."
Group B occurs prior to the "Day of wrath."

Conversely, in Group B, there is no reference to Satan.
In Group A, Satan is bound for a thousand years.

In Group B, He comes for His own.
In Group A, He comes with His own.

In Group B, He comes in the air.
In Group A, He comes to the earth.

In Group B, He claims His bride.
In Group A, He comes with His bride.

In Group B, the Great Tribulation follows.
In Group A, the Tribulation is interrupted and the Millennium follows.

The Harpazo (Rapture)

Surprisingly, Group B—the Harpazo, Greek, commonly called "the Rapture," from the Latin—was promised by the Lord in His final hours (John 14) and was remarkably detailed by Paul (1 Thessalonians 4:12–17; 1 Corinthians 15:51–53).

There are, of course, a number of things that good conservative scholars have different views on. However, from a careful exegetical study of Paul's second letter to the Thessalonians, chapter 2, an important sequence can be noted:

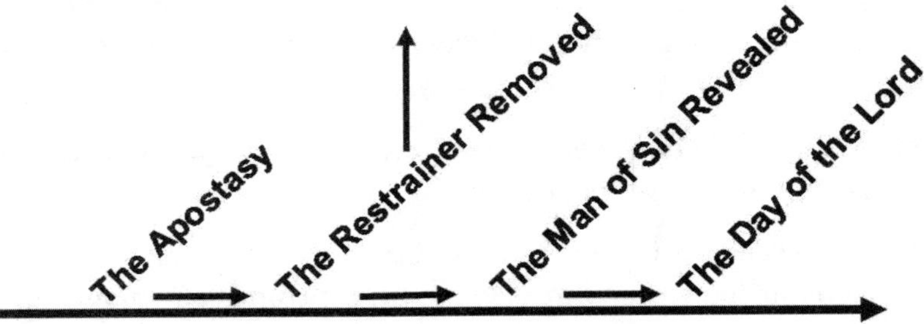

For that day shall not come, except there come a falling away first.[22] v.3

He who now [restraineth] will [restrain], until He be taken out of the way. v.7

And then shall that Wicked One be revealed. v.8

(Note: the "Restrainer" is the Holy Spirit as He indwells the church believer.)

The removal of the Restrainer is a prerequisite to the Wicked One being revealed. He, in turn, is a prerequisite to the Seventieth Week of Daniel commencing, which is concluded by the Great Tribulation, which is interrupted by the Second Coming and the establishment of the Kingdom.

Rapture Imminent

Other than the predicted widespread apostasy of the nominal churches, there appears to be no prerequisite events that must precede the Rapture. We are clearly taught throughout the entire New Testament to expect Him at any moment. This is called "the Doctrine of Imminence." It stands as a rebuttal to both Post-Tribulation and Mid-Tribulation eschatological views since they require precedent events to His return.

Second Coming Prerequisites

In contrast to the Rapture, there are a number of events that must precede the Second Coming in power and to establish the Kingdom. There are at least seven years of history detailed in the passages concerning the "Seventieth Week" that Gabriel described to Daniel (Daniel 9:24–27). The final 3 ½ years—42 months, 1260 days, the most documented period in both the Old and New Testaments—labeled by the Lord Himself as "the Great Tribulation" (Matthew 24:21, 22) are climaxed by His return. In fact, the Old Testament highlights the very purpose of this "time of Jacob's trouble":

> I will go and return to my place, till they acknowledge their offence, and seek my face: in their affliction they will seek me earnestly.
>
> —Hosea 5:15

This is God speaking: in order to *return* to His place, He must have *left* it! The "offence" is singular and specific. It will take this time of affliction for Israel to repent and petition His return.

(This may also explain Satan's continuing attempts to thwart the plan of God through his anti-Semitism. If he can wipe out the faithful remnant of Israel he may believe that he can prevent this essential prerequisite petition.)

It appears that the Lord is destined to return *twice:* first to gather the church; and then, subsequently, to fulfill the promises to Israel.

Caveats

There are many differing views—even among well informed and competent conservative scholars—that one will encounter throughout any study of Eschatology. What makes eschatological studies so challenging is that, to have validity, your own eschatological views need to harmonize with the entire corpus of Scripture.

So it will be crucially important to study your Bible thoroughly, be precise in your definitions, and carefully draw your own conclusions. Draw upon the best expertise available, but cautiously formulate your own perspectives, anchored in the bedrock of Scripture. It is far too important to delegate to others. Your best protection is "the whole counsel of God." Avoid "single verse theology."

Remember: God always rewards the diligent.

Good hunting. The King is coming! *Baruch HaShem!* Praise His Name!

(These notes were excerpted from Briefing Packages and DVDs available from Koinonia House, www.khouse.org.)

What Is Justification?

Justification means we are guaranteed an entrance to heaven on the basis of what *Christ* has already done. *He is the righteous and holy One*. He has simply imputed to us *His* righteousness and *His* holiness; however, our character, our actions, and our deeds have not necessarily changed yet. In other words, it's a *fact* that we have been set apart and made holy unto God; however, in real life experience, nothing really has changed.

Once we are "justified," God begins the long process of experiential sanctification where He must literally *make us* righteous, holy and set apart in character, action, and deed. *He* is the One who will accomplish these things in our lives by His power of resurrection. We are the ones, however, who must continually choose to let Him do so. These changes in our character don't happen automatically. *We* must allow God to remake us into righteous and holy vessels reflecting Him in all our actions. It's His will to do so and He gives us the power to do it, but *we* must make the moment-by-moment choice to "put off" the old man and "put on" the new.

This is called the process of sanctification—learning to walk in the newness of His Life.

Some Christians are quick to allow God to sanctify them and the change is quite noticeable. Others, however, seem to take a lifetime. And, still others, never do. The Word of God says that we are the "elect according to the foreknowledge of God the Father, *through sanctification of the Spirit* unto obedience" (1 Peter 1:2).

So, *justification* is a "free gift" that we receive as a result of our believing in Christ, whereas, *sanctification* is a process we must all participate in and show by our actions and our character that we *are* being conformed into His image and that our soul *is* being transformed. Sanctification is the time we turn from our sin and self and embrace not only all that He has done *for us*, but all that He wants to do *in us.*

"Justification" will definitely get us into heaven. It opens the door for us, *but sanctification is what the Lord will judge us on at the Bema Seat*. Experiential sanctification will allow us to be presented to Christ as pure virgins and to inherit the kingdom with all its rewards. If we haven't learned "holiness" *here*, however, it will be too late to learn it when we get *there*.

What Is Sanctification?

Experiential sanctification (*hagiasmos*, Strong's #38) is "the process by which God conforms us back into His image," the image that was lost when Adam and Eve sinned (Romans 8:29). *It's the means God uses to set us apart and to make us holy, prepared, and "fit" for the coming kingdom* (John 17:19). The process of sanctification purifies us, separates us from sin, and consecrates us to God. 2 Thessalonians 2:13 tells us "God has chosen us to salvation through experiential sanctification of the Spirit."

Sanctification is the lifelong process by which we become those overcomers who inherit the Millennial Kingdom.

Sanctification means being cleansed of any sin or self that would contaminate our soul. It's that time where we are emptied of our "self," and then filled back up with Christ's Life. It's the process of learning to exchange lives with Christ. As we give Him ours, He gives us His (1 John 2:1–2). *Sanctification refers to an inward change (a metamorphosis) brought about apart from the natural strength of the individual.* This inward change is brought about by *His* spirit. "For this cause I have raised you up to show in thee My power" (Exodus 9:16). It's His power that sanctifies us, that changes us and that makes us new creations, but it's *our* choice that allows God to accomplish it. It's not automatic (1 Peter 1:15–16).

Experiential sanctification is the means by which God's Spirit highlights the self-centered things we do and then shows us how to replace them with His Life. *Our fulfillment, our meaning, and our significance in this life and the next all rest upon this transformation process.* God's will is that we might show *by our actions* (our "Spirit-led" works) that we *are* "new creations" in Him and that He lives in us. This demonstrates that we have not only applied the Blood to the doorposts of our house, we have also expelled the leaven.

God's will is that our *new* spirit be freed from all soulish influences so that *His* Spirit can freely direct our lives (James 1:19–22). Scripture validates this: "Having, therefore, these promises, dearly beloved let us *cleanse ourselves from all filthiness of the flesh and spirit*, perfecting holiness in the fear of God" (2 Corinthians 7:1. See also Leviticus 20:7; Romans 12:1). Sanctification is the process that makes this happen.

God's purpose for sanctification is that we might be "conformed into the image of Christ." The Greek word for *conformed* is *summorphos* (Strong's #4832), which means "to be jointly formed or fashioned unto." It's from the root word *sun*, which means "union, resemblance or completeness," and *morphe*, which means "adjustment or shape." *Experiential sanctification is the process by which we are shaped or fashioned into His resemblance.*

God wants us conformed into His image so that we might produce the "fruit" that will make us "prepared" and "fit" not only to attend the wedding festivities in heaven, but also to rule and reign with Him in the Millennial Kingdom here on earth.

The measure of our usefulness to the Lord in the future kingdom will be found in the measure of our sanctification here and now.

Circumcision

Deuteronomy 30:6 is a very interesting Scripture verse. God says here that He is going to *circumcise* His people's hearts so they might love Him "with all their heart and all their soul." (See also Deuteronomy 10:16.) In this context, *circumcision* means "spiritual circumcision"—circumcision of the heart, not of the body. Romans 2:29 validates this: "He is a Jew, which is one inwardly; and *circumcision is that of the heart*, in the spirit and not in the letter; whose praise is not of man, but of God."

Spiritual circumcision simply means that the Spirit of God has been allowed to cut around the heart and expose any sin or self. It means constantly allowing God to expose and then, "put off" our old nature and "put on" the new. The idea here is a full surrender and a total commitment to the Lord. Colossians 2:11 explains: "In whom also ye are circumcised with the circumcision made without hands, in the putting off the body of the sins of the flesh by the circumcision of Christ." Circumcision is simply a sign of the covenant relationship between God and man.

Back in Old Testament times, an uncircumcised man was "cut off" from his people (Genesis 17:14). *Cut off* (Strong's #3772) means "severed from or *cut off from fellowship*." This person was not killed, but simply "cut off" from fellowship and driven out from the family. *Because* he *was the one who broke the covenant, he was removed from receiving any further blessings*. This is an interesting parallel to what we have been talking about throughout this book.

The process by which the Lord made a covenant in the Old Testament is also quite fascinating. Again, it was by cutting. Genesis 15:17 tells us that the Israelites would cut an animal into pieces and then walk through the cut-up parts, which pledged that person's faithfulness to the covenant. In the New Testament, however, God gives us a *new* covenant. Hebrews 8:10 tells us that God puts "His laws into our minds and writes them in our hearts." This is saying that God inscribes (or cuts) His law of Love in our hearts so that our previously vague ideas about holiness, righteousness, and purity can become clearly understood realities in our lives.

Circumcision, therefore, has more to do with "sanctification" than it does with "justification." It has to do with our obedience to address anything that prevents our loving God. Circumcision means to continually "put off" the old man and to "put on" the new one. It means to moment-by-moment renew our minds so that we can be transformed into Christ's image and we can love others as He desires. Colossians 2:11 says, "We are circumcised with the circumcision made without hands, in the *putting off the body of the sins of the flesh* by the circumcision of Christ." (See also Philippians 3:3.)

When we put all this together, it makes perfect sense. If Abraham in the Old Testament (who was already saved) had not been circumcised, he would not have inherited the promises. Thus, *circumcision was not an act of saving faith, as he already had "heaven," it simply guaranteed him joint heirship. It was Abraham's inheritance that was in question with circumcision, and the appropriation of that blessing was conditioned upon his obedience* (Genesis 22:15–18).

The same principles apply to us!

> Godliness is profitable unto all things, having promise of the life that now is, and of that which is to come.
>
> —1 Timothy 4:8

Knowing God Loves Us

Before we can go any further in God's *sanctification process*, we must know without a doubt that the Father loves us. We must be assured that Christ has not only laid down His Life expressly to give us His Love, but that He has also called us to be His vessels of Love to others. If we know and have a living experience of these things, then we will have the confidence and the trust to lay our wills and our lives down to Him and love Him daily in return (i.e., allow the sanctification process to proceed).

The Bible says: "Hereby perceive [know] we the love of God, because He laid down His life for us" (1 John 3:16).

How Do We Know God Loves Us?

When I (Nancy) first began teaching *The Way of Agape*, I focused in on the two great commandments. "Thou shalt love the Lord thy God with all thy heart, and with all thy soul, and with all thy mind . . . and thou shalt love thy neighbour as thyself" (Matthew 22:37–39). After several years of hearing the reactions of the women in those classes, however, I realized there is no way we can learn to love God or others until we *first* know and experience that God loves us. Knowing that God loves us is the *foundation* of our faith. Without first being able to experience His Love and acceptance for ourselves, we're not going to be able to move forward in the sanctification process.

In other words, we can't lay down our lives to God and love Him, if we don't really think He loves us. This principle is true no matter how long we have been Christians, no matter how many people we have led to the Lord, no matter how many Scriptures we know or the number of Bible studies we have led. If we don't know that God loves us personally, we'll be unable to grow simply because we don't trust Him enough to yield our lives to Him.

This doesn't mean that God is not in our hearts, loving us. He is! It just means we won't have that daily, living experience (personal, touching, loving intimacy) of encountering and seeing His handprint and His Love at every turn. This is one of the reasons why so many of us are not experiencing God's abundant Life after being Christians for many years. It all goes back to the fact that we really don't know God loves us.

(If you are stumbling in this area, we recommend the book *The Way of Agape*, especially chapter seven, "Knowing God Loves Us.")

Scriptures That Prove He Loves You

The following Scriptures are paraphrased with emphasis added. You can pray these Scriptures or simply copy them down so when doubt about His Love overwhelms you, you can bring them out and read them over and over. Then you must make those "faith choices" to believe what you have just read.

Herein is Love, not that we loved God, but that He loved us and sent His Son to be the propitiation [substitute offering] for our sins. (1 John 4:10)

He bowed the heavens also, and came down. (Psalm 18:9)

He sent from above, He took me, He drew me out of many waters. (Psalm 18:16)

The Lord appeared unto me saying, "Yea, I have loved thee with an everlasting Love." (Jeremiah 31:3)

I have engraved thee upon the palms of my hand. (Isaiah 49:16)

I will never leave thee or forsake thee. (Hebrews 13:5)

For the mountains shall depart and the hills be removed; but my kindness [chesed] shall not depart from thee, neither shall my covenant of peace [rest] be removed, saith the Lord that hath mercy on thee. (Isaiah 54:10)

As the heaven is high above the earth, so great is His Mercy [lovingkindness] towards them that fear Him. (Psalm 103:11)

Many are the afflictions of the righteous. But the Lord delivers them out of them all. He keepeth all his bones; not a one of them is broken. (Psalm 34:19–20)

When you pass through the waters [trouble] I will be with you; and through the rivers, they won't overflow you; when you walk through the fire, you won't be burned; neither shall the flame kindle upon thee. For I am the Lord . . . You are precious in My sight and I love you. (Isaiah 43:2–4)

God commendeth His Love toward us in that, while we were yet sinners, Christ died for us. (Romans 5:8)

For God so loved the world, that He gave His only begotten Son. (John 3:16)

Greater Love hath no man than this, that a man lay down his life for his friends. (John 15:13)

Behold, what manner of Love the Father hath bestowed upon us, that we should be called the sons of God. (1 John 3:1)

Having loved His own which were in the world, He loved them unto the end. (John 13:1).

What shall separate us from the Love of Christ? Shall tribulation, or distress, or persecution, or famine, or nakedness, or peril, or sword? . . . I am persuaded that neither death, nor life, nor angels, nor principalities, nor powers, nor things present, nor things to come, nor height, nor depth, nor any other creature shall be able to separate us from the Love of God which is in Christ Jesus, our Lord. (Romans 8:35, 38–39)

When we know that God loves us, we're able to daily surrender ourselves to Him and allow His process of sanctification to proceed.

Who We Are *in Christ*

It's not only important in the sanctification process to know that God loves us, it's also important to know *who we are in Christ*. Our identity and security must be *in Christ*, not in ourselves or others or in the the things we do. If we know who we are in Christ, then when we fail, we won't be devastated, because our identity will still be intact. If we are insecure in God's Love and who we are *in Him*, however, then when we fail, we will have the need to cover it up and somehow try to earn His Love again. Our fulfillment and meaning in life only comes from knowing God loves us and from being assured of our identity in Him.

The following Scriptures validate our identity in Christ. Again, you can pray these when doubt overwhelms you. (If you continue to struggle in this area, we would again recommend reading *The Way of Agape*, chapter six, "Our True Identity and Security.")

The Word of God states that if we are *born again,* then we are:

Reconciled to God (2 Corinthians 5:18)

A son of God (1 John 3:1)

A new creature (2 Corinthians 5:17)

Called of God (2 Timothy 1:9)

Chosen (Ephesians 1:4; 1 Peter 2:9)

The temple of the Holy Spirit (1 Corinthians 6:19)

Holy and without blame before Him in Love (Ephesians 1:4)

A partaker of His divine nature (2 Peter 1:4)

In Christ Jesus by His doing (1 Corinthians 1:30)

Accepted in the Beloved (Ephesians 1:6)

Beloved of God (Romans 1:7; 1 Thessalonians 1:4)

Complete in Him (Colossians 2:10)

Alive with Christ (Ephesians 2:5)

The apple of my Father's eye (Deuteronomy 32:10; Psalm 17:8)

Forgiven of all my sins and washed in His Blood (Ephesians 1:7; Hebrews 9:14; Colossians 1:14; 1 John 1:9; 2:12)

Healed by the stripes of Jesus (1 Peter 2:24; Isaiah 53:5)

Delivered from the power of darkness and translated into God's kingdom (Colossians 1:13)

Set free (John 8:31-33)

Kept by God and the evil one does not touch me (1 John 5:18)

Free from condemnation (Romans 8:1)

Dead to sin (Romans 6:2,11; 1 Peter 2:24)

God's workmanship created in Christ Jesus for good works (Ephesians 2:10)

Being changed into His Image (2 Corinthians 3:18)

Victorious (Revelation 21:7)

Strong in the Lord (Ephesians 6:10)

More than a conqueror (Romans 8:37)

The righteousness of God in Him (2 Corinthians 5:21)

The light of the world (Matthew 5:14)

An ambassador for Christ (2 Corinthians 5:20)

The salt of the earth (Matthew 5:13)

Sealed with the Holy Spirit of promise (Ephesians 1:13)

Joint heirs with Christ (Romans 8:17)

Raised up with Christ (Ephesians 2:6)

Established to the end (1 Corinthians 1:8)

Firmly rooted, built up, established in the faith, and abounding with thanksgiving (Colossians 2:7)

In this world as He is (1 John 4:17)

Knowing who we are in Christ keeps us secure in Him, no matter what circumstances we face.

Sanctification Is God's Will

Experiential sanctification, therefore, is God's will for every one of our lives. Scripture again validates this: "For this is the will of God, even your *sanctification*" (1 Thessalonians 4:3). The teachings surrounding the sanctification of the soul are the central subject of most of the Epistles from Romans to Jude. Sanctification is how our souls are transformed and saved: "Lay apart all filthiness and superfluity of naughtiness, and receive with meekness the engrafted word, which is able to *save your souls*" (James 1:21). Apart from this sanctification process, it's very difficult to properly understand the central message of the Epistles (Hebrews 2:3; 10:35–39). In other words, when God speaks of the "saving of souls," it's not the "new birth" He is referring to. He is speaking about the cleansing, renewing, and transforming of those who already believe.

God's will is that we might make the constant "choice" to let Him sanctify us. If we make this choice, He will give us the power to make it happen in our lives. For this to occur, however, we must make 1 John 1:9 a major part of our lives: "If we confess our sins, He is faithful and just to forgive us our sins, and to cleanse us from all unrighteousness." Confession simply means owning the sin—taking personal responsibility for it. Then God can constantly renew and transform us.

Following our new birth, God deals with us on an entirely different plane—as servants, with a view toward the kingdom. Sanctification is the highway to joint heirship with Christ.

Obeying God's Will

Experiential sanctification, therefore, is God's will. And even though we might not *feel* like obeying God's will, we must choose to do *so by faith* because we know He loves us and has the best in mind for us. If we want to be overcomers, we really have no other choice.

The Greek word for *obey* is *hupakouo* (Strong's #5219), which means "*to open in the sense of opening a door*." It comes from the root word *to hear,* to listen or to heed. Thus, the "obedience" we are to render to God is the obedience of not only *hearing* His will, but actually *doing* His will.

A perfect example of obedience is, of course, the Lord. He obeyed His Father's will in spite of how He felt, in spite of what He wanted, and in spite of all the hindrances He encountered in His life, because He knew the Father loved Him. His death on the cross is the highest expression of obedience there is. Jesus willingly submitted to His Father's will and by the power of the Spirit was obedient unto death (Philippians 2:5–8). Thus, Scripture tells us, "He learned obedience by the things He suffered" (Hebrews 5:8). Jesus chose to obey His Father's will regardless of the consequences. We must do the same!

The Difference Between "Obeyers" and "Followers"

We could call spiritual Christians "obeyers" because that's really what they are. The Lord told Samuel that "obedience is better than sacrifice," and that "disobedience [or rebellion] is as the sin of witchcraft" (1 Samuel 15:22–23). Thus, according to Scripture, any action we do that lacks in obedience is really a "fall." Matthew 7:21–23 says, "Not everyone that saith unto me, Lord, Lord, shall enter into the kingdom of heaven but *he that doeth the will of My Father* which is in heaven. Many will say to Me in that day, Lord, Lord, have we not prophesied in Thy Name? And in Thy Name have cast out devils? And in Thy Name done many wonderful works? And then will I profess unto them, *I never knew you.*"

This is a pretty tough Scripture.

The Pulpit Commentary surprisingly says, "Not *all* followers of Christ will be saved. They *all* say, 'Lord, Lord';" they *all* call themselves by the holy name of Christian; but not *all* can enter into the kingdom of glory at the last. For our Father which is in heaven is the King of heaven; and *none can enter into His kingdom but those who do His will*" (vol. 15, p. 291).

Now "followers" can be just that—followers, and not necessarily believers. Judas might be an example. Obeying God not only entails following Him, but also includes *denying ourselves*, picking up our crosses, and walking in His footsteps (Luke 9:23). Judas, obviously, never went that far. He was a follower only.

God is not saying that we must obey Him *perfectly* in order to enter the kingdom. Only Jesus is that perfect! God is saying that as best we can, we must deny ourselves and give ourselves over to Him. When we do fail, He will be there to pick us up, dust us off, and—if we allow Him to—once again fill us with Himself. Jesus' Love gives us the freedom to fail and the freedom to try again.

But how do we do that?

In chapter twelve, we examined the four steps to giving things to God, turning around, and going His way. We explored how we acknowledge our wrongs, how we confess them, repent of them, and then, how we give them to God. We examined what it means *on a practical level* to surrender our wills and our lives to the Lord (1 Corinthians 11:28; Romans 6:11–13; 13:14).

> I beseech you therefore, brethren, by the mercies of God, that ye present your bodies a living sacrifice, holy, acceptable unto God, which is your reasonable service. And be not conformed to this world: but *be ye transformed* by the renewing of your mind, that ye may prove what is that good and acceptable, and perfect, will of God.
>
> —Romans 12:1–2

Christ wants us not only to receive His Life in *our spirit* through faith at our new birth, He also wants us to maintain that new Life in *our soul* through obedience. To obey Christ means we must continually *choose* to set aside *our own reason, our own thoughts,* and *our own opinions* and, by faith, *choose* to do His will.

Hindrances to Obeying God's Will

We will encounter many *hindrances* when we choose to obey God's will of sanctification. First of all, there is the *world* and all its pressures. Then, of course, the *enemy* with all his schemes. But one of the biggest obstacles to obeying God's will is the *flesh* which is made up of our soulish or natural thoughts, emotions, and desires, which are basically inclined toward self-centeredness. We call it our "self-life" or our "flesh."

God wants both our "self-life" and our physical life to be completely surrendered to Him, so that "His Life" from our new spirits and hearts can come forth and begin to transform our souls. This, again, is that *exchange of life* we talked about in chapter eight. This must all be done by the power of the Holy Spirit because, quite frankly, "self" cannot cast out "self." Therefore, there must be a divinely prompted *self-emptying* process.

The flesh takes on many forms, such as self-confidence, self-esteem, self-pity, self-defense, self-vindication, self-centeredness, self-accusation, self-pleasing, self-assertiveness, self-boasting, self-expression, self-indulgence, self-satisfaction, self-admiration, self-congratulations, self-excusing, self-justification, self-righteousness, self-complacency, self-reflection, self-glory, self-love, and selfishness. Galatians 5:19–21 expands this list of "works of the flesh" and tells us that those who do such things will *not* inherit the kingdom.

When we refuse to recognize, confess, and repent of the above things, we will quench God's Spirit in us and block His Life from coming forth. The trouble here is not with our inability to recognize, confess, and repent of our sin, but with *our own unwillingness* to do so.

Hindrance #1: Our Own Will

The particular portion of our "flesh" that seems to hinder God's will of experiential sanctification more than any other is our *own* will and desires. All it takes is a simple *no* from our self-life and God's will is immediately quenched.

Our will is like the "inner power" of man. Martin Luther called it "the most excellent part of man" (*Bondage of the Will*). Our will is the principal part of our makeup because it's the *power to determine what we are going to do* and the *power to direct our lives*. In other words, our will determines our actions.

Christians are the only ones who really have the choice to either go God's way *or* their own way. That's their moment-by-moment free choice. Nonbelievers, as we mentioned before, can make whatever choice they want to, *but none of them have the* authority *to go against what they naturally feel or what they think, because they don't have another* power *source within them to perform anything different from how they feel.* So, no matter how much they talk about "free choice," they really don't have one!

Christians, on the other hand, do! We don't have to be carried on by the tide of our emotions and make "emotional choices." We can be honest with God and say, "I don't want to do this; I don't feel like it; I don't love them; I don't want to forgive them," and so forth. "But I know I have Your authority to say 'nevertheless, *not* my will, but Thine,' and Your power to accomplish Your will in my life. The incredible thing about "faith choices" is that God, in His timing and way, will eventually change our emotions to match or align with the choices we have made and make us genuine.

Philippians 2:13 validates that God Himself is in us not only to *will* but also to *do*.

So union with Christ not only involves a union of our spirits, but also a continuous union of our wills by His authority and power.

(Read more about God's delegated authority and power on page 340.)

Hindrance #2: Our Own Understanding

Another huge hindrance to our obeying God's will of sanctification is our own understanding. As humans, we process everything that happens to us through our own "natural" reasoning.

When a thought first comes into our minds, an automatic chain reaction occurs: our *thoughts* stir up our emotions, our *emotions* then influence our own will, and our *will* then produces our *actions*. This is why it's important to be aware of our thinking. If we can catch our negative thoughts when they first occur, we will be able to stop the chain reaction *before* it even begins (2 Corinthians 10:5). But when we don't "take every thought captive," we end up being carried on by the "tide of emotion," quenching God's Spirit, and ending up operating out of our own understanding.

Our own reason, however, can often become a stumbling block, because God quite frequently accomplishes His will in a way that's completely opposite to the way *we* think He should. Consequently, much of the time we are left confused by His actions. God seems to enjoy making things totally "impossible," *before* He finally accomplishes them in His timing and way. God does *not* need to give us a reason for His actions. He is God! Our responsibility is simply to trust and obey Him no matter what He does. This takes faith, not our own natural understanding.

In the past we always walked according to our own thoughts. Now, however, we must trust that whatever God does, it is done according to His plans and no questions need be asked (Jeremiah 29:11). Even though we may not understand His methods or His ways, we must still trust and obey Him. Even when He acts in an unconventional manner, He is under no obligation to tell us *why* or *for what*. Our only response should be to say, "Lord, Your ways are higher than my own (Isaiah 55:9). I don't understand, but I lay that on the altar. Do what You want with me." Then finish with this commitment prayer, "Though You slay me, yet I will trust You" (Job 13:15).

Satan is a master at using our own understanding to confuse us, discourage us, and enslave us. Many of us have experienced this firsthand. When our own natural reasoning fails, we quickly fall into the enemy's trap of confusion and unless we recognize what is happening, we'll end up captured.

We must be aware that at any given moment, our thoughts will either be controlled by our own understanding (allowing the enemy to gain access) or be controlled by the Spirit of Christ. This is again why God exhorts us in 1 Corinthians 10:5 to "bring into captivity every thought to the obedience of Christ; and have in a readiness to revenge all disobedience." This is an exhortation to *catch our negative thoughts and know exactly what to do with them.*

(See the Four Sanctification Steps on pages 342-346.)

Freedom is found only by leaving our natural thoughts at the Cross and being recaptured by God's. Then His will of sanctification can proceed undeterred.

Hindrance #3: The Power of Sin

Another huge obstacle to obeying God's will of sanctification is the "power of sin" that dwells in our souls and bodies and continually causes us to *walk by the flesh*. It's an invisible law that gravitates us to sin and causes us to break God's law (1 John 3:4). The power of sin is an actual energy force or governing principle that dominates our flesh. It's an organized power that dwells in our unredeemed bodies and unsanctified souls whose whole intent and purpose is to cause us to veer off course and "miss the mark." That "mark" is what Philippians 3:14 describes as "*the mark of the high calling of God.*" It's being able to rule and reign with Christ in the coming kingdom! (It's the hope of our salvation.) *Missing the mark simply means missing our calling.* Therefore, it stands to reason that the power of sin is going to constantly try to cause us to veer off course and miss the purpose of our calling.

Sin is a power that we cannot overcome in our own natural selves (Romans 7:21). At least not without God. This power of sin overcomes every "natural" man and woman because they cannot defeat it or conquer it in their own power. As we said before, at our new birth (justification) we become freed from the "penalty of sin," but not the "power of sin." *The whole process of sanctification is learning how to overcome the power of sin that dwells in our flesh.* This is why God gives every believer the freedom to choose whom they will follow: Will we allow our self-life (our old nature) to rule and to produce *wood, hay, and stubble*—"works of the flesh"—in our lives; or will we permit our new nature (God's Life in us) to rule and to produce *gold, silver, and precious stones*—"works of righteousness"—in our lives?

It's important to understand that when we begin to depend more and more upon God's resurrection power to perform His will in our lives, a huge internal war will explode between the *Spirit of God* in our spirit trying to create the "new man," and the *power of sin* in our souls and bodies, determined to keep the "old man" reigning. This occurs because we now have two natures. Before we were born again, we had only *one* nature and thus, there was no conflict. But after our conversion, we find ourselves with *two* natures—God's Life in our hearts empowered by His Spirit and our "self-life" in our souls empowered by the power of sin.

Listen to how Romans explains it:

> I find then a law, that, when I would do good, evil is present with me" . . . For that which I do I understand not; for what I would, that do I not; but what I hate, that do I. If, then, I do that which I would not, I consent unto the law that it is good. Now then, it is no more I that do it, but [the power of] sin that dwelleth in me.
>
> —Romans 7:21, 15–17

At our new birth, our "old self" is *positionally* crucified with Christ (John 17:21–23; Colossians 2:9–13). However, *experientially* this is not the case at all. We haven't yet learned how to put to death the deeds of the body or how to be cleansed and renewed. We still live by the flesh empowered by the power of sin (Romans 8:13). Thus, the pull of the "self-life" is still tremendous.

Even though the Bible gives us knowledge of what sin is, there's still a basic conflict in every believer between the desire to do good and the inability (or the powerlessness) to do so. In other words, something in our basic human nature (the power of sin) holds us back from doing good and from overlooking the faults of others. Our human reaction tends toward being self-centered, resentful, bitter, and angry. These are all part of our natural soul that the power of sin absolutely embraces.

Consequently, a huge war is going on in our souls between *our own wills* and desires (the "flesh") pulling us one way and *the Spirit of God* pulling us another. Paul warned us about this conflict: "*I see another law in my members* [power of sin], *warring against the law of my mind* [power of God], and bringing me into captivity to the law of sin which is in my members. O wretched man that I am! Who shall deliver me from the body of this death?" (Romans 7:23–24).

The Bible accurately describes the natural man, the old man, or the flesh as powerless, hopeless, and loveless. But it also gives us the solution to dealing with it and how to get back to peace with God (Romans 5:1; Colossians 3:15). Paul said: "I thank God *through Jesus Christ our Lord that we can be set free*" (Romans 7:25). Paul was saying here that Jesus is our

Deliverer, our Savior, and the only One who can bring us life, liberty, and acceptance. Implementing His authority and His power in our lives is the only thing that will set us free!

One of the reasons we, as Christians, don't run to God's Word more often to help us implement this power and authority, is because His Word also reproves and corrects us. And most of the time we don't want to hear the truth about ourselves. It's much easier to blame things on other people and not look inwardly. John 3:19 tells us, "Men love darkness rather than light because their deeds are evil." We naturally tend toward self-defensiveness, over-rationalization, and suppression.

Jesus made atonement for our sins by shedding His own blood on that Cross two thousand years ago. He paid the ultimate price and there is nothing more needed for our justification. In order to be experientially sanctified, however, we must allow the Lord to daily expose our "self-life" (anything fleshly or self-centered) and then we must nail these things to the Cross (i.e., appropriate what He has already done for us). This is called a co-crucifixion with Christ or a co-death with Him. Romans 12:1–2 tells us how we are to do this: "I beseech you therefore, brethren, by the mercies of God, that ye present your bodies *a living sacrifice*, holy, acceptable unto God, which is your reasonable service." In other words, we are to put ourselves on the Altar (or at the Cross) and leave ourselves there, never to be removed.

Therefore, Christ is the only One who can overcome the power of sin in our lives because He is the only One who can change our hearts, renew our minds, and transform our souls. In other words, He's the only One who can heal us from the inside out. *The Cross is His instrument to do this because it deals directly with the power of sin.* Scripture puts it this way: "For the preaching of the Cross is to them that perish foolishness; but unto us who are saved it is the power of God" (1 Corinthians 1:18). And Romans 8:2 tells us that only the law of the Spirit of Life (power of God) can set us free from the law of sin and death (the power of sin). So, the bottom line is: we don't overcome the power of sin, we are *delivered from it by the Cross* and by God's resurrection power in us.

Recognizing this struggle between the *power of sin* that resides in our souls and bodies and the *power of God* that dwells in our spirits is of the utmost importance (Romans 8:3–13). If we don't understand this conflict or how to resolve it, we will succumb to the flesh every time. In chapter twelve, we explored the exact steps to overcoming the power of sin, as well as the flesh and the world.

One final thought: the more of Christ's Life we can experience, the less the power of sin will have a hold on us.

Hindrance #4: The Power of the Enemy

In addition to the power of sin hindering us from obeying God's will of experiential sanctification, one more force is at work against us, and that's demonic power or the power of darkness.

In Genesis 2:17 God gave Adam and Eve one very simple rule—they were *not* to eat from the Tree of Good and Evil. He told them that if they did, they would surely die. God set them in the Garden of Eden to be obedient servants warning them that the tree before them held the choice of life and death.

The enemy, however, watched for an appropriate opportunity (just as he does with us) to pounce on them and cause them to disobey God's commands. And he found one. He subtly tempted Eve with something she really wanted, "the knowledge of good and evil" (Genesis 3:1–7). She eventually succumbed to his lies and, as a result, died spiritually. Adam followed suit.

What's so sad is that *before* this, Adam and Eve had "abundant life." They walked with the Lord and had an intimate relationship with Him. But after their fall, they were spiritually separated from Him and had only "death" to look forward to. Satan's promises *never* come true! Wisdom is *never* attained by disobedience to God's Word. *As a result of Adam and Eve's sin, the entire world has fallen under the power of the enemy* (1 John 5:19) and ever since there has been a perpetual struggle between Satan's forces and mankind. All of Satan's dealings with us can be traced back to this one act of disobedience by Adam and Eve. He wants to cripple us with his inserted lies, fear, and doubt so that we won't obey God, we won't follow Him and we won't be able to overcome. But Christ promises to deliver us—if we choose to let Him—and extend the fatal blow to the enemy. *Christ is the only One who has the overcoming power to destroy the evil one* (Hebrews 2:14).

It's important to recognize that as we mature in the Lord and begin to be experientially sanctified as God desires, the spirits of darkness will become even more fierce. Satan does not fear "intellectual understanding" of spiritual things; what he fears is a Christian with a "life-changing" experience. *He fears Christian overcomers, Christ-likeness, and the results of sanctification.* When our life begins to change from self-centeredness to other-centeredness, from human love to God's Love, and from human understanding to God's wisdom, the enemy becomes ferocious.

The only way we can overthrow the power of the enemy is by a force greater than ourselves, the resurrection power of Christ (Ephesians 6:13). Thus, obeying God's will of sanctification is critical. It determines what benefits, if any, we'll have in the coming kingdom. It also determines our inheritance, our position of authority, our rewards, and our intimacy with the Lord in that kingdom.

How God Enables Us to Obey His Will

The Power and Authority of the Believer

Because the Lord knows the importance of moment-by-moment choices to obey His will, He not only has given us His resurrection *power* to accomplish that will in our lives, He has also given us the *authority* to obey His will even when we don't feel like it.

The Greek word for this kind of *authority* is *exousia* (Strong's #1849), which means "the right to exercise power or the right of the person in charge" (Matthew 9:6; 2 Corinthians 10:8). This authority originates with God because He is obviously the Person in charge. He is the ultimate source of all authority (Romans 9:21). He simply passed that authority on to Christ, and through Christ that authority was passed on to His disciples and then to us (John 10:18).

A frequent question is: Do we have the authority to choose to *do* something that we really don't feel or want to do? Is this a legitimate choice? Can we override our real feelings?

The answer is yes! Absolutely!

We not only have God's authority (*exousia*) to make choices we don't feel, we also have His strength (*kratos*) to implement those choices in our lives (Philippians 2:13). In chapter nine, we talked about the *kratos* power of God enabling us to "rein in our emotions" so we can make faith choices. If we didn't have this ability, God's power would be of no use to us.

This is saying that, as believers, we have God's authority to implement His power. In other words, it's His power and His authority, but because He lives in us we can implement that same authority and power (1 Corinthians 6:12; 2 Corinthians 4:7). Like Jesus, we have the authority and power not only to lay our lives down but also authority and power to pick them back up again (John 10:18). The right to exercise this type of power comes from "ownership."

"As many as received Him, to them gave He power to become the sons of God, even to them that believe on His Name" (John 1:12). These are called *sonship rights* (Romans 8:14-15; Galatians 4:7).

The Dictionary of New Testament Theology says, "Our authority is founded in the rule of Christ" (vol. 2, p. 610). We exercise that power only by the authority or the dominion *God* has given us. *The Word of God gives us the authority, and the Spirit of God gives us the power.* These phenomenal gifts are ours through our new birth. Whether we use them or not, however, is up to us.

It's through God's authority and power that we receive the ability not only to overcome our flesh (our old human nature), but also the world and the enemy. This is called "delegated authority."

Delegated Authority

Delegated authority is the means God uses to execute His will (Matthew 16:19; 12:29; 1 Peter 5:8–9; James 4:7–10; Revelation 12:11; Luke 10:19; Psalm 149:8). As we said, it's *His* will and *His* power to accomplish it (Matthew 28:18), but, it is still chosen, implemented, and then performed through us. Delegated authority is not easy, because it requires the complete emptying of self and the subsequent submission to God's will. In other words, we must be totally cleansed of all known sin and self.

Those who represent God's authority must continually seek restoration, reconciliation, and love, even though they themselves are rejected, stepped on, and refused. God does not use proud souls to demonstrate His delegated authority, but only those who are humble and willing at all costs to serve Him.

Peter is a good example of this. Christ gave Peter the delegated authority to be a part of the miracle of Pentecost when the Holy Spirit of power fell upon three thousand believers. Peter was anointed and allowed to share the gospel. (See Acts 2:14–36; 38–40.) *The Pulpit Commentary* comments on this: "It was needful in the early church that one should be chosen to be the chief office bearer and leader of the body of believers. Peter's faith, character and zeal made him a perfect candidate to fulfill this role" (vol. 15, p. 137).

In like manner, Jesus has given that same authority and power to us (Luke 10:1, 17–19; Mark 6:7, 13). Delegated authority is the means God uses to execute His will (Revelation 3:7; Isaiah 22:22). Christ has given us His authority to bind the enemy from touching our lives (i.e. forbid him entrance) and then, His power to loose (free) the strongholds. Because of Christ, we, too, have the keys to the closet of the temple of our body, either to bring freedom or to impose bondage.

Delegated authority comes from an unction above. It means being a representative of Christ who, because of His indwelling, has power to overcome the world, the flesh, and the devil (1 John 2:27).

Faith Choices

As New Testament believers, we are given a portion of the same delegated authority and power that Christ's disciples had in Acts. The Holy Spirit came upon them, just as He does us. Christ is the One who gives us that authority. Scripture says that if we *abide* in Him, that same authority and power will be ours. The delegated authority and power of God are truly the "keys to the kingdom" (Matthew 16:19).

Delegated authority is implemented in our lives by learning to make "faith choices,"—nonfeeling choices to do God's will regardless of our circumstances, other's reactions, or our emotions. These can also be called "contrary choices" because they are usually contrary to how we feel, what we think, or what we want. *"Faith choices" or "contrary choices" are simply the means by which we exercise God's authority*. It is saying, "Not as I will, but as Thou wilt" (Matthew 26:39). In other words, *we* make the choice, *He* then implements it in our lives.

How many of us, however, are really practicing this principle? How many of us really understand the power and authority we have in Christ? How many of us are daily making choices to follow Christ simply out of obedience? Not very many. This is why we are not seeing more overcomers in the body of Christ today or more of God's power manifested in our homes, our churches, or our communities. Many of us have not been taught how to use the incredible gifts God has given us; therefore, we've been unable to put them into practice in our lives. As a result, we've not learned how to become *overcomers*, but, in fact, have actually been *overtaken by* the world, the flesh, and the devil.

Once we understand the importance of making faith choices to follow God, regardless of how we feel or what we think, we'll see our lives changed, our marriages renewed, and our broken hearts healed (Luke 4:18). It is *God's Word* that gives us the authority, and then His Spirit that gives us the power to implement these choices in our lives.

Nonbelievers can make all the nonfeeling choices they want to, but it will not do them any good, because they don't have the authority or the power of God to perform *anything different* from what they feel or what they think. Christians, however, do! Because we have Christ's divine nature—His Life—in us, we have His authority to choose His will, regardless of how we feel, and then His power to perform that will in our lives, even if we are weak (2 Peter 1:3; Luke 21:19; Philippians 2:13). The authority to "put off" our sin and self, and then the power to "put on" Christ's Life belongs to God Himself, but He has commissioned us as the bearers of His authority (Ephesians 4:22–27).

Suffice to say, the way we overcome the world, the flesh, and the devil is by making "faith choices" to do God's will regardless of how we feel, and then by God's resurrection power implementing that will in our lives. Making a faith choice by itself is not enough, we must have God's power behind that choice to accomplish His will.

The Bible emphasizes the fact that before God can ever entrust us with His authority in the kingdom to come, we must have shown our faithfulness to implement His will here on earth. Thus, the manner in which we personally multiply the authority and power the Lord has entrusted to us on earth will determine just how much power and authority we will have in the Millennial Kingdom.

Remember, however, true authority is always exemplified in Love.

The Four Sanctification Steps

In order to enter God's presence, we must not only be believers with the Spirit of God in our hearts, we must also be *clean*. Even if we are true believing Christians, we cannot just walk into the Holy Place any time we feel like it. God is holy and will commune with us only when we, too, are holy. He cannot abide where there is any corruption, sin, or self. Thus, in order to enter His presence and worship Him as He desires, we must first *put off* any sin and self and *put on* Christ. In other words, in order to respond the way God would have us respond in a difficult situation, we must be clean.

We must never confront someone unless we are a cleansed vessel. If we are not clean, it will be the flesh working, not the spirit, and the encounter will go poorly. *Self, no matter how polished it is, does* not *accomplish a thing!* The other party will immediately sense our judgmental attitude, react from his defenses, the truth will be hidden, and we'll sink even deeper into the pit than we were before. If we can get clean first, then we can respond from God's Love, His wisdom, and power. The other person will sense our unconditional acceptance, respond from his heart, and the situation will have a chance to turn around.

The following, then, is a brief overview of the four specific steps required to cleanse our hearts so that God's Life can come forth. Again, they are based on the steps that the Priests of Solomon's Temple took in the Inner court in order to deal with their sin and be reconciled to God. (If you want an even more in-depth explanation of how these steps work, we recommend taking a look at our textbook *Be Ye Transformed.*)

1. *Acknowledge negative thoughts or emotions to the Lord.* The first step we must take in order to be a cleansed vessel, is to *recognize and acknowledge any negative thoughts or emotions that have occurred.* It's important to "take these thoughts captive" (2 Corinthians 10:5), look at them, and allow God to give us His discernment about them. We must not *vent* these things to others nor *push them down* into the hidden part of our soul, but simply ask the Lord to expose what's *really* going on.

This is what the priests did at the Lavers of Bronze in the Inner Court of Solomon's Temple. The lavers themselves were made of women's looking glasses (mirrors of polished metal). Thus, as the priests bent over the lavers to wash their hands, what they actually saw was their own reflection in the mirrored lavers. The priests' actions are symbolic of what the Lord requires us to do. We are to ask Him not only to expose what's going on in our *conscious thoughts and emotions*—the surface things that we *can* see—but we must also ask Him to shed light on the *buried things* in our souls, the root causes that we *cannot* see.

Our surface emotions are often just the symptoms of a much deeper cause. If the real root problem can be exposed, and subsequently gotten rid of, the surface emotions will not occur again either. If we deal only with the external emotions and never the root causes, however, the surface problems will continue to come back. It is essential that we always ask the Lord to expose any hidden root issues.

Whenever we find ourselves hurt, angry, resentful, envious, critical, self-centered, prideful, ungrateful, anxious, afraid, confused, bitter, judgmental, or filled with any ungodly emotion, we must stop, get alone with the Lord, and go through these steps. Ask the Lord to expose what is really going on. He is the only One who can cleanse our sin—and also the only One who can take those things from us "as far as the east is from the west" and completely heal us.

As was shared earlier, thoughts are the most important ingredient of our makeup. This is where the battle is waged. The reason our thoughts are so important is that they are the first to be triggered in the chain reaction of our soul: our thoughts spark our emotions, our emotions cause our desires (or our choices), and our choices determine whose life will be lived in our souls. This is why God tells us to "take every thought captive" (2 Corinthian 10:5).

It's also important to understand that our first, original negative thought is not sin. It's what we choose to do with that negative thought that makes it sin or not. If we immediately recognize the thought as ungodly and give it over to the Lord, we have *not* sinned and His Life can continue to flow. If, however, we mull that negative thought over and over again in our minds, we will need to confess it and repent of it because it has already quenched God's Spirit in us.

2. *Confess and repent to the Lord and forgive others.* The second essential step in becoming a cleansed vessel is to *confess and repent of all that the Holy Spirit has shown us and, in addition, unconditionally forgive anyone who has wronged us.*

(This step is really part of step 1. But because so much goes on here, we've taken the liberty to separate it into two steps.)

Confession simply means "owning" our sin and acknowledging that what we have done, either ignorantly or knowingly, has quenched God's Spirit in us. It's sin; therefore, we must confess ownership of it. The Hebrew Bible translates *confession* as "*spreading our hands*." In other words, we must "come clean" and confess all.

Repenting means choosing to turn around from following what those negative thoughts and emotions are telling us and, instead, choosing to follow what God wants. This critical step of confession and repentance is our *own responsibility*. As 1 John 1:9 says, "If *we* confess our sins, [then] *He* is faithful and just to forgive us our sins."

This is the step, however, that many of us seem to leave out when we give things over to the Lord. Certainly, we acknowledge our hurts, fears, and doubts to Him, but often we forget to admit our own responsibility in the situation. This is why so many of the things we've given to the Lord often come back. If we *don't* do our part by confessing and repenting of them, God is hindered from doing His—taking them away.

> I *acknowledged* my sin unto Thee, and mine iniquity have I not hid . . . I will *confess* my transgressions unto the Lord; and *Thou forgavest the iniquity of my sin.*
>
> —Psalm 32:5; 103:12

Part of this second step of confession and repentance is that we must also unconditionally forgive others for whatever ill they have done to us. Unforgiveness is one of the many things that quenches God's Spirit in us and blocks His Life from coming forth. It also hinders God from working *in* us and *through* us. The way we release God to change our situations is by unconditionally forgiving the other party, *whether or not he has asked for it.*

Now, don't misunderstand us, we are not pardoning these people by doing this. We don't have the authority to do that. That's God's responsibility. *He* is the judge and He alone decides their future. When we unconditionally forgive them, we are simply releasing them to Him, so that *He* can judge them righteously, and also *so that our response to their sin won't become a stumbling block in us.*

> If ye forgive men their trespasses, your heavenly Father will also forgive you: But if ye forgive not men their trespasses, neither will your Father forgive your trespasses."
>
> —Matthew 6:14–15

Both of the above steps (1 and 2) occur at the *Lavers of Bronze* in the Inner Court of Solomon's Temple.

3. *Give everything to God that is not of faith.* Once God has revealed our ungodly thoughts and emotions and we have confessed our responsibility in them, the third essential step is that we must *give everything that is not of faith over to Him.* God will not violate our free will by forcibly taking these things from us; we must willingly sacrifice and choose to hand them over to Him. This is the "putting off" of the "old man" found in Ephesians 4:22–24.

God wants us to give to Him—to sacrifice to Him—everything in us that is not of faith, so that it can be purged and cleansed by His blood (Romans 12:1–2). This is exactly what the priests did at the Brazen Altar as they sacrificed their offerings to the Lord. Scripture gives us a vivid picture of what happened: "Now when Solomon had made an end to praying, the fire came down from heaven and consumed the burnt offering and the sacrifices; and the glory of the Lord filled the house" (2 Chronicles 7:1).

Being a *living sacrifice* means offering God the best of what we have to offer—ourselves! His Word tells us that offerings like this rise to Him as a sweet-smelling savor (Exodus 29:18, 25). This sweet savor was the difference between Cain and Abel's offering. Abel followed God's instructions and his sweet-smelling sacrifice was accepted. Cain, on the other hand, didn't obey God's prescribed order and, thus, his offering was rejected. It had no sweet aroma.

Most of the things we give to the Lord are of the flesh and we'll experience them gone in a few days, if we are faithful to go through the above cleansing steps. When we give Him our sin, He promises to take it "as far as the east is from the west" (Psalm 103:12). Some of the things the Lord might expose, however, could be longstanding strongholds of the enemy and these will take a little time to actually experience a healing. So don't be dismayed if certain thoughts and feelings seem to reappear even after you have given them to God.

The truth is that the Lord takes our sin the moment we give it to Him, but often *our feelings don't align with those choices immediately.* And this is where Satan tries to make us think that God is not faithful and that He has not cleansed us. Satan uses these in-between times—between the time we choose to give ourselves to God and the time the Lord finally aligns our feelings with our choices—to try to confuse, discourage, and destroy us. *God*, on the other hand, lets us go as long as He knows is wise, to test us and strengthen our faith. He is constantly asking us: "Will you trust Me in spite of what you see, feel, or think?"

This is the step where the priests sacrificed their offerings on the Brazen Altar.

4. *Read God's Word and replace lies we have believed with His Truth.* The fourth essential step in dealing with our sin and self is that we must *read God's Word and replace the lies we have believed with His Truth.* We must remember that God is the only One who can *cleanse, sanctify, and heal our souls* completely by His Word.

Remember, it was at the Molten Sea—a huge bathtub that held thousands of baths—where the priests immersed themselves bodily in order to receive a total cleansing. They had become all blood splattered while sacrificing their offerings at the Brazen Altar. Now they needed a complete bodily bathing in order to be thoroughly cleansed.

In like manner, after we have confessed, repented, and given everything to the Lord, we too are "bloody" and "torn apart" and in desperate need of God's complete healing power. Only reading or reciting Scriptures from the Word of God can totally restore us at this point, and only the Lord can wash us "with the washing of water by the Word" (Ephesians 5:26).

For this reason, it is very helpful to memorize appropriate Scriptures for this particular step, so that if we are away from our Bibles, we can still put the Word of God in our innermost part where the lies have been. Scriptures like Psalm 32:5: "I have acknowledged my sin unto Thee, and mine iniquity have I not hid . . . I have confessed my transgressions unto the Lord; and Thou forgavest the iniquity of my sin." All of Psalm 51 is good, also 1 John 1:5–10, Galatians 2:20, and 2 Corinthians 7:1 are wonderful Scriptures to remember and memorize.

After we have gone through these four steps—recognized and acknowledged our sins, confessed, and repented of them, given them over to God, and read His Word—we can be confident that He will cleanse us, align our feelings with our faith choices, and perform His will through us.

At this point our bodies are cleansed and our spirits purified, and we have *put on* the "beauty of Christ's own holiness" (Psalm 96:7–9; Psalm 29:2). Just like the priests, we have changed our clothes and can now boldly enter the Lord's presence and worship Him.

If you are interested in exploring this area further, we suggest getting the little book *The Key*, which gives you more information on giving things to God. Or if you want to delve into this area in-depth, we recommend the textbook *Be Ye Transformed.*

Abiding in Christ

Abiding simply refers to the degree of intimacy and fellowhip we have with the Lord (John 15:10).

The word *abide* (Strong's #3306) means "to stay in, give place to and continue to dwell in." It's critical we *abide* in Christ in order to produce more fruit. John 15:7-8 tells us "If ye abide in Me, and My words abide in you, ye shall ask what ye will, and it shall be done unto you. Herein is My Father glorified, that ye bear much fruit; so shall ye be My disciples."

The Pulpit Commentary, commenting on John 15 says: *"These words are addressed to the disciples, not to unconverted men"* (vol. 17, p. 69). It goes on to say that "It's possible to be in a relationship with the true vine—to be in it and a part of it—and, *yet to bring forth* no *fruit*." These would be believers who are *justified*, but not *experientially sanctified.*

All this stresses the necessity of a believer abiding in the Lord in order to continue in a vital connection and draw life from Him. John 17:21–23 confirms this: "That they may be one; as Thou, Father, art in Me, and I in Thee, that they also may be one in us . . . even as we are one: I in them, and Thou in Me, that they may be made perfect in one."

To abide in Christ means that we have no known or unjudged sin, nor any unconfessed "self-life" (self-centeredness, etc.). In other words, we are open, cleansed, waiting, listening, and fellowshiping with Him—we are ready at any moment to be used by Him. This is abiding in Christ. It's only natural to assume then that if we *don't* have fellowship with the Lord and abide with Him *here* on earth, it will be very difficult to have fellowship with Him and abide with Him *there* in the coming kingdom.

If we don't abide, John 15 tells us that we will not only be unfruitful, but we can also become shriveled, *withered* (Strong's #3583), and dried up. Christ takes the unfruitful and withered branches away and casts them into fire, which is symbolic of judgment. Fire tries our works, as we read in 1 Corinthians 3:13. We will be asked: Was your work done in the flesh or was it done by the Spirit? Was it "silver, gold, and precious stones" or was it "wood, hay, and stubble?" 1 Corinthians 3:15 tells us *If* it is the latter, we will suffer the loss of opportunity, position, and our hopes in the Millennial Kingdom, *but* we will still be saved. Here again, it's our works that go through the fire, *not* us.

The Word tells us that these "unfruitful" believers will be "ashamed" at His coming because they will be found "naked" (1 John 2:28).

Living Examples

Scripture tells us that *the kingdom of God is experienced in power* in contrast to mere words (1 Corinthians 4:20). In other words, *this power must be shown forth in our lives, not just in our words.* Words about power have very little meaning, unless they are accompanied by a personal manifestation of that power through faith.

"The message" a man brings, is literally the man himself! "For our Gospel came *not* unto you in word only, but also in power" (1 Thessalonians 1:5). And we must do the same. Preaching should have as its goal exhibiting the power and authority of Christ, not an eloquent sermon that simply highlights the speaker's intelligence and cleverness. *Truth without power becomes doctrine only.* Truth is where the "word" and the "deed" match and become one. Paul said:

> Brethren, when I came to you, [I] came not with excellency of speech or of wisdom, declaring unto you the testimony of God. For I determined not to know anything among you, except Jesus Christ, and Him crucified. And I was with you in weakness, and in fear, and in much trembling. And my speech and my preaching were not with enticing words of man's wisdom, *but in demonstration of the Spirit and of power; so that your faith should not stand in the wisdom of men, but in the power of God.*
>
> —1 Corinthians 2:1–5

There's the key! If Paul believed and taught this, how much more should we also. *Our faith in God's ability to do the impossible is the means by which God's power is enabled to work.* Knowing that when God is involved, "*all things are possible.*" Again, it's *His* overcoming power, but it's *our* faith that implements it. However, much of our faith, even today, rests upon what we can *see* and *feel*. God knows that we can never truly live by faith as long as we are being manipulated by our senses. His Word reveals that the further removed we can get from our faith resting on the things that we see and feel, the more deeply we will enter into a life of real faith in God, manifested by His Love.

Three Seasons in a Believer's Life

(1 John 2:12–14)

There are three seasons in a Christian's life:

1. "*Little children*" are in the early stages of their spiritual life. They have newly come to Christ. They are sons who have been forgiven and Christ's Name is the ground upon which they are forgiven. They have had their sins washed away by the blood of Christ because they have believed on Him. They know the Father and, thus, the *dunamis* power of God. Their sins are forgiven for His name's sake and thus, they are promised to be with the Lord in the kingdom.
2. "*The young men*" are strong and have the Word of God in them. They have not only overcome sin, but also the wicked one. In other words, they know how to use the delegated authority (*exousia*) and power (*kratos*) of Christ to rein in their emotions so that the life of Christ can come forth.
3. "*The fathers*" have known the Lord for a long time and have an intimate relationship with Him. This stage is characterized by intimate knowledge and application of that knowledge. It shows that they have overcome the flesh and the indwelling power of sin. Thus, they are "more than conquerers" because they experience the overcoming power (*ischus*) of God in *all* areas of their lives. These saints did not stop with the salvation of their spirits, they have also allowed God, through the sanctification process, to bring salvation to their souls. These are truly overcomers who will hear the precious words, *"Well done, good and faithful servant . . . enter the joy of the Lord"* (Matthew 25:21, 23).

What More Can We Do?

In this process of sanctification, what are some of the other things Scripture tells us to do:

Wait for Him—Hebrews 9:28; 1 Corinthians 1:7; Romans 8:19, 23, 25; Galatians 5:5; Philippians 3:20; 1 Thessalonians 1:10

Give diligence to being approved—2 Timothy 2:15; Hebrews 4:11

Do "spiritual" works (works done by the power of the Holy Spirit in us)—1 Timothy 6:18. We are saved without works, but we enter the kingdom by spiritual works.

Stay watchful—Luke 21:36; Mark 13:35; Matthew 24:43; Revelation 16:15

Always be in prayer—Luke 21:36

Looking for the "blessed hope"—Titus 2:13; Jude 21

Endure trials and temptations—James 1:12; Hebrews 12:1; Mark 13:13; James 5:7–8; Hebrews 6:12

Love others with Agape Love—Matthew 22:37–39; 2 Timothy 4:8

Be holy—1 Peter 1:15–16; 2 Peter 3:14; 1 Thessalonians 5:23

Be ready—Matthew 24:44; Luke 12:40

Abide in Him—1 John 2:28; 1 Corinthians 3:14

(Much of this material is taken from *Believers Sharing or Forfeiting Christ's Glorious Reign* by W. F. Roadhouse, InTheBeginning.org.)

The Sons of Zadok

In Ezekiel's vision of the future Millennial Temple, the original priests of Levi (or Eli), who ministered in the first and second temple, are replaced by the "sons of Zadok" (Ezekiel 44:10–16). The Zadok priests are the faithful and obedient ones who will *minister directly to Christ.*

At the time of Ezekiel's vision, the presence of God had departed from the earlier temples because of Israel's (and its priests') disobedience and unfaithfulness. The Eli priests had not persevered in their faith, but had actually caved into the belief of the conquering nations—hardening their hearts toward God and being overtaken by the world. They had soiled their garments by distancing themselves from the Lord. One could say they "became naked" and their real heart motivation was exposed. Matthew 15:8 expresses it perfectly: "This people draweth near unto Me with their mouth, and honoreth Me with their lips, but their heart is far from Me." Consequently, they had lost the presence of God.

This is what the word *ichabod* in 1 Samuel 4:21 means: "The glory is departed from Israel."

In Ezekiel's Temple, absolute holiness will be required to be the Zadok priests. These priests will know the difference between the holy and the profane, and they will demonstrate this knowledge not only spiritually, but also physically, in the future Millennial Temple (Ezekiel 44:23).

In like manner, we run the risk of becoming like the old Eli priests when we become unfaithful, disobedient, and thus "naked" before the Lord. Therefore it's critical we learn how to become spiritual sons of Zadok who are able to remain in an intimate fellowship with the Lord, even to the very end, and who put righteousness and faithfulness before everything else. When we become clothed with the "garments of righteousness" (works done by the Spirit of God in us), that righteousness will flow like a river to all with whom we come in contact. Love and righteousness are always interconnected.

Spiritual sons of Zadok quickly judge themselves so that God's Spirit will *not* be quenched even for a moment. They are uncompromising, unspotted, and unwrinkled believers. They live a separated life, always applying the blood of Christ without which the glory of God will again depart. They are humble and lack notoriety. They desire to please only the Lord. These sons demonstrate to others—not only spiritually, but also physically—the difference between the holy and the profane. Kindness and all the fruit of the Spirit exude from their lives. They only operate in the power of God, not in the flesh. They keep themselves in constant communication with the Lord, always keeping their spiritual fountains clean and clear. By doing this, they give glory to God, never taking it for themselves. The fear of the Lord overrides everything else in their lives.

To be a son of Zadok will cost a person his entire life—his thoughts, his will, and his emotions. But these can be gladly given, because in exchange, he then will be clothed with the "beauty of Christ's holiness."

(For a more in depth discussion of this subject, be sure to see the book *The Sons of Zadok* in the bibliography.)

Sacrifices in Ezekiel's Temple

Interestingly, the sacrificial system will be restored in Ezekiel's temple in remembrance of what Christ did on the Cross. Isaiah referred to this: Isaiah 56:7—59:21 and also in 66:20–22. Jeremiah did the same (33:18) as did Zechariah (14:16–21). From these passages it is obvious that this sacrificial system is distinct from the Mosaic system, but will involve animal sacrifices as well as other forms of worship. In other words, in Solomon's Temple the sacrifices *looked forward* to what Christ was going to do and to commemorate the redemption that would be accomplished at the Cross, whereas, in Ezekiel's Temple, the sacrifices will be *in remembrance of* what Christ has already done. It will be a commemorative act looking back on the work accomplished by Jesus on the Cross. The Cross of Christ will *always* be the central issue in the life of a believer. Offerings in this temple will be no different. They will commemorate all that Christ has done for us.

Sacrifices are and always have been symbolic, *not* efficacious—meaning they never could take away any sin; they only pointed to the One who could. Sacrifices were a covering or a ceremonial cleansing to purify objects contaminated by sin, which then enabled God to dwell among His people and allowed them to fellowship with Him. The old system of sacrifice was purely ceremonial. It did *not* resolve the problem of a guilty conscience. The new system will do likewise. As the old, it will require the purification of the flesh. No one will be able to approach a holy God in unsanctified flesh. The sacrifices will help restore fellowship with God.

In the Millennium the feasts of Passover, Pentecost, Tabernacles, and the keeping of the Sabbath will also be celebrated. Thus, sacrifices during the Millennium will serve two purposes: 1) They will serve as a continuous memorial that the Messiah *has* come, His blood *has* been shed, and atonement *has* been made for our sins, and 2) They also will provide believers with a perfect opportunity to worship and praise Him for all He has done. Peace offerings will also be given that will involve the whole family (Ezekiel 43:27).

The offering of these sacrifices is a major focal point of opposition, not only with the current Jewish establishment but also with many Christians. The question they raise is: Why should sacrifices be observed if Christ's once-and-for-all sacrifice fulfilled the Old Testament expectations? This is a good question. The answer is, these millennial sacrifices will serve as a memorial looking back on the offering of Christ, with a retrospective meaning just as we do with the Lord's Supper. These sacrifices are *not* expiatory; neither were the Mosaic sacrifices. They only are commemoratory, pointing to the reality of Christ.

Seven Judgments in Scripture

1. *Judgment of Believer's Sins*—takes place at the Cross (1 Peter 2:24; 3:18; Romans 5:9; 2 Corinthians 5:21; Galatians 3:13; Hebrews 9:26-28; 10:10, 14–17).

2. *Self-Judgment*—part of the sanctification process. If we constantly judge ourselves, we won't have to be judged later by the Lord (1 Corinthians 11:31).

3. *Judgment of Believer's "Works"*—takes place at the Bema Seat of Christ (Romans 14:10; 2 Corinthians 5:10; Matthew 12:36; Galatians 6:7; Ephesians 6:8; Colossians 3:24–25). The result will either be a *reward* of inheriting positions of authority in the coming kingdom or a *loss*—barely entering the kingdom (Colossians 3:24; 1 Corinthians 3:11–15; 2 Corinthians 9:6).

4. *Sheep and Goat Judgment*—judgment of Gentiles living at the time of the Second Coming. This judgment occurs immediately after the return of Christ. Those who pass this judgment will enter the Millennial Kingdom because they cared for "the brethren" during the Tribulation (Matthew 25:31–46).

5. *Judgment of those living in Israel at the Second Coming*—determines their place in the Millennium (Zechariah 13:8–9; Isaiah 1:24–31). Determines who will receive blessings and who will not (Psalm 50:1–7; Ezekiel 20:33–44; Malachi 3:2-5; 4:1–2).

6. *Judgment of Angels*—occurs after the Millennium (Jude 6).

7. *White Throne Judgment*—judgment of the wicked and the dead at the end of the Millennium (Revelation 20:11–15). The test is the possession of eternal life.

(Information taken from *The Millennial Kingdom*, John Walvoord, p. 276–295 and the *Scofield King James Bible*, p. 1351.)

Glossary

Abiding in Christ - Abiding means to stay under, to endure, or to continue in fellowship with the Lord even during difficult times. It means to stay clean, with no known sin or unconfessed self-life. Abiding means staying an open and yielded vessel for His use.

Abundant Life - Experiencing God's Life in place of our own. Loving with His Love, experiencing His wisdom and relying upon His strength.

***Agape* Love** - The supernatural Love of God that is part of His eternal Life. We receive this unconditional, one-sided, freeing, and other-centered Love at our new birth. *Agape* is God Himself.

Agapao - "Totally giving ourselves over to something," either to something good like God and others; or, to something bad such as darkness, the world, or the praise of men, etc.

Altar of Sacrifice - In Ezekiel's temple this altar is called *Ariel*, which means "Lion of God." The sacrifices given on this altar will be a memorial to what Christ has done for us.

Armor of God - The "warfare clothing" we must have on in order to "be strong in the power of His might" so that we can withstand the enemy's arrows. It's His truth, His righteousness and Love, His gospel, His shield of faith, His helmet of salvation, His sword of the Spirit, and then, our praying in the Spirit and watching in supplication for all saints.

Authority (*Exousia*) - The right of the person in charge, which of course, is the Lord, to exercise power. The power is the Lord's, but the choice to implement it is our own.

Authority and Power of the Believer - God not only has given us His strength (His Power) to do His will regardless of how we feel, He has also given us His authority to choose His will, regardless of how we feel. The Word of God is what gives us this authority and the Spirit of God is who gives us the power. This authority and power of Christ is how we overcome the world, the flesh, and the devil. Together, they are the "keys to the kingdom."

Baptism of the Spirit – This is when the Spirit of God comes upon us (*epi*) for the sake of empowering. This infilling of the Spirit gives us power to become witnesses for Christ, not just in words, but with our lives.

"Being Ready" - Being watchful and prepared for Christ's imminent return. Being ready means having partaken *of* Christ's Life, bearing "fruit," and thus, being fit and worthy for the kingdom reign. It's being clothed with the appropriate wedding garments (Revelation 19:7–8).

Bema Seat of Christ - The place where Christ will judge all believers and their works. This is where He will judge our fitness and our worthiness to inherit positions of authority in the kingdom. The works that will be judged will either be wood, hay, and stubble, which will be burned and cause "loss"; or gold, silver, and precious stones, which will withstand the fire and be rewarded. (See Judgment Seat of Christ.)

"**Bitter Water**" - When a believer makes an emotional choice that quenches God's Spirit in their heart, "self-life" (or bitter water) will come forth from their lives.

Body of Christ - Made up of all true believers, both past, present, and future, who have accepted Christ as their Savior, believed upon Him, and received His Spirit in their hearts.

Carnal (secular, nominal) Christian - An unfaithful, disobedient, and unprepared Christian who is independent, self-confident, and self-reliant. This is a believer in whom there has been no life transformation. Instead of overcoming the world, the flesh, and the devil, they have been overcome by the same. They are "soulish" Christians who do things their own way, not God's. They call themselves Christians, but they do not live His Word.

Castaway - (Strong's #96, *adokimas*) means "unapproved, rejected, worthless, and reprobate." It's someone who has been tested and has been found unworthy. He failed the test and thus, is cast out. He ran the race, but failed to win the prize.

Cast Out - (Strong's #1544, *ekballo*) Someone who is sent away, rejected and thrown out with force, like the man without the wedding garment in Matthew 22:1–14.

Christ's Image Carved into us - Being conformed into His image by the carving and the cutting away of the "flesh" by the Holy Spirit.

Circumcision - Continually "putting off" our old man and "putting on" the new one. It means to moment-by-moment renew our minds so that our souls can be transformed into Christ's image. It has more to do with the *sanctification process* than with *justification.*

Condemnation - Accusations from the enemy that push us further away from God (Romans 8:1).

Conviction - Exhortation from the Lord in His Love that reveals our sin, but will ultimately draw us closer to Him (John 16:8).

Co-reigning with Christ - Believers who become co-heirs of Christ's kingdom because of their faithfulness and perseverance. They will hold positions of authority in the Millennium helping Christ rule over the nations.

Crowns - A symbol of rulership, a reward. There are five crowns one can earn—an incorruptible crown, a crown of rejoicing, a crown of Life, a crown of glory, and a righteous crown.

Davidic Covenant - The unconditional covenant between David and the Lord that assures the Jewish people of an eternal homeland. This will begin to be fulfilled in the Millennium Kingdom.

Delegated Authority - The means by which God executes His will. It's His will and His power, but it's chosen and implemented through us.

Disciple - A learner, student or follower of Christ. This person may or may not be saved. In order to truly partake *in* Christ's Life, a disciple must become "born again." In order to partake *of* Christ's Life, however, a disciple must not only receive His Life in his heart, but also live His Life out in his soul.

Double-minded - A believer who is living *two lives*. God's Life is still in this believer's heart, but because he has made emotional choices to follow His own will and not Gods, "self-life" (bitter water) is showing forth in his soul.

***Dunamis* Power of God** - Part of the eternal Life of Christ that we receive in our spirits and hearts when we are born again. It comes from the Source of all power, God. It is His divine ability and His supernatural strength to do what He has asked. This is the power we must rely upon to do the "good works" required for inheriting the kingdom.

Empowering of the Spirit - The time that the Spirit of God comes *upon us* for the sake of divine empowerment. Sometimes it is called the "baptism of the Spirit."

Entering the Kingdom - Those who are "justified" by God (born again) will *enter* the Millennial Kingdom and be a subject there. We have that eternal security.

Eternal Life - This is the supernatural Life of God that we receive when Christ's Spirit comes to reside in our hearts as a result of our invitation and our confession of sin. Eternal Life consists of God's (*Agape*) Love, His (*dunamis*) power, and His supernatural wisdom.

Exchanged Life - After our self-life has been crucified and set aside, the Life of Christ is freed to come forth from our hearts. This doesn't happen automatically. We must make the constant choice to relinquish and surrender ourselves. In other words, we give God our life, He then gives us His.

Faith - To put trust in. Faith is not only believing God's promises, it's also trusting our very lives to Him to do all that He wants. Faith is the means by which God's divine power works in us. Faith comes in the form of a constant choice.

Faith Choices - Nonfeeling choices to obey God's will, no matter what we think or feel. God's Word tells us that we have *His* authority to make these kinds of contrary choices and then, *His* power to perform them. Faith choices are how we exercise God's authority and His power. It's the way we overcome the world, the flesh, and the devil.

Filled with the Spirit - A believer who has made a faith choice to deny himself, pick up His cross, and follow Christ (regardless of how he feels or what he wants), so that God's Life is free to come forth.

Flesh - That natural, self-centered part of us—the old man—that is made up of our natural soul and our physical body. It's our life apart from God, i.e., our self-life.

Foolish - In Scripture, this means being unprepared, worthless in character, or full of darkness. Another term for foolish is *double-minded.*

Forsaking All - Willing to surrender everything that stands in the way of God's Spirit working through us.

Free Choice - Only Christians have "free choice" because only they have a different power source within them to produce something different from what they naturally think, feel, or want to do.

"Fruit" - That which is produced by the Spirit of God through us. These are deeds of righteousness and godly actions prompted and performed by the Spirit of God in our hearts. They occur as a result of exchanging lives with Christ.

Garment - Scripture speaks of two different kinds of garments. The *Garment of Salvation* is the one Christ puts on us at our new birth (Isaiah 61:10). This is our "external garment." The second Scriptural garment is the *white linen garment* made up of the believer's own "righteous works" (Revelation 19:7–8). This is our "internal garment" and the one that is required for admittance to the Wedding celebrations.

"Gold, silver, and precious stones" - (1 Corinthians 3:14–15) "Spiritual works" done by the believer through the power of the Holy Spirit that bring glory to God.

Glorification - This is the part of salvation that will happen in the future when Christ comes back the second time and gives us new spiritual bodies. This is where He saves our bodies from the *presence of sin.*

God's Glory - A manifestation of the Holy Spirit or the presence of God. In the Old Testament, God's glory manifested itself in the Shekinah Glory. In the New Testament, God's glory manifests itself when a believer is filled with the Holy Spirit.

Glorifying God - This simply means reflecting Christ's image, showing forth His Love and His wisdom, and operating by His power.

Grace - Unmerited favor that has been bestowed upon us by God as a "free gift." Grace cannot be earned. It brings us to God and enables us to believe. It's what the Law could never do. By grace we are saved.

"Hope of our Calling" - (Ephesians 1:17–18) Inheriting the coming Millennial Kingdom and ruling and reigning with Him eternally is the reason God has called us. This is the hope of our calling.

Hope Realized - Understanding and embracing the purpose of our calling here and now, and allowing it to determine our actions. That hope then becomes a "tree of Life" (Proverb 13:12).

***Ischus* Power of God** - The physical strength and ability God gives us to do His will. It's divine empowerment. We are to yield our natural ability and depend upon God's strength in order to do His will. Scripture says only when we are weak, can we be made strong.

"I know you not" - The Greek word for *know* here is *oida*, which means "personal intimate knowledge." The five foolish virgins in Matthew 25 did not know the Lord intimately, nor did He know them.

Indwelling of the Spirit - In response to our personal invitation, the Spirit of God comes *in us* and *indwells* us. At this time, the Spirit of God unites our spirit with His and gives us a brand-new spirit.

Inheritance - There are two kinds of inheritance. One belongs to every believer because he is a son of God. It's called a *sonship inheritance*. The other inheritance is called an *inheritance from the Lord* and is conditioned upon the life that the believer lives on earth. This inheritance is earned by merit and the recipient will receive a reward (joint heirship) in the kingdom. This inheritance is in addition to salvation and is conditioned upon obedience.

Inheriting the Kingdom - Those faithful and obedient Christians who have learned how to overcome the world, the flesh, and the devil by the authority and power of Christ are the ones who will inherit the Millennial Kingdom. These are the ones who will rule and reign with Christ. The deciding factor is how we live our life here and now.

Judgment Seat of Christ - The place where Christ will judge a believer's "fruit," his faithfulness, and his perseverance. The outcome of this judgment will determine his place, his role, and his status in the coming kingdom. This is God's gateway to the Millennium. (See Bema Seat.)

Justification - This is our "born again" experience. It means to be declared not guilty because of what Christ has done for us on the Cross. He paid the penalty for us. He is the righteous One. He simply imputed that righteousness to us as a "free gift." No works are needed. This is where we are saved from the *penalty of sin*.

Keys to the Kingdom - The authority of Christ to make a "faith choice" and His power to implement that choice are the "keys to the kingdom" because of the *chain reaction* that follows. Applying His authority and power leads to being sanctified; which in turn leads to being a partaker of Christ's Life; which leads to overcoming the world, the flesh, and the devil and eventually, to co-reigning with Him in the coming kingdom. Not applying these keys will prevent our being sanctified, partaking, overcoming, and inheriting the kingdom.

Kingdom of God - A spiritual kingdom that focuses on our relationship to the King, who rules and reigns in our hearts. The essential feature of this kingdom is holiness and deliverance from sin. It's an invisible kingdom where Christ transforms the believer into His image by a sanctification process.

Kingdom from Heaven - This physical kingdom will merge with the Kingdom of God at the end of the age fulfilling God's plan to come down and dwell among us. This kingdom will be centered in Jerusalem where Christ will rule the earth from His Throne.

Kingdom Perspective - This is the framework, attitude, or outlook we all must have as believers regarding the end times and the literal Millennial Reign of Christ. This outlook is critical because it's the basis upon which we make our moment-by-moment choices today, which will ultimately determine our eternal destiny there.

***Kratos* Power of God** - The ability God has given us to "reign in our self-life" in order that His Life may come forth. It's called Spirit-control. It's Christ's overcoming power to make faith choices to yield ourselves and act out of His Life, rather than our own.

Laboring to Enter In - The road of experiential sanctification that leads to Millennial inheritance is one of toil and labor and striving. Scripture says that we enter into that inheritance only through much tribulation.

The Law - God's rules and regulations. The Law's purpose was to lead people to God. The Law tells us what His will is. The five books of Moses (the Law) was good and pure and shows us our sin, but it never will lead anyone to salvation.

Legalism - Keeping the law by doing "good works." Trying to "work" our way to heaven. Not relying upon the Spirit to produce good works, but accomplishing such in the flesh.

"Life from Death" - God's Life will only flow from our hearts when we have yielded ourselves totally and experienced a co-death with Christ.

Loving God - Surrendering our own sin and self to Christ so that He can live His Life out through us is what loving God is all about. Loving God means totally giving ourselves over to Him for His use, as a cleansed and open vessel.

Mark of the High Calling of God - (Philippians 3:14) The goal of the race. Reaching the finish line. Becoming overcomers who not only inherit the coming Millennial Kingdom, but who also rule and reign with Christ there.

Marriage Feast - This occurs on earth after Christ returns a second time. Many saints (including those from the Old Testament) will attend this feast.

Millennial Kingdom - That literal thousand-year reign of Christ upon the earth where Satan is bound, the temple is rebuilt, and Israel is reestablished.

Millennial Temple - (Ezekiel's Temple) The literal temple, where Christ will rule and reign from, that will be built in Jerusalem during the Millennium. It's sometimes called Ezekiel's Temple because he was the prophet to whom God gave the plans. The purpose of this temple is to demonstrate holiness and righteousness.

"Outer Darkness" - (Strong's #1857) This does not speak of "hell." Nor is it a place where unbelievers go (1 John 2:9-11). It's the place where the unfaithful and disobedient believers will dwell during the Millennium while they re-learn experiential sanctification. It's a separate place, another room or region outside of the light of the presence of the Lord.

Overcomers - Those faithful, obedient, and persevering believers who are not only "partakers *in* Christ's Life," but also "partakers *of* His Life. In other words, they live His Life (share His Love, depend upon His wisdom and are empowered by His Spirit), not just talk about it. They are not perfect, but they constantly recognize their choices and know how to go God's way. They know how to overcome the world by faith in the Word of God, the flesh by a co-death with Christ on the Cross, and the devil by the blood of Christ. Jesus is the real Overcomer, but as they continually allow Him to live His Life out in them, they, too, can become overcomers. They have died to self and they now live to please the Lord by a holy and blameless life. An overcomer is faithful, obedient, and persevering.

"Overcoming the World" - We overcome the world—the lust of the flesh, the lust of the eye, and the pride of life—by having *faith* to give ourselves over to the Lord and trusting in His Word. We overcome the world by not loving it, but instead loving God. We refuse the world by denying ourselves and having faith in His promises.

"Overcoming the Flesh" - We overcome the flesh and its resident power of sin by Christ's authority and power to *flee* it. By making faith choices to nail our sin and self to the Cross (by crucifying the flesh), we free ourselves from its grasp. We must not only acknowledge our sin and self, we must also confess and repent of it, and then lay it at the Cross.

"**Overcoming the Devil**" - We overcome the enemy by God's *dunamis* power to *fight* him. We are to apply the blood of Christ, depend upon the delegated authority of Christ, and lay our lives down before the Lord (Revelation 12:11).

Partakers *of* Christ's Life - Persons who not only receive Christ's eternal Life in their spirits when they are born again, but who also live His Life in their souls, sharing it and passing it on. They are not only recipients of His Life, but also carriers of His Life.

Penalty of Sin - The wages of sin is death. Only by being "justified" through Christ's substitutionary death can we be declared righteous and overcome the penalty of sin.

Power of Sin - An energy force that dominates our "flesh" (our soul and body). The power of sin is an organized power that dwells in our unredeemed bodies and unsanctified souls, whose intent and purpose is to cause us to "miss the mark." (The "mark" is being conformed into Christ's image so we can eventually rule and reign with Christ.) Only experiential sanctification overcomes the power of sin.

Power of God - This supernatural power is a part of the Life of God that was given to us at our new birth. It's the divine ability to do God's will even when we are weak. (See God's resurrection power.)

Presence of Sin - At the end of this age, we won't have to fight the motions of the flesh nor the presence of sin because our bodies will be glorified. Satan and his demonic hordes will be bound and we will finally be freed from sin's influence.

Preparation - The preparation the Bible talks about is the readiness needed to inherit the Millennial Kingdom. It means "putting off" of the flesh and the "putting on" of Christ on a moment-by-moment basis. It's called the process of sanctification—learning to be holy and righteous in character and deed and, thus, partakers of Christ's Life.

Perseverance - Persistent submission in a situation that is out of our control. It's another word for patience or forbearing.

Purgatory - According to Catholic doctrine, *purgatory* is an intermediate hell or place of punishment located in Hades. This unscriptural doctrine comes from 2 Maccabees 12:41–46, not from the Bible.

Quenching the Spirit - This happens to a believer who has a new spirit and a new heart. But because he makes emotional choices to follow what he wants rather than what God wants, God's Life (His Spirit) is quenched or blocked in his heart and prevented from coming forth.

Rapture - The surprise catching up of the saints by Christ to be with Him forever (1 Thessalonians 4:16–18).

Refilled with the Spirit - After we have been indwelt and empowered by God's Spirit, we must daily be *refilled* with His Spirit. This means choosing to continually "put off" our sin and self and "put on" Christ, not letting the Spirit get blocked or quenched.

Reflecting His Life - When we are partakers *of* Christ's Life, His Life will manifest itself in our lives and touch all those around us. Others will see Christ's Love in us, hear His wisdom, and know we operate in His power.

Rest of God - A place as well as an experience. The rest of God has two applications. In the *present*, it means resting in the completed work of Christ (allowing Christ to live His Life out through us). In the *future*, it means participating in the Millennium with Christ. Having finished the work that God gave us to do while here on earth and completing our battles in overcoming the world, the flesh, and the devil, we will be able to rest in the Lord's kingdom (Matthew 11:28–29; Hebrew 4).

Rewards - Prizes or honors given out at the Bema Seat of Christ. Rewards are earned by merit and are a payment for work well done. Colossians 3:24 call these the "reward of inheritance." These are levels of responsibility that will be given to us.

River of Life - Christ is the Source of the River of Life. This river is a picture of God's Life (His Spirit) filling a believer and then overflowing to all that that believer comes in contact with.

Ruling and Reigning with Christ - Holding positions of authority or levels of responsibility that Christ will extend to us in the future Millennial Kingdom.

Salt of the Earth - *Salt* refers to a believer and to his spiritual condition. In a Spirit-filled Christian it is emblematic of the holiness of God. In a carnal Christian, however, salt is said to "lose its savour" and must be "thrown out."

Salvation (Complete) - The salvation of our spirit occurs at our new birth where we are saved from the *penalty of sin* (justification). The salvation of our soul—where we are saved from the *power of sin*—is a lifelong process of learning how to set aside our self-life so that Christ's Life can come forth (experiential sanctification). The salvation of our body occurs at the second coming of Christ where we are saved from the *presence of sin* (glorification).

In the Old Testament, saints were saved by belief alone; however, in the New Testament believers are indwelt by and sealed with the Holy Spirit who, then, becomes our "Enabler" in the sanctification process that leads us to complete salvation.

Sanctification (Experiential) - This is the part of salvation where we are saved from the *power of sin*. It's the lifelong process of actually making us righteous and holy in character and deed, which is what determines our inheritance. It's learning how to "put off" the flesh and "put on" Christ in practice. It's applying the four Sanctification Steps (recognizing our sin and self, confessing and repenting of it, giving it to God, and replacing it with His Word). This is where God actually transforms our souls and we become living examples of Him, reflecting His Love and His power. The goal is to make us more like Christ.

Self-life - Our own natural thoughts, emotions, and desires that are usually contrary to God's Life in us. Self-life is our old nature, the old man, or the flesh.

Spiritual Christian - This is a true disciple of Christ who is a partaker *of* Christ's Life and totally dependent upon the Holy Spirit for everything. He's a believer who is filled with God's Spirit and bearing much "fruit." All his works are done in the power of the Spirit, not his flesh. He is a believer who is obedient, faithful, and persevering and thus, able to overcome the world, the flesh, and the devil. He is not perfect, but at least he recognizes his sin and chooses to turn around and follow God.

The Separate Place (the *gizrah*) - A separate enclosure or space or room to the west of Ezekiel's temple, used for objects that have become unclean or unholy as they must be "cut off" from the sanctified things. Such items can later be cleansed and restored.

Single-minded - A believer who is living *one life*. Because he is making "faith choices," God's Life from this Christian's heart is freely coming forth, filling his soul and flowing out to all he meets.

Strongholds - Old memories, rejections, lifelong insecurities, crippling fears, or any other thing that we have not dealt with or given to God, but simply pushed down and buried. These become the enemy's hideouts and the holes he uses to keep us his captives.

Sweet Water - Because a Christian makes faith choices to follow Christ, irregardless of how he feels or what is happening in his life, God's Spirit (the sweet water) can freely flow.

Strength in Weakness - Scripturally, *weakness* does not mean feebleness or inability, but simply a yielding and a complete relinquishment of self to God. Only when we are yielded, can God be strong through us.

Suffering - This occurs when we choose to deny ourselves, pick up our cross, and follow Christ. Suffering means "barring ourselves from following what *we* want, feel, and desire, and choosing instead to follow Christ.

Ten Talents - (Matthew 25:14–30) The talents in this parable were not a gift, but represented a special privilege or stewardship that was given to each of the servants in accordance with their own capabilities. They were a loan. Each servant, however, must decide for himself what he wanted to do with his talents.

Ten Virgins - Ten *believers* who were waiting for Christ's return. However, only five of them were prepared and fit to enter into the Wedding ceremony when He did appear. The door was shut to the other five virgins who were unprepared (Matthew 25:1–13).

Treasure - The "treasure" that the Bible speaks of is God's eternal Life and it is free for the asking (justification). But in order to obtain *the inheritance* that goes along with it, it will cost us everything (experiential sanctification).

Tribulation - That seven-year period of time on the earth that Scripture says will be more terrifying than any other time in history; there will be famine, earthquakes, persecution, hatred, and lawlessness.

True Disciple – A disciple who has not only partaken *in* Christ's nature, but who is partaking *of* His Life (His Love and His wisdom). Not just a follower of Christ, but a follower who is actually living His Life and experiencing His power.

"Two Gates" - There is one gate at the entrance to the Kingdom of God and another at the end of our walk with God, i.e., the Judgment Seat of Christ. This is the gateway that determines our inheritance in the coming kingdom.

Unprofitable - (Strong's #888) means "unmeritorious or useless." This is used of the unprofitable or lazy servant in Matthew 25:14–30.

Water of Life - Waters that flowed from the Throne room of God in Ezekiel's Temple out to all the land of Israel, thereby, healing everything in its path. Water is the symbol of "spiritual life." In like manner, we are to be filled with that water of Life, and then let it flow from our lives to all those around us.

Weakness - According to Scripture, weakness is a complete yielding and reliance upon the Spirit of God. A person who is totally relinquished to God is said to be "strong in the power of His might."

Wedding Ceremony - Only those who are prepared, ready, and fit ("worthy") may enter the Wedding Ceremony, which occurs immediately after the Judgment Seat. Only a few people will attend this event. These believers must have on the proper Wedding garments, not only the "righteousness of Christ" (justification), but also the "righteous acts of the saints" (acquired through the process of sanctification).

"Weeping and Gnashing of Teeth" - This refers to the unimaginable regret, remorse, and sense of shame that carnal and disobedient Christians will experience in the Millennium as they look back over their wasted lives.

"Wise" - Saints who have prepared themselves. They are living only one life (God's) and thus, are single-minded. Because they have made "faith choices," God's Life is freed to come forth.

Wood, Hay, and Stubble - (1 Corinthians 3:12–13) These are "fleshly works" done by a believer in his own power, not Christ's. They bring glory to the man, not the Lord.

Works of the Flesh - Works done in and by our own natural strength and ability without depending upon God's Spirit. Things that are motivated by our own *self*-centeredness ("wood, hay, and stubble").

Works of the Spirit - That which is motivated by Christ's Life in us and performed by *His* power through us. These are good and righteous deeds that are done in the power and ability of the Holy Spirit ("gold, silver, and precious stones").

Zadok Priests - Priests who had remained faithful when Solomon's Temple was destroyed. The Levi priests, who had rebelled, will be replaced in Ezekiel's Temple by the sons of the Zadok priests. They are the ones who will minister to the Lord.

Bibliography

Bibles:

The Scofield Holy Bible, King James Version, Oxford University Press, New York, NY, 1969.

The Companion Bible, King James Version, Zondervan, Grand Rapids, MI, 1974.

The Interlinear Bible, Hebrew, Greek, English, Associated Publishers, Wilmington, DE, 1976.

The International Inductive Study Bible, Precept Ministries, Harvest House, Eugene, OR, 1993.

The Septuagint Version, Greek and English, Sir Lancelot C. L. Brenton, Zondervan, Grand Rapids, MI, 1970.

ISV (*International Standard Version*), The ISV Foundation, Davidson Press, Paramount, CA, 2008.

Technical Helps:

Botterweak and Ringren, *Theological Dictionary of the Old Testament,* Eerdmans, Grand Rapids, MI, 1975.

Bromiley, Geoffrey W., *Theological Dictionary of the New Testament,* Eerdmans Publishing Company, Grand Rapids, MI, 1964.

Brown, Colin, Editor, *Dictionary of New Testament Theology,* Vols.1–3, Zondervan, Grand Rapids, MI, 1967.

Bruce, F. F., Editor, *The International Bible Commentary,* Zondervan, Grand Rapids, MI, 1979.

Buttrick, George Arthur, Editor, *The Interpreters Dictionary of the Bible,* Abington, Nashville, TN, 1962.

Delitzech, Keil, Editor, *Commentary on the Old Testament,* Eerdmans, Grand Rapids, MI.

Dillow, Joseph, *The Reign of the Servant Kings,* Schoettle Publishing, Hayesville, NC, 1992.

Douglas, J. D., *New Bible Dictionary,* Tyndale Publishers, Wheaton, IL, 1982.

Douglas, J. D., *New Bible Dictionary,* 2nd Edition, InterVarsity Press, Leicester, England, 1982.

Encyclopedia Britannica, University of Chicago, Chicago, IL,1985.

Encyclopedia Judaicia, Keter Publishing House, Jerusalem, Israel.

Halley, Henry H., *Halley's Bible Handbook,* Zondervan Publishing House, Grand Rapids, MI, 1961. Pages 413-456.

Jameson, Fausset & Brown, Editors, *Commentary of the Whole Bible,* Zondervan, Grand Rapids, MI, 1974.

Kittel, Gerhard, Editor, *Theological Dictionary of the New Testament,* Eerdmans Publishers, Grand Rapids, MI, 1964.

Martin, Ralph, *Dictionary of Later New Testament and Its Development,* InterVarsity Press, Leicester, England, 1997.

Mounce, William D., *Complete Expository Dictionary,* Zondervan, Grand Rapids, MI, 2006.

Orr, James, Editor, *The International Standard Bible Encyclopedia,* Eerdmans, Grand Rapids, MI, 1939.

Pfeiffer, Charles, *The Wycliffe Bible Commentary,* Moody Press, Chicago, IL, 1962.

Richman, Chaim, *The Holy Temple,* The Temple Institute, Jerusalem, Israel, 1997.

Spence, H. D. M., Editor, *Pulpit Commentary,* Vols. 1–23, Eerdmans, Grand Rapids, MI, 1950.

Strong, James, *Strong's Expanded Exhaustive Concordance of the Bible,* Thomas Nelson, Nashville, TN, 2001.

Thayer Greek/English Lexicon of the New Testament, Associated Publishers, Grand Rapids, MI, 1889.

Unger, Merrill, *The New Ungers Bible Handbook,* Moody Publishers, Chicago, IL, 2005.

Vine, W. E., *Vine's Complete Expository Dictionary, Old & New Testament,* Thomas Nelson, Nashville, TN, 1984.

Walvoord, John F., *The Bible Knowledge Commentary,* Chariot Victor Publications, Wheaton, IL, 1997.

Walvoord, John F., *The Bible Knowledge Commentary of the Old Testament,* Victor Books, Wheaton, IL, 1985.

Wuest, Kenneth S., *The Expanded Translation of the Greek New Testament,* Eerdmans, Grand Rapids, MI, 1961.

Wuest, Kenneth S., *Word Studies in the Greek New Testament,* Vols. 1–3, Eerdmans, Grand Rapids, MI, 1945.

Zodhiates, Spiros, *The Complete Word Study New Testament (with Parallel Greek),* AMG Publishers, Chattanooga, TN, 1992.

All Other References from:

Alcorn, Randy, *Heaven,* Tyndale House Publishers, Carol Stream, IL, 2004.

Barnhouse, Donald Grey, *The Invisible War,* Zondervan, Grand Rapids, MI, 1965.

Baughman, Ray C., *The Kingdom of God Visualized,* Shepherd Press, Birmingham, AL, 1972.

Benware, Paul, *The Believers Payday,* AMG Publishers, Chattanooga, TN, 2002.

Beshore, E. Kenton, *The Millennial Apocalypse and Armageddon,* 21st Century Press, Springfield, MA, 2001.

Bevere, John, *Driven by Eternity,* Warner Faith Books, New York, NY.

Brandt, Henry, *Breaking Free,* Harvest House Publishers, Eugene, OR, 1994.

Buchanan, Alex, *Heaven and Hell,* Sovereign World, Kent, England, 1948.

Chafer, Lewis Sperry, *Salvation,* Zondervan, Grand Rapids, MI, 1975.

Chambers, Oswald, *Our Brilliant Heritage,* Discovery House, Grand Rapids, MI, 1998.

Chitwood, Arlen L., *The Judgment Seat of Christ,* The Lamp Broadcast, Inc., Norman, OK, 2001.

Chitwood, Arlen L., Editor, *Selected Writings of A. Edwin Wilson,* Schoettle Publishing Co., Hayesville, NC, 1981.

Chitwood, Arlen, L., *The Spiritual Warfare,* The Lamp Broadcast, Inc., Norman, OK, 2005.

Chitwood, Arlen L., *Search for the Bride,* The Lamp Broadcast, Inc., Norman, OK, 2001.

Chitwood, Arlen L., *Salvation of the Soul,* The Lamp Broadcast, Inc., Norman, OK, 2003.

Chitwood, Arlen L., *The Most High Ruleth,* The Lamp Broadcast, Inc., Norman, OK, 2004.

Chitwood, Arlen L., *Jude - Acts of the Apostles,* The Lamp Broadcast, Inc., Norman, OK, 1999.

Chitwood, Arlen L., *The Study of Scripture,* Schoettle Publishing, Norman, OK, 2005.

Connor, Kevin J., *Mystery Parables of the Kingdom,* Distributor Publications, Victoria, Australia, 1996.

Day, Ashley, *Exploring Galatians,* Author House, Bloomington, IN.

Dodson, Kenneth, *The Prize of the Upcalling,* Schoettle Publishing, Miami Springs, FL, 1989.

Dunahoo, Charles H., *Making Kingdom Disciples,* P. R. Publishing, Phillipsburg, N.J.

Evans, Tony, *What a Way to Live,* Word Publishing, Nashville, TN, 1997.

Freeman, Hobart E., *Deeper Life in the Spirit,* Faith Publications, Warsaw, IN, 1970.

Fruchtenbaum, Arnold, G., *Footsteps of the Messiah,* Ariel Press, Tustin, CA, 1982.

Fruchtenbaum, Arnold, G., *Israelology,* Ariel Press, Tustin, CA, 1989.

Fruchtenbaum, Arnold, G., *The Missing Link in Systematic Theology,* Ariel Press, Tustin, CA.

Govett, Robert, *Govett on the Parables,* Schoettle Publishing, Mission Springs, FL,1989.

Govett, Robert, *Christ's Judgment of the Saints,* Conley and Schoettle Publishing, Miami Springs, FL, 1985.

Govett, Robert, *Rewards According to Works,* Schoettle Publishing, Miami Springs, FL, 1989.

Greenwood, Glen, *A Marriage Made in Heaven,* Word Publishers, Dallas, TX, 1990.

Harmon, James, *The Coming Spiritual Earthquake,* Prophecy Countdown, Maitland, FL, 1993

Hodges, Zane, *Grace in Eclipse,* Redencion Viva, Dallas, TX, 1985.

Howard, Rick, *The Judgment Seat of Christ*, Naioth Sound and Publishing, Woodside, CA, 1990.

Huegel, F. J., *Forever Triumphant,* Zondervan, Grand Rapids, MI, 1958.

Jeffries, Grant, *Heaven,* Frontier Research Publications, Toronto, Canada, 1992.

Johnson, Carl G., *The Account Which We Must Give,* Regular Baptist Press, Schaumburg, IL, 1990.

Kroll, Woodrow Michael, *It Will be Worth It All,* Loizeqaux Brothers, Neptune, NJ, 1977.

La Haye, Beverly, *Spiritual Power for Your Family,* Charisma House, Lake Mary, FL.

La Haye, Tim, *Charting the End Times,* Harvest House, Eugene, OR, 2001.

La Haye, Tim, *The Popular Bible Prophesy Workbook,*

Lang, G. H., *The Revelation of Jesus Christ,* Schoettle Publishing Co., Hayesville, NC.

Lang, G. H., *First Born Sons,* Schoettle Publishing Co., Hayesville, NC, 1997.

Lang, G. H., *Picture Parables,* Schoettle Publishing, Hayesville, NC, 2008.

Larson, Steven, *Heaven Help Us,* Nav Press, Colorado Springs, CO, 1995.

Levitt, Zola, *A Christian Love Story,* Dallas, TX, 1978.

Luther, Martin, *Bondage of the Will,* translated by J. I. Parker, O.R. Johnston, Revell, Grand Rapids, MI, 1957.

Maxwell, L. E., *Born Crucified,* Moody Press, Chicago, IL, 1945.

McTernan, John P., *Only Jesus of Nazareth Can Sit on the Throne of David,* Xulon Press, Liverpool, PA, 2005.

Missler, Nancy, *The Way of Agape,* King's High Way Ministries, Coeur d'Alene, ID,1995.

Missler, Nancy, *Be Ye Transformed,* King's High Way Ministries, Coeur d'Alene, ID, 1996.

Missler, Nancy, *Faith in the Night Seasons,* King's High Way Ministries, Coeur d'Alene, ID, 1999.

Moody, D. L., *The Overcoming Life,* Bridge-Logos, Orlando, FL, 2007.

Murphy, Dr. Ed, *Handbook for Spiritual Warfare,* Thomas Nelson Publishers, Nashville, TN, 2003.

Nee, Watchman, *Spiritual Authority,* Christian Fellowship Publishers, New York, NY.

Nee, Watchman, *The Spiritual Man,* Christian Fellowship Publishers, New York, NY, 1968.

Nee, Watchman, *Secrets to Spiritual Power,* compiled by Sentinel Kulp, Whitaker House, Sunneytown, PA, 1999.

Neighbour, R. E., *If By Any Means,* Conley and Schoettle Publishing Co., Miami Springs, FL, 1985.

Oliver, C. R., *The Sons of Zadok,* Ransom Press, Bonita Springs, FL, 2000.

Panton, D. M., *The Judgment Seat of Christ,* Schoettle Publishing, Hayesville, NC, 1984.

Pearl, Michael, *The Eight Kingdoms,* N G J Ministries, Pleasantville, TN, 2006.

Pentecost, Dwight J., *Things to Come,* Zondervan, Grand Rapids, MI, 1958.

Rhodes, Ron, *The Wonder of Heaven*, Harvest House, Eugene, OR, 2009.

Schmitt, John W., *Messiah's Coming Temple,* Kregel Publications, Grand Rapids, MI, 1997.

Shreve, Mike, *Our Glorious Inheritance,* Deeper Revelation Books, Cleveland, TN, 1991.

Simpson, A. B., *The Land of Promise,* Christian Publications, Camp Hill, PA, 1996.

Simpson, A. B., *Wholly Sanctified,* Christian Publications, Camp Hill, PA, 1991.

Somerville, Robert S., *The God Contracts*, Xulon Press, 2005.

Stanley, Charles, *Eternal Security: Can You Be Sure,* Walker and Co., New York, NY, 2000.

Tamez, Elsa, *The Scandalous Message of James*, Crossroads, New York, NY, 1985.

Tozer, A. W., *The Knowledge of the Holy,* Harper and Row, San Francisco, CA, 1961.

Wall, Joe L., *Going for the Gold,* Moody Press, Chicago, IL, 1991.

Walvoord, John E., *The Millennial Kingdom,* Zondervan, Grand Rapids, MI, 1959.

Whipple, Gary, *Shock and Surprise: Beyond the Rapture,* Schoettle Publishing, Hayesville, NC, 1992.

Whipple, Gary, *The Matthew Mysteries,* Schoettle Publishing Co., Hayesville, NC, 1995.

Wigglesworth, Smith, *God's Power Today,* Whitaker House, New Kensington, PA, 2000.

Wilson, Edwin A., *Selected Writings of A. Edward Wilson,* Schoettle Publishing Co., Hayesville, NC, 1996.

Yohannan, K. P., *Reflecting His Image,* Gospel for Asia, Carrollton, TX, 2004.

Articles:

A. M., Group, *A Layman's Perspective, Entrance into the Kingdom,* Lawrence, KS, Feb.'92.

Constable, Dr. Thomas L., *Notes on Ezekiel,* Sonic Light, 2007 Edition, www.soniclight.com.

Dolphin, Lambert, *The Temple of Ezekiel,* May 31, 1995, Lambert@ l dolphin.org.

Finley, Gavin, *The Sheep Goat Judgment,* End Time Pilgrim, www.endtimepilgrim.org.

Finley, Gavin, *The Parable of the Ten Virgins,* End Time Pilgrim, www.endtimepilgrim.org.

Govett, Robert, *The Race and the Crown,* Tracts on the Kingdom, Schoettle Publishing, Hayesville, NC.

Govett, Robert, *The Gift and the Prize,* online.

Johnson, Ron, *The Centrality of the Jewish Temple in the Affairs of God, Israel and the Nations, Part Two: Future Temples,* Oroville Evangelical Free Church, Oroville, CA.

Lang, G. H., *Ideals and Realities,* Schoettle Publishing, Hayesville, NC, 1988.

Legge, Pastor David, *The Millennial Temple,* Ezekiel, Part 22, Preach the Word.

Millennial Temple, *Israel's Levitical Priesthood is Once More Alive,* Bible Study Manuals, Ezekiel 40–48, online.

Newberry, Thomas, *Types of the Temple,* The Brazen Sea,

Roadhouse, W. F., *Believer's "Sharing or Forfeiting" Christ's Glorious Reign,* Toronto, Canada.

The Heavenly Calling, *The Outer Darkness,* Lamp Broadcast Inc., Norman, OK, July 1984.

Wilson, Edwin, *Selected Writings of A. Edwin Wilson, Ruling and Reigning, The Unfaithful Christian,* Schoettle Publishing, Hayesville, NC, 1996.

Wilson, A. E., *The Bride of Christ,* online.

Booklet:

Crawford, Scott, *The Five Warnings for Believers, Word of Truth,* Schoettle Publishing Co., Hayesville, NC, 2006.

End Notes

Preface

* The Barna Group
www.barna.org/FlexPage.aspx?Page=BarnaUpdateNarrowPreview&Barna UpdateID=295 (accessed 2/11/09).

Chapter One: Prologue

1. Hebrews 3:14.
2. Revelation 20:6; Daniel 7:27; 2 Timothy 2:12.
3. See also: Revelation 2:7, 11, 26–28; 3:5, 12, 21; 19:7–9; Hebrews 12:17; Matthew 5:3 & 10; 1 Corinthians 3:13-15; 2 Corinthians 5:10; Act 20:32; 2 Timothy 2:12; James 1:12; 1 John 4:17.
4. Colossians 1:25–26.
5. Charles Stanley, *Eternal Security*, 180.
6. Paul N. Benware, *The Believer's Payday*, 2.
7. Erwin Lutzer, *Your Eternal Reward*, 15, 18.
8. Tim La Haye, *The Popular Bible Prophecy Workbook.*
9. Spiros Zodhiates, *The Complete Word Study New Testament*, 25.
10. Grant Jeffries, *Heaven*, 165.
11. John Walvoord, *The Millennial Kingdom*. Kenneth Wuest, *Expanded Translation of the Greek New Testment. Thayer's Greek/English Lexicon.*
12. *A Layman's Perspective*, February 1992, page 1.
13. Revelation 2–3.
14. Ephesians 1:9–10, also 17-18; Psalm 8:4–9; 1 John 3:1–3; 1 Peter 1:13; Luke 14:14; 20:35–36.
15. Acts 17:11.

Chapter Two: Eternal Security

1. Genesis 1:26–27; 5:3; 9:6; Hebrews 2:7–8.
2. Isaiah 14:12–17.
3. Genesis 3:14–19; Romans 5:12, 18–19.
4. John 14:3, 18–21.

5. John 6:51; Hebrews 2:9; 9:22–24.
6. 1 Timothy 2:6.
7. Acts 2:24.
8. John 4:10; Revelation 22:17.
9. John 1:12; 3:16; Romans 5:8–9; 6:23.
10. Jeremiah 31:31–34; Ezekiel 36:24–28; Hebrews 8:6–13.
11. John 1:11–13; 3:18; 5:24; Ephesians 2:5, 8; Isaiah 53:10–11; Hebrews 9:11–12; Romans 4:5–8; 5:1, 9–10, 18.
12. Ephesians 1:13–14; 2:8–9; John 3:16, 36; 5:24; Romans 8:38–39.
13. Matthew 16:25–27; 1 Peter 1:9.
14. 1 Thessalonians 4:16–17; 1 Corinthians 15:51–53; Philippians 3:20–21; 1 John 3:2.
15. John 5:24; Ephesians 2:5.
16. Matthew 16:25–27; 1 Thessalonians 4:3; 5:23; 1 Peter 1:9; James 1:21.
17. 1 Thessalonians 4:3–4; Romans 6:19, 22; Hebrews 12;14; 1 Corinthians 1:30; 2 Thessalonians 2:13; 1 Peter 1:2; Ephesians 1:4.
18. Matthew 24:14; Luke 4:43; 8:1; 9:1–6; Acts 8:12; Hebrews 4:8.
19. Ephesians 1:4–7.
20. Titus 3:8.
21. 1 Timothy 1:19; 1 Corinthians 5:5; Romans 8:6.
22. Romans 8:38–39; John 3:5, 14–16, 18, 36.
23. Romans 8:17; 2 Timothy 2:12; James 2:5.
24. www.brainyquote.com/quotes/quotes/j/johngreenl385048.html (accessed 2/11/09).
25. Charles Stanley, *Eternal Security*, 124–125, 293.
26. Ephesians 4:1.
27. Matthew 24:13.
28. Matthew 16:25–26.
29. Ephesians 2:8.
30. 1 Thessalonians 5:23; 1 Peter 1:9; James 1:21; Hebrews 10:39.
31. 1 John 3:2.

Chapter Three: Inheritance

1. Galatians 3:29.
2. 1 Peter 1:4.
3. Luke 15:24.
4. Revelation 2—3; Hebrews 6:12: Leviticus 21:8.
5. Hebrews 3—4.
6. American Book Co., 348–349.
7. Hebrews 11:8; 6:12; Acts 26:18.
8. Ephesians 1:18; Colossians 1:12; Revelation 21:7.
9. Tony Evans, *What a Way to Live*, 180.
10. Romans 8:17; 2 Timothy 2:12; Revelation 2:26; 21:7.
11. Matthew 5:5; 25:34; Revelation 21:7.
12. *The Popular Bible Prophecy Book*, 47.
13. Joshua 14:8–9; 22:1–5.
14. Revelation 14:13; Deuteronomy 30:15–20.
15. Romans 6:23; Ephesians 2:8; John 17:2.
16. Colossians 1:12; 3:24; Ephesians 1:18.
17. Matthew 6:33; Hebrews 6:1–19; 10:23.
18. Joseph Dillow, *Reign of the Servant Kings*, 346, 349, 352.
19. Spiros Zodhiates, *The Complete Word Study New Testament*, 25. Kenneth Wuest, *Greek New Testament*, 90. Charles Stanley, *Eternal Security*, 90, 124–125
20. 2 Thessalonians 1:5, 11; Luke 20:34–36.
21. 2 Peter 3:11, 14; 1 Thessalonians 2:10–12; 3:13; 4:1,7; 2 Thessalonians 1:11.
22. Hebrews 6:12–15; Ephesians 5:5.
23. 2 Timothy 4:8; 1 John 2:28; Matthew 24:4; James 1:12.
24. Hebrews 10:35; 1 Corinthians 9:24–27.

Chapter Four: Who Are the Overcomers?

1. Revelation 21:7; Colossians 1:12.
2. Proverbs 3:18; 11:30.

3. Revelation 20:6, 14; 21:8.
4. Numbers 31:16; Joshua 13:22; 2 Peter 2:15–16; Jude 11.
5. Revelation 13:8; 20:12.
6. Philippians 4:3; Matthew 10:32.
7. Jeremiah 1:18; Galatians 2:9; 2 Chronicles 3:17; 1 Kings 7:15.
8. 1 Peter 4:12–13; 2:21–23.
9. *Word Studies in the Greek New Testament*, vol. 3, 114–115.
10. Martyn Lloyd Jones, *Life in the Spirit*, 78–80, 363–364, 370.
11. Hebrews 12:1; Luke 6:22–24.
12. Matthew 5:1–12; 6:1–13; Revelation 3:21; 11:18; 22:12; Luke 14:12–14; Phillipians 3:14.
13. Romans 6:23; Ephesians 2:8; John 3:15–16; 17:2; 1 John 5:11.
14. Colossians 1:12; 3:24; Ephesians 2:10; Revelation 21:7.
15. Luke 16:16; Mark 9:1; Matthew 4:17
16. 2 Thessalonians 1:5; Matthew 6:33; Colossians 3:23–24.
17. Psalm 16:11.
18. Psalm 21:6; Ephesians 5:27; Colossians 1:22; 1 Thessalonians 3:13; 5:23.
19. Charles Stanley, *Eternal Security*, 90, 124–125.
20. *Expanded Translation of the Greek New Testament*, 18.
21. *Your Eternal Reward*, 74, 77.
22. *Thayer's Greek / English Lexicon*, 226.
23. Matthew 18:12; 22:13; 25:30.
24. Spiros Zodhiates, *The Complete Word Study New Testament*, 25.
25. *The Bible Exposition Commentary*, vol.1, 92.
26. Zane Hodges, *Prophecy Study Bible*, article by Tony Evans, 1234.
27. Hebrews 12:6; 1 Corinthians 11:31–32.

Chapter Five: Thy Kingdom Come

1. Matthew 6:10, 13; Acts 1:6; cf. Psalm 45, 46, 47, 48.
2. Carl Johnson, taken from *The Account Which We Must Give,* 11.

3. Genesis 12:1–4; confirmed Genesis 13:14–17; 15:1–7,18-21;17:1–8.
4. Deuteronomy 30:3; Genesis 15:18.
5. 2 Samuel 7:8–17; 23:5; Psalm 89:34-37.
6. Jeremiah 31:31; Hebrews 8:8.
7. Isaiah 65, et al.
8. He uses both in two adjacent verses: Matthew 19:23, 24.
9. Matthew 19:28; Luke 22:30.
10. Revelation 7.
11. Revelation 21.
12. Matthew 12:23–45.
13. Matthew 13:10–17, 34–35.
14. Daniel 9:25; Luke 19:41, 42.
15. "Fullness of the Gentiles" is the completion of the Church; not to be confused with the "Times of the Gentiles": the domination of the Gentiles beginning with Nebuchadnezzar and climaxing with the Antichrist.
16. Psalm 2:45; 110; Isaiah 2:1–5; 4:1–6; 11:1–9; 12:1–6; 30:18–26; 35:1–10; 60; 61:3–62—62:4; Jeremiah 23:3–8; 32:37–44; Ezekiel 40—48; Daniel 2:44–45; 7:13–14; 12:2–3; Micah 4:1–8; Zechariah 12:10—14:21.
17. Psalm 2; 110; Revelation 12:5; 19:15; Philippians 2:6–11.

Chapter Six: Kingdom Events

1. More specifically this is called "the 70th Week of Daniel," of which the last 3 1/2 years is called "the Great Tribulation" (Matthew 24:15, 21).
2. Matthew 16:27; Luke 14:14; 1 Corinthians 3:9–15; 4:5; 9:18–27; 2 Timothy 4:8; Revelation 22:12; 1 Peter 4:17; Hebrews 10:30–31.
3. Matthew 16:27; Revelation 22:12.
4. Matthew 27:19; Acts 12:21; 18:12; 25:6, 12; Romans 14:10–12.
5. Matthew 24:42–51; 25:14–30; Mark 8:34–38.
6. Matthew 16:25; Luke 9:25; Philippians 3:8.
7. Matthew 16:27; 18:23–35; Luke 16:2; 6:37; Hebrews 4:13; 1 Corinthians 3:6–8, 12-15; Revelation 2:23; 22:12; Ephesians 6:8-9; Colossians 3:22–25.

8. Romans 14:10; 2 Corinthians 5:10.
9. Jeremiah 17:10; Revelation 2:23; 1 Corinthians 3:13.
10. "The Outer Darkness in Matthew and it's Relationship to Grace," *The Journal of the Grace Evangelical Society,* autumn 1992, vol.5:2.
11. Psalm 89:14; Ecclesiastes 12:14; Romans 2:5–6.
12. *Word Studies in the Greek New Testament*, 126.
13. Romans 2:16; 1 Corinthians 4:5; Matthew 6:1–4; Hebrews 4:12–13.
14. Matthew 24:45; 25:23; Luke 16:10a; 1 Corinthians 4:2; Revelation 2:10.
15. Matthew 12:36–37; Luke 12:2–3.
16. 1 Corinthians 3:13–15; 2 Corinthians 5:10; Galatians 6:7; Revelation 2:23; Colossians 3:23–25.
17. Paul Benware, *The Believer's Payday,* 2.
18. Steve Larson, *Heaven Help Us*, 25.
19. Matthew 16:24–27; 24:45–51; 25:14–30.
20. 1 Corinthians 3:8; 2 Corinthians 9:6; Colossians 3:22–25.
21. Matthew 25:14–30; Revelation 3:16.
22. John 15:6; Matthew 24:51.
23. 2 Timothy 2:12; Revelation 2:26; 3:21.
24. Matthew 25:34; Acts 20:32; Galatians 3:18; Colossians 1:12.
25. 1 Corinthians 3:8; 2 Corinthians 5:10; 1 Timothy 5:18b; Matthew 10:41–42; 11:11; 16:27; Luke 12:42–44; 2 John 1:8; Mark 9:41; 2 Timothy 2:19–20.
26. Charles Stanley, *Eternal Security: Can You Be Sure*? 192.
27. Luke 12:33-34; 18:22; Mark 10:21.
28. Matthew 25:21, 23; Luke 19:17.
29. 1 Corinthians 9:25; 1 Thessalonians 2:19; 2 Timothy 4:8.
30. Much of this material was taken from *The Encyclopedia Judaica* on marriage.
31. Matthew 25:1–12; 2 Corinthians 11:2; Ephesians 5:26; 1 John 3:2–3; Revelation 19:7–8; Isaiah 62:5; Jude 24.
32. Ephesians 3:4–5; Romans 16:25–26; Colossians 1:23; 2 Thessalonians 1:5, 11.
33. 1 John 1:6–7; 2:3–6; 4:8.

34. Revelation 14:4; 2 Corinthians 11:2.
35. *The Pulpit Commentary*, vol. 15, 492.
36. Leviticus 8:10; 21:12; 1 Samuel 10:1.
37. *The Dictionary of New Testament Theology,* vol.3, 116.
38. Revelation 3:10; 1 John 1:7; Hebrews 11:5; 12:14; Luke 9:62; 21:36; Matthew 5:3; 2 Peter 3:11, 14.
39. *The Ever Increasing Demands of Faith*, August 25, 2008.
40. G. H. Lang, *Picture Parables*, 378.
41. Revelation 1:6; 5:10.
42. Matthew 16:24–26; 19:28–29; Romans 8:17; Revelation 2:26–27.
43. Matthew 5:20.

Chapter Seven: The Millenial Temple

1. Zechariah 6:12–13; Isaiah 2:2–4; 27:13; 56:6–8; 66:20.
2. Isaiah 2:3; 60:13; Daniel 9:24; Joel 3:18; Haggai 2:7–9.
3. Micah 4:1; Isaiah 2:2–3.
4. Joel 3:18; Ezekiel 47:1–12.
5. William Welty, <isv.org/about_us/bios/william.htm>.
6. Isaiah 66:20; Obadiah 1:17; Zechariah 8:3.
7. 2 Corinthians 6:16; Ezekiel 43:1–2.
8. Pat Jeppersen, one of Chuck's rabbinical advisors from Spokane, Washington.
9. *The Theological Dictionary of the Old Testament*, 459–461.
10. Matthew 18:12; 22:13; 25:30.
11. Hebrews 12:17; Matthew 8:12; 22:13; 24:51; 25:30.
12. 1 Corinthians 3:11–15; 2 Corinthians 5:10; 1 John 2:28.
13. The Ark and the Mercy Seat described in the Throne room are always spoken of as being separate. The Seat of Mercy is what defines the location of the Holy of Holies. Some suspect this Mercy Seat will be the actual throne upon which Christ will sit during the Millennium.
14. *The Temple of Ezekiel*, Lambert Dolphin, page 3.
15. 1 Samuel 2:35; 2 Samuel 8:17; 15:24–29.

Chapter Eight: Partakers *of* Christ's Life

1. Romans 8:9–17; Galatians 5:16.
2. Colossians 1:27; Philippians 1:21.
3. Galatians 5:25; Ephesians 3:16–19.
4. Galatians 5:22; Matthew 7:17; James 5:7, 18; Romans 6:21–22.
5. *The Pulpit Commentary*, vol. 15, 297.
6. Luke 6:43–44; Matthew 12:33; 3:10.
7. 1 Corinthians 8:3; 2 Corinthians 5:10–11, 14; Hebrews 10:30–31; 2 Peter 1:3–11.
8. 2 Timothy 4:10; Luke 6:32; 11:43; 1 John 2:15.
9. John 14:21; 15:9–10.

Chapter Nine: God's *Dunamis* Power

1. 1 Chronicles 29:11; Psalm 66:7; Revelation 7:12.
2. Matthew 19:26; Mark 10:27; Luke 18:27; Mark 9:23; Jeremiah 32:27.
3. Exodus 6:1; 10:1; 11:1; 7:10–14.
4. 2 Corinthians 13:4; Luke 4:14; 4:36; Acts 10:38.
5. Daniel 3:17; Hebrews 7:25.
6. 2 Timothy 1:12; Jude 24–25; 1 Peter 1:5.
7. Ephesians 3:16, 20; Colossians 1:11; 2 Timothy 1:7.
8. John 20:22; Luke 11:13; Ezekiel 36:26; Romans 8:9: 1 Corinthians 3:16; 6:19–20.
9. Hebrews 11:27; Acts 2:25; Job 42:5.
10. 1 Corinthians 7:37; Galatians 5:16.
11. Ephesians 3:16; 2 Samuel 22:33; Psalm 18:32; 2 Corinthians 8:11.

Chapter Ten: Strength in Weakness

1. Ephesians 6:10; 2 Corinthians 12:10; Isaiah 40:29–31; Psalms 138:3; Hebrews 11:34b.
2. Isaiah 53:12; Philippians 2:8–9; Hebrews 2:8–9.
3. 2 Corinthians 11:30; Galatians 6:14; Exodus 9:16; Jeremiah 9:24; 1 Corinthians 1:31.
4. Exodus 15:11; 1 Peter 1:15–16; 1 Thessalonians 5:23.

5. Luke 16:15; Galatians 5:16–21; Romans 16:17; Ephesians 5:3–5; 1 Corinthians 6:9–10.
6. 1 Corinthians 3:15; Galatians 5:21; Ephesians 5:5; Matthew 25:28–30.
7. 1 Corinthians 3:15; 2 Corinthians 5:10; Matthew 10:33; 25:12; 2 Timothy 2:12.
8. Matthew 24:1, 3; Mark 13:3–4; Luke 21:7.
9. Acts 1:8; 13:46–48; 15:14–18.
10. Matthew 7:5; 1 Peter 2:1–2; Luke 12:42–46.
11. Matthew 8:12; 22:13; 25:30.
12 Matthew 8:12; 22:13; 25:30.
13. 2 Corinthians 5:11; Revelation 2:23; Colossians 3:25.
14. *The Pulpit Commentary*, vol. 15, 358, vol. 16, 338.
15. Matthew 8:12; 22:13; 25:30, 51.
16. 1 Corinthians 3:4; Matthew 26:70–72, 74; Mark 16:14; Psalm 95:8; Hebrews 5:11.
17. 2 Corinthians 7:10; Revelation 2:5; 1 John 1:9.
18. Galatians 5:21; 1 Corinthians 6:9; Matthew 21:43; 2 Timothy 2:12; Ephesians 5:5.
19. John 12:24–25; Matthew 16:24–25.
20. 1 John 2:28; 2 Peter 3:14; Matthew 25:10; Luke 12:40.
21. 1 Timothy 6:14; Revelation 2:25.

Chapter Eleven: Faith—the Means of God's Power

1. Romans 4:20–21; Joshua 23:14.
2. Matthew 24:13; 2 Timothy 2:10.
3. Matthew 24:13; Mark 13:13.
4. 2 Corinthians 13:5; 1 Corinthians 11:28.
5. *A Layman's Perspective*, 9.
6. *The Pulpit Commentary*, vol. 15, 297.
7. Romans 11:6; Ephesians 2:8; John 1:12–13; 3:16; 5:24; 20:31; Romans 5:15; 10:10; 2 Corinthians 9:8; 2 Thessalonians 2:16.
8. Romans 5:2; Ephesians 2:8.

Chapter Twelve: What Is an Overcomer?

1. Joel 2:32; Psalm 34:4.
2. Luke 12:5; Romans 9:21.
3. Luke 10:19; John 10:17–18; Matthew 28:18–20.
4. 1 Corinthians 6:12; 10:13.
5. Romans 8:14–15; Galatians 4:7.
6. From *The Dictionary of New Testament Theology*, vol. 2, 610.
7. 1 John 1:7; 2:14; Romans 8:2; Revelation 12:11.
8. Galatians 5:16; Ephesians 2:3.
9. Some of this material has been excerpted from Donald Grey Barnhouse, *The Invisible War*, 179–186.
10. 1 John 2:15–18; 3:1; 5:19.
11. Some of this material has been taken from Donald Grey Barnhouse, *The Invisible War*, 179–186.
12. 2 Timothy 2:11; 1 Peter 4:13.
13. Revelation 2:10; 3:10; Acts 14:22; Matthew 19:27–29.
14. 2 Corinthians 11:23; 1 Peter 4:12–13.
15. 2 Timothy 2:22; 1 Corinthians 6:18; 1 Peter 2:11.
16. Ephesians 1:7; 2:13; Colossians 1:14.
17. John 12:31; 14:30; 16:11.
18. D. L. Moody, *The Overcoming Life*, 68, 327.
19. Hebrews 2:14; Matthew 12:28–29.
20 Matthew 16:19; 12:29; Mark 3:27; Psalm 89:40.
21. *The New International Dictionary of New Testament Theology*, vol. 1, 651.
22. Isaiah 22:22 (refers to the Kingdom of David; see chapter 5); Matthew 18:18; Revelation 3:7.
23. Ephesians 6:13; Luke 21:15; Acts 6:10.
24. 1 Timothy 6:12; James 4:7.
25. Interestingly enough, *Agape* was another name for the Egyptian goddess Isis whose center of pagan worship was Rome. Isis, along with her husband Osiris (known as Logos) and their son, Hermes, were

classically called "the trinity" (a counterfeit to the Father, Son, and Holy Spirit). It was said that Isis' supernatural powers superseded all other pagan gods combined. An inscription upon her statue reads: "*I am the queen of the country; and whosoever I* bind*, no man can* loose." (*The Pulpit Commentary,"* vol. 15, 137).

Chapter Thirteen: The Return of His Glory

1. Deuteronomy 31:17; 1 Samuel 4:21, "Ichabod"; Ezekiel 9:3.
2. Isaiah 60:13; Joel 3:18; Micah 4:2; Haggai 2:7–9; Zechariah 6:12–14; 14:16.
3. *The Pulpit Commentary*, vol. 12, 379.
4. Leviticus 11:44; 19:2; 20:7; 1 Peter 1:15–16.
5. John 4:14; 7:37–38; Psalm 36:9.
6. Isaiah 11:9; Habakkuk 2:14.
7. Ezekiel 36:35; 47:12; Isaiah 35:1–2, 6–7; Joel 3:18.
8. Acts 1:8; Ephesians 5:17–18.
9. Revelation 21:6; John 7:38; Revelation 8:11.

Chapter Fourteen: Personally Reflecting His Glory

1. Ezekiel 9:3; 10:4, 18–19; 11:22–23.
2. Hebrews 4:1–11; 10:37–38.
3. Hebrews 6:6; Psalm 95:11.
4. Kevin J. Conner, *Mystery Parables of the Kingdom.*
5. 1 Corinthians 9:25; 1 Timothy 6:12; 2 Corinthians 5:9.
6 Ephesians 2:10; Revelation 19:7–9.
7. Hebrews 2:1–4; 3:7–14; 6:4–8; 10:26–39; 12:25–29.
8. Much of this material is taken from *The Pulpit Commentary*, vol. 16, 10–11.
9. 2 Timothy 4:7; 1 Corinthians 9:25; 1 Timothy 6:12; Hebrews 12:1–2; Colossians 1:29.
10. *The Pulpit Commentary*, vol. 15, 309.
11. Charles Stanley, *Eternal Security*, 90.
12. *The Pulpit Commentary*, vol. 22, 463.
13. *The Millennial Apocalypse*, 318.

14. Revelation 3:17; 2 Corinthians 5:3; Matthew 22:11.
15. *Pulpit Commentary*, vol. 15, 359.
16. Joseph Dillow, *The Reign of the Servant Kings,* 346.
17. James 1:4; 1 Peter 1:9; 5:10.
18. 2 Corinthians 5:10; Romans 14:10–12.
19. Revelation 2:26–27; 3:11–12.

Supplemental Notes

20. "Are the Constants of Physics really constant?" *Scientific American,* June 2005.
21. *Israel Today*, April 6, 2007.
22. Some point out that the Greek may be alluding to the Rapture here, but that is not critical to our case.

Acknowledgments

We are deeply indebted to the writings of Joseph C. Dillow, whose *The Reign of the Servant Kings* awakened us to the realities involved in being "overcomers." Furthermore, we owe an even greater indebtedness to our dear friend Louis Schoettle, whose diligence and initiatives introduced us not only to Dillow, but also Govet, A. Edwin Wilson, Michael Pearl, and others. Their insights, despite our differences in views on several critical topics, nevertheless proved to be of paramount value in our research on so many polemical issues.

We are also deeply indebted to Dr. William Welty and the resources of his team completing the *International Standard Version* translation, for their counsel and tutorial assistance in resolving many of the subtle exegetical issues.

Any errors, however, are entirely our own. We flee for refuge to our traditional trademark admonition to "receive the Word with all openness of mind, yet search the Scriptures daily to prove whether those things are so!" (Acts 17:11).

The Lord has blessed us with encouragements resulting from many of our previous publications; however, never have we both, together, felt as drawn and compelled to call these particular insights to the attention of our faithful friends. We pray that they will prove to be a blessing to all of us who are seeking to qualify as "overcomers, indeed"!

In the Name of our Coming King,

Chuck and Nan Missler
(On our 52nd Wedding Anniversary)

Topical Index

New Heavens & New Earth

Outer Darkness

Overcomers

Overtaken

Overcoming Results

Parables

Partakers

Perseverance

Power

Prayer

World

Worthy

* * *

Miscellaneous

Scriptures

Supplemental Notes Index

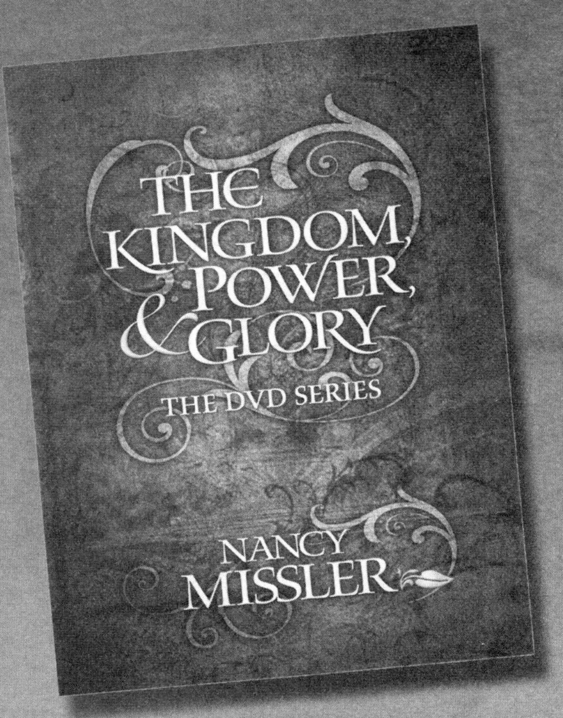

DVD - $59.95

Scripture tells us that we are to "prepare ourselves" for Christ's soon return.

What exactly does this mean?
What's at stake?
What if we aren't prepared?

Being ready, fit and prepared will dramatically affect our role, our position and our place of responsibility in the future Millennial Kingdom.

In this 14 hour DVD, Nancy shares, not only the Scriptural importance of ***why*** we need to be "prepared," but also ***what*** we need to do to be prepared.

What is the King's

The King's High Way is
dedicated to encouraging and
Christians how to "walk out" their
passion is to focus on the practical
application of Biblical principles. Learning how to really love as Jesus loved; how to renew our minds so our lives can genuinely be transformed; and how to develop authentic, unshakable faith throughout our night seasons. Scripture says we are to prepare ourselves for Christ's soon return. (Isaiah 62:10)

For more information, please write to:

The King's High Way Ministries, Inc.
P.O. Box 3111
Coeur d'Alene, ID 83816

or call:

On the Internet:
http://www.kingshighway.org

The King's HIGH Way